French Culture and Society

Other titles in *The Essentials* series

Forthcoming

French Culture and Society
The Essentials

Michael Kelly
School of Modern Languages
University of Southampton

A member of the Hodder Headline Group
LONDON

Co-published in the United States of America by
Oxford Unversity Press Inc., New York

First published in Great Britain in 2001 by
Arnold, a member of the Hodder Headline Group,
338 Euston Road, London NW1 3BH
http://www.arnoldpublishers.com

Co-published in the United States of America by
Oxford University Press Inc.,
198 Madison Avenue, New York, NY10016

British Library Cataloguing in Publication Data
A catalogue record for this book is available from the British Library

Library of Congress Cataloging-in-Publication Data
A catalog record for this book is available from the Library of Congress

ISBN 0 340 76024 9

1 2 3 4 5 6 7 8 9 10

Production Editor: James Rabson
Production Controller: Martin Kerans
Cover Design: Terry Griffiths

Typeset in 10/12pt Minion by J&L Composition Ltd, Filey, North Yorkshire
Printed and bound in Great Britain by MPG Books Ltd, Bodmin, Cornwall

What do you think about this book? Or any other Arnold title?
Please send your comments to feedback.arnold@hodder.co.uk

Contents

Preface

France is a favourite subject of study and discussion throughout the English-speaking world. There are many reasons why this should be so. It is home to one of the world's major languages; it has a rich cultural heritage; it is an influential presence on the international political stage; it is the fourth largest economy in the world; it is a leading player in scientific and technological development; it has had a complex and fascinating history; it is a popular tourist destination; its wine and food set standards for the rest of the world; the list could go on.

Whatever the reason for wanting to know more about France, this glossary aims to provide a handbook of concise and relevant information, and a springboard for further investigation. It will be useful for many types of reader, and especially for students, whether or not they have a knowledge of the French language. It has been the aim of contributors to write entries in a clear and jargon-free style, to provide explanations of technical terms, and to give translations of French expressions.

The glossary covers a wide range of topics relating to French culture and society since the end of the First World War, though in many cases background is sketched in from earlier periods, where this is important. Some entries deal with historical topics, while others deal with issues of current concern, but the aim is always to illuminate France as it has now become. France is intimately linked with many other countries, by history and by current affairs, and many entries discuss the 'French connection' with them. But they do not attempt to offer an extensive account of other countries, even those French-speaking countries in Africa or the Americas that increasingly feature in world news, or figure in academic programmes.

Longer entries deal with around 340 significant topics. Most of them are written by the thirty-six contributors, each of whom is a specialist in her or his field. Their names are shown in the entries they wrote, and details of their specialist interests are given in the Notes on contributors. Some 450 shorter entries offer biographical information on individuals and brief outlines of other topics. These, and all other unattributed material, are the work of the editor, who has tried to ensure the accuracy of all the information included. We have sought to convey the essentials, but we have necessarily been selective, and hope that many readers will want to pursue our suggestions for further enquiry. Since it aims to provide a handbook, and route map for discovering France, the glossary can be used in several ways.

In *dictionary* mode, a reader may simply look up relevant entries in their alphabetical location, from the **A.B.C.** music hall to Zinedine **Zidane**. They include a brief statistical profile of **France** in the year 2000.

In *exploratory* mode, a reader may follow the cross-references from one entry to another. All words in small capitals are also headwords (or close cognates) for other entries. Readers wishing to pursue these connections will find that each entry leads to other avenues of enquiry, enabling them to build up a larger picture.

In *thematic* mode, a reader may wish to read a group of entries covering a general area of French life. The longer entries on significant topics were selected to provide an overview of France since the end of the First World War (1918), dealing with historical topics, with social and political topics, and with ideas and movements in culture. The main thematic groupings are described in the outline of Themes.

In *library* mode, a reader may take up the suggestion to consult other works providing more extensive discussion of the topic at hand. Many of the longer entries are followed by abbreviated suggestions for Further reading, pointing to useful books, articles or websites mostly in English, but sometimes in French. The full form of these references is given in the Bibliography.

Themes

The longer entries can be read in the following main thematic groupings:

Historical topics

Historical periods or moments

In rough chronological order: Third Republic, *entre-deux-guerres* (inter-war period), Popular Front, *drôle de guerre* (Phoney War), Occupation, Vichy regime, Liberation, Provisional Government, Fourth Republic, Cold War, Fifth Republic.

Significant events

Algerian War, Blum-Byrnes agreement, *Chambre bleu horizon*, decolonization, Dien Bien Phu, Dunkirk, *Épuration*, Évian agreements, *l'Exode*, 6 February 1934, Holocaust, Maginot Line, Marshall Plan, May '68, Munich 1938, putsch (April 1961), Resistance, Rif War, Spanish Civil War, Stavisky affair, STO (labour conscription), Suez Crisis, Tours Congress, Paris Peace Settlement, Wall Street Crash.

International relations

Africa, Algeria, America, Britain, China, Czechoslovakia, Europe, Germany, Hungary, Indo-China, Pacific, Poland.

Social and political topics

French-speaking countries and selected French towns and regions

Alsace-Lorraine, Belgium, Brittany, Canada, Corsica, DOM (overseas departments), France 2000, Lyon, Marseille, Paris, Provence, regionalism, Switzerland, TOM (overseas territories).

Social groups

Bourgeoisie, *cadres* (executives), class, élites, *employés* (white collar workers), *paysans* (farmers, peasants), race and ethnicity, students, workers (and the working class).

Education

Collège de France, École normale supérieure, education, *grandes écoles*, universities.

Themes

Economy

Bureaucracy, capitalism, the economy, economic policies, employment, Fordism, the franc, inflation, privatization, Taylorism, trade unions, *les trente glorieuses* (post-war prosperity), work-time.

Trade, industry and transport

Agriculture, audiovisual industry, automobile industry, decentralization, GATT, globalization, industrialization, Industry (Ministry), liberalism, modernization, nationalization, railways, space programme, technology.

Issues

Army, assimilation, atomic weapons, *banlieue* (suburbs), *bidonvilles* (shanty towns), collaboration, colonialism, democracy, Eurocentrism, exclusion, immigration, imperialism (and Empire), integration, memory (and commemoration), nation, neo-colonialism, nuclear deterrent, revolution, *sans-papiers* (unauthorized foreigners), state.

Political movements

Action française, anarchism, anti-colonialism, anti-communism, anti-fascism, anti-Semitism, Communist Party, *Croix-de-feu*, ecologists, fascism, Free French, *Front national*, *le gauchisme*, Gaullism, *intégrisme*, Maoism, MLF (*Mouvement de libération des femmes*), *le Milice*, MRP (*Mouvement républicain populaire*), NATO (North Atlantic Treaty Organization), OAS (*Organisation de l'armée secrète*), pacifism, *poujadisme*, *Parité*, PPF (*Parti populaire français*), PSU (*Parti socialiste unifié*), radicalism (*Parti radical*), RPF (*Rassemblement du peuple français*), RPR (*Rassemblement pour la République*), Socialist Party, *tripartisme*, Trotskyism, UDF (*Union pour la Démocratie Française*).

Private life

Abortion, *Choisir* (Choose), contraception, everyday life, family, gender, happiness, health, homosexuality, *jouissance*, love, masculinity, MLAC (*Mouvement pour la libération de l'avortement et de la contraception*), morality, sexuality, social security, women, youth.

Religion

Atheism, Catholicism, Islam, Judaism and Jewishness, *laïcité* (religious neutrality), Protestantism.

Ideas and movements in culture

Concepts

Absurd, alienation, author, the body, canon (literary), civilization, commitment, critical theory, culture, deconstruction, *écriture* (writing), identity, ideology, the imaginary, intellectuals, intertextuality, myth, orientalism, the Other, subject and subjectivity, universalism.

Genres

Autobiography, abstract painting, architecture, art, *bande dessinée* (comics), *chanson* (song), cinema, concerts, detective fiction, jazz, music (classical), music (popular), music-hall, novel, painting, photography, posters, science fiction, sculpture, short story, theatre, thriller, western.

Cultural movements

Avant-garde, *cinéma du look, Beur* culture, cubism, Dadaism, *écriture féminine* (women's writing), existentialism, feminism, futurism, humanism, *les Hussards*, Marxism, *mode rétro*, naturalism, *Négritude, nouveau roman* (new novel), *nouveau théâtre* (new theatre), *nouveaux philosophes* (new philosophers), *nouvelle critique* (new criticism), *nouvelle vague* (new wave cinema), personalism, post-modernism, post-structuralism, realism, socialist realism, Situationism, structuralism, Surrealism, youth culture.

Disciplines

Anthropology and ethnography, chemistry, engineering, linguistics, literary history, philosophy, physics, psychoanalysis, semiology, sociology.

Cultural institutions

Académies, archives, *ciné-clubs*, the cock (Gallic), *Comédie française*, concert halls, Culture (Ministry), film festivals, film studios, Institut de France, *grands travaux* (public works), Jeanne d'Arc, libraries, Louvre museum, *maisons de la culture* (culture houses), Marianne, museums (and art galleries), *Musée d'Orsay*, postage stamps, Pompidou Centre (Beaubourg), prizes (literary), publishing, theatre festivals, theatres, *Théâtre National Populaire* (TNP).

Media and communications

Broadcasting regulation, censorship, documentaries, information technology, Internet, journalism, media and mass media, Minitel, news, press (daily), press (weekly), radio (state), radio (independent), satellite and cable broadcasting, television, television drama.

Language

Argot (including *verlan* and *tchatche*), creole, dictionaries, *franglais*, French language, Francophonie, *patois*, regional languages, spelling, standardization (of the French Language).

Leisure and consumption

Café, carnival, cities, Club Méditerranée, *colonies de vacances* (holiday camps), consumerism, *cuisine* (food and gastronomy), cycling, Euro-Disney, fashion, football (clubs), football (national team), holidays, leisure, night-clubs, Olympic Games, rugby, sport, stadia, tennis, Tour de France, tourism, transport, urban planning, wine, winter sports.

Notes on contributors

Margaret Atack is Professor of French at the University of Leeds. Her publications include *Literature and the French Resistance: Cultural Politics and Narrative Forms 1940–1950* (1989), *Contemporary French Fiction by Women: Feminist Perspectives* (co-editor, 1991), and *May 68 in French Fiction and Film: Rethinking Society, Rethinking Representation* (1999).

Nicholas Atkin is Senior Lecturer in History at the University of Reading. He has published widely on twentieth-century France and is the author of *Church and Schools in Vichy France, 1940–1944* (New York, 1991) and *Pétain* (London, 1998). He is about to publish a short study on the Occupation, together with a monograph *The Forgotten French: Exiles in the British Isles, 1940–1944*.

Rodney Ball is Senior Lecturer in French in the School of Modern Languages at the University of Southampton, where he teaches General and French Linguistics. Topics on which he has recently published include current lexical and grammatical tendencies in French, language attitudes, and the prescriptivist tradition. His book, *The French-speaking World: A Practical Introduction to Sociolinguistic issues* (London: Routledge) appeared in 1997, followed in 2000 by *Colloquial French Grammar* (Oxford: Blackwell).

Bill Brooks is Head of the School of Modern Languages at the University of Southampton, and is a Senior Lecturer in French. He has published books and articles on French eighteenth-century literature and thought. In recent years his research interests have focused on the evolution of French republican political culture in the post-modern period, with a particular emphasis on the external relations of France with Europe and Africa since 1989.

Jackie Clarke is Lecturer in French Studies at the University of Southampton. Her current research explores attempts by technical élites to construct a new social and economic order in France in the 1930s and 1940s. She has published articles on the inter-war rationalization movement and is working on a book entitled *Modernity and Crisis: Engineering a New France from the Great Depression to Vichy*.

Susan Collard is a Lecturer in French in the School of European Studies at the University of Sussex. She teaches a range of courses on twentieth-century French history and politics as well as on the politics and institutions of the European Union. Her research interests focus currently on cultural politics and policy in France with a special interest in the Mitterrand presidency.

Martyn Cornick is Reader in Contemporary French Studies at the University of Birmingham, UK. He teaches and researches in the area of French intellectual history, especially Jean Paulhan and the *Nouvelle Revue française* (*Intellectuals in History, Jean Paulhan and the NRF, 1925–1940*, Atlanta and Amsterdam: Rodopi, 1995), as well as Franco-British perceptions. He is also editor of the quarterly *Modern and Contemporary France.*

Máire Cross is Professor of French at the University of Sheffield. Her publications include *Early French Feminisms, 1830–1940* (with Felicia Gordon) and *The Feminism of Flora Tristan* (with Tim Gray). Her research interest covers the history of nineteenth-century political ideas and the politics of feminism in contemporary France.

Hugh Dauncey has worked in France at ESCAE and ENSCP Bordeaux, Paris VII and ENA and is currently Senior Lecturer in French Studies at the University of Newcastle upon Tyne. He teaches contemporary French politics, economics, society and history and has published on French science and new communications technology as well as on aspects of French popular culture – most specifically radio and television – and sport.

Christopher Flood is Professor of European Studies at the University of Surrey. He is author of *Pensée politique et imagination historique dans l'œuvre de Paul Claudel* (1991) and of *Political Myth: A Theoretical Introduction* (1996). He has co-edited *Political Ideologies in Contemporary France* (1997), *Currents in Contemporary French Intellectual Life* (2000), and collections of essays on the politics of French intellectuals (1993, 1998, 2000). He is co-editor of the *European Horizons* series with University of Nebraska Press.

John Flower is Professor of French at the University of Kent. Formerly Professor of French at the University of Exeter he has also taught at the universities of Nanterre, Bordeaux and Avignon. Has published widely on the work of François Mauriac and on literature and politics in modern France. He is editor of the *Journal of European Studies* and of the Berg French Studies series. His non-academic writing includes books on Provence, Lombardy and Burgundy.

Hilary Footitt writes on the Liberation of France and on women in politics. Her publications on France and the Second World War include *The Politics of Liberation: France, 1943–45*, with John Simmonds (Leicester: Leicester University Press, 1988). She has written on the first women members of the French Assembly (*les 33 Glorieuses*) and, most recently, on women in the European Parliament: *Women, Europe and the New Languages of Politics* (London: Continuum International, 2001).

Jill Forbes is Professor of French at Queen Mary College, University of London. She works on French culture, cinema and media and her most recent books are *Contemporary France: Essays and Texts on Politics Economics and Society* (London: Pearson, 2000), with Nick Hewlett and François Nectoux, and *European Cinema* (Palgrave, 2000) with Sarah Street.

Charles Forsdick is James Barrow Professor of French at Liverpool University, and has previously lectured at Glasgow University. He has published on exoticism, colonial and postcolonial literature in French, postcolonial theory, travel literature, and the modern French novel. He is author of *Victor Segalen and the Aesthetics of Diversity* (Oxford: Oxford University Press, 2000).

Ted Freeman is Senior Lecturer, Department of French, University of Bristol. Since 1989 he has been Editor of Bristol Classical Press's French Texts series (Duckworth Publishers), and is the author of a number of studies and editions of twentieth-century authors and movements, most recently *Theatres of War: French Committed Theatre from the Second World War to the Cold War*, (Exeter: University of Exeter Press, 1998).

Bertram M. Gordon is Professor of History and Acting Provost and Dean of Faculty, Mills College, Oakland, California, USA. He is the author of *Collaborationism in France during the Second World War* (Ithaca, New York: Cornell University Press, 1980), the editor of *The Historical Dictionary of World War II France: The Occupation, Vichy and the Resistance, 1938–1946* (Westport, CT: Greenwood Press, 1998). His recent articles include 'The decline of a cultural icon: France in American perspective', *French Historical Studies*, 22:4 (Fall 1999), 625–51. He also writes on the history of gastronomy, tourism, and the 1968 French student revolt.

Claire Gorrara is Lecturer in French at Cardiff University. She has published mainly on gender, history and literary representations of the Second World War, most notably *Women's Representations of the Occupation in Post-1968 France* (Basingstoke: Macmillan, 1998). She is currently working on French detective fiction and is writing a cultural history of the post war French *roman noir*.

Johnnie Gratton is Statutory Lecturer in French at the National University of Ireland, Dublin. He is the author of *Expressivism: The Vicissitudes of a Theory in the Writing of Proust and Barthes* (Legenda, 2000), and co-editor of *Modern French Short Fiction* (Manchester: Manchester University Press, 1994), *La Nouvelle hier et aujourd'hui* (Paris: L'Harmattan, 1997), and *Subject Matters: Subject and Self in French Literature from Descartes to the Present* (Amsterdam: Rodopi, 2000). His articles include studies of Barthes, Breton, Colette, Proust, Sarraute, and Jean-Loup Trassard.

Laurence Grove is Lecturer in French at the University of Glasgow, having previously studied and taught at the University of Pittsburgh and Middlebury College (Vermont). His main research interest is a historical approach to text/image forms in French culture, principally the emblem books of the Early Modern period and the *bande dessinée* from the 1930s onwards. His current book project, *The Emblematic Age*, compares and contrasts these two forms.

David Hanley has taught at Ulster, Reading and Cardiff universities as well as Nanterre and Poitiers. He is the author of books and articles on French and European politics, especially parties: *Contemporary France* (1984), *Keeping Left?: CERES and the French Socialist Party* (1986); *Christian Democracy in Europe* (1992). He has a forthcoming book on *Party, Society and Government; Republican Democracy in France* (Berghahn), and has been guest columnist for *La Croix* for 16 years.

Geoff Hare is a Senior Lecturer in French at Newcastle University. He has published extensively on French radio and television, including issues of regulation, policymaking and the impact of new technologies. More recently he has written on the organization and impact of the World Cup on French society, and on the links between media and sport. He is a Vice President of the British Federation of Alliance Françaises.

Alec G. Hargreaves is Professor of French and Francophone Studies in the Department of European Studies at Loughborough University. His publications include *Voices from the North African Immigrant Community in France: Immigration and Identity in Beur Fiction* (Oxford and New York: Berg, 1991; 2nd edition 1997), *Immigration, 'Race' and Ethnicity in Contemporary France* (London and New York: Routledge, 1995) and, co-edited with Mark McKinney, *Post-Colonial Cultures in France* (London and New York: Routledge, 1997).

Nicholas Hewitt is Professor of French and Director of the Institute of Modern Cultural Studies at the University of Nottingham. He has written extensively on French literary, intellectual and cultural history from 1918 to 1960. His last major work was a biography of Céline, published in 1999.

Diana Holmes is Professor of French at the University of Leeds, where she teaches film and the nineteenth- and twentieth-century novel. She is the author of works on French women writers including books on *Colette* (1991), *French Women's Writing 1848–1994* (1996), and *Rachilde* (forthcoming). She also writes on French cinema, and co-edits a series on French Film Directors for which she co-authored the volume on Truffaut.

Michael Kelly is Professor of French at Southampton University, UK. He is Associate Editor of the journal, *French Cultural Studies*, co-editor of the journal *Language and Intercultural Communication*, and joint editor of books *French Cultural Studies: An Introduction* (Oxford: Oxford University Press, 1995) and *Pierre Bourdieu: Language, Culture and Education* (Bern: Peter Lang, 1999). He has published widely on French culture and society, and intellectual history, including books on Catholic, Marxist and Hegelian thought. He is currently completing a monograph on the Nationalization of French culture in 1945.

Bill Kidd is Reader and Head of French at the University of Stirling. He has written extensively on twentieth-century French literature and ideology (Vercors, Mauriac,

Aragon, Bernanos), on culture and iconography, and war and memory. He is the author of *Les Monuments aux morts mosellans de 1870 á nos jours* (Metz: Editions Serpenoise, 1999), an illustrated monograph on the changing problematics of commemoration in Lorraine, and co-editor of *Contemporary French Cultural Studies* (London: Arnold, 2000).

David Looseley is Senior Lecturer in French at the University of Leeds. He has published widely on French culture, policy and institutions. His book *The Politics of Fun: Cultural Policy and Debate in Contemporary France* was funded by the Leverhulme Trust and published in 1995 (Oxford: Berg, reprinted in paperback 1997). He is currently completing an AHRB-funded history of popular music and the music industry in contemporary France, which also focuses on cultural debate.

John Marks is Reader in French in the Department of Modern Languages at Nottingham Trent University. His main research interest is post-war philosophy and social theory in France and Europe. His publications include *Gilles Deleuze: Vitalism and Multiplicity* (London: Pluto Press, 1998) and he is the co-editor of *Deleuze and Literature* (Edinburgh: Edinburgh University Press, 2000).

Lucy Mazdon is a Senior Research Fellow at the University of Southampton. She has published a number of articles on French film and television. She is the author of *Encore Hollywood: Remaking French Cinema* (London: BFI, 2000) and the editor of *France on Film: Reflections on Popular French Cinema* (London: Wallflower Press, 2000).

James Minney teaches French language at the University of Southampton. His research interests include regional languages in France, questions of language and identity and non-standard varieties of French. He has recently completed a PhD thesis on the Flemish movement of French Flanders and the maintenance of Flemish.

Pam Moores is Senior Lecturer in French and Director of Undergraduate Programmes in the School of Languages and European Studies at Aston University. She has researched and published on the nineteenth-century novelist, journalist and Communard, Jules Vallès, and on the contemporary French media. Her publications focus on media personalities in politics, French newspapers, the street press, and analysis of media coverage of French election campaigns.

Keith Reader is Professor of French at the University of Glasgow. He has written widely on French cultural studies, including books on *Intellectuals and the Left in France since 1968* (1987), *The May 1968 Events in France* (1993), and *Régis Debray* (1995). He co-edited the *Encyclopedia of Contemporary French Culture* (1998).

Michèle Richman teaches courses on French identity and contemporary youth culture at the University of Pennsylvania. Her research focuses upon the French tradition of a self-reflexive critical discourse forged through comparison with cultural others. Publications relating to Bataille, Barthes, Durkheim, Mauss, Leiris, and the Collège de sociologie include *Reading Georges Bataille: Beyond the Gift* and the forthcoming, *Not for Primitives Only: French Modernity and the Reinvention of the Sacred from Durkheim to the College of Sociology.*

David Scott holds a personal chair in French (Textual and Visual Studies) at Trinity College Dublin. He has published widely on literature, painting, semiotics and textual and visual studies, and organized many exhibitions on arts and design. His books include *Pictorialist Poetics* (1988), *Paul Delvaux* (1992) and *European Stamp Design: A Semiotic Approach* (1995). A study on the early modern poster, *Figures de l'affiche*, is forthcoming. An editor of *Word & Image* and *l'image*, he is president of IAWIS/AIERTI.

Max Silverman is Professor of Modern French Studies at the University of Leeds. He is a specialist in the areas of immigration, race, nation and citizenship, the city, cultural theory and debates, and colonial and post-colonial theory and cultures. He has written two monographs, *Deconstructing the Nation: Immigration, Racism and Citizenship in Modern France* (London: Routledge, 1992) and *Facing Postmodernity: Contemporary French Thought on Culture and Society* (London: Routledge, 1999). He has also edited a collection of essays under the title *Race, Discourse and Power in France* (Avebury, 1991) and has published numerous chapters in books and journal articles on the above topics.

Steven Ungar is a Professor of French and Comparative Literature at the University of Iowa. His research includes books and articles on Jean-Paul Sartre, Roland Barthes, Maurice Blanchot, and French colonial cinema. He is working on a book-length study of urban spaces and everyday life, with emphasis on post-Second World War French literature and film.

Susan Weiner is Associate Professor of French at Yale University, where she teaches courses in twentieth-century cultural studies. She is the author of *Enfants Terribles: Youth and Femininity in the Mass Media in France, 1945–1968* (Baltimore: Johns Hopkins University Press, 2001) and the editor of an issue of *Yale French Studies*, 'The French Fifties' (December 2000). Her articles have appeared in *French Cultural Studies, Contemporary European History, Yale French Studies*, and *Sites*.

Acknowledgements

I should like to thank my thirty-six contributors who found the time to distil their knowledge into the painfully short space allocated for the entries. Without exception, I was helped and supported by their generosity of spirit, and in the process learned a great about France. I am especially grateful to Hugh Dauncey, Diana Holmes and Máire Cross, who helped enormously by taking on several extra entries when another contributor had to withdraw at a late stage.

I am grateful to my colleagues in the School of Modern Languages at Southampton, particularly Bill Brooks, and in the Subject Centre for Languages, Linguistics and Area Studies, particularly Liz Ashurst. They supported and encouraged me while I was working on the glossary, sometimes at the expense of other commitments. I was very glad to have the constant help and encouragement of my editor at Arnold, Elena Seymenliyska, who shepherded the process through to completion with patience and good humour. I am also grateful to the British Academy for the award of a Senior Research Fellowship, without which I would not have been able to complete the editing within a reasonable time frame.

I should like to acknowledge the good counsel and good company of many academic colleagues in Britain, Ireland, America and France, who have nourished my love and knowledge of France, and contributed in less tangible ways to this glossary. Though it may be invidious to single out individuals, I should like particularly to thank Jill Forbes, Nick Hewitt and Brian Rigby, with whom I have shared *un bout de chemin* on the intellectual journey of French cultural studies. I should also like to record my debt to the late Donald Charlton, my *patron* at Warwick, whose teaching and scholarship set an inspiring example.

My immediate family has borne most of the personal brunt of the task, putting up, among other things, with my early mornings and late nights at the computer. I could not have carried the enterprise through without their love and understanding, and this book is theirs in more ways than one: I therefore wish to dedicate it to Jo, Tom and Paul.

Michael Kelly
Southampton
November 2000

A.B.C. 1934–64. The most successful Paris music-hall venue from the 1930s to the 1950s. It occupied the premises of the former Plaza theatre, located on the Boulevard Poissonnière, which were subsequently turned into a cinema.

Abetz, Otto 1903–58. German ambassador in Paris (1940–44). A passionate francophile during the 1930s, he was a lavish promoter of cultural collaboration during the Occupation. He was tried and imprisoned after the war (1949–54).

Abortion The practice of abortion (*avortement* or *Interruption Volontaire de Grossesse*) was an illegal and imprisonable offence in France until 1975. French anxiety about low birthrates, particularly after the First World War had severely reduced the young male population, was a determining factor in anti-abortion policies. The right-wing Vichy government (1940–44), which idealized maternity and promoted the moral and patriotic virtues of large families, made abortion an offence punishable by death and executed one *faiseuse d'anges* (abortionist – literally 'maker of angels') in 1943. Simone de Beauvoir shocked conservative opinion in 1949 by defending women's right to safe, freely chosen abortion, in *Le Deuxième sexe*. Beauvoir pointed out that despite the law there were as many abortions as births each year in France, and that the law merely served to make what could be a safe medical intervention into a dangerous, back-street ordeal for all but the richest women.

The second wave of the women's movement, the Mouvement de Libération des Femmes (MLF), made women's right to control their own bodies a central campaigning theme. In 1971, 343 women, most of them well known (the list included, for example, the actress Catherine Deneuve and the novelist Françoise Sagan, as well as de Beauvoir herself) published a manifesto in the Nouvel Observateur, declaring that they had all had illegal abortions. The *Manifeste des 343* marked the beginning of the campaign for the legalization of abortion. The year 1971 also saw the formation of the MLA (*Mouvement pour la Libération de l'Avortement*) and of a similar group Choisir. At the *Procès de Bobigny* (Bobigny Trial), four women accused of involvement in the abortion of a minor (the victim of a rape) were successfully defended by the feminist lawyer Gisèle Halimi, while crowds of women demonstrated for repeal of the anti-abortion laws outside the court. In November 1974, the then Minister of Health, Simone Veil, introduced a law to legalize abortion, and against fierce opposition from the Church and the conservative Right succeeded in gaining a parliamentary majority. The *loi Veil* became law provisionally in 1975, was confirmed in 1979, and after further feminist lobbying, abortion was made reimbursable by the Sécurité Sociale in 1982. Catholic and Extreme Right opposition to abortion continues, with a few cases of violent attacks on abortion clinics, which led to the 1993 law criminalizing failure to respect a woman's legal right to abortion. (**Diana Holmes**)

1

Further reading

Cook and Davie (1999). See Chapter 3, 'Gender', by Catherine Rodgers. Duchen (1986) Laubier (1990).

Abstract painting   Although in some ways Impressionism and CUBISM helped pave the way for it, abstract painting has never figured as prominently in twentieth-century French ART as in other modern art traditions. In the analytical Cubism of BRAQUE and PICASSO, the sight of the real object was never lost in the intense analysis to which its spatial aspects were submitted, while in the work of LÉGER and MATISSE, a primary preoccupation with form and colour never obliterated the human figure. A strong figurative component has thus been sustained through the various avant–garde movements with which PARIS has been centrally associated in the 1850–1950 period.

This does not of course mean that abstract painting – whether the geometric forms of Kandinsky, Malevich and Mondrian or the freer styles of some FUTURIST and SURREALIST artists – was not closely associated with modern French painting. The colour experiments of the Post-Impressionists and the Fauves, clearly anticipated the abstract potential of colour, while the cubism of late Cézanne and early Braque pointed to the scope of pure form. But that close connection between artists, architects and designers that characterised the avant-garde in Germany (the Bauhaus), the Netherlands (De Stijl) and Russia (Constructivism) and which seemed to promote a deeper understanding of pure plastic values, had no equivalent in the modern French tradition.

Of course, there were many individual French or Paris-based artists who made their reputation as abstract artists, including Jean Fautrier and Serge Poliakof in the 1940s, and Nicolas de Staël and Georges Mathieu in the 1950s. But none of them received the acclaim of Braque or Matisse or the American abstract expressionists. The one outstanding post-war French abstract painter was Yves Klein, whose mono-chrome canvases of the 1950s (particularly those in 'Klein blue') took abstract art to its logical conclusion. However, even Klein signalled a returning to the figure through his body paintings and his presentation of real objects powdered in Klein blue pigment. (**David Scott**)

Further reading

Kandinsky, (1970) and Kandinsky (1989).

Absurd   Philosophical notion at the heart of much twentieth-century literature and theatre. The word originally meant 'out of harmony' before acquiring its popular meaning of 'ridiculous'. One of the first major French writers to use the term in its modern sense of 'alien', 'defying reason', is André MALRAUX: 'the undeniable proof of the absurdity of our existence is the certainty of death' in *La Voie royale* (*The Royal Way*, 1930). It reached its widest public through Albert CAMUS's essay *Le Mythe de Sisyphe* (*The Myth of Sisyphus*, 1942): man lives alone in an alien, imperfect and godless universe that defies reason, thwarts his desire for happiness, and guarantees only one thing, that he will die. This perception can be blindingly sudden. Thereafter,

Camus argues, 'absurd man' has a number of choices: (1) violent, homicidal rebellion, the wrong choice taken by the eponymous hero of his play *Caligula* (1945); (2) physical suicide, rejected by Camus because it is a capitulation to the absurd; (3) spiritual and intellectual suicide, such as a recourse to religion; and (4) a conscious decision to 'preserve' the absurd, live life to the full and experience a limited but intense form of HAPPINESS. The absurd is better exemplified in Camus's novel *L'Étranger* (*The Outsider*, 1942) than in his plays. Likewise SARTRE's *La Nausée* (*Nausea*, 1938) is a brilliant fictional treatment. The 'new' dramatists of the 1950s developed a radically non-realist style more appropriate to the philosophy than did Camus and Sartre themselves. The plays of BECKETT, IONESCO, ADAMOV and others are often referred to collectively as the 'Theatre of the Absurd', or NOUVEAU THÉÂTRE (New Theatre). (**Ted Freeman**)

Further reading

Esslin (1991). A brilliant if uneven study of the whole phenomenon. Hinchcliffe (1969). Succinct and helpful, more focused on France than Esslin.

Absurd, Theatre of the   See NOUVEAU THÉÂTRE

Académie française   See ACADÉMIES, INSTITUT DE FRANCE

Académies   The word *académie* is derived from the name given (after the hero Academus) to a sanctuary in an olive grove just outside Athens in Ancient Greece, where Plato spent time thinking and teaching philosophy. The word came to be used to describe a school or place of learning, until the Renaissance when it also became associated with the learned societies that were becoming increasingly fashionable.

The word has two main uses in France. The first, as in English, describes learned academies of various kinds, but refers also implicitly to the five former Royal Academies that now constitute the INSTITUT DE FRANCE. They are the *Académie Française*, the *École National Supérieure des Beaux Arts*, the *Académie des Inscriptions et Belles Lettres*, the *Académie des Sciences* and the *Académie des Sciences Morales et Politiques*. The Academies were created under the French monarchy in the seventeenth century in order to establish central authority and censorship over particular aspects of cultural life: language, writing, poetry, dance, sculpture, architecture and painting. This established a tradition of *académisme* in French cultural life: a tendency towards conformity to centrally prescribed rules and taste, which still influences much artistic creation today. The Academies, and in particular the *Académie Française*, represent an élite cultural and scientific establishment, membership of which indicates the highest possible recognition by the French state of an individual's professional achievement and scholarly distinction.

The second usage of the word *académie* is as the name given to the geographic and administrative divisions of the state education system, of which there are 25, each one under the responsibility of a *Recteur*. (**Susan Collard**)

3

Further reading

See the website of the *Académie française*: www.academie–francaise.fr

Action Française   Founded in 1898 at the height of the Dreyfus Affair, Action Française (AF) was initially one of the committees formed by anti-Dreyfusard intellectuals. It outlived the Affair and changed itself into a league in 1905, seeking wider membership. From 1908 onwards it produced a daily newspaper as well as other publications. It also established an institute dispensing ideological instruction. Its early members were from diverse political traditions, including republicanism, but the group was converted to monarchism and rejection of the THIRD REPUBLIC by Charles MAURRAS, who became the leading ideologue of the French extreme Right, influencing several generations of nationalists. Maurrassian doctrine involved a paradoxical application of positivistic philosophical method to theorizing reactionary traditionalism. It rejected the ideas of the Enlightenment. It rejected the liberal, democratic principles of the French Revolution. It advocated a hereditary monarchy with extensive executive powers, decentralized local government, CATHOLICISM to underpin moral order, corporatist economic organization and an absolute commitment to national security. AF attracted substantial support with its polemics against the Republic, its denunciations of secularism and its attacks on groups such as JEWS, Freemasons, PROTESTANTS and parasitic foreigners who were allegedly undermining the national interest. Having rallied to the national truce between political enemies during the First World War, it reached the height of its activity during the early 1920s, but was severely damaged by the condemnation of Maurras's writings announced by the Vatican in 1926. In the 1930s it was overshadowed by newer anti-parliamentary groups. However, the opportunity to exercise real influence on government arose with the advent of the VICHY REGIME in 1940. Several of Marshal PÉTAIN'S closest advisers were from AF and the programme of the National Revolution bore a strong Maurrassian imprint. The newspaper continued to be published until it was closed by the PROVISIONAL GOVERNMENT in the summer of 1944. It was ironic that Maurras, the ultra-patriot, was tried and imprisoned after the Liberation on grounds of intelligence with the enemy and denunciation of resisters. His movement has continued to have a vestigial existence since the war. **(Christopher Flood)**

Further reading

Weber (1962). This remains a classic study.

Adamov, Arthur   1908–70. Russian-born writer and playwright. His early austere and anguished plays were influential in the theatre of the ABSURD. His later plays, like *Paolo Pauli* (1957) adopted a more REALIST style and followed Brecht in offering criticism of contemporary society.

Africa   The relationship between France and Africa raises moral and political questions at every stage of its history. Begun after 1492, French links with Africa were developed by Louis XIV's Finance Minister Colbert and involved French trading posts in Africa in the Atlantic slave trade.

Although the French Revolution abolished the slave trade and slavery in 1793 for a short period, it only finally ended in 1848. The French colonial presence in Algeria and Senegal began again in 1830, and was expanded across West and Central Africa in 1880s and 1890s. At its height, 73 per cent of the landmass and 40 per cent of the population of the French empire were in West and Equatorial Africa. Having defined empire as a 'civilizing mission' under the THIRD REPUBLIC, France presented itself in Africa as the guardian of native rights against other predatory European states. The reality was colonial domination, with African children required to learn French and embrace French history and culture. In this way a francophile African élite was educated, with a flowering of francophone African writers and leaders.

The decolonization of Sub-Saharan Africa in 1960 was peaceful, in contrast to the violence of Algeria. Power in these countries with their dependent economies passed into the hands of African ÉLITES, with close cultural, linguistic and personal ties to élites in France. Bilateral co-operation agreements between individual leaders of African states and Metropolitian France on trade, defence and culture ensured the continued political influence and domination of France throughout the post-colonial period and encouraged corruption and fraud on either side. The first social-ist President of the FIFTH REPUBLIC promised a new deal for Africa in 1981, and made initial attempts to increase development aid and replace bilateral co-operation agree-ments with a multilateral approach within a wider European and international framework. However, support for corrupt dictators like Mobutu, former President of Zaïre, and for a genocidal government in Rwanda, has seriously damaged the credi-bility of the French civilizing mission in Africa. (**Bill Brooks**)

Further reading:

Bayart (1984). Still the most authoritative overview available. Verschave (1998). A highly critical perspective.

Agrégation   The highest competitive national examination in the state education sys-tem. Originally designed to fill teaching posts in the main subject areas in *lycées*, it is now used as a qualification for university teachers, researchers and other professions.

Agriculture   France was traditionally an agricultural society, and remains one of the world's largest agricultural exporters (second only to the United States). Up to the Second World War, around one-third of the population worked on the land, produc-ing a quarter of the national wealth. Production methods remained predominantly traditional, and based on small family-owned farms. Much of France's national pride stemmed from agriculture, and in particular from the reputation of its wine and food. Under the VICHY REGIME, MARSHAL PÉTAIN promoted a *retour à la terre*, to restore traditional values, and also to meet the food production quotas set for the occupying Germans. After 1945, agriculture was targeted for modernization, since it was hard-pressed to feed the population during the post-war period of shortages and rationing, and since productivity was falling noticeably behind other countries. Farms were modernized to adopt intensive methods of production, through mecha-nization, fertilizers and land redistribution, to create larger, more productive and more profitable units. This was accelerated by entry into the Common Market (1957), and France played (and still plays) a major role in defining the terms of the Common Agricultural Policy (CAP), with its complex structure of regulations and incentives. Modernization was successful in meeting its aims, but rural depopulation accelerated as workers migrated to towns and industry, in what became known during the 1950s as *l'exode rural* (rural exodus). The numbers of people working on the land have continued to decrease, and now account for only 2 per cent of the population (a farming community of around one million). Although successive governments (and the CAP) have declared a policy of supporting medium-sized family farms, agriculture has increasingly become 'agribusiness'. Production has been reorganized into larger units, and those units have in turn become components of a much larger industry. Agricultural activity is determined by a shrinking number of large companies, that have largely industrialized the main 'upstream' processes (such as supply of seeds, fertilizer, animal feed), and 'downstream' processes (such as distribution and marketing of produce). They increasingly regulate production itself, through setting quotas, defining the standards and quality of the produce required, and often through direct managerial control. (**Michael Kelly**)

Further reading

Forbes *et al.* (2001). A very useful textbook on many aspects of French society. Mendras and Cole (1991). Focuses on the social history of France and the break–up of traditional social structures.

Algeria   Prior to independence in 1962 following the ALGERIAN WAR, Algeria was the most prized possession in France's overseas empire. French COLONIZATION had been based on military conquest beginning in 1830. The violent nature of Algeria's transition to independence left a complex legacy of mutual distrust. The single-party state established in 1962 by the *Front de Libération Nationale* (FLN) sought to reduce the country's reliance on France by cultivating new commercial and political partners in the Soviet bloc and elsewhere, and by pursuing a policy of Arabization in educational and other spheres, replacing French as far as possible by the use of Arabic. In practice, French remained widely used, Algeria continued to receive significant amounts of French development aid, and growing numbers of Algerian migrant workers took up job openings in France in the face of high unemployment and low living standards in Algeria.

The Algerian authorities officially halted labour migration to France in 1973, but the expatriate population there continued to grow as families became settled. Algeria benefited from large rises in the prices paid for its oil and gas exports during the 1970s, but economic improvements were not sustained. By the late 1980s, the FLN's hold on power was being weakened by the rise of Islamist (Islamic fundamentalist) groups capitalizing on popular discontent over economic mismanagement and political corruption. A state of virtual civil war broke out within Algeria during the 1990s, spilling over into France in 1995 with a terrorist bombing campaign by disaffected youths of immigrant origin working under the orders of Algerian Islamists who accused France of backing the Algerian government. These events helped to fuel popular stereotypes of IMMIGRATION and ISLAM as threats to the national identity and security of France. (**Alec Hargreaves**)

Further reading

Stora (1994). A concise and balanced account.

Algerian War   Armed struggle against French rule launched by Algerian nationalists in 1954, culminating in the independence of ALGERIA in 1962. The last and most bloody chapter in French DECOLONIZATION, it provoked· a terminal crisis in the FOURTH REPUBLIC, bringing the return to power in 1958 of Charles DE GAULLE and the beginning of the FIFTH REPUBLIC.

The Algerian nationalist guerrillas were led by the *Front de Libération Nationale* (FLN). They were faced by a large, well-equipped French army, including many conscripts, whose superior numbers were insufficient to outweigh the popular antagonism generated by the colonial system among Algeria's mainly Muslim indigenous population. The minority white settler population, whose privileged position could not be sustained without the French army and its political masters in Paris, was unwilling to contemplate Algerian independence. With the French military suffering growing casualties and adverse publicity over the use of torture in the interrogation of nationalist suspects, political and public opinion in France began to weaken in its commitment to the war. In 1958, backed by senior army figures, *pied-noir* (white settler) activists challenged the government in France, provoking a political crisis that enabled de Gaulle to assume power. But he soon began preparing the way for Algerian independence, which was eventually agreed under the ÉVIAN AGREEMENTS of 1962. By this stage, army dissidents and *pied-noir* activists had grouped within the OAS *Organisation de l'armée secrète* (Secret Army Organisation), and had adopted a scorched earth policy, launching violent attacks against French as well as Muslim targets. Independence in the summer of 1962 was marked by the mass exodus of the *pieds-noirs*, mainly to France. (**Alec Hargreaves**)

Further reading

Rioux (1990). A detailed survey of the impact of the Algerian war on France. Stora (1993). A lucid narrative on the main stages of the war.

Alienation   A first distinction obtains between alienation as a state of estrangement or disaffection, and as a critical concept. Instances of the former were frequent among surviving army veterans of the First World War. Literary expressions of alienation related to this 'war to end all wars' included Henri BARBUSSE's *Le Feu* (*Fire*, 1916) and passages in the 1924 Manifesto of SURREALISM that called for revolt against the values of reason and good taste among an ageing generation of middle-class patriots. Louis-Ferdinand CÉLINE's *Voyage au bout de la nuit* (*Journey to the End of Night*, 1932) provided a singular brutal vision of the war, which its narrator characterized as an international slaughterhouse.

Clandestine activity against GERMANY and the VICHY REGIME during the 1940–44 OCCUPATION often transformed alienation into organized RESISTANCE. By 1945, essays and fiction by Jean-Paul SARTRE, Albert CAMUS, and Simone de BEAUVOIR linked alienation as a universal condition to a Parisian EXISTENTIALISM that evolved through the mid-1960s in the fiction and plays of Samuel BECKETT as well as the absurdist theatre of Eugène IONESCO. During the same period, Frantz FANON's *Peau noire, masques blancs* (*Black Skins, White Masks*, 1952) analysed the psychological effects of racism on non-whites in France while Henri LEFEBVRE's *Critique de la vie quotidienne* (*Critique of Everyday Life*, 1947) drew on Hegel and Marx to contend with disaffection of a capitalist modernity that commodified identity in the form of material possessions.

Students and workers who went into the streets to protest against government policies in the spring of 1968 responded to alienation in the form of a dissidence whose intensity recalled partisan militancy between the wars. A prolonged estrangement involved the mixed reception that greeted workers, especially those from North and Sub-Saharan AFRICA, imported to provide cheap labor with ambivalence and hostility. Another was evident in the music, literature, and cinema of self-styled BEUR youths at odds with the cultures of their North African parents and those of a more or less white France unwilling or reluctant to accept them. (**Steven Ungar**)

Further reading

Ben Jelloun (2000); Fanon (1967); and Lefebvre (1991).

Alleg, Henri Born 1921. Communist journalist, whose account of his torture at the hands of the French ARMY in Algiers, *La Question* (1958), fuelled domestic opposition to the ALGERIAN WAR.

Alsace-Lorraine The hyphenated territory of Alsace-Lorraine, as distinct from Alsace *and* Lorraine, the subject of a defiantly anti-German popular song, was a product of France's defeat in the Franco-Prussian war (1870–71) and German annexation of the *départements* of Alsace (the Haut-Rhin and Bas-Rhin) and the Moselle *département* of Lorraine. Incorporated as Reichsland Elsass-Lothringen, an annexation ratified by the Treaty of Frankfurt in May 1871, it covered some 14,000 sq km. and included much of Lorraine's considerable coal, iron and steel capacity as well as the major provincial capitals of Strasbourg and the strategically important Metz. The territory was and to some extent remains bisected internally from north–west to south–east by a long-standing linguistic frontier between French and German (and two variants of *PATOIS*). Alsace, virtually bilingual in 1871, was largely germanophone by 1918. This was partly because of the emigration of middle-class French elements and the arrival of German-speakers. French irredentist feeling was maintained by exile organisations in PARIS, and locally by branches of the 'souvenir Français' and the largely though by no means exclusively pro-French CATHOLIC CHURCH. The territories were restored to the *mère patrie* (Mother country) in 1918 but re-integration was conducted in a high-handed, almost colonial manner, provoking local hostility and fuelling local autonomist movements. The region successfully resisted attempts in 1924 to impose the Republic's secular schooling legislation from which it has been protected by annexation and where, uniquely in France, the pre-1871 Concordat survives to this day. During the Second World War, Alsace-Lorraine endured a second, much more brutal annexation under the Nazi regime, including racial deportations and the forcible incorporation of its citizens into the Wehrmacht, known later as the '*Malgré nous*'

(Against our wishes). It returned definitively to France in 1945. Today, the border is no longer an issue, but by a predictable paradox, Alsace returned one of the highest pro-Maastricht votes (over 65 per cent) in the 1992 referendum, while offering significant electoral comfort to the anti-European *FRONT NATIONAL*. (**Bill Kidd**)

Further reading

Silverman (1972).

Althusser, Louis   1918–90. Philosopher. His structural and 'anti–humanist' interpretation of MARXIST theory, expressed in *Pour Marx* (*For Marx*, 1965) was influential in the 1960s and 1970s. His theory of the human SUBJECT and IDEOLOGY is still influential. His career ended in 1980 when he killed his wife in a bout of depression.

America   The relationship between France and America is characterized by discourses on either side of the Atlantic that allude to political and cultural difference and promote national exceptionalism. A continuation of the historic European rivalry between the French and the Anglo-Saxon worlds adds another dimension to what are often close cultural and political affinities.

Both are proud republics, but their practice of the liberal political theories of the Enlightenment differs. In American democracy the liberty and rights of the individual predominate in a federal republic, while in France the role of the unitary republic places limits on the rights of the individual subordinated to the general will. At the end of the eighteenth century, America fought for independence from English colonial domination with some military assistance from France. Shortly afterwards, France threw off despotism through a revolutionary struggle. Both then became possible models for the democracies that have followed across the world. The Republics are about the same age but American economic and military influence has increased dramatically. The history of the once powerful French STATE is much longer, but its power has declined significantly since the First World War.

In the twentieth century, America became the pre-dominant Western liberal democracy largely responsible for the LIBERATION of a humiliated France in 1944, the reconstruction of Europe in the post-war period, and, with the exception of Vietnam, enforcer of DECOLONIZATION. The rise of America thus coincided with the decline of France as a world power. France has responded by seeking to protect and expand its cultural influence while taking on the challenge of the American economic way, first through the promotion of national champions by the state, and since 1983 by public and private partnerships powerful enough to operate in a global free market. Since 1989 many French intellectuals have equated Americanization with globalization, regarding it as a universalism which directly threatens the uniqueness of the French republican model. The rivalry is far from over, and each republic remains acutely aware of the other. (**Bill Brooks**)

Further reading

Tocqueville (1887). This nineteenth-century classic gives a fascinating perspective which has scarcely aged. Baudrillard (1988). An individual philosophical and cultural analysis.

AMGOT   Allied Military Government of Occupied Territories. The planned administrative structure, favoured by the United States, to be set in place after the Allied landings in 1944. It implied that France was to be regarded, like GERMANY, as a defeated enemy and subject to Allied occupation. The plan was vehemently opposed by DE GAULLE, and with the assistance of Churchill, was eventually shelved.

Amsterdam-Pleyel movement   1932–39. A campaign aiming to promote peace and oppose FASCISM. Led by the writer Henri BARBUSSE, it was controlled by the COMMUNIST PARTY, and attracted support mainly from intellectual circles.

Anarchism   A political doctrine claiming that individuals are capable of organizing the peaceful regulation of their affairs without any interference from the STATE, religion, or laws. French anarchists Pierre-Joseph Proudhon (1809–65) and Georges Sorel (1847–1922) were influential in Europe and beyond. The former opposed the regimentation of the workers by industrial capitalism and the authoritarian dogma of MARXISM. His book *Qu'est-ce la propriété? (What is Property?* 1840) containing the riposte *'La propriété c'est le vol '* ('Property is theft') gave a misleading subversive reputation to this marginal ideology. Proudhon's social conservatism was nowhere more evident than in his misogyny. His scheme of a decentralized administration with co-operatives and workshops as ideal economic units found great appeal in France where small-scale production units lasted well into the twentieth century. During the early THIRD REPUBLIC French nihilist anarchists imitated Russians using terrorist action to destroy the State. Louise Michel, a Communarde deportee until 1880, was a prominent pacifist anarchist, frequently imprisoned for her inflammatory speeches. More widespread was the doctrine of anarcho-syndicalism, theorized by Georges Sorel. The idea of the general strike as the ultimate weapon with which to overthrow capitalism and the state appealed to many workers alienated from bourgeois reformist parliamentary socialism. The advent of war in 1914 ensured the demise of anarcho-syndicalism in France although it re-emerged in republican Spain of the 1930s and later in some Latin American countries. The anti-establishment movement of MAY '68 gave a fresh impetus to anarchism which continues to support anti-nuclear demonstrations, for example, at Malville in 1978, and to encourage acts of civil disobedience against militarism and, most recently, against globalization, for example, at Millau in 2000. Anarchists are now scattered and marginal, although very articulate in their consistent criticism of the establishment. (**Máire Cross**)

Further reading

Jennings (1990). Contains a section on the development of anarcho-syndicalism and its subsequent influence on French trade unions. Tombs (1999). Provides an excellent account of this dramatic episode in revolutionary history, explains its historical importance for the Left, in particular its symbolism of direct action for anarchists, Marxists and others.

Annales   Historical journal, founded in 1929, the *Annales d'histoire économique et sociale (Annals of Economic and Social History)* introduced a new approach to the study of history, emphasizing long-term social processes rather than high-profile political events, and using interdisciplinary methods to discuss broad themes.

Anouilh, Jean 1910–87. Prolific playwright who wrote for almost fifty years and had great popular success with both comedies and tragedies. His most performed plays are about anguished and solitary figures like *Antigone* (1944), and *L'Alouette* (*The Skylark*, 1959) about Joan of Arc.

Anthropology (and ethnography) Its emergence as an academic disicpline in the late nineteenth century coincides with those of other social sciences such as SOCIOLOGY and with policies linked to overseeing the overseas territories France occupied as colonies and protectorates. Until almost 1950, anthropology was equated in large part with physical anthropology while ethnography referred to the systematic description of data collected through fieldwork in purportedly 'primitive' cultures outside France. Claude LÉVI-STRAUSS's *Elementary Structures of Kinship* (1949) introduced an alternative model in which anthropology became a general theory of human societies grounded on comparative analyses of ethnographic materials formerly referred to in terms of ethnology. The ambitions Lévi-Strauss held for what he later called structural anthropology challenged the pre-eminence of history and philosophy within the post-war reconfiguration of human sciences whose new interdisicplinarity attributed key roles to LINGUISTICS and PSYCHOANALYSIS.

Theorists of structural anthropology competed through the 1970s with proponents of the 'New History' (*nouvelle histoire*) to assume control of the mission that sociology in the tradition of Émile DURKHEIM and his nephew, Marcel MAUSS, had held as the prime arbiter of total social facts. At the same time, anthropologists such as Georges Balandier, Alfred Métraux, Marcel Griaule, Michel LEIRIS and Louis Dumont contributed significantly to ongoing applied research at the level of ethnology. Since the mid-1970s, studies by Michel DE CERTEAU and Marc Augé have revised earlier models of the human sciences by drawing variously on methods and materials from history, sociology and anthropology to support their respective inquiries into the structure of everyday life and the anthropology of supermodernity. (**Steven Ungar**)

Further reading

Augé (1995). A provocative study at the intersection of anthropology, critical theory, and recent works on spatiality. De Certeau (1984). A modern classic in the making: provocative in its implied revision to notions of urban space and the subversive potential of 'operations' at the core of daily life. Lévi-Strauss (1969). A major text. See also his *Tristes Tropiques* (1955) for a sense of his impact on post-war thought and literature.

Anti-colonialism Anti-colonialism is the political and intellectual struggle against the institutions of COLONIALISM. Its principal aim is to resist and overthrow colonial domination in order to restore local control. Anti-colonialism is the main political movement that triggered DECOLONIZATION. Although after the First World War there were isolated anti-colonial voices in metropolitan France, these were concerned more with fighting colonial brutality than with challenging the ingrained ideology of Empire itself. They were, as result, largely incapable of influencing public opinion. The inter-war years were in fact a golden age for the French Empire, with the desire for expansion being replaced by a sense of consolidation as rapidly expanding air travel provided crucial communication links. On the eve of the Second World War, many French believed that the country would find salvation in its Empire, from where they would draw troops, wealth and prestige. Such a belief focused more on MYTH than reality and ignored the growing anti-colonialism that had developed after 1918 both in the colonies and among colonial subjects in France itself. Resentment was often simmering in the Empire beneath a surface of apparent obedience. Colonial troops serving in the First World War, for instance, were horrified by their experience of Europe and began to question what they had been taught about the superiority of French CIVILIZATION. Inspired by the Russian Revolution and the post-war movement to grant self-determination to subject peoples, various anti-colonial movements emerged in the 1920s and 1930s, especially in North Africa and Indo-China. They were often accompanied by rebellions, as in the case of Yen Bay in Vietnam in 1930. After the Second World War, the anti-colonial movement developed even more rapidly and confounded any plans to rebuild France by further development of its colonies. The struggle for independence in Indo-China ended in 1954 with the French defeat at DIEN BIEN PHU and Indo-China was freed from French control. The trauma of the ALGERIAN WAR (1954–62) and the creation of an independent ALGERIA represented the triumph of anti-colonialism, although certain critics see the DOM-TOM as an anachronistic, neo-colonial legacy of Empire. (**Charles Forsdick**)

Further reading

Betts (1991). A concise account of the concrete effects of anti-colonialism and the dismantling of the French Empire. Césaire (2000). Césaire's classic analysis of the destructive impact of colonialism on both colonizer and colonized, first published in French in 1950.

Anti-communism   Opposition to communism, which spread after the Bolshevik revolution of 1917. In France the PCF (*Parti communiste français;* COMMUNIST PARTY) founded after a split in 1920 within the SFIO (SOCIALIST PARTY) challenged the revolutionary credentials of existing left-wing ideologues, the RADICALS and later the socialists. This provoked hostile reactions in the struggle for party supremacy of the revolutionary and parliamentary Left. However, the strongest anti-communist sentiment came from the ruling classes, Church leaders and right-wing politicians. Their hatred of communists was founded on fear of their take-over of power and of their desire to end the exploitation of the working class through the transfer of the privately owned means of production (factories, land, finance) to public ownership. Anti-communist measures included financial sabotage of democratically elected governments and legislation against the PCF. Antagonism to the PCF-backed *FRONT POPULAIRE* government of 1936 resulted in a flight of capital abroad. Hitler and Stalin's pact of non-aggression in 1939 provoked anti-communist measures in France, extended by the VICHY REGIME. These included arrests and deportation, as well as repression of the party and trade unions. DE GAULLE outmanoeuvred the PCF as the liberator of PARIS and pre-empted any possible Communist revolution in 1944, as the PCF was by then a well-armed RESISTANCE group especially in the south of France, and gained the greatest number of votes at the polls in 1945. Opinion towards communists polarized further in France in 1947 with the international ideological conflict known as the COLD WAR, between East and West. Anti-communism was not quite so hysterical in France as was American McCarthyism in the 1950s. It polarized opinion among intellectuals as there seemed to be no middle ground between communism and capitalism until 1968, when a more libertarian Left emerged, critical of the PCF's dogmatism and democratic centralism. Following the electoral demise of the PCF in the 1980s and the collapse of communism in the East, French anti-communism has also declined. **(Máire Cross)**

Further reading

Hewlett (1998). Contextualizes the ideological debates between Right and Left of which anti-communism was an integral part after 1945. Vinen (1996). Contains a detailed account of inter-party ideological strife before 1945.

Anti-fascism   Opposition to existing fascist regimes outside France or to the threat of an imminent take-over within France, in the defence of democracy and human rights. The first successful anti-fascist group was formed to halt the threat of French FASCISM as a result of the fascist dictatorships in Italy, where Mussolini had been in power since 1922, in Germany, where Hitler took over in 1933, and in Spain, where Franco eventually gained victory in 1939. The alliance of SOCIALISTS (*Section française de l'Internationale ouvrière*), RADICALS (*Parti radical*) and the COMMUNIST PARTY (*Parti communiste français*) marked the end of the communists' attacks on the bourgeois parties of the 1920s. This was a result of an order by the Comintern (Communist International), issued from the USSR, for communists to combat fascism by entering a broad-based electoral coalition. Anti-fascist unity in 1935 included Republicans, Republican-socialists, the *Ligue des droits de l'homme* (Human Rights League), the CGT and CGTU trade unions, former servicemen's associations and intellectual anti-fascist committees. This unity led to the election of the *FRONT POPULAIRE* government in June 1936 which proceeded to legislate against the Far Right *Ligues*, although the timidity of the BLUM government in 1936 prevented it from intervening to help republican Spain against Franco. The short-lived left-wing government antagonized many capitalists and the ruling classes, who later accepted defeat and collaboration with Hitler's regime from 1940 to 1944. Since 1945 anti-fascism has been restricted to a small number who maintain a vigil against the threat of fascism. In the name of the 1789 republican tradition of liberty, equality and fraternity, France has accepted victims of fascist regimes such as those of Franco's Spain in 1939 and Pinochet's Chile in 1973, although many refugees from Spain found themselves deported to Germany in 1940. From the 1980s onwards, small anti-fascist associations across Europe have re-emerged to condemn as neo–fascist the racist policies of the Far Right in France and elsewhere. **(Máire Cross)**

Further reading

Jackson (1988). Provides an historical account of the formation of the anti-fascist coalition. Soucy (1995). Provides a detailed analysis of French pro-fascist groups in the inter-war period.

Anti-Semitism   Publicists of the nationalist Extreme Right were the main exponents of ideological anti-Semitism in twentieth-century France, although anti-Semitic prejudice spread far more widely. On the extreme right, hatred of the THIRD REPUBLIC and of the heritage of the Revolution was often entwined with old religious, moral and/or social stereotypes which portrayed the JEWS as evil Christ-killers, debased blasphemers, materialistic parasites and cunning, self-interested schemers. Feeding on actual or imagined politico-financial scandals involving Jews, these images were accompanied by conspiracy theories of Jewish machinations to subvert France and the rest of the world by manipulating the forces of LIBERALISM, secularism, capitalism and socialism to atomize and eventually dominate society. Newer, deterministic racial theories also gave a veneer of scientificity to cultural prejudices. The monarchist league *ACTION FRANÇAISE* bridged the pre-1914 period and the inter-war years in this regard. Some of the other anti-parliamentary leagues of the 1920s and 1930s also propagated anti-Semitism, as did fascist intellectuals such as Robert BRASILLACH and Lucien Rebatet. Léon BLUM, Jewish leader of the Socialists and first Prime Minister of the POPULAR FRONT government in 1936, attracted loathing as an alleged harbinger of national decay and Judaeo-Marxist revolution. Independent of German pressure, the VICHY REGIME enacted legislation restricting the rights of Jews, confiscating property, revoking the citizenship of recently naturalized Jewish immigrants, placing foreign Jews in concentration camps and eventually co-operating in the mass deportations of some 75,000 Jews to the German death camps. For a period after the war these matters were not extensively aired in public. However, as the history of Vichy was increasingly re-examined from the 1970s onwards, accompanied by the trials of Klaus BARBIE, Paul Touvier and Maurice Papon on charges of crimes against humanity, the extent of France's anti-Semitic past was dragged back into the public gaze. At the same time, the Extreme Right, though hampered by laws against incitement to racial hatred and against denial of crimes against humanity, still played on anti-Semitic themes. Jean-Marie LE PEN and other *FRONT NATIONAL* publicists specialized in discursive strategies catering to anti-Semitic stereotypes while staying just inside the law and allowing their authors to deny what they were doing. (**Christopher Flood**)

Further reading

Birnbaum (1992). Covers most of the period. Zuccotti (1999). Useful on French anti-Semitism in general as well as on French treatment of Jews during the Occupation. Marrus and Paxton (1981). Still a valuable source on the wartime period.

Apostrophes 1975–90. Cultural chat show, chaired by Bernard Pivot on *Antenne 2* TELEVISION station.

Aragon, Louis 1897–1983. Writer. As a leader of the SURREALIST movement, his *Paysan de Paris (Paris Peasant,* 1926) was particularly influential. He joined the COMMUNIST PARTY (1927) and became its leading cultural figure in France. He wrote many novels, volumes of poetry and criticism, and played a leading role in the literary RESISTANCE. He edited the review *LES LETTRES FRANÇAISES* (1953–72) and had a powerful political role within the PCF.

Architecture The architecture of contemporary France is a mosaic resulting from the evolution of time, the influence of outside cultures, the specificities of localities and contemporary practical needs. The great *châteaux* of the Loire valley benefited from the influence of Italian culture in Renaissance France (the two-way staircase at Chambord is by Da Vinci). The imposing symmetry of Versailles epitomizes the Classicism of Louis XIV's absolutism, the expression of power through simplicity. The boulevards of Paris created by Baron Haussmann in the 1850s and 1860s originally resulted from the need to sanitize the city's slums.

Many of the recent constructions that dominate France's cities come as a result of post–war necessity. Northern towns that were heavily bombed required hasty rebuilding, thus the concrete functionality of town centres such as those of Brest or Amiens. Population expansion called for cost-effective housing, but whereas English town planners often built outwards, in France they went up. The high-rise HLM, *Habitations à Loyer Modéré*, the equivalent of British council housing or American projects, perhaps reflect the French urban tendency to live in apartments rather than houses. Wealthier French dwellings are often concentrated within the cities, with the less well-off occupying schemes in the suburbs (*banlieues*).

In terms of the monumental and public, recent French architecture has been dominated by MITTERRAND's GRANDS TRAVAUX. This series of grand-scale work aims at architectural excellence within a Republican context. The style is grandiose but unashamedly modern, as in the glass pyramid of the LOUVRE (designed by Ieoh Ming Pei), the giant book-shaped towers of the Bibliothèque nationale de France (by leading French architect Dominique Perrault) or the Grande Arche de la Défense, a 300 000 tonne hollow cube (designed by Otto von Spreckelsen). Critics, however, have labelled the projects exorbitant, often impractical on a functional level and Parisian rather than French.

Architecture in France is overseen by the *Institut Français d'Architecture* (French Institute of Architecture). As with other artistic domains, training is highly centralized. The architecture section of the *École des Beaux Arts* (Fine Arts School) often dominates, although the end product is generally noted for its audacity and non-conformism. (**Laurence Grove**)

Further reading

See the website of the Pompidou Centre: www.centrepompidou.fr. The National Museum of Modern Art's section of the website includes areas on the architecture of contemporary France through reference to their collections. There are pages in English and links to related sites.

Archives   Each of France's *départements* has its own archive, situated in the *préfecture*, in which local and official documents are housed. The term 'archive' in French properly applies in the first instance to these, but there are numerous other facilities of much broader-based interest of which it can also be used. Library facilities in France traditionally centre upon specialist collections in PARIS, while French provincial university libraries tend to be much less well stocked than their British or American counterparts, or often indeed than the main municipal library. The new *Bibliothèque Nationale* is named after President François MITTERRAND, of whose GRANDS TRAVAUX it was the apogee. Opened on the Tolbiac site in 1996, it represents a vast technological and logistic improvement on its predecessor in the Rue de Richelieu, while the Bibliothèque publique d'information in the POMPIDOU CENTRE (Beaubourg) reopened in 1999 in completely refurbished space, with state-of-the-art computer facilities. Access to the latter is free, but this tends to be the exception; a fee is payable not only to use the Bibliothèque Nationale, but for access to the majority of municipal libraries.

The *Vidéothèque de Paris* in Les Halles, recently rechristened the Forum de l'image, makes available a comprehensive array of films and (to a lesser degree) television programmes set in Paris. The *Bibliothèque du film* (BIFI) in the Rue du Faubourg Saint–Antoine is now a world-class archive, with completely open access to books and a growing range of films viewable on video. Most if not all of these archives have their catalogues on-line, further proof that a library culture which for long seemed sadly behind the times is now moving into the twenty-first century. (**Keith Reader**)

Further reading

See the websites of the BPI and the BN: www.bpi.fr and www.bnf.fr

Argot, verlan and tchatche   In its strictest sense, which goes back to the Middle Ages, *argot* refers to secret words and expressions used by criminal and other marginal or specialized groups. Such items may pass into wider conversational use, and even cease to be colloquial altogether (*cambrioleur*, 'burglar', for example). So *argot* is now usually just a general equivalent of 'slang', though the older meaning survives in expressions like *argot militaire* ('military argot'). French has an extensive repertoire of *argotique* alternatives to standard terms – more than English possibly, at least as regards everyday objects (*valoche*, 'suitcase', *lourde*, 'door', etc.).

The ghettoization of immigrant teenagers in high-rise estates has relaunched the secret vocabulary tradition, particularly in the form of *verlan* ('backslang'). This involves making ordinary words like *musique*, 'music' or *femme*, 'woman', unrecognizable by interchanging syllables or individual consonants (*zicmu, meuf*). *Verlan* is itself backslang for *(à) l'envers* ('back-to-front'). When combined with English items, especially from the drug and rock scenes, and with traditional *argot*, the result is a quick-fire, up-to-the-minute style of adolescent speech known as *le tchatche*. Thus: *Cool man, on s'nedo rencart au féca pour dreprend un godet*: '*ne te fâche pas, nous nous sommes donné rendez-vous au café pour prendre un verre*' ('take it easy, we've arranged to meet at the pub for a drink').

Inner-city ghetto talk has come to be imitated by speakers who are neither IMMI-GRANTS nor teenagers nor residents of high-rise estates, but are very susceptible to MEDIA trends. When used in this way, often with an admixture of fashionable intellectual terminology, it is sometimes referred to as *le français branché* ('plugged-in French'), or less flatteringly as *le parler faux jeune* ('fake youth talk'). Meanwhile, the youngsters in their ghettos coin new 'secret' items, increasingly Arabic-based, which in their turn may pass from *tchatche* into more general use, and even into DICTIONARIES. (**Rodney Ball**)

Further reading

Merle (1996). An entertaining introductory account.

Army The army has influenced France as an institution, through individuals in political office, and through shared experiences of compulsory National Service. Only occasionally has the army played determining roles in politics, but stewardship of ATOMIC WEAPONS and consequent proximity to the Presidency cemented its importance.

The First World War proved that the army, though long-time monarchist or bonapartist, would defend the Republic. The 1919 CHAMBRE BLEU HORIZON – the colour of the old army uniform – was right-wing, as France gloried in victory, but faltering inter-war prosperity caused by recession and slow MODERNIZATION, led disaffected *anciens combattants* (former soldiers) to join political leagues such as the CROIX-DE-FEU, contesting the integrity of politics and Republicanism. The army, still dominated by aristocratic officers, hesitated between the Republic and monarchist factions such as the ACTION FRANÇAISE. When the THIRD REPUBLIC foundered (1940), Marshal PÉTAIN (*Action française* sympathizer and First World War hero), and General DE GAULLE claimed France's leadership.

Although de Gaulle rekindled democratic politics in 1944–45, before quitting office (1946), the army influenced post-war politics mainly through colonial wars in INDO-CHINA and ALGERIA. Defeat in Indo-China (1954) made the army desire 'victory' in the ALGERIAN WAR, to regain honour, but plotting of army generals, their mysterious role in returning de Gaulle to office and ending the FOURTH REPUBLIC (1958), and PUTSCH (1961) tainted the army's reputation. Under de Gaulle and successive presidents, atomic weapons and NUCLEAR DETERRENCE gave the army renewed importance and direct access to the powerful Presidency of the FIFTH REPUBLIC.

The end of compulsory National Service in 1997 concluded France's tradition of linking armed forces and nation through a 'Republican' people's army of young (male) conscripts. France's newly 'professionalized' army faces this, as well as budget cuts and moves towards European defence, in defining its identity. (**Hugh Dauncey**)

Further reading

Waites (1984). This puts the army in a broader context.

Aron, Raymond 1905–83. Liberal sociologist and journalist. A friend of SARTRE and a prominent intellectual figure after 1945 in his own right, he distinguished himself by his popularizations of SOCIOLOGY and his attacks on MARXIST ideas.

Art Art in France has a rich history of innovation and patronage from the Middle Ages onwards. François I (1494–1547), for example, provided a catalyst for the French Renaissance by encouraging the influx of Italian art and artists, among them Leonardo da Vinci. The seventeenth century saw the court patronage of such artists as Philippe de Champaigne, Nicolas Poussin and Charles Le Brun, as well as the creation of the Academy of Painting and Sculpture (*Académie de Peinture et Sculpture*, 1648). The *salons* of the eighteenth and nineteenth centuries further institutionalized the production and display of art and accompanied the success of the Neo-Classical (e.g. Ingres, David) and Romantic (Delacroix, Géricault) styles. None the less it was reaction against the establishment that led to Impressionism and Post-Impressionism.

Counter-reaction accounts for much of the French-dominated movements of the twentieth century. DADA and SURREALISM (BRETON, DUCHAMP) can be read as reactions against the nonsensical atrocities of the First World War. The case of surrealism, with its close links between automatic writing, political activity, dream-like paintings and mixed-media creations, stands as a good example of the dependency of French (and all) art upon other disciplines and influences. This has happened in spite of the strictly compartmentalized French education system.

The post-1945 period has seen heavy and inspirational French involvement in movements often classed as North American domains: Alain Jacquet's photo mock-up of Manet's *Déjeuner sur l'herbe* (Lunch on the grass, 1964) epitomizes Pop-Art and Bertrand Lavier's fridge-based sculpture *Brandt sur Haffner* (1975) is a clear example of Conceptual Art. Current French artists of note include Niki de SAINT-PHALLE (*Nouveau Realisme*), Ben (Swiss but working in France, Installation Art) and Jacques Monory (Narrative Figuration).

Despite the irreverence of much French art, it is often the product of a closed and institutionalized system. *The École des Beaux Arts* near the SAINT-GERMAIN area in Paris generally remains the training ground for artists and critics alike and the country's system of galleries, dealers and outlets (e.g. the National Museum of Modern Art in the POMPIDOU CENTRE) are very much PARIS-based. (**Laurence Grove**)
See also PAINTING.

Further reading

www.louvre.fr The Louvre website includes all aspects of French art up to the mid-nineteenth century. There are pages in English and links to related art sites.
www.centrepompidou.fr. The section of this website on the National Museum of Modern Arts gives general information, through reference to their collections, on many aspects of contemporary French art. There are pages in English and links to related sites.

Art galleries   See MUSEUMS.

Artaud, Antonin   1896–1948. Theatre director and writer. He was best known for his advocacy of a 'theatre of cruelty', developed in *Le Théâtre et son double* (*The Theatre and its Double*, 1938), which called for plays to engage their audience emotionally.

Assimilation   A process of cultural change generally understood to mean the adoption of a dominant cultural model by disempowered groups together with their abandoning of previously distinctive cultural values and practices. During the colonial period, assimilation served as a synonym for the *mission civilisatrice* (civilizing mission) by which French ÉLITES frequently sought to justify authoritarian rule overseas. After DECOLONIZATION, the word tended to slip into disuse, but the underlying idea has often been implicit and sometimes explicit in the debates over RACE and ethnicity surrounding the settlement in France of IMMIGRANT minorities originating in former colonies. Many non-immigrants believe these new minorities should assimilate, meaning that they should adopt the cultural codes which are dominant in France and abandon linguistic, religious and other cultural traits characteristic of their countries of origin.

In the colonial context, the idea of assimilation was based almost literally on a black-and-white view of different cultural norms. French and more generally European values and practices, transplanted into the colonies by white settlers, were assumed to be far superior to those of the indigenous populations, who were also distinguished by darker skin colours and other 'racial' features. In the post-colonial period, Extreme-Right parties such as the FRONT NATIONAL have argued that immigrant minorities of Third World origin are culturally inassimilable and should therefore be expelled from France. In the wider debate concerning these post-colonial minorities the word most commonly used is now 'INTEGRATION' rather than 'assimilation'. For some, particularly on the right of the political spectrum, the two words are largely interchangeable. Others, generally more to the left, take a less hierarchical view of integration, arguing for a process of mutual cultural adaptation on the part of majority and minority ethnic groups. (**Alec Hargreaves**)

Further reading

Gaspard (1992). This article positions 'assimilation' in the wider debate over ethnic relations in France.

Association des Écrivains et Artistes Révolutionnaires (AEAR)   1932–39. Cultural

association sponsored by the COMMUNIST PARTY, which sought to draw writers and artists into political activity. It published a journal, *Commune*, and attracted prominent figures in literature, painting and theatre.

Atget, Eugène   1857–1927. Photographer. He spent twenty-five years taking around

7000 photographs, mainly of old PARIS. He regarded himself as a provider of useful documents, and only after his death was he recognized as perhaps the greatest precursor of photographic modernism. See also PHOTOGRAPHY. (**Johnnie Gratton**)

Atheism   The belief that there is no God. It is often distinguished from agnosti-

cism, which declines to believe that there is or is not a God, and should also be distinguished from anti-clericalism, which involves hostility to the Church, and can be found among believers and non-believers. With the separation of the Church from the STATE at the beginning of the twentieth century, atheism was no longer punishable by law, and the radical philosophical traditions of the eighteenth century Enlightenment came back into fashion in France. Militant atheism was widely promoted by liberal parties who wished to eliminate the influence of the Church in public and private life, especially in the areas of HEALTH, EDUCATION and science. It was taken up by many in the SOCIALIST and COMMUNIST movements after the First World War. They adopted Marx's dictum that religion is the 'opium of the people', a narcotic which gives comfort but stops people from taking action to improve the conditions in which they live. It was also taken up by many scientists, who regarded religious beliefs as superstitions, and saw them as an obstacle to scientific enquiry.

The dominant CATHOLIC CHURCH responded with active campaigns against atheism, arguing that it was a danger not just to organized religion but also to individual moral integrity and to social order. The Second Vatican Council (1962–65) modified this approach, and adopted an attitude of dialogue to build relations between Catholics and non-believers, and to encourage co-operation with them on social issues as well as on the ethical issues arising from scientific and technological advance. In response, the parties of the Left and the scientific community attenuated their hostility to religion, regarding it as a private matter for individuals. Some intellectuals argued that atheism was not an essential component of science, or of MARXIST theory, but merely the ideological climate in which they had historically developed. In the latter part of the century, the resurgence of fundamentalist approaches to religion, both Catholic and increasingly ISLAMIC, have challenged the truce with atheism. (**Michael Kelly**)

Further reading

Chadwick (2000). A useful collection of essays on social and intellectual aspects of Catholicism.

Atomic weapons   France was the fourth country to acquire atomic and nuclear capabilities, testing her first A-bomb in the Algerian Sahara in 1960. France's independent NUCLEAR DETERRENT strategy has required constant development of her nuclear arsenal and the nuclear industry (military and civil) has been an important, if sometimes much-contested aspect of France's techno-industrial MODERNIZATION. Nuclear weapons remain central to French defence, although conventional forces and new technologies such as satellite observation compete for defence funding. Preparatory work on atomic weaponry was done during the FOURTH REPUBLIC, but final decisions to proceed with production were taken by DE GAULLE on his return to power in 1958, accompanied by the creation of a *secrétariat d'État aux questions atomiques et spatiales* (Office of Secretary of State for Atomic and Space Matters). The *Commissariat à l'énergie atomique* (CEA, Atomic Energy Commission), founded in 1945, and the defence procurement agency collaborated on warheads for air delivery by Mirage bombers, sea-based ballistic missiles created by the SPACE PROGRAMME carried by France's nuclear submarines (SNLE) and silo-based land missiles on the Plateau d'Albion. During the 1970s, France prepared her acquisition of tactical nuclear weapons, in reflection of evolving doctrines of French deterrent strategy and the possible use of Hadès tactical missiles in European conflict as a 'final warning' of France's readiness to use her deterrent force. Throughout the life of the strategic deterrent, nuclear weapons have been constantly modernized in response to needs for smaller multiple missile heads and more accurate targeting. The CEA and nuclear lobby claim that logistically complex warhead programmes and mastery of nuclear TECHNOLOGY have stimulated the French ECONOMY, but critics suggest that nuclear weapons funding has deprived other sectors. Until 1996, when France finally abandoned nuclear warhead testing in the Pacific, French refusal to limit testing at Mururoa and Fangataufa atolls focused attention of protesters on the warhead programme and brought France into conflict with PACIFIC countries. (**Hugh Dauncey**)

Further reading

Howorth (1984). Deals with French nuclear defence policy and anti-nuclear movements.

Audiovisual industry   The audiovisual industry traditionally comprises TELEVISION, RADIO and CINEMA. Recently it has been extended by developments in new media such as the Internet. The audiovisual landscape, known in France as the 'PAF' or *paysage audiovisuel français*, is an extremely important part of French culture, playing a major role in the construction and dissemination of national IDENTITIES.

The importance of the audiovisual industry is underlined by long-standing STATE involvement. Television and radio remained virtual state monopolies until the 1980s. The film industry was not controlled by the state in the same way. However, state intervention was introduced to support cinematic production as early as the 1920s.

The audiovisual industry became a vital tool in the SOCIALIST administration of the 1980s. Socialist cultural policy placed a firm emphasis on national culture, its international role and its protection from external threat. Central to this cultural crusade were the audiovisual media, particularly television and cinema. Various forms of state support (for example financial aid for the film industry) and intervention (government praise for specific films such as Claude BERRI's *Germinal* of 1993 for example) bear witness to the importance of the audiovisual industry.

These various forms of support and intervention reveal a very French conception of audiovisual production. In France television, film and radio are generally considered to be more than just industries and as such in need of protection from market forces. This understanding, combined with the role of audiovisual production in the construction of a national culture, came to a head in the GATT (General Agreement on Tariffs and Trades) discussions of 1993. Whereas American negotiators advocated the application of the principles of free trade to the audiovisual industries, the French called for 'cultural exception', the continuing state protection of audiovisual production. These very different positions highlight the national importance of the audiovisual industries in France and the role they have long played in France's struggles with the United States. See also AMERICA. **(Lucy Mazdon)**

Further reading

Hayward (1993). A useful history of French cinema which emphasises its role in the construction of national identities. Kuhn (1995). Provides an overview of the main developments in the media industries, including television and radio.

Auriol, Vincent   1884–1966. Socialist politician, elected first President of the FOURTH REPUBLIC in 1946.

Author   The prestige enjoyed by the figure of the literary author extends a tradition instituted in 1634 when Cardinal Richelieu created the French Academy (*ACADÉMIE FRANÇAISE*) to edit a DICTIONARY and a grammar of the FRENCH LANGUAGE. Since 1900, the Academy's role as a prime site of legitimation for literary authors has been challenged by PUBLISHING houses, journals and mass MEDIA from the daily press to TELEVISION. Legitimation has also occurred in the form of annual PRIZES and awards and in critical editions such as the Bibliothèque de la Pléiade. After 1945, critics and theorists redirected concerns with the literary work (*œuvre*) toward the process of writing (*ÉCRITURE*) often at odds with authorial intention. The programme of COMMITTED writing as promoted by Jean-Paul SARTRE in his post-war monthly, *Les Temps Modernes*, equated the literary author with the poet in opposition to the writer of prose who contended directly with social and political issues.

Two decades later, Roland BARTHES set the author (*écrivain*) apart from the writer-scribe (*écrivant*) and speculated on writing as an intransitive verb in order to argue that the birth of the reader occurred at the cost of the author. Around the same time, Michel FOUCAULT identified an author-function resulting from discursive practices that governed the production of texts. In 'The Laugh of the Medusa' (1975), Hélène CIXOUS asserted the specificity of women's writing in an early formulation of what she soon theorized as feminine writing (*ÉCRITURE FÉMININE*). Recent proponents of genetic criticism (*critique génétique*) have returned to the literary author by tracing the creative process in the form of textual variants in what some have seen as a variation of the practice, promoted a century earlier by Gustave Lanson (1857–1934), of reading the work via the life of the author. (**Keith Reader**)

Further reading

Debray (1981). Traces writers' evolving roles from 1880 to (1980), during three ages or cycles dominated by the university, the publishing house and the media. Sartre (1988). A grand synthesis and historical model of literary practices; dated yet still provocative.

Autobiography   Autobiography is traditionally identified with the practice of housing one's temporally disparate experiences within a unifying narrative form. In recent years, this understanding of autobiography as 'life writing' has expanded to take in the diverse range of discursive practices that constitute the broader field of 'self-writing'.

The history of modern French autobiography is a patchy affair. Of the many autobiographical works published before 1945, few continue to be highly regarded. While GIDE's *Si le grain ne meurt* (If it Die, 1926) has long been viewed as a classic, works by COLETTE such as *La Naissance du jour* (*Break of Day*, 1928) and *Sido* (1929) have received only belated recognition. The shared theme of struggle to achieve a measure of personal freedom and authenticity recurs in Michel LEIRIS's *L'Age d'homme* (*Manhood*, 1939). Here, however, the use of juxtaposition and association as structuring principles yields a remarkably original experiment in self-portraiture.

Leiris subsequently went on to write the four volumes of *La règle du jeu* (*The Rules of the Game*), widely held to be one of the richest explorations of autobiography in any modern literature. Thematically this work often intersected with the spate of post–war autobiographical writing sponsored by EXISTENTIALISM. Jean GENET, Simone de BEAUVOIR, and Violette Leduc all produced important works, with Sartre's *Les mots* (*Words*, 1963) forming a high point. As STRUCTURALISM replaced existentialism, so autobiography lost its intellectual legitimacy, only to regain it with the publication of *Roland Barthes by Roland Barthes* (1975), at once a critique of autobiographical premises and an affirmation of autobiographical possibilities. Various blends of critique and affirmation went on to characterize the 'new' autobiography, whether exemplified by Georges PEREC's *W ou le Souvenir de l'enfance* (*W or the Memory of Childhood*, 1975), Nathalie SARRAUTE's *Enfance* (*Childhood*, 1983), or Marguerite DURAS's *L'Amant* (*The Lover*, 1984). By the final decades of the twentieth century, the lure of autobiography became so unusually strong that it drew certain writers, such as Annie ERNAUX and Pierre Bergounioux, away from fiction altogether, and drew others, such as Serge Doubrovsky and Christine Angot, towards the frontier zone known as 'autofiction'. (**Johnnie Gratton**)

Further reading

Keefe, and Smyth 1995. Sheringham 1993.

Automobile industry   The automobile industry reflects major industrial, economic and social transformations in France. Post-war iconic cars such as the RENAULT 2CV, 4CV, the CITROËN DS, and the Renault R4 and R5 marked French society, and were emblematic of their times and of the social groups to whom they gave mobility. As car production became globally competitive in the 1980s and 1990s French firms collaborated with foreign producers. The World Wars were instrumental in developing France's car industry. Mass production instituted during the 'war economy' of 1914–18 was implemented in the inter-war period by Renault and Citroën, reinforcing France's European industry leadership. Renault and Citroën were technically innovative, but in the 1930s, high taxes on cars and the government emphasis on RAILWAYS slowed industry expansion.

The OCCUPATION (1940–44) and the COLLABORATION of car producers such as Renault caused industry reorganization after 1945. Renault underwent NATIONALIZA-TION as the Régie-Renault, and several smaller producers merged. During the 1950s Renault, Citroën, Peugeot, Panhard and Simca were encouraged by governments to target different market sectors. Renault (economy models) built the 4CV (1946) and successive *voitures sociales* (social cars). Peugeot (mid-sector) produced the 203 (1949). Citroën (luxury) marketed *tractions avant* (front-wheel drive cars) and the ground-breaking DS19 (1956). Citroën also produced the inexpensive 2CV (1949) designed pre-war for France's small farmers, and by the 1970s producers had diversified their ranges. Despite the massive success of the R4 (1961) which offered affordable load-carrying, the R5 (1972), a safe style for women, and the Citroën GS (mid-range), high-tech exports were weak, especially to the USA. During the 1970s, mergers concentrated production around Renault and PSA Peugeot-Citroën. Automated fabrication has reduced employment in car production, and international collaboration has weakened the *exception française* of the automobile industry, but it still reflects French socio-economic MODERNIZATION, and current problems of manufacturing industry. French STATE aid to Renault in particular has brought France into conflict with EU industry and competition policy, which is inspired by LIBERALISM. (**Hugh Dauncey**)

Further reading

McLintock (1983). A history of Renault cars.

Avant-garde   A French word meaning 'vanguard', the advance division of an army. The term was first applied to ART in the 1820s by the French socialist Saint-Simon, who believed that the artist was essentially an agent of progress and emancipation. Since Saint-Simon's time, the concept of the avant-garde has undergone numerous revisions in response to changing artistic theories and practices. Clement Greenberg, the major art critic of the 1950s and 1960s, argued that modernism, as reflected in the evolution of painting from Manet to abstract expressionism, was all about exploring the possibilities of one's medium. 'Avant-gardeness', therefore, was essentially a matter of formal and technical innovation. A very different view emerged in Peter Bürger's influential *Theory of the Avant-Garde* (1974), a book that restores the militant note struck by Saint-Simon. Only by being REVOLUTIONARY, anti-institutional, and concerned to reintegrate with life, can art fully merit description as 'avant-garde'.

Bürger's view makes sense in the French context because it appears to be supported by modern French cultural history. The French experience, centred upon PARIS, includes not only *artistic* movements that match his criteria (especially DADA and SURREALISM), but also, crucially, *intellectual* movements such as EXISTENTIALISM, STRUCTURALISM, and the entirely Paris-based variant of POST-STRUCTURALISM known as *TEL QUEL*. All of these movements became, like Paris itself, sites of convergence between literature and ideas, aesthetics and ethics, art and politics. And in this dynamic of convergence, perhaps, lies the most valuable legacy of modernist avant-gardism.

By the last quarter of the twentieth century, with French left-wing politics in disarray and with the waning of intellectual confidence in all-encompassing systems of thought, new uncertainties were making avant-gardism look arrogant and pretentious. Moreover, fresh approaches to art history were changing our image of avant-garde movements: had they not always been male-dominated groups motivated by elitist desires? In the light of such questioning, the contemporary shift in idiom from heroic 'avant-garde' to practical 'cutting edge' speaks volumes. (**Johnnie Gratton**)

Further reading

Bürger (1984); Compagnon (1994). This is critical of both Greenberg and Bürger, makes an interesting case for distinguishing modernism from avant-gardism. Wood (1999). A balanced and informative survey, with several essays on manifestations of avant-gardism in France.

Avignon Festival   Founded in 1947 by Jean VILAR, this is the largest of France's publicly funded summer arts festivals, and focuses on music, theatre and dance. See THEATRE FESTIVALS.

Aymé, Marcel   1902–67. Novelist who wrote whimsical and at times acerbic stories of French life, often with country settings. He came under attack at the LIBERATION for his right-wing sympathies. His collection of short stories, *La Passe-muraille* (1943) is still popular.

Aznavour, Charles   Born 1924. A popular French singer and songwriter who won an international following in the 1950s for his relaxed rendering of romantic themes.

B

Baccalauréat   School-leaving certificate, comprising a number of subjects, whose nature and relative importance varies according to the emphasis (Letters, Natural Sciences, etc.) of the programme. The written and oral examinations are administered nationally. Success in obtaining an overall average pass mark in the *bac* or *bachot* is an entry qualification for university and for many white collar jobs. The government has set a target of 80 per cent pass rate by 2000, and has come close to meeting it.

Bachelard, Gaston   1884–1962. Philosopher and historian of science. He examined radical breaks in the development of knowledge, and analysed the meanings of important archetypal themes in culture and society, such as the four elements (earth, water, air, fire), for example in *Le psychanalyse du feu* (*The Psychoanalysis of Fire*, 1938).

Baker, Joséphine   1906–75. American-born black singer and dancer, who was popular for her sexy performances and exotic costumes in the 1920s, particularly in her MUSIC-HALL show, *la Revue nègre*.

Balladur, Édouard   Born 1929. Gaullist politician. He was Finance Minister 1986–88 and Prime Minister 1993–95.

Bande dessinée   The *bande dessinée* ('drawn strip') might be the closest linguistic equivalent to the comic strip, but sociologically the two are vastly different. In France the 'BD' is commonly referred to as the Ninth Art, it occupies an important section in any main bookshop, and statesmen such as DE GAULLE or JOSPIN have invited comparison with BD characters. The form also has its national institution in Angoulême, where the large-scale BD festival takes place annually in the last weekend of January.

Recent critics have been eager to trace the BD back to the Bayeux Tapestry and beyond, although the illustrated narratives of Rodolphe Töpffer (1799–1846) are generally given as starting point. In the 1930s syndicated imports that appeared in children's weeklies (such as *Mickey, Robinson*) recorded heavy sales. However American imports were limited during the war, and then afterwards through the COMMUNIST-inspired 1949 law on Children's Publications. The 1950s saw the success of French BDs in journals such as the communist *Vaillant* or the Catholic *Cœurs vaillants*. In 1959 René GOSCINNY, now of Astérix fame, instigated *PILOTE*, a magazine that gradually turned the form towards an adolescent audience, prefiguring the indisputably adult-aimed productions of the 1960s, such as *Barbarella*. The 1980s and 1990s saw the switch from magazines to albums as the predominant BD form.

It should be stressed that the BD is a francophone rather than a French obsession, one of the strongest traditions being in Belgium. Early Brussels productions include the adventures of Tintin and the long-running journal *Spirou*, which introduced such characters as the Smurfs (*Les Schtroumpfs*) and Lucky Luke. Brussels also boasts a national BD centre.

Current *bandes dessinées* cover an enormous range of styles, themes and ideas. Sci-fi ecliptic narratives have been mastered by Moebius (Jean GIRAUD). Claire BRETÉCHER has covered feminist issues in her simply-drawn bourgeois characters. Political and social issues have been broached by Lax (*Chiens de fusils* on Northern Ireland) and Jo (albums on AIDS), among others. There is also a vast market for pornography and violence in BD form.

The BD is an area of modern culture where France has beaten American imports. Indeed the Gauls' resilience might be gauged in the success of the Parc Astérix as compared with the trouble-stricken Disneyland Paris (formerly EURO-DISNEY). **(Laurence Grove)**

Further reading

Look at the website of the National Centre in Angoulême. It includes pages in English and links to a host of other BD sites: www.cnbdi.fr

Banlieues   Literally, suburbs. In current usage, the term commonly denotes disadvantaged urban areas associated with stereotyped images of immigrants and social deviance, notably criminality. Understood thus, the *banlieues* are connoted similarly to 'inner-city' areas in Britain and the USA. This meaning of the term is a fairly recent phenomenon, closely related to the politicisation of IMMIGRATION, RACE and ethnicity during the 1980s and 1990s. Until then, *banlieue* was a generic term embracing suburban areas as a whole, including well-to-do as well as less affluent districts. This broader meaning is still in circulation, but media usage has transformed the everyday connotations of the word by focusing on socially deprived neighbourhoods, containing dense concentrations of minority ethnic groups.

This semantic change is linked to longer-term developments in migratory flows, socio-economic conditions, housing policy and the wider political context. The minorities most associated with the *banlieues*, as currently understood, are of Third World origin. Until the 1970s, these groups were under-represented in *habitations à loyer modéré* (HLM), publicly run housing equivalent to council housing in the UK and housing projects in the USA. Government action to eradicate BIDONVILLES (shanty towns) and other sub-standard forms of housing in which immigrant workers were concentrated coincided with the rise of family settlement among minorities of Third World origin. Increasingly, these were housed in high-rise HLM blocks, generally situated in outlying suburbs. During the 1980s and 1990s, these districts experienced particularly high unemployment rates together with sporadic outbreaks of violence between disaffected youths and the police. The stigmatization of these neighbourhoods in media reports and political discourse helped to turn the *banlieues* into a synonym for social problems and ethnic tensions. **(Alec Hargreaves)**

Further reading

Hargreaves (1996).

Barbara 1930–97. Singer and song-writer. She was popular in the 1960s for her *femme fatale* persona and emotional songs such as *Nantes* (1964), which evokes the death of her father.

Barbie, Klaus 1913–91. Chief of the Gestapo in LYON (1942–44), known as the 'butcher of Lyon', since he was responsible for massacres of civilians, large-scale torture, including that of Jean MOULIN, and the deportation to concentration camps of many JEWS and RESISTANCE members. He became a prosperous ship-owner, but was eventually found and extradited from Bolivia. He was sentenced to life imprisonment in 1987 after a high-profile trial for crimes against humanity.

Barbusse, Henri 1873–1935. Writer. Celebrated for his best-selling anti-war novels, *Le Feu* (*Fire*, 1916) and *Clarté* (*Light*, 1919), he became a leading figure of the intellectual Left, and a staunch supporter of COMMUNISM.

Bardot, Brigitte Born 1934. Actress whose starring role in Roger Vadim's film *Et Dieu créa la femme* (*And God Created Woman*, 1956) established her as France's answer to Marilyn Monroe in the 1950s and 1960s. She later became an animal rights campaigner.

Barrault, Jean-Louis 1910–94. Actor and director. He was a powerful actor on stage and screen, and an influential director, using every available aspect of the performing arts in 'total theatre'. He directed plays by most major French dramatists of the post-war period.

Barre, Raymond Born 1924. Centre-Right politician. An academic economist, he served as a European commissioner (1967–72) as a minister, and as Prime Minister (1976–81) under GISCARD D'ESTAING. He stood unsuccessfully for President in 1988.

Barrès, Maurice 1862–1923. Writer. A conservative novelist and essayist, who influenced the intellectual Right during the inter-war period.

Barthes, Roland 1915–80. Writer and cultural critic. He challenged the traditional institutions of literature, preferring the more open concept of ÉCRITURE (writing). He developed an influential critique of the MYTHS and meanings in the MEDIA and EVERYDAY LIFE, in *Mythologies* (1957), and was an influential figure in French CRITICAL THEORY.

Bataille, Georges 1897–1962. Writer and ethnographer. His early analyses of non-Western societies led him to explore the role of culture in society, and his subsequent writings reflect deeply on issues of sacrifice, transgression and exoticism.

Baudrillard, Jean Born 1929. Social theorist. His studies of CONSUMER society have focused on the importance of symbolic systems, and the alienating effects of progress and modernity. He has been influential in POST-MODERNIST criticism.

Bazin, André   1918–58. Film critic. His analyses of film genres and the aesthetics of CINEMA have been widely influential, and he was co–founder in 1951 of the leading French film magazine, *CAHIERS DU CINÉMA*.

Beaubourg   See POMPIDOU CENTRE.

Beauvoir, Simone de   1908–86. Novelist and philosopher. She was a leading figure in the EXISTENTIALIST movement and a life-long partner of Jean-Paul SARTRE. Her novels and autobiographies are widely read, but her most enduring achievement is *Le deuxième sexe* (*The Second Sex*, 1949) which is regarded as the founding text of modern FEMINIST thought.

Bécaud, Gilbert   Born 1927. Singer and song-writer. An energetic stage performer, he was popular from the mid-1950s, particular for romantic ballads like *Et maintenant* (What now my love?).

Beckett, Samuel   1906–89. Irish-born writer. He spent most of his career in France, and wrote in English and French. Best known for *En attendant Godot* (*Waiting for Godot*, 1953) his plays, novels, poems and films became increasingly austere and minimal as he explored the limits of language, communication and identity. He was awarded the Nobel Prize in 1969.

Belgium (French in)   The three language communities of Belgium comprise French, Dutch and German speakers respectively (there are also many immigrant languages, with no official status). But the communities correspond only partly to the three administrative regions of this recently federalized country. These are: Wallonia in the south, with 3.3 million francophone Walloons and, along the German border, the 68 000 Belgian germanophones; Flanders in the north, with 5.9 million Flemings, who speak Dutch (the term 'Flemish' is best reserved for local dialects); the national capital, Brussels, an enclave inside Flanders, with a population (950 000) that is four-fifths French-speaking.

In Flanders public services are provided in Dutch only, while French has sole official status in Wallonia (the German speakers have special arrangements). Both languages are official in Brussels, where administrative offices, street signs, etc. are bilingual. Upwardly mobile francophone *Bruxellois* have recently been abandoning large areas of the inner city to the immigrants and moving into more affluent Flemish territory just outside the bilingual area, which they are demanding should be extended. The demand is rejected by the Flemings, determined to resist any expansion of bilingualism (the Brussels 'oil stain', as they call it).

There are many such disputes between the two communities, and striking economic disparities: prosperous, 'high-tech' Flanders is a world away from the derelict former mining districts of Wallonia. Indeed, the continued viability of Belgium as a unitary state is increasingly being called into question. But most francophones are unenthusiastic about closer links with France: their ties are increasingly with their immediate local district. It is noticeable in this connection that distinctive regional accents, rarer and rarer in northern France, continue to flourish in Wallonia, even in urban areas. However, the traditional Walloon and Picard dialects are nowadays in sharp decline, despite valiant efforts to preserve them. (**Rodney Ball**)

Further reading

Blampain *et al.* (1997). A comprehensive linguistic survey. Pavy (1999). Deals with community and identity issues.

Belmondo, Jean-Paul   Born 1933. Actor. One of France's most respected film actors, who has made over sixty films from *A bout de souffle* (*Breathless*, 1959) to *Les Misérables* (1995).

Benda, Julien   1867–1956. Writer. Best known for his essay *Le Trahison des clercs* (*Treason of the clerks*, 1927), which attacked INTELLECTUALS for their compromises with the political and commercial world, he went on to become a prominent campaigner for peace and against FASCISM.

Benveniste, Émile   1902–76. Linguist. One of France's major contributors to LINGUISTIC theory, his work developed the tradition of Saussure, and has been influential in literary criticism.

Bérégovoy, Pierre   1925–93. Socialist politician. Finance Minister and Prime Minister (1992–93) under MITTERRAND, he committed suicide after a heavy electoral defeat.

Bergson, Henri   1859–1941. Philosopher. His analysis of time, memory and human consciousness and his concept of *élan vital* (life force) were influential in the early twentieth century, though he is generally remembered for his short essay on laughter (*Le Rire*, 1900). Interest in his ideas was revived during the 1990s by philosophers like DELEUZE.

Bernanos, Georges   1888–1948. Catholic writer. Best known for his novels of the struggle between good and evil in country settings, such as *Journal d'un curé de campagne* (Diary of a Country Priest, 1936), he was also an influential essayist in the polemical tradition of Catholic moralists.

Berri, Claude   Born 1934. Film director. He is best known for his film adaptations of literary works, especially the internationally successful 'heritage' films *Jean de Florette* and *Manon des sources* (1986).

Besson, Luc   Born 1959. Film director. His films specialize in violence and action, often inspired by Hollywood, where he has been based since his science-fiction success *Le Cinquième Élement* (*The Fifth Element*, 1997).

***Beur* culture**   Forms of cultural expression associated with second-generation members of the Maghrebi (North African) minority in France. '*Beur*' is a VERLAN (backslang) expression formed by inverting and partially truncating the syllables of the word 'Arabe'. To avoid the often pejorative connotations of 'Arabe' inherited from the era of COLONIALISM, youths of immigrant origin began calling themselves 'Beurs' during the late 1970s. The word entered general circulation in the mid-1980s, when media usage often linked the term to social problems stereotypically associated with IMMIGRATION such as poor housing, poverty and crime. For this and other reasons, many second-generation Maghrebis now reject the term.

Among the earliest artistic activities of the 'Beur' generation were amateur theatre groups playing to local audiences from the mid-1970s onwards. Like later 'Beur' artists, they performed essentially in French, with a sprinkling of Arabic and Berber expressions borrowed from parental cultures. They have also been heavily influenced via the MASS MEDIA by anglophone, especially American, cultural models. Mehdi Charef's novel *Le Thé au harem d'Archi Ahmed* (*Tea in Archi Ahmed's Harem*, 1983) and its subsequent adaptation as a film, with the slightly modified title of *Le Thé au harem d'Archimède* (*Tea in Archimedes's Harem*, 1985), helped to launch a significant and still growing body of literary and cinematic work. During the 1990s, artists of Maghrebi origin in bands such as Assassin and IAM were among those contributing to the rise of rap as one of the most popular forms of music in contemporary France. (**Alec Hargreaves**)

Further reading

Hargreaves (1997). A detailed literary study drawing on interviews and unpublished documents. Hargreaves and McKinney (1997). Includes chapters on film, television, literature and music.

Beuve-Méry, Hubert 1902–89. Journalist. He served as correspondent with Le TEMPS in the 1930s, and as director of studies at the URIAGE Leadership School (1940–42). He became founding director of *Le MONDE* in 1944, a post he held till his retirement. His editorials and his Centre-Left stance on current affairs were highly influential in French political life.

Bibliothèque nationale de France See LIBRARIES, ARCHIVES.

Bidault, Georges 1899–1983. Christian democratic politician. A prominent RESISTANCE figure, he helped to found the Christian Democrat MRP Party in 1944 and served as a senior minister and Prime Minister (twice). He supported the return to power of DE GAULLE in 1958 but opposed the independence of ALGERIA, as a result of which he spent six years in exile (1962–68).

Bidonvilles Shantytowns, typically consisting of huts built of wood and corrugated iron, lacking basic amenities such as mains supplies of water, gas and electricity. Amid the post-war housing shortage, *bidonvilles* sprang up on plots of spare land in many French cities during the 1950s and 1960s. They were built mainly by IMMIGRANT workers, filling gaps in the labour market, for whom no housing provision had been made. Ironically, many of these immigrants were employed in the construction industry, but the new housing which they helped to build went primarily to the majority ethnic population. At their height in the mid-1960s, French *bidonvilles* were officially estimated to contain 75 000 inhabitants. According to unofficial estimates, the figure was at least three times higher. One of the biggest groups of *bidonvilles*, in the Paris suburb of Nanterre, contained 10 000 residents.

Graphically depicted in Bourlem Guerdjou's film *Vivre au paradis* (Living in Paradise, 1999), living conditions in *bidonvilles* were squalid. Without proper sanitation, they were breeding grounds for disease. Makeshift heating arrangements were a constant fire risk. Following media coverage of fires, which had claimed a growing number of lives, legislation was passed in 1964 aimed at clearing the *bidonvilles* and rehousing their inhabitants. It was to be another ten years before the last of the main *bidonvilles* was cleared. Some smaller pockets, known as *micro-bidonvilles*, endured long after this. Many inhabitants were rehoused initially in *cités de transit* (transit estates), which were somewhat better but still temporary accommodation. In some cases they remained there as long as twenty years before gaining access to permanent housing, often in publicly run tower blocks in areas now known as the BANLIEUES. **(Alec Hargreaves)**

Further reading

Lallaoui (1993). A vividly illustrated study placing the *bidonvilles* in the wider context of post-war French housing developments.

Blanchot, Maurice   Born 1907. Writer and critic. His works explore the nature of writing, to which he ascribes a privileged role in articulating human SUBJECTIVITY and ethical concerns.

Blin, Roger   1907–84. Actor and theatre director. He is best known for his experimental theatre, and his work in theatre of the ABSURD (*NOUVEAU THÉÂTRE*), with writers like BECKETT and GENET.

Bloc national   Centre-Right electoral coalition, which secured a majority in the post-war elections of November 1919, and governed until 1924.

Bloch, Marc   1886–1944. Historian. Co-founder of *ANNALES* (1929), his study of medieval society (*La Société médiévale*, 1939–40) remains a classic. He was active in the RESISTANCE, and was shot by the Gestapo.

Blum, Léon   1872–1950. Socialist politician. A literary scholar and moralist, he was a follower of Jean Jaurès, and an opponent of COMMUNISM. He directed the SOCIALIST PARTY newspaper, *Le Populaire* from 1920, and led the POPULAR FRONT government as Prime Minister (1936–37). Arrested by the VICHY government and prosecuted unsuccessfully, he was deported to Buchenwald concentration camp. On his return, he served again in government, including briefly as Prime Minister. His socialist HUMANISM, expressed in the essays of *A l'échelle humaine* (*On a Human Scale*, 1945) became his party's guiding philosophy.

Blum-Byrnes Agreement   This is the name commonly given to an appendix to the post-war agreement on a range of economic issues between France, represented by former Prime Minister Léon Blum and the United States, represented by Secretary of State James Byrnes. It was signed in Washington on 28th May 1946. The appendix, called an 'Understanding' in the English text and '*Arrangement*' in the French, set out the provisions under which American films could be imported into France. Instead of limiting the number of dubbed foreign films which could be imported, the 'agreement' instituted a 'screen quota' whereby exhibitors were obliged to set aside a number of weeks per quarter (initially four, and raised to five in 1948) for the screening of films produced in France. It was initially welcomed by the film industry, especially the distributors who were keen to satisfy public demand for American films banned from France during the Occupation.

From 1947 onwards the 'agreement' was widely denounced as a form of American imperialism and as a plot to destroy the French cinema. This move was led by the Communist press and by the numerous members of the film industry, especially the technicians, who were close to the Communist Party, but it was not confined to them. In this way a MYTH grew up around the 'agreement', which was fed by the political polarizations of the COLD WAR but which has been regularly repeated since then. According to the myth, Blum 'sold out' the French film industry to the Americans. However, as Jeancolas has pointed out, the number of reserved weeks approximately corresponded to what the French industry was capable of supplying to distributors at the time, since production capacity badly needed MODERNIZATION and had been severely damaged by the war. Recent interpretations of the 'agreement' therefore stress how far it protected rather than damaged French CINEMA during its crucial period of reconstruction. **(Jill Forbes)**

Further reading

Jeancolas (1993). A meticulous and authoritative account. Portes (1986). One of the first attempts to evaluate the 'agreement' dispassionately.

Bobino   1812–1985. Large concert hall in the Montparnasse district of Paris, used as a major venue for popular music.

Bocuse, Paul   Born 1926. Chef. Based near LYON, he became a celebrity chef in the 1970s, and is associated with *la nouvelle cuisine.*

Body (*le corps*)   In the twentieth century French thinkers have made an important contribution to the rethinking of Descartes' mind–body dualism. Inspired by Husserl's concept of the body, MERLEAU-PONTY's phenomenology explores the connections between body, action and perception. The fact that the 'body-subject' is both a producer and product of historical meaning means that human beings are agents who can transform society, but are also bodies which carry the 'sedimentation' of social institutions and traditions. Merleau-Ponty shows that we are not just consciousnesses which observe the world, but also bodies which are immersed *in* the world.

A second generation of French thinkers used new insights in the fields of PSYCHOANALYSIS, social history, literary theory, and FEMINIST theory, to develop this work on the body. By showing that the body produces drives and is implicated in power structures, they go even further than Merleau-Ponty in calling into question Descartes's tendency to privilege the mind over the body. Jacques LACAN shows how the early development of the ego is connected to the infant's growing understanding that it has a body. Michel FOUCAULT's work on social institutions such as the prison, the clinic, and the school, explores the ways in which the body becomes an important site for the production of power/knowledge in the modern era. His later work on 'techniques of the self' suggests ways in which an ethical conception of the body might be opposed to what he sees as the moral UNIVERSALISM of the Judaeo-Christian tradition. Julia KRISTEVA, an important figure in French feminist theory, attempts to establish new connections between the body and language, and Luce IRAGARAY explores ways in which feminine sexuality might produce a language which contrasts with the 'phallic' and centred language of masculine sexuality.

The pace of contemporary technological change poses a new set of philosophical questions relating to the body, and some theorists have drawn upon French thinkers to speculate about the possibility of a 'post-human' or 'cyborg' body. (**John Marks**)

Further reading

Featherstone *et al.* (1991). A wide-ranging collection concerning the significance of the body in contemporary social theory. Welton (1999). A comprehensive reader which deals with the body in twentieth-century Continental philosophy, with useful accompanying essays.

Bœuf sur le toit, Le   A Right Bank Paris night-club, popular with the cultural avant-garde during the inter-war period.

Bonnefoy, Yves   Born 1923. Poet and art critic. His poetry is highly disciplined, in the classical tradition of Paul VALÉRY. Like his criticism, it often meditates on philosophical themes, especially consciousness and the nature of existence.

Boulez, Pierre   Born 1925. Composer and conductor. France's leading figure in the field of contemporary MUSIC, his work is often complex and conceptual. He draws widely on other performing arts and on technological advances, and develops his energetically experimental approach at the IRCAM, which he founded in 1975.

Bourdieu, Pierre   Born 1930. Sociologist and social critic, noted for his theory of distinction, in which individuals try to increase their social, cultural and symbolic capital within whatever field they are operating. He has recently become one of France's most prominent dissenting intellectuals, supporting a number of protest movements.

Bourgeoisie   The wealthiest CLASS in French society. Originally, the term applied to the merchants living in towns (*bourgs*), but as the social role of the aristocracy declined, it was extended to include all property-owning groups. Politically, the bourgeoisie has usually been identified by its opponents as the small élite of rich capitalists who exercise undue influence in national life. Culturally, it has been identified with the comfortable lifestyle and moral complacency of the middle classes, lampooned for example in BUÑUEL's film *Le Charme discret de la bourgeoisie* (*The Discreet Charm of the Bourgeoisie*, 1972).

Bové, José   Born c.1953. Environmentalist activist. Hailed as the new Astérix, he became a celebrity after leading the French lobby in demonstrations at the G7 meetings in Seattle, brandishing a Roquefort cheese, and then symbolically dismantling the building site of McDonald's restaurant in his home town of Millau, for which he was given a three month suspended jail sentence in July 2000. (**Máire Cross**)

Further reading

Bové (1999).

Braque, Georges   1882–1963. Artist. A founder of CUBISM, with PICASSO, he worked with many writers and poets.

Brasillach, Robert   1909–45. Writer. A journalist with ACTION FRANÇAISE (from 1931) and *Je suis partout* (from 1937), he was a passionate advocate of FASCISM, and became a prominent COLLABORATOR during the OCCUPATION. He wrote literary criticism and several novels. He was tried and executed for treason at the LIBERATION.

Brassaï   1899–1984. Photographer. Romanian-born, he was initially close to the SURREALISTS, and became famous for his unusual and often dream-like shots of PARIS, presented in albums like *Paris de nuit* (*Paris by Night*, 1933).

Brassens, Georges   1921–81. Singer and songwriter. The leading figure in French CHANSON with Jacques BREL during the 1950s and 1960s, he sang to his own guitar accompaniment, and combined personal sentiment and social comment in erudite and racy lyrics, which often harked back to Mediterranean and medieval inspirations.

Brel, Jacques   1929–78, Singer and songwriter. Alongside Georges BRASSENS, the leading figure in French CHANSON during the 1950s and 1960s. He was an energetic and dramatic concert performer, specializing in big ballads, like *Ne me quitte pas* (If you go away, 1962), which became a transatlantic hit for Nina Simone. He also performed in both films and stage musicals.

Bretécher, Claire   Born 1940. Cartoonist. Co-founder of the *Écho des savannes* magazine (1972), she is best known for observing the foibles of middle-class life in several series of *planches* (single-page cartoon strips), including *Les Frustrés* (The Frustrated Ones, from 1974), which appeared weekly in *Le NOUVEL OBSERVATEUR*.

Breton, André   1896–1966. Writer. Poet and novelist, he launched the SURREALIST movement with *Manifeste du surréalisme* (*Surrealist Manifesto*, 1924) and remained its leading theorist, the 'Pope of surrealism', despite high-profile quarrels with other members. His volumes of poetry, like *Les champs magnétiques* (*Magnetic Fields*, 1920), and novels like *Nadja* (1928) and *Arcane 17* (1944) explore themes of language, love and freedom.

Briand, Aristide   1862–1932. Politician. Several times Prime Minister, he was active in Franco-German reconciliation after the First World War.

Britain   Historically Britain and France have not always enjoyed cordial relations. From the medieval period onwards, and despite the common ancestry of the peoples inhabiting their territory, the two countries were rivals. Rival nations tend to define their respective identities in terms opposing each other's characteristics, and the French and British were not exceptional in this. Yet this should not obscure the fact that the two nations have often been drawn towards one another, for instance when British fashions or customs were admired by French Anglophiles, or when French manners and ideas were praised by British Francophiles. From the twelfth to the eighteenth centuries, however, the two nations were often at war. The Hundred Years' War (1337–1453) produced one of France's most enduring historical figures, JOAN OF ARC, whose actions were subsequently mythologized in order to symbolize French resistance to British oppression. The peak of Anglo-French hostility was reached during the Revolutionary and Napoleonic Wars (1792–1815), when the countries' armies and navies were often engaged in combat. Indeed, in France the myth and slogan of 'Perfidious Albion' ('Albion' being a classical attribution derived from the white cliffs of the south coast) were revived during this period for propaganda purposes. The French First Republic and Empire were portrayed as representing the very opposite of British monarchic tyranny and oppression. As for the British, during the nineteenth century and into the twentieth century, the memory of the upheaval of the French Revolution was often invoked in order to reinforce the powerful sense of political superiority that tended to prevail in conservative Victorian circles. Around the turn of the century (1900), however, the hostile atmosphere receded and a period of rapprochement began, culminating in the signing of the *Entente cordiale* (amicable agreement) in 1904. This paved the way towards military co-operation, and in 1914 the British fought alongside the French as allies. The military and political alliance lasted for the rest of the twentieth century, including co-operation on overseas ventures such as the abortive SUEZ CRISIS and the Gulf War. During the Second World War, Britain supported the Free French, under DE GAULLE, against the VICHY regime of Marshal PÉTAIN. French post-war attitudes have been coloured both positively and negatively by Britain's political and cultural closeness to the United States. (**Martyn Cornick**)

Further reading

Bell (1996); Bell (1997); Cornick (1994); Gibson (1995).

Brittany   Brittany is the large Atlantic peninsula, which forms the Western extreme of mainland France. Celtic in origin, it was independent until 1532 and retained relative autonomy until the French Revolution when it was split (like the rest of France) into *départements*. The current population numbers 2.79 million. Brittany has been a region since 1959 and is now made up of four *départements*: Côtes d'Armor, Finistère, Île-et-Vilaine and Morbihan. Historically, Brittany also includes a fifth, Loire-Atlantique, which is now included in the Pays de Loire region. The two main cities in Brittany, at its two eastern and western extremes, are Rennes (the academic and administrative capital) and Brest (a naval centre, with a growing engineering and electronics industry). The economy relies heavily on AGRICULTURE (especially pigs, cattle, poultry and market gardening). Half of the fish caught in France are landed in Brittany, and about 20 per cent of the population rely directly or indirectly on the maritime economy.

Brittany changed radically during the twentieth century. Rural depopulation led to rapid urbanization and caused a steady exodus of Bretons to PARIS. Sensitivity to its peripheral, isolated location and to the implications of centralized national administration has led to a growth of interest in Breton identity. There is an increasing awareness that the future prosperity of the area depends on political and cultural activism. A number of groups campaign for greater autonomy or even for independence. The *Front de Libération de la Bretagne* (Brittany Liberation Front), particularly active in the 1970, is a banned organization that continues to attack public buildings and other symbols of the Republic. The Breton language is still spoken by a number of older Bretons, but only in 1951 was its teaching permitted in schools for the first time. The bilingual schools belonging to the *Diwan* movement are becoming increasingly popular. In many ways, contemporary Brittany is still torn between tradition and modernity; however, with an expanding TOURIST industry, an increasing number of small and medium-sized companies and a growing sense of regional identity, its future remains promising. (**Charles Forsdick**)

Further reading

Cousquer and Picard (1996). A useful survey of Breton history, culture, politics and economics. Well illustrated and containing up-to-date statistics and other information. Range of exercises for each chapter.
Le Lannou (1978). A concise account of Breton history which provides particular focus on the region's economic development and the transformations of its agricultural industry.

Broadcasting (regulation and deregulation)   A Higher Broadcasting Council (*Conseil supérieur de l'audiovisuel* or *CSA)* now regulates French RADIO and TELEVISION, a function traditionally exercised by ministers. Under the 1982 law on 'freedom of communication', MITTERRAND ended the STATE monopoly on radio and television broadcasting and set up the first regulatory body (*la Haute autorité*). To lessen direct political influence on radio and television, this 'High Authority' was to act as a buffer between broadcasters and government. The very political interference that the creation of an independent Regulator was meant to stop soon showed itself again, in the transformation of the *Haute autorité* into the *Commission Nationale de la Communication et des Libertés* (CNCL) by the Chirac government (1986) and then into the CSA by the Rocard government (1989). The CSA is composed of nine members appointed by the President of the Republic and the Presidents of the National

Assembly and Senate. Among its functions are: to award licences to private radio and television stations; to appoint managing directors of public (state) stations; to oversee fairness of electoral communication and pluralism of access to broadcasting in general; to maintain standards of public decency; and to monitor cultural quotas for French language songs on radio.

Deregulation refers to the process of opening up the French media to new channels and stations run by independent franchise-holders in competition with existing state-owned channels. For radio, this had occurred even before the passing of the 1982 law when a temporary licensing body set up by Mitterrand's government authorized many 'local private radios'. For television, deregulation began in practice in the mid-1980s with the PRIVATIZATION of TF1 and the creation of new private terrestrial and SATELLITE and cable channels. **(Geoff Hare)**

Further reading

Kuhn (1995). Authoritative overview of broadcasting's relations to the state and policy making. Barbrook, (1995).

Buffet, Bernard   1928–99. Artist. Often associated with the EXISTENTIALIST movement, his figurative paintings include distinctively spiky line drawing, and were widely reproduced in posters during the 1960s and 1970s.

Buñuel, Luis   1900–83. Film director. Influential Spanish-born film maker, his long career began with the SURREALIST classic *Un chien andalou* (*Andalusian Dog*, 1928, made with Salvador Dali) and includes *Le Charme discret de la bourgeoisie* (*The Discreet Charm of the Bourgeoisie*, 1972).

Bureaucracy   French bureaucracy is reputed for impenetrability and inefficiency, but in the 1990s attempted to modernize and become more productive as the STATE aimed to reduce spending and improve relations between citizens and administration. Civil service and public sector have traditionally faced overmanning and inefficiency, and the meritocratic legitimacy of recruitment has been questioned. Civil service recruitment has been traditionally by competitive examination, theoretically guaranteeing selection on merit for public service. Entry to the highest echelons of the administration has been easiest from highly selective GRANDES ÉCOLES, notably the *École libre des sciences politiques* (which, after 1945, became the *Institut d'études politiques de Paris*) and the *Ecole nationale d'administration* (ENA). Studies of family origins of students of these schools show they facilitate social reproduction of cultural and professional ÉLITES, and thus that the bureaucracy is not meritocratic. ENA was created (1946) to provide the technocratic elite considered necessary to lead France's MODERNIZATION, and feeds the most prestigious of the *grands corps administratifs* (main administrative departments) such as the *Conseil d'État, Inspection des Finances, Cour des Comptes*, and the diplomatic service. Political instability before the war and during the FOURTH REPUBLIC may have encouraged French people to consider the bureaucracy itself as the state. FIFTH REPUBLIC governments have been stable, but boundaries between state and bureaucracy are blurred by senior civil servants' career crossovers between administration and politics. In particular, personal cabinets of ministers, staffed mainly by seconded civil servants, form a permeable interface between politics and the bureaucracy. Another controversial crossover is *pantouflage*, the entry into the private sector of civil servants. In the 1990s, governments of Left and Right addressed the evident sclerosis of the civil service and the public sector, with the intention of reducing public spending. However, planned reforms of public-sector employment, and particularly of the retirement regimes for state employees, provoked major resistance from influential TRADE UNIONS. (**Hugh Dauncey**)

Further reading

Birnbaum, (1982). Deals with élites, government and bureaucracy.

Butor, Michel   Born 1926. Writer and critic. His early novels, such as *La Modification* (1957) were hailed are exemplars of the *NOUVEAU ROMAN*, with dense and complex texts which made heavy demands on the reader and explore the relationships between time, space and consciousness.

Cable broadcasting   See SATELLITE AND CABLE BROADCASTING.

Cachin, Marcel   1869–1958. Communist politician. Editor of *L'HUMANITÉ* (1919–57) and a supporter of Lenin, he was a *député* for most of the inter-war period, and a senior member of the PCF until his death.

Cadres   A new managerial CLASS, which emerged in France in the mid-twentieth century, and which can be seen as both the product and the agent of major socio-economic changes which have taken place, particularly since the Second World War.

The literal meaning of the word *cadre* is frame, or framework, which points to one of the defining aspects of the professional role of the cadre. In contrast with, for example, a lawyer who is part of a partnership, or someone who runs a small business, the cadre is defined by his/her role as part of the fabric of a large organizational framework. In twentieth-century France, as elsewhere, large companies have tended to replace small businesses. Thus, the emergence of *les cadres* as a new middle class should be seen as one of many social changes which has accompanied the development of mass production and mass consumption in France this century.

Considerable interest has focused on the IDEOLOGY of *les cadres* before and after the Second World War. It was during the depression years of the 1930s, in a period of profound conflict between labour and employers, that the new middle class began to form organizations to defend its status and promote its social vision. Claiming to speak from a position of neutrality between WORKERS and employers, these organizations aspired to transcend class conflict by seeking technical/managerial solutions to social and industrial problems. Of course, such ambitions also served to legitimize their own role as technicians and managers and to promote practices which ultimately served the interests of the employer more than the worker. As large companies continued to displace smaller businesses during the decades of rapid economic growth which followed the war, the importance of the *cadre* continued to grow. It is in this period that the *cadre*, the embodiment of the values of efficiency and productivity which underpinned post-war growth, figures most prominently in French cultural production as the object of both fascination and criticism.(**Jackie Clarke**)

Further reading

Boltanski (1987).

Café   In France, as in most European countries, cafés have long played an important part, not merely in urban (and village) leisure activity, but also as centres for cultural interaction. In the twentieth century, particularly in PARIS, the Golden Age of the café was in the inter-war years and the immediate post-war period. In the 1920s, the great cafés of Montparnasse, like the Coupole and the Dôme attracted an influx of American tourists and writers in exile, such as Hemingway, Scott Fitzgerald or Gertrude Stein, in addition to avant-garde painters like PICASSO. The Closerie des Lilas on the corner of the Boulevard du Montparnasse and the Boulevard Saint-Michel was also an important centre for writers.

By the 1930s, intellectual activity moved to the cafés of the LATIN QUARTER and SAINT-GERMAIN-DES-PRÈS, due to the proximity of the University, publishing-houses and political meeting-halls such as the Mutualité. After the Liberation, Saint-Germain-des-Près was the centre of French intellectual life, with the EXISTENTIALISTS adopting the cafés LE FLORE and LES DEUX MAGOTS as their headquarters, and with right-wing writers and intellectuals using the Brasserie Lipp on the opposite side of the Boulevard Saint-Germain. The HUSSARDS frequented the Rhumerie Martiniquaise further down the boulevard. These cafés, with their distinctive political and artistic followings and character, were not merely important centres for intellectual and artistic discussion; they also served as places of work, with establishments providing pen and paper, and on occasions, special rooms, for their intellectual clients.

After the 1960s, however, the cafés began to lose their role as meeting places for artists and intellectuals, due to the changes in the urban structure and in the means of communication. (**Nicholas Hewitt**)

Further reading

Lottman (1982). A discussion of intellectual activity in Paris from 1936 to 1960, with considerable detail on Parisian cafés.

Cahiers du cinéma   Monthly film magazine. Founded in 1951, it gave an early forum to future *NOUVELLE VAGUE* directors. Strongly politicized by MAY '68, it later returned to a less partisan approach, becoming France's most successful and informative film journal.

Camus, Albert 1913–60. Writer. Best known for his concept of the ABSURD (the inherent meaninglessness of life), expressed in novels like *L'Étranger* (*The Outsider*, 1942) and essays like *Le Mythe de Sisyphe* (*The Myth of Sisyphus*, 1942). He was influential as editor of the newspaper COMBAT, wrote several plays, and had a high-profile quarrel with his friend SARTRE after the publication of *L'Homme révolté* (*The Rebel*, 1951). He received the Nobel Prize in 1957.

Canada (French in) The largest group of native French speakers outside France are the 6 000 000 francophone *Québécois* (formerly 'French Canadians') concentrated along the St Lawrence valley in Quebec province, with their main urban centres in Montreal and Quebec City. Montreal has a sizeable anglophone population too (30 per cent), and many immigrant languages are spoken there. Otherwise the province is close to 100 per cent francophone, apart from the Arctic regions, populated by Inuit-speaking native Americans. Conversely, there are smaller groups of francophones elsewhere in Canada – notably 230 000 in New Brunswick and 480 000 in Ontario. Overall, French speakers make up 25 per cent of Canada's population.

Colonists from western France were the first Europeans to settle in North America (from around 1600), but were soon heavily outnumbered by the British, the colony of 'New France' being absorbed into Canada in 1763. Nevertheless, as a homogeneous, Catholic, very rural population, the French speakers succeeded in clinging on to their language, religion and culture. By the mid-twentieth century, having become increasingly urbanized, secular and middle class, they were asserting their identity more forcefully. One consequence was that in 1969 French was made the co-official language of bilingual federal Canada. (In practice, 40 per cent of francophones claim proficiency in English, whereas only 8 per cent of anglophones claim proficiency in French.) By contrast, in the 1970s it became Quebec government policy to reinforce the status of French within the province by discouraging bilingualism.

There has been much speculation that Quebec might leave the Canadian Federation altogether, though this is not currently on the agenda, following two negative referendum results. But French is now the province's sole official language (neighbouring New Brunswick is officially bilingual), French-language film and literature flourish, businesses have been induced to switch to operating in French, and many disgruntled anglophones have moved away. (**Rodney Ball**)

Further reading

Edwards (1998). A comprehensive survey. *Le Québécois de poche* (1998). A lively pocket guide to Quebec French.

Canard enchaîné, Le Satirical newspaper, founded 1915. Witty and allusive, it specializes in lampooning political manoeuverings and current affairs, and in investigative JOURNALISM, particularly where this uncovers scandals within the STATE apparatus.

Cannes Film Festival   Initiated in 1939, to compete with the Venice festival, it was effectively launched in 1946 and has become one of the most important annual FILM FESTIVALS in the world. Held now in May, it attracts several thousands of visitors, including stars, directors, producers, critics and enthusiasts.

Canon (literary)   The literary canon is based on the idea of a selection of key texts which are, in Harold Bloom's words, 'authoritative in our culture' because of their aesthetic and, perhaps, moral value. Bloom's so-called 'western canon' is extremely Anglocentric, placing Shakespeare at its pinnacle and including only four French writers – Montaigne, Molière, PROUST and BECKETT. Nevertheless, Bloom's description of the canon as 'the choice of books in our teaching institutions' shows not only that it is necessary, because 'who reads must choose', but that it is also pertinent to France since the rise of a French canon is closely associated with the spread of formal EDUCATION. In the seventeenth century the *ACADÉMIE FRANÇAISE* assembled a catalogue of the 'most celebrated books' written in French but this was with a view to using them as source works for its DICTIONARY rather than as recommended educational reading. The creation of the national canon is usually thought to have begun in the eighteenth century with the beginnings of the study of literature in educational establishments, and to have taken more concrete shape in the nineteenth century as education became compulsory.

Although debates about 'canon formation' are more frequently associated with American than with French schools and UNIVERSITIES, quarrels about the relative national merits of different authors are in fact extremely common in France. Thus the canon became politicized after the French defeat in the Franco-Prussian War of 1870 was attributed to the decline of national moral values. Literary education was then expected to take on a patriotic colouring and to instruct school pupils in the glories of the NATION. In the post-war period the inclusion in the canon of women writers such as Marguerite DURAS or of Francophone authors has sometimes been challenged as a form of misplaced political correctness, while interpretations of accepted canonical writers, such as Racine, have frequently been contested. More recently, debates have focused on whether popular literature can be considered canonical. (**Jill Forbes**)

Further reading

Bloom (1994). Essays on twenty-six canonical authors preceded by an essay on 'the canon'. France (1995). Contains an illuminating introduction on the selection of material together with an entry on the canon. Hollier (1989). Numerous references to the canon illustrate the American approach to the topic.

Capitalism   A form of society in which the main wealth is privately owned capital, and in which economic, social and political life are organized so as to encourage the increase of that wealth. In a capitalist society, all activities (including goods and services) tend to become commodities, which can be traded, usually for money.

For much of the twentieth century, the idea of capitalism was used mainly by the Left to describe and criticize modern French society, and in particular the financial and industrial sectors of the ECONOMY. Following MARXIST ideas, they argued that wealth was produced by exploiting WORKING PEOPLE, and was concentrated in the hands of a smaller and smaller group of rich capitalists. They also pointed to the economic cycles of expansion and contraction, and the effects of competition, all of which had damaging effects on the lives of ordinary people.

Anti-capitalist views were also aired by the French Right, especially during the 1930s. Many CATHOLICS saw capitalism as immoral, legitimizing the expression of greed. Royalists saw it as the triumph of the BOURGEOISIE who had led the Revolution of 1789 and wished to destroy traditional social structures and values. FASCISTS saw it as a scheme to enable JEWS and freemasons to seize control of French society by secretly manipulating the financial levers of power.

Though all these hostile views can still be found in France, there has been, since the international collapse of communism in 1989, a growing willingness to defend capitalism as an effective system for distributing wealth and encouraging innovation. Most politicians now agree that there is no alternative to capitalism, and whereas LIBERALS argue for a free, or a lightly regulated, market, SOCIALISTS defend a mixed economy with state investment and regulation to protect people against the excesses of the market. (**Michael Kelly**)

Cardin, Pierre   Born 1922. Fashion designer. He participated with Dior in launching the post-war NEW LOOK, and later launched ready-to-wear ranges. He was noted in the 1960s for his futuristic designs, inspired by astronauts and science-fiction films.

Carné, Marcel   1909–96. Film director. Noted for his atmospheric and poetic films, he was particularly popular in the 1930s and 1940s. Several of his films are regarded as cinema classics, especially *Les Enfants du paradis* (*Children of Paradise*, 1943–45).

Carnival   A term derived from the work of the Russian literary theorist Mikhail Bakhtin, who develops it in his analyses of the work of Rabelais and Dostoevsky in particular. Carnival, whose model is the ancient Roman Saturnalia, refers to a time at which all established societal hierarchies and distances are suspended. Eccentricity, profanation, parody, the Dionysiac affirmation of transience and relativity are characteristic of what for Bakhtin is a major mode of modern literature in particular. The term became extremely influential in French theoretical discourse, particularly that associated with the grouping around *TEL QUEL*, in the aftermath of the MAY '68 events which seemed such a perfect illustration of it. The writing of such as Joyce and BATAILLE was praised for its carnivalesque qualities, while DERRIDEAN DECONSTRUCTION and *ÉCRITURE FÉMININE* alike drew widely upon the liberating and dehierarchizing possibilities opened by the notion. The original sense of carnival to refer to a kind of street theatre or masquerade further suggests its contribution to the increasingly important fields of GENDER and performance studies, which Bakhtin's work pre-dates.

In the process of its popularization, however, the term lost some valuable precision. Carnival time can exist as such only because the established order will necessarily reassert itself once the carnival is over, rethroning the temporarily dethroned and reinstating what had been overturned – something illustrated by the denouement of May. In this respect the mode of carnival is emphatically one of parody rather than of the post-modern, 'all bets are off' pastiche to which it is too often assimilated. Perhaps because its abusive extension has weakened its force, but also perhaps because it has been to a degree subsumed under the wider rubric of performance studies, carnival is less omnipresent now in theoretical discourse than a few years back. But in its more precise sense the term is still an extremely valuable one. (**Keith Reader**)

Further reading

Bakhtin (1968).

Cartel des gauches   Centre-Left electoral coalition which secured a majority in the parliamentary elections of 1924 and provided governments until 1928.

Cartier-Bresson, Henri   Born 1908. Photographer. From the 1930s to the 1960s he took photographs of a wide range of subjects, and became known as a photo-journalist and DOCUMENTARY photographer, with a strong sense of artistic composition.

Castelnau, General de   1851–1944. Politician. Leader of the conservative National Catholic Federation during the inter-war period, and a leading figure on the nationalist Right.

Catholic Church   CATHOLICISM.

Catholicism   While, since 1905 and the Law of Separation of Church of State, France has remained a lay country, Catholicism has retained its status as the principal religious faith. Although at a local level the Catholic Church's presence and influence may be limited (recruitment to the priesthood is low) and regular religious practice remains very sporadic, nationally it has an impressive hierarchical organization. Statements and directives by the Episcopal Assembly and by influential figures such as the Archbishop of Paris are given prominent coverage by the media and are heeded by many. Catholic INTELLECTUALS readily participate in major social and political debates. *La Croix* (*The Cross*), the daily Catholic paper, has a wide distribution. For centuries, associated closely with the monarchy, aristocracy, and the political Right, the Catholic Church during the last 100 years has become increasingly open to social and democratic values. The worker-priest experiment of the mid-twentieth century is a prominent illustration. Since the Second Vatican Council, it has in general adopted more tolerant and liberal positions. One example is that mass is regularly held in French instead of Latin with the priest directly addressing his congregation. Although this trend is popular with many, a number of revolutionary groups remain critical of the hierarchy's inability to go further. The trend has also encouraged the resurgence of a traditional Catholicism whose supporters reject modern developments, are opposed to ecumenicalism, and practise Catholicism as it was known in the mid-nineteenth century, sometimes, in defiance of Papal and Episcopal authority. Such groups now exist in all *départements* and are often associated with the extreme political Right. In addition to internal divisions, the Catholic Church is increasingly challenged by other faiths, and by ISLAM in particular, to which there has been a significant number of conversions. (**John Flower**)

Céline, Louis-Ferdinand 1894–1961. Writer. His novel *Voyage au bout de la nuit* (*Journey to the End of Night*, 1932) presented a bleak picture of the world after the First World War, but in a racy and sophisticated style which made him a major author. Compromised by his right-wing and ANTI-SEMITIC writing during the OCCUPATION, he drew on his wartime experience in a series of experimental novels.

Censorship Censorship is the process of supervising and controlling information and ideas that are circulated within society. Traditionally, it refers to books, newspapers and periodicals, plays, films, television and radio programmes, and news reports. For most of the last century, the main source of censorship in France has been the STATE, through various agencies and laws, such as the 1949 law restricting publications aimed at children. The exception was the period 1940–44, when the German occupying authorities issued the 'Otto Lists' (named after the ambassador, Otto ABETZ) banning over 1000 book titles. At the same time, the VICHY Ministry of Information ran a censorship service which imposed strict restraints on cultural activities and on what could be published in the press.

Material has mainly been censored officially on grounds of being immoral or obscene, or injurious to children or national security. During the OCCUPATION, this was routinely extended to include anything written by, or favourable to, Jews or Communists. Wartime censorship was strict and visible, but after the LIBERATION, many of the powers were retained by successive French governments. They were used less conspicuously, except in times of emergency, such as the ALGERIAN WAR, when books and journals were frequently banned before distribution. Radio and television were state monopolies until the 1970s, and current affairs programmes were always subject to close political control, a fact which shocked many when protesting journalists at ORTF revealed the extent of political intervention, and the consequent self-censorship of programme makers.

During the 1990s, censorship of the Internet was the subject of much debate, with courts ruling that portal providers should either remove offending pages from overseas websites (for example, material related to Nazi memorabilia), or block French citizens from accessing them. In addition to the state, censorship of various types has been used by churches and political parties. For example, the Vatican's Index of Forbidden Books, now discontinued, limited what CATHOLICS should read, or tolerate, as did the French Church's detailed classifications of films and television programmes. Party political censorship often operates at local level, and was shown in the controversial measures by the NATIONAL FRONT to remove left-wing publications from municipal libraries in Orange and Marignane (1997). (**Michael Kelly**)

Centre Pompidou See POMPIDOU CENTRE

Certeau, Michel de 1925–86. Cultural historian. A Jesuit priest, he wrote scholarly studies in the history of religion and science, but has been most influential through his analyses of EVERYDAY LIFE and its often neglected practices which can reveal a great deal about social reality.

Césaire, Aimé   Born 1912. Poet, playwright and politician. A SURREALIST and leader of the NEGRITUDE movement during the 1930s, his *Cahier d'un retour au pays natal* (*Return to my Native Land*, 1939) became a classic of the black consciousness movement. As well as writing plays, he was also a *député* and mayor in his native Martinique.

CFDT *(Confédération française démocratique du travail)*   A major trades union congress. Formed in 1964 when the majority of delegates voted to leave the Catholic CFTC (*Confédération française des travailleurs chrétiens*). It has generally been close to the SOCIALIST PARTY.

CGT *(Confédération général du travail)*   Traditionally the largest of the French trades union congresses. It has generally followed the political lead of the COMMUNIST PARTY (PCF).

CGTU *(Confédération général du travail unitaire)*   1922–36. Communist-led union which broke away from the socialist-led CGT, after the two political movements separated. It rejoined the CGT on the eve of the election of the *FRONT POPULAIRE* government.

Chaban-Delmas, Jacques   (1915–2000). A Gaullist politician, and mayor of Bordeaux (1947–95). Several times a Minister and President of the National Assembly, he was Prime Minister (1969–72) and stood unsuccessfully for President of the Republic in 1974.

Chabrol, Claude   Born 1930. Film director. Launched in the NOUVELLE VAGUE, he has made nearly seventy films, of which *Les Cousins* (*Cousins*, 1959) and *Le Boucher* (*The Butcher*, 1970) are the most admired.

Chagall, Marc   1887–1985. Artist. A Russian-born post-impressionist painter, he was noted for his use of folk motifs and religious themes.

Chambre bleu horizon   So-called after the colour of the First World War French infantry uniform, the *Chambre bleu horizon* (Sky Blue Chamber (of Deputies)) was elected in December 1919, producing a decisive swing to the Right and prompting historians to draw parallels with the Restoration *chambre introuvable* (1815) and the parliaments elected after the revolutionary *Commune* (1871). Of 616 seats, the *Bloc national* secured 433, the Left 180. Led by politicians who had migrated from the pre-war 'Left' such as CLEMENCEAU, Millerand and BRIAND, the former included a significant proportion of practising Catholics and, sitting for the first time since 1871, *députés* for the newly recovered territories of ALSACE-LORRAINE. The Left extended from HERRIOT'S RADICALS, who in practice occupied a centrist position on most issues, to Léon BLUM's SOCIALIST PARTY (SFIO), subsequently outflanked by the new COMMUNIST PARTY, founded at the TOURS CONGRESS in December 1920. The composition of the Chamber, and widespread anxiety about the Soviet revolution of 1917, symbolized by the mythical *homme au couteau entre les dents* (man with a knife between his teeth) whose image had featured in the electoral campaign, influenced the decision to re-establish diplomatic relations with the Vatican, broken off after the separation of Church and State in 1905. Much more pressing issues were the peace settlement, national security and economic reconstruction. Industrial production quickly returned to pre-war levels and the 8-hour, 6-day week was a welcome measure of social justice, though the 5-day week and paid holidays had to wait until 1936 and women's suffrage, another contentious issue, until 1944. However, differences over taxation policy hampered efforts to deal with the huge fiscal burden of war debt, while the understandable inclination to 'make Germany pay' produced Prime Minister's POINCARÉ's controversial and ultimately abortive occupation of the Ruhr (1923). The April 1924 elections ushered in a new legislature of the Centre-Left and a coalition government, the short-lived *CARTEL DES GAUCHES*, weakened in turn by its mishandling of another aspect of unfinished Franco-German business, the extension of the Republic's secular legislation to Alsace-Lorraine. (**Bill Kidd**)

Further reading

McMillan (1992).

Chanel, Gabrielle 'Coco'   1883–1971 Fashion designer. The most successful woman designer of the 1920s, she challenged tradition by dressing women in trousers and jackets, previously reserved for men, rejecting corsets and tight-fitting clothes, and popularizing cheap costume jewellery. Compromised during the Occupation, she made a comeback in the 1950s and is best known for the striking but simple lines of her 'little black dresses', her 'Chanel No. 5' perfume, and the company logo based on her initials.

Chanson   Although *chanson* literally means song, it has acquired the secondary connotation of a specifically French genre. Hence the common retention of the term in English. In this second sense, lyrics have greater importance than in Anglo-American songs. There is also a narrative element and a degree of social observation. Stage performance is often theatrical, the singer 'interpreting' the song in character: the word *interprète* means both singer and actor.

From 1900, the *chanson* of the Paris MUSIC-HALL was generally equated with frivolity or sauciness (Dranem, MISTINGUETT, Maurice CHEVALIER) and, in the 1930s, with grim urban melodrama (Fréhel, Édith PIAF). But during that decade, the singer-songwriter Charles TRENET invented a more whimsical, 'poetic' style, overflowing with a *joie de vivre* now associated nostalgically with the *FRONT POPULAIRE* era. Trenet was the blueprint for the singer-songwriter who has dominated *chanson* since the 1950s, exemplified in three iconic stars: Jacques BREL, Georges BRASSENS and Léo FERRÉ. In their songs, often labelled 'poetic' or 'text' songs, Trenet's verbal acrobatics were extended to produce a broader palette of emotions and comment.

After American rock'n'roll hit France around 1960, pop and its French derivatives (Johnny HALLYDAY, Sheila) became the norm, though the big three remained popular, even after their deaths. In the 1970s, however, a new generation of singer-songwriters emerged, raised on Brassens or Ferré but equally comfortable with pop (Francis Cabrel, Jean-Jacques Goldman, RENAUD, Alain Souchon). Renaud became the star of the 1980s, playfully fusing rock idioms with the vocabulary, settings and accordion of pre-war *chanson*. This helped spawn a number of experimental bands (Pigalle, Louise Attaque, *Les Têtes Raides*) who have redefined *chanson* with an ironic post-punk sensibility; while recent solo artists (Miossec, Dominique A) have set their self-penned, introspective work to driving or hypnotic electronic sounds. Of the 1970s generation, Goldman is now the most successful. But it is conceivably in these postmodern hybrids that the future lies, as long as sound is not allowed to obscure sense. (**David Looseley**)

Further reading

Rioux (1994). A substantial historical introduction.

Char, René   1907–88. Poet. Linked in the 1930s with SURREALISM, his prose poems are dense and philosophical. Active in the RESISTANCE, he was popular and respected in the post-war period. The poems of *Fureur et mystère* (*Fury and Mystery*, 1948) were written, but not published, during the OCCUPATION.

Charlie-Hebdo   Founded 1970. A satirical weekly paper, known for its vulgar and offensive cartoons, lampooning political figures and current affairs.

Chautemps, Camille   1885–1963. Centrist politician. A leading figure in the RADICAL PARTY, he served in most inter-war governments, including three short periods as Prime Minister. He was tainted by accusations of scandal, incurred disgrace for his role in the collapse of 1940, and spent his last 20 years in America.

Chemistry   The French chemical industry ranks second in Europe and French chemical companies figure high in world rankings. The industry employs 250 000 people and is important for France's scientific independence. Chemistry has been crucial to French INDUSTRIALISATION and TECHNOLOGY, and major chemicals firms have undergone NATIONALIZATION and PRIVATIZATION under different ECONOMIC POLICY. During the First World War, the backwardness of French industrialization and technology meant that France had no real explosives industry or chlorine capability. In the inter-war period the chemicals industry developed as basic chemistry exploited national natural resources such as salt (Camargue, Nancy) and potassium (Mulhouse – including potassium in Alsace ceded to France by the Versailles Treaty). French chemical research was strong, exemplified by the Nobel prizes of Irène Curie and Frédéric Joliot (1935), but the relative weakness of the industry inhibited applied research and industrial development, and archaic agricultural practices limited demand for chemical fertilizers. As with industry generally, industrial and agricultural MODERNIZATION (1945–75) transformed French chemistry, as France developed her *capitalisme chimique* of high-tech science, STATE investment in public sector companies and a growing private sector. The postwar boom was particularly noticeable in fertilizers and pesticides for agriculture, plastics, paints and lacqueurs for manufacturing, soaps and beauty products for household consumption, and pharmaceuticals. The fundamental importance of petrochemicals was favoured by France's oil and gas resources in ALGERIA and at Lacq (near Pau in the Pyrennees). It also facilitated the growth of leading firms such as the *Compagnie française des pétroles* (French Oil Company) and Elf-Aquitaine. In 1982, the socialist administration nationalized Rhône-Poulenc and Péchiney-Uginé-Kuhlmann and the proportion of state-owned chemical companies reached 85 per cent in recognition of the industry's strategic importance. Rhône-Poulenc was privatized in 1993, and in the mid-1990s figured with CEA-Industrie in the top ten world chemical companies. (**Hugh Dauncey**)

Chevalier, Maurice   1888–1972. Popular singer, with a relaxed and cheerful style, who became internationally adopted as an image of Frenchness, through songs such as 'Thank heaven for little girls'. He also starred in films and musicals. Despite criticism of his wartime concert appearances in Germany, his career continued to blossom and he starred in numerous films and musicals.

Chevènement, Jean-Pierre   Born 1939. Socialist politician. Leader of the left-wing socialist republican (CERES) faction of the SOCIALIST PARTY since 1966, he has held several ministerial posts since 1981.

Chiappe, Jacques   1878–1940. Prefect of police for Paris (1927–34), he was dismissed after being compromised by involvement in the STAVISKY AFFAIR. He then entered politics as a right-wing nationalist.

China   Since it first sustained contact with France in the eighteenth century, China has occupied a changing yet privileged position in French culture and foreign policy. China represents one of the principal, non-European OTHERS which continues to fascinate metropolitan France and by which it has attempted to define itself. In the nineteenth century, a succession of French diplomats, missionaries, traders and travellers spent time in China and permitted a variety of forms of economic, political and cultural exchange. France was granted a 'concession' in Shanghai in 1849, and it was hoped that this coastal enclave for mainly commercial activity would allow the steady expansion of French trade in China. Similarly, it was hoped that the French colonies in INDO-CHINA (the regions of Tonkin, Annam and Cochin-China) would provide a route into the Chinese Empire. The real opening up of relations occurred, however, after the suppression of the Boxer Rebellion in 1900 when French troops were part of the international force that occupied Beijing. France began to invest in Chinese railways and to establish major banking interests in the country.

In the First World War, many Chinese workers were employed at the Front, and after the War increasing numbers of Chinese students attended French universities. All French concessions were handed back to the Chinese in 1945 and France lost its final toeholds in a country that had once been a major object of imperial desire. Events in

China – the Revolution of 1912 and Mao Zedong's victory in 1949 – had repercussions for French colonial interests in Indo-China. China provided weapons for the VIET MINH, for example, and played a key role in the Indo-Chinese war. DE GAULLE, as part of what have been called his 'politics of grandeur', eventually recognized the Chinese Communist government in 1964 and attempted to create a special relationship with a country then isolated from the other major world powers. A new period of cultural exchange began, with a number of French intellectuals visiting MAOIST China. After Nixon met Mao in 1972, France signed massive deals with China for the import of advanced technology. France retains strong commercial ties with China as this vast and increasingly important country opens up progressively to the West. (**Charles Forsdick**)

Chirac, Jacques   Born 1932. Gaullist politician, long-standing leader of the RPR party, and mayor of PARIS, he held several ministerial posts, and was prime minister in 1974–76 and again in 1986–88. Elected President of the Republic in 1995.

Choisir   Founded on the belief that women should have the right to choose their own biological destiny and to control their own bodies, *Choisir* (Choose), a legal reform movement, was the idea of a lawyer, Maître Gisèle Halimi, who defended the women in the Bobigny trial in 1973 as part of the campaign for the right to ABORTION on demand. It started as a preventative move in defence of the 343 signatories of a declaration, who had blatantly publicised their flaunting of the 1920 law outlawing abortions (see MLAC). Halimi successfully campaigned on this single issue which hitherto had never been discussed in the formal political arena. Although the movement was successful in politicizing issues pertaining to sexual matters, it was only partially successful in obtaining the right to abortion up to ten weeks. Since then, the founders have continued to campaign to change the restrictive laws on women's sexuality, in order to make abortion and CONTRACEPTION more freely available particularly for the majority of women who cannot afford to resort to private means to procure an abortion abroad, which has always been a possibility for the wealthy. *Choisir* also campaigned to have rape further criminalized and defends victims of violence and rape. Although *Choisir* was successful in mobilizing women into a protest movement, the radical FEMINISTS in the MLF disagreed with their single-issue approach and dissociated itself from them. Halimi subsequently become elected as one of the few women deputies in the Assemblée nationale. (**Máire Cross**)

Further reading

Jackson (1996). This biography of a prominent feminist activist provides good background on the complex debates within the feminist movement in the 1970s which the successful group *Choisir* had provoked. *Quel président pour les femmes?* (1981). This gives an idea of the influence of the association *Choisir* on the 1981 presidential election.

Christian democrats   See MRP.

Ciné-clubs   The *ciné-club* movement in France has had two periods of cultural significance. The first was in the 1920s when clubs were formed to view banned works by

Soviet directors such as Eisenstein, Pudovkin and Dziga Vertov. These then had an immense influence on French DOCUMENTARY film-making. The second was at the LIBERATION and during the period of reconstruction up to the mid 1950s when the film critic André BAZIN was at the centre of 'cultural animation' movements such as the *Jeunesses cinématographiques* (Cinematic youth), which he founded in 1943. Bazin was also active in the film club at IDHEC, the national film school opened in 1944, for which he wrote a series of film notes (fiches) some of which are still in use as pedagogic tools today. Bazin's activities, however, were most closely linked with *Travail et culture*, a branch of the *Peuple et culture* movement associated with the French COMMUNIST PARTY and with the CGT trade union. Through this organization he visited schools, factories and union meetings in order to screen films, deliver lectures and organize often heated debates with audiences in these venues. *Travail et culture* aimed at 'the creation of a proletarian class consciousness' but it received government support since it was considered a valuable agent of democratization and education and an important contributor to the work of national reconstruction. Bazin and his collaborators also took their film education programmes abroad, especially to the French-occupied zone of Germany as part of the re-education programme.

Alongside such journals as *L'Écran français* and *La Revue du cinéma* the *ciné-club* movement made a major contribution to the creation of a film culture in post-war France by persuading audiences to take films seriously and to study them closely. In this way, the *ciné-club* movement contributed to the creation of an audience capable of appreciating and analysing film and therefore one that would be receptive to movements such as the NOUVELLE VAGUE. (**Jill Forbes**)

Further reading

Andrew (1978). A biography of Bazin, containing an account of his *ciné-club* activities and a brief history of the club movement. Rigby (1991). Contains details of the origins and activities of *Peuple et culture*.

Cinema   Since its invention, cinema has always played an important role in French culture. Thanks to the entrepreneurial skills of Charles Pathé, French films dominated world markets before 1914 and the French film industry remains the largest in Europe and one of the largest in the world after Hollywood. Among France's most aesthetically significant film movements are the AVANT-GARDE of the 1920s, poetic realism in the 1930s and the NOUVELLE VAGUE in the late 1950s and early 1960s. The close association between experimental cinema and the plastic arts in the silent period is found in films such as René CLAIR's *Entr'acte* (*Interlude*, 1924), Fernand LÉGER's *Ballet mécanique* (*Mechanical Ballet*, 1924), and Germaine Dulac's *La coquille et le clergyman* (*The Seashell and the Clergyman*, 1930). With sound cinema, the poetic realist masterpieces of Marcel CARNÉ, such as *Le jour se lève* (*DAYBREAK*, 1939), with their sympathetic portraits of everyday tragedy and powerful evocations of life in the city, turned Jean Gabin into a powerful symbol of the French working man. The *nouvelle vague* movement transformed the way films were made and popularized the image of a new, youthful, often PARISIAN lifestyle across the world. Since the Second World War the French government has invested in the cinema as a means of creating a certain image of France and promoting the use of the FRENCH LANGUAGE. Through selective subsidy for films of artistic merit, and through the promotion of support for distribution, dubbing and sub-titling, as well as quotas of films screened on television, the French government has been at the forefront of the defence of national and European cinemas against Hollywood dominance. Its most significant victory was the policy of 'cultural exception' which allowed 'audiovisual products' to be exempted from the provisions of the 1993 GATT round. (**Jill Forbes**)

Further reading

Hayward (1993). Provides a sometimes idiosyncratic but always stimulating overview of the history of French cinema. Williams (1992). Written from an American perspective, it is particularly informative about French cinema before the Second World War.

Cinéma du look   Also known as the 'Forum des Halles' cinema, after the space that has from the late 1970s onwards been the focal point of Parisian street style. It is characterized by techniques and filmic language borrowed from TELEVISION and the video clip, large-scale budgets (unusually for films dealing primarily with youth) and a sophisticated range of special effects. Its leading proponents are Jean-Jacques Beineix, Luc BESSON and Léos Carax. Beineix's work, best known through *37°2 la matin* (*Betty Blue*, 1986), is heavily layered and stylized, concentrating on image rather than plot as in a totally different way the *nouvelle vague* had done before him, and often heterosexually explicit. Besson derives his inspiration from the American cinema and has often adopted an almost aggressively anti-*cinéma d'auteur* stance. He eulogizes escape into (literally) the Parisian underworld (*Subway*, 1985) or the depths of the ocean (*Le Grand Bleu* (*Big Blue*), 1988), in a style as romantic and transcendental as it is POST-MODERNIST. Carax's preoccupation with disaffected youth issued in what was then the costliest French film of all time, *Les Amants du Pont-Neuf* (*The Lovers of the Pont-neuf*, 1991), which was criticized for its glamorization of life on the PARIS streets.

Latterly the *cinéma du look* seems to have run out of steam. Beineix has not made a film for a decade; Carax's follow-up to *Les Amants du Pont-Neuf*, *Pola X* (1999), was universally badly received; and Besson is now to all intents and purposes a Hollywood film-maker, as *The Fifth Element* (1997) illustrates. Greater budgetary caution in large part accounts for this, along with the emergence of grittier and more realistic films about the problems facing youth, of which Matthieu Kassowitz's *La Haine* (1995) is the archetype. (**Keith Reader**)

Further reading

Austin (1996). Places this cinema well in context.

Cities   The myth that France is a predominantly rural country was exploded in 1931, when the urban population for the first time exceeded that of the countryside. Since then, and particularly since the Second World War, the urban population has continued to grow.

The major beneficiary of this, often uncontrolled, urban growth has been PARIS, which has traditionally sucked in the population from the rest of the country as well as creating a monopoly of power, financial strength, talent and amenities. This led to the phenomenon which the planner Jean-François Gravier called *Paris et le désert français* (*Paris and the French desert*, 1947). The only rivals to the power of the capital were the great regional centres of LYON and MARSEILLE, although, as late as 1968, of all regional cities, only Lyon had a population of over a million. Smaller regional centres, however, continued to exert considerable economic, political and cultural power in their locality, due primarily to their great distances from the capital: there are no major regional cities less than 200 kilometres from Paris.

Since the 1980s, however, the situation has changed. François MITTERRAND's REGIONAL bill of 1982 devolved real economic and political power to the provinces and, by extension, to regional capitals, whose mayors were traditional powerful figures both locally and nationally. At the same time, Paris ceased to exert such a powerful attraction as a place to live and work, replaced by cities such as Grenoble, Nice, Toulouse or Montpellier, centres of France's high-tech industries. In the North, Lille has been able to reinvent an identity as a European transport and commercial centre. In consequence, regional cities have attempted to become as lavish as Paris in their provision of outstanding ARCHITECTURE and cultural facilities. (**Nicholas Hewitt**)

Further reading

Thompson (1970). Contains an excellent description of the growth of French cities up until 1970. Winchester (1993). Has a useful chapter on the urban system.

Citroën   Automobile manufacturer. Founded by André Citroën (1878–1935), the company introduced mass production methods into France. Well known for its innovative models of the post-war period such as the 2CV (*deux chevaux*) and DS ('*déesse*'), it remains a major car maker.

Civilization   According to the French dictionary entry, *civilisation* as a noun first appeared in the early part of the eighteenth century (1734) as a derivative of the verb *civiliser* (to civilize), that predated it by over two centuries (1558), and referred to the process whereby an entire people passed from one state to a more evolved one, as gauged by moral, intellectual, artistic, and technological development. As a product of the Enlightenment, the notion of *civilisation* was informed by the evolutionary models of society directed toward social change. By the end of the eighteenth century, however, this radical critical edge was subsumed under an alleged UNIVERSALISM that generalizes the world-view of the European BOURGEOISIE by occulting its CLASS and national specificity. In the post-revolutionary period it was recuperated by Napoléon for his imperial ambitions under the banner of the *mission civilisatrice* (civilizing mission). The process of becoming civilized was henceforth linked to the ideology of progress as the defining trait of Western superiority. This cultural bias persisted well into the twentieth century, when the socio-ethnologist Marcel MAUSS pointed out in 1930 that the criteria for defining *civilisation* are always Western.

Commonly associated with the great monuments of high culture, such as architecture, art, literature, music, philosophy, the definition of civilization actually encompasses the more global sense of an 'ensemble of social phenomena (religious, esthetic, scientific, technical) common to a large society or group of societies'. Yet, this relatively neutral dictionary presentation's insistence upon the size of the agglomeration relegates small, tribal societies to civilization's antithesis: nature or barbarism.

Until very recently, *cours de civilisation* (civilization classes) was the term commonly used for courses devoted to French culture and society aimed at foreign students, or courses of 'background' information about foreign countries for French students. That traces of the hierarchical and teleological connotations of *civilisation* persist within current usage is illustrated by the Robert Dictionary's primary illustration for the term: 'The progressive civilization of Oceanic peoples'. (**Michèle Richman**)

Further reading

Elias (2000).

Cixous, Hélène   Born 1937. Writer, literary critic, and leading French FEMINIST. She developed the practice of *ÉCRITURE FÉMININE* (feminine writing) as a new way of writing about sexual difference and the construction of SUBJECT identity,

Clair, René   1898–1981. Film director. He made successful and internationally admired sentimental comedies on strongly French themes, including *Un chapeau de paille d'Italie* (*An Italian Straw Hat*, 1927) and *Silence est d'or* (*Silence is Golden*, 1947).

Clarté   1919–28. Political and literary journal, founded by Henri BARBUSSE, It acted as the focus for a movement of avant-garde INTELLECTUALS, including MARXISTS and SURREALISTS, who criticized traditional French culture and BOURGEOIS society.

Class   Classes are large groups in society, which are mainly formed by their different economic circumstances, but are also marked by social, political and cultural differences. Identifying with a particularly class gives people a sense of belonging to a community, with shared values and lifestyle. Class ranks along with NATIONALITY, ethnicity and GENDER as one of the most powerful sources of cultural identity. Until the 1950s, small farmers (*PAYSANS*) and farm-workers were the biggest grouping, followed by industrial WORKERS or *prolétaires*. Since the nineteenth century, French people have been acutely conscious of class differences, especially when these have led to open conflicts. The 1930s were a particularly class-conscious period, when a severe economic crisis made life very difficult for large numbers of working people. They saw a great contrast with the life enjoyed by the wealthy minority, or 'BOURGEOISIE', who were thought to be led by *les deux cent familles*, the 200 richest families in France. The previously divided political groups of the Left and Centre combined in a POPULAR FRONT movement, which was elected to government in May 1936, with a programme of social reforms to help the working class. During the Second World War and the LIBERATION period, class conflicts were largely suppressed, but re-emerged in 1947, and have had fluctuating prominence since then, with a second peak in the 1970s after the MAY '68 events. In the present, class differences continue to be reflected in the privileged position of social ÉLITES, and in social problems such as unemployment and homelessness. Class issues are often expressed in debates on issues such as inequality (*les inégalités*), job insecurity (*la précarité*), urban crime (*l'insécurité*) and EXCLUSION. **(Michael Kelly)**

Further reading

Mendras and Cole (1991). Focuses on the social history of France and the break-up of traditional class structures.

Claudel, Paul 1868–1955. Poet and dramatist. A convert to CATHOLICISM, he used Christian symbolism to overlay realist action, in plays like *Le Soulier de satin* (*The Satin Slipper*, 1929), and linked love and passion with metaphysical themes of redemption and suffering. A career diplomat, he also published many volumes of poetry.

Clémenceau, Georges 1841–1929. Politician. Leading figure of the early THIRD REPUBLIC, several times Prime Minister, he presided over the PARIS PEACE SETTLEMENT, but failed to be elected President in 1920.

Clément, Catherine Born 1939. Writer and journalist. Her essays have been influential, in combining LACANIAN PSYCHOANALYSIS with MARXIST theory. She has also written several novels.

Clément, René 1913–95. Film director, popular in the 1950s, whose best-known film, *Jeux interdits* (1953) is still remembered for the theme tune played on classical guitar.

Clouzot, Henri–Georges 1907–77. Film director. His controversial war-time film, *Le Corbeau* (1943) gave a characteristically dark picture of French life.

Club Méditerranée Club Méditerranée (Club Med) is an organization of 'vacation villages' offering idyllic getaways in exotic sites around the world in carefully constructed environments built around French food and wine. A product of the post-Second World War TOURISM boom, Club Med became famous in the 1970s for its hedonistic *bouffer, bronzer, et baiser* (eat, tan, and make love) romanticized Polynesian vacations, but it struggled in the 1980s and 1990s.

Begun in Majorca in 1950 by Gérard Blitz, a Belgian diamond cutter and champion swimmer, Club Med was intended to make seaside vacations available to all Europeans. Four years later, Blitz formed a partnership with Gilbert Trigano, a French entrepreneur who had been a RESISTANCE leader during the OCCUPATION. At first, guests slept in surplus army tents and cooked their own food. During the French economic expansion of the 1960s, Club Med villages were advertised as the escape from the commercial urban rat race. By the 1970s, Club Med attracted mainly young singles and couples in quest of sex and sun.

The ageing of the baby boom generation and the fear of AIDS in the early 1980s, together with the development of sex tourism in Thailand and elsewhere, made it difficult for Club Med to maintain its market niche. Its advertising shifted toward families. In 1993, Trigano appointed his son Serge as chief executive. A changing travel market and cheaper competition cut into Club Med sales. Serge was forced out in 1996, after Club Med, with 115 resorts in 37 countries, announced the largest financial loss in its history.

A year later, Philippe Bourguignon, who had helped turn around the strike-prone, debt-laden Euro-Disney theme park, was brought in as head. Bourguignon reorganized the resorts into 78 'family' and 7 'adult' villages. Revenues rose in Europe but continued to lag in America. Serge Trigano criticized Bourguignon for 'Disneyfication' and Americanization, while Club Med struggled to shed its hedonistic image and compete with larger travel organizations in a demographically older market increasingly oriented towards 'cultural' tourism. (**Bertram M. Gordon**)

Further Reading

Faujas (1994).

Cock, Gallic   The *coq gaulois* is the oldest of the French national symbols, dating back to the Roman period when a simple play of words – the latin *gallus* means both cock and inhabitant of Gaul – led to the attributes of the farmyard animal – valour, vigilance, fertility, sexual prowess – being transferred to the Gauls and then the French. The cock's association in Roman mythology with Mercury, god of commerce, the arts and eloquence, further enhanced its symbolic potential. It later became associated positively with Christian religious values and, thereafter, with the French monarchy. Despite these latter associations, however, the farmyard connections of the bird – France's historic rivals, with their national symbols of lions or eagles were not slow to deride it as a domestic fowl presiding over a dung-heap – precluded it from taking a dominant position in royal and, later, French republican insignia.

The Gallic cock's fortunes in the twentieth century have remained mixed. It has appeared as a national icon on French definitive stamps only twice, commemorating the LIBERATION in 1944 (when it appeared juxtaposed with the acronym 'RF' and the Lorraine Cross) and making a three-year run in 1962–65. The painter Gérard Garouste invented a comic icon fusing the Gallic cock, Marianne and a sheaf of wheat in a stamp commemorating the bicentenary of the French Republic in 1992, while its most spectacular recent philatelic appearance was in 1994 when, as symbol of French commerce, it shook hands with the British lion (also symbolizing trade) to mark the completion of the Channel Tunnel. Perhaps its most famous association this century is with sport, where as a *coq sportif* it decorates rugby shirts, is the trademark of a major sportswear brand, and was the *Footix* mascot for the 1998 Football World Cup. But in today's urban industrial society, the cock's association with rural France may, despite its long and noble pedigree, militate against its wider use as a national symbol. (**David Scott**)

Further reading

Pastoureau (1998).

Cocteau, Jean   1889–1963. Writer, artist and film director. He first became known as a poet, but wrote several short novels, like *Les Enfants terribles* (*Dreadful Children*, 1929), and plays which, like *La Machine infernale* (1934), often drew on classical mythology. Active in many areas of the arts, he became a respected and popular film director, whose *La Belle et la bête* (*Beauty and the Beast*, 1945) is now a classic.

Cohabitation   The term used to describe the arrangements under the FIFTH REPUBLIC, when the President and Prime Minister (and therefore the government) come from opposed political groupings, as has happened on three occasions,

Cohn-Bendit, Daniel   Born 1945. German-born political activist who played a leading role in the events of MAY '68. Now a leading ecological activist and member of the European Parliament.

Cold War   In the long-lasting campaign of intimidation and propaganda waged between the United States and the Soviet Union that began with the Allied victory and only ended with the collapse of COMMUNISM in the early 1990s, French foreign policy as well as popular and intellectual opinion did not automatically gravitate to either side. The French position was a complex one, in large part due to the wartime experience of bombardment and the Nazi OCCUPATION. Not until a decade after the LIBERATION did the perception that the USSR posed a greater threat than Germany to French security decisively change.

On the heels of the Nazi Occupation came American Liberation, though FOURTH REPUBLIC leaders from Charles DE GAULLE on were reluctant to toe the line of their American saviours. Beginning with his famous speech of August 1944, De Gaulle consciously shaped French policy and national self-perception as independent. But those same years saw the articulation of new and renewed ties between France and both the United States and the Soviet Union. For those with wartime memories, the strong presence of French Communist Party members in the ranks of the Resistance made a break with the Soviet Union unthinkable. Economic assistance in rebuilding the nation, however, would come from the United States. The May 1946 talks in Washington between Leon BLUM and Secretary of State James Byrnes yielded the BLUM-BYRNES AGREEMENT: in exchange for American financial aid, France accepted the 'Open Door principle', which sought to end restrictive trade practices and thus reduce the Communist influence. With the March 1947 establishment of the Marshall Plan, French policy made a marked shift towards alliance with the United States. It was, however, less the decisions of policy-makers than the central place occupied by Left INTELLECTUALS in French culture, their self-identification as REVOLUTIONARIES and accompanying anti-Americanism, that made France's specific experience of the Cold War less a matter of international relations than one of internal ideological conflict. The cultural war *par excellence* in post-Second World War France lasted well into the 1980s. (**Susan Weiner**)

Further reading

Souton (1994). Presents the views of orthodox historians alongside his own in an analytical chronology of events and attitudes. Judt (1992). Discusses the reluctance of French intellectuals on the Left to speak out against Soviet policies. Freeman (1997). Examples of the cultural impact of the Cold War.

Colette, Sidonie–Gabrielle 1873–1954. Writer. Her novels, like *Chéri* (1920) explore personal relationships, often in frank and intimate detail. Her explorations of hypocrisy, corruption and male domination of WOMEN initially incurred disapproval, as did her unconventional lifestyle. She subsequently became an influential figure in literary circles.

Collaboration In common use, collaboration refers to the French who worked for Nazi Germany during the Second World War, especially during their 1940–44 OCCUPATION of France. The word actually means 'working together,' which can be either positive or negative. Its secondary definition is the more common one of treason. As times change, so do evaluations of collaboration and collaborators. The French writer Paul Morand served as an ambassador for the collaborationist VICHY REGIME, was punished after 1945, but his work has since regained popularity.

Most discussions of collaboration focus on public cases, such as the writer Robert BRASILLACH, who was executed in 1945, and 'horizontal collaborators', women who had sexual relations with German soldiers and were punished at the LIBERATION. Some, such as the Vichy official Maurice Papon, went unpunished for decades, others were never sanctioned.

Collaborators acted for many reasons, ranging from expectation of personal gain after the French defeat in 1940, when it appeared that Nazi Germany had won the war, to sincere belief in the Nazi New Order. After the German attack against the Soviet Union in 1941, many collaborators acted from an aversion to COMMUNISM. Collaborators came from throughout the French political spectrum. In 1940, even the Communists thought they could work with the Germans. As the tide of battle turned against Germany, especially after the Allied landing in French North Africa in November 1942, many collaborators began to entertain doubts but some continued to support Germany through the liberation of France in the summer of 1944. A small number even followed the retreating German army into exile in Germany, where they were dispersed only after the Nazi defeat in May 1945. Collaborators who survived the war often defended their actions, saying that their activity had spared the French even harsher sanctions by the German occupiers. (**Bertram M. Gordon**)

Further reading

Gordon (1980); see also his 'Collaboration', in Gordon (1998), for how collaboration has been interpreted since the war. Hirschfeld and Marsh (1989). Essays mainly on the cultural side of collaboration.

Collège de France A unique state-funded institution, concerned with the development of specialised research and its dissemination through an open teaching programme. Although the name only dates from 1870, the Collège owes its existence to François 1er who in 1530, at the instigation of Guillaume Budé, appointed six *lecteurs royaux* in disciplines (Hebrew, Greek and Mathematics) that were not then recognized by the *Université de Paris* (SORBONNE). The *Collège Royal* which subsequently developed, managed to retain its autonomy from the university establishment, despite the close proximity to the Sorbonne of its own dedicated building (completed in 1778 under Louis XV). Today the *lecteurs* have become professors, of which there are currently 52, spanning a range of disciplines in the Humanities as well as the Physical and Social Sciences. Most of them are directors of research centres or laboratories, not all of which are located in the Collège itself. They are required both to pursue original research and to make their results available to the general public through open courses, mainly held at the Collège, but also, more recently, at affiliated institutions in France and sometimes abroad. An average of 5000 people attend such lectures and seminars every year, and numbers are rising.

Traditionally a very franco-centric and gender-biased institution in its ethos and outlook, the Collège adopted a range of measures in the 1990s designed to enhance its international vocation and reputation. In addition, a programme of renovation of the outdated and overcrowded buildings of the Collège was included as one of François MITTERRAND's *GRANDS TRAVAUX* in 1991, thus highlighting the state's desire to make the Collège a prestigious forum for discussion at the heart of the international research community. A large amphitheatre, library and state of the art conference facilities are among the new provisions.

Some of France's most illustrious names have been members of the Collège de France, though Albert Einstein declined a Chair in 1933. Current professors include Pierre BOULEZ, Pierre BOURDIEU, Claude LÉVI-STRAUSS and Emmanuel LE ROY LADURIE. (**Susan Collard**)

Further reading

See the Collège's extensive website: www.college-de-france.fr

Colonialism   Whereas IMPERIALISM usually describes the theory of empire and the attitudes of a dominant metropolitan centre to its distant possessions, colonialism, which can be seen as an inevitable and concrete result of imperialism, is the physical act of settling those distant territories. Settlement would usually begin in a major military or commercial location or on a coastal periphery and then spread, according to local circumstances, via conquest, exploration or steady annexation. The implications of settlement were twofold. On the one hand, French nationals were suddenly transported to places radically different from metropolitan France, either as permanent settlers (*colons*) or as missionaries, colonial officials, troops and traders. On the other hand, contact with French people, language and culture had lasting and often irreversible effects on the colonized culture and its indigenous population. French colonial policy was one of either 'assimilation' or 'association', the former implying the imposition of French administrative structures on individual colonies, the latter involving systems of government which combined French and indigenous control. Association supposedly allowed a greater degree of local autonomy, although this usually involved the appointment of puppet rulers by the French.

Common to most French colonial activity was the Eurocentric assumption that European norms in culture and politics should be imposed universally. The *mission civilisatrice* (civilizing mission) considered that colonized countries were inferior and required the imposition of French culture, education, justice and technology. One of the most obvious examples of such a strategy can be seen in the denigration of local languages and the promotion of French as a language of social advancement. Consequently, there are now as many speakers of French outside France (mainly in the former colonies and DOM-TOM) as there are in metropolitan France itself. The resultant existence of hybrid, francophone cultures can be seen as a persistent legacy of French colonialism. Those who describe the current period as one of post-colonialism are often accused of being prematurely celebratory since they ignore the existence of NEO-COLONIALIST tendencies in contemporary international relations. **(Charles Forsdick)**

Further reading

Aldrich (1996). A clear and well-researched account of French colonialism in the nineteenth and twentieth centuries. Ferro (1997). A comprehensive account of European colonialism, from conquest to independence, which provides a specific focus on a number of French examples.

Colonies de vacances *Colonies de vacances* (vacation colonies) were summer vacation camps established for lower-class urban children to learn the value of outdoor group activities and experience presumedly healthier country air. School vacations were legally recognized in 1834 in France, and they gave rise to concerns about idleness in 'degenerate' cities.

The first *colonie de vacances* is said to have been created by Wilhelm Bion, a Zürich pastor, who sent 68 children into the nearby mountains in 1876. Established with crusading zeal by religious charities, early colonies in France served both girls and boys. By 1883, camps run by the public schools had also appeared. In 1902, the Paris *Colonie de Vacances* Committee alone sent 5329 of a total 142 287 school children to experience a rigorous hygienic rural outdoors regimen in camps with activities organized to instill in the children a sense of rootedness in the French soil. The camps also began attracting middle-class children, sent to share the open-air camping experience, which came to be considered a vital part of their education. School teachers and tourism interests joined to promote the camps.

Colonies de vacances continued to grow during the inter-war years and the state played an increasingly important role. In 1923, the national committee administering the colonies was granted legal recognition. POPULAR FRONT legislation in 1936 provided for paid two-week vacations for all French workers, stimulating the tourist trade with its plethora of scout, youth hostel, Touring Club, and *colonie de vacances* activities. More than 5000 colonies enrolled over 100 000 children. The camps survived the Second World War but a cultural shift in the 1970s away from regimented group camping, together with the enhanced affordability of CLUB MÉDITERANÉE and other vacations outside France, closed the era of the *colo*. Now in decline, they are none the less still visible in country areas during the summer, and provide seasonal employment for students as *moniteurs* (supervisors). **(Bertram M. Gordon)**

Further reading

Rauch (1996); Lavenir (1999).

Coluche 1944–86. Actor and comedian, whose performances parodied the conservatism and hypocrisy of the French middle classes. As a satirical gesture, he stood for President in 1981. He later helped to found the RESTAURANTS DU CŒUR.

Combat 1941–47. Newspaper. Founded as the clandestine paper of the RESISTANCE movement of the same name (1940–43), it became an important daily newspaper after the war, especially under Albert CAMUS, its first post-war editor.

Comédie française The oldest professional national theatre company in France, based since 1790 in a theatre originally built by Victor Louis, adjacent to the Palais Royal. It was created in 1681 by *lettre de cachet* under Louis XIV, who sought to fill the void left by the death in 1673 of Molière, whose troupe had been the main provider of court entertainment. The *Comédie française* brought together two previously rival theatre troupes: the Théâtre Guénégaud (a regrouping of Molière's troupe), and the Hôtel de Bourgogne. The king's patronage enabled him to exercise considerable censorship.

After the disruption of the Revolution, Napoleon, by the 'decree of Moscow' in 1812, gave the company a new and unique status, based on the organization of the 'Confrérie de la Passion'. It became an association of actors who are shareholding members (*sociétaires*), run by an administrator appointed by the government, a status it still retains today, when roughly 75 per cent of its funding comes from the Ministry of CULTURE.

The role of the *Comédie française* had traditionally been as *gardien du répertoire*: to preserve and to present to the public a repertoire of French classic playwrights such as Molière, Corneille, Racine, Marivaux and Beaumarchais. It claims to have over 3000 plays in its repertoire, which it puts on using the practice of alternating performances in the Salle Richelieu adjacent to the Palais Royal. More recently, it has included some foreign and more contemporary playwrights such as SARTRE, Stoppard, IONESCO and Brecht, using two new theatres made available to it since 1993: Le Vieux Colombier and Le Studio-Théâtre.

It is often referred to as *La Maison de Molière* because his plays have been so frequently put on, and every year on the anniversary of his birth, the actors pay homage to his memory after the performance. (**Susan Collard**)

Further reading

See the company's website: www.comedie-francaise.fr

Comité national de la Résistance (CNR) 1943–44. Representative body bringing together most organizations involved in the RESISTANCE. Its Charter (1944) outlined a series of social and economic reforms, many of which were introduced at the LIBERATION.

Commitment Intervention in public debate on the part of writers, artists and others in the public sphere not directly involved by profession with politics. The English term translates the French noun *engagement*, with frequent usage in English for the adjectival form *engagé*. The phenomenon dates from the late nineteenth century with antecedents in the seventeenth- and eighteenth-century literary figures Blaise Pascal and Voltaire. The more recent meaning derives from turn-of-the-century protests on the part of writers, artists and others, who were opposed to the trial and conviction of Colonel Alfred Dreyfus on charges of treason. *Dreyfusards* based their actions in moral concerns and the threat to human rights represented by ANTI-SEMITISM of which they saw Dreyfus as a victim. Throughout the first third of the century, commitment was synonymous with protests against the status quo, equated in most cases with progressive political and social causes such as PACIFISM and DECOLONIZATION.

Following the August 1944 LIBERATION of Paris, Jean-Paul SARTRE and others on the COMMUNIST and non-Communist left sought to prolong solidarity among wartime RESISTANCE groups into permanent involvement with social justice. Sartre politicized the function of the writer within a programme of committed writing (*littérature engagée*) whose initial mission was to denounce and militate against threats to human freedom. Between 1945 and 1970, the Sartrean model and various left-wing offshoots dominated commitment, as its proponents spoke out on issues ranging from nuclear war and self-determination for ALGERIA to union-busting, torture and sexism. Post-war commitment also replaced intervention in the form of writing with more direct and militant activism.

Since the mid-1970s, *NOUVEAUX PHILOSOPHES* (new philosophers) such as Bernard-Henri LÉVY and André GLUCKSMANN have used the popular PRESS, television and film to militate against threats to human rights such as the Gulag phenomenon in Soviet Russia and more recent genocide in former Yugoslavia. The *MÉDECINS SANS FRONTIÈRES* (Doctors without borders) have likewise maintained high media visibility as an activist organization dedicated to treating victims of war and genocide around the world. (**Susan Ungar**)

Further reading

Poster (1975). Traces the evolution of the Sartrean model of commitment since 1945. Schalk (1979). Examines inter-war debates along a broad ideological spectrum from left to right.

Communism   See COMMUNIST PARTY.

Communist Party   A political movement of the Left, founded at the Congress of TOURS in 1920. As in other developed countries, the French labour movement, and the various SOCIALIST PARTIES attached to it, developed strongly at the end of the nineteenth century. The 1917 Bolshevik Revolution in Russia had great influence on the movement, and when its leader, Lenin, invited other countries to follow his revolutionary path, a part of the French socialist party voted to accept. They became a section of the Moscow-based Communist International, *Section française de l'internationale communiste* (SFIC), and then the *Parti communiste français* (PCF). From then onwards, relations with the non-Communist socialist parties were always difficult, and overshadowed by the bitterness of the initial split. Organized in a highly disciplined way, following the principle of 'democratic centralism', the PCF became an effective and militant party, and secured powerful influence in the trades unions, in political campaign groups, and in social movements. During the 1930s it joined forces with the socialists in the reforming POPULAR FRONT movement, and was prominent in the ANTI-FASCIST movements. Its obedience to Stalin plunged it into crisis when he signed a non-aggression pact with Hitler in 1939. The party was banned in France, and its leader Maurice THOREZ fled in exile to Moscow. During the German OCCUPATION, after initial hesitations, the PCF re-emerged as one of the main forces in the RESISTANCE, and went on to form part of the post-war government.

For most of the COLD WAR it received around a quarter of the votes in elections, but was politically isolated and frequently attacked for its unwavering support of the Soviet Union. Its ideological influence remained strong, however, and it was active in many opposition and protest movements. Since 1981, it has twice been a junior partner in socialist governments, though its popular support has fallen to around 10 per cent of the vote, and other groups have taken over its protest role. As a disciplined party with little tolerance for internal disagreements, it has been distinguished by the number of leading members who have left or been excluded, and the number of prominent national figures, especially writers and artists, who have supported it without joining it. (**Michael Kelly**)

Further reading

Adereth (1984). A useful history in English, written from a sympathetic point of view. Caute (1964). Very detailed, particularly on the pre-war period, with a wealth of anecdote. Bell and Criddle, (1994). A highly critical account. Hazareesingh (1991). An analytical account, showing the disillusion and decline of the recent period.

Compagnons de la chanson   1944–80. A close harmony male singing group who drew on the French folk traditions and gained an international reputation in the 1950s.

Concert halls   Auditoria for professional music, classical or popular. France has around 400, though many more multi-purpose venues exist where music is performed. In comparison with London or Berlin, Paris is poorly equipped for large classical concerts. Its major symphony hall, *la Salle Pleyel* (1927), can accommodate 2300 but the acoustics are considered unsatisfactory. Other suitable venues are the Champs-Elysées and Châtelet theatres, though here too acoustics and the Italianate stages create problems. Mitterrand's GRANDS TRAVAUX (grand building projects) promised a major new hall at the *Cité de la Musique* (La Villette), but the project fell victim to cuts. One hall was built, with excellent acoustics but seating for only 1000. Chamber music and recitals are better provided for in the capital, including in some unexpected places, such as the MUSÉE D'ORSAY and the LOUVRE. Outside Paris, efforts have been made locally to improve provision. A number of cities now offer state-of-the-art halls in conference centres (Nice, Strasbourg) or converted buildings (Metz, Nancy, Toulouse). Other venues are also available, from municipal theatres to the former MAISONS DE LA CULTURE.

After the closure of many MUSIC-HALLS earlier in the century, adequate facilities for popular music were lacking until recently. In Paris, two historic music-halls, l'OLYMPIA and BOBINO, have now been rebuilt and in 1984 le Zénith, purpose-built for popular music, opened at La Villette, accommodating over 6000. With government aid, other cities followed suit and Zéniths now operate in Caen, Pau, Marseille and elsewhere. Some smaller venues have also been developed, including 125 government-sponsored *Scènes de musiques actuelles* (present-day music theatres). But there is still a shortage of the more intimate venues for less well-known performers.

It could be argued that CDs, downloadable music and festivals reduce demand for traditional concert halls. But French musicians, administrators and governments still seem to believe in the importance of the organized indoor concert as both an aesthetic and a civic experience. (**David Looseley**)

Further reading

D'Angelo (1997). Contains details of concert halls and other musical provision.

Concerts   Paris has traditionally not been a musical venue as important as London, Berlin or Vienna, but recent developments have done much to alter this. The new *Opéra de la Bastille* (1990) and the *Cité de la Musique* at La Villette (1995) are now recognized as significant international venues, despite the aesthetic and political controversy with which the former has been surrounded. Olivier MESSIAEN and Pierre BOULEZ, composer and composer-conductor, respectively, have been not only France's major concert-music figures of the post-war period, but equal in status to any of their European or American counterparts. The refurbishment of the old Opera House, previously an acoustic joke, has been another important factor. The provinces too have benefited, as the *Opéra de Lyon* illustrates. All France really lacks now is a symphony orchestra on a par with the London Symphony or the Berlin Philharmonic, though the Orchestre de Paris runs these close.

JAZZ, on the other hand, has since the LIBERATION found its second home in France more than in any other European country. Beloved of the EXISTENTIALISTS, it was also the subject of much critical controversy, as in the debates in the late 1940s, between Hugues Panassié and Charles Delaunay, the former denouncing bebop, the latter championing it. France had also been home to the Quintette du Hot Club de France, the apogee of string jazz, thanks above all to the inspired guitar-playing of Django REINHARDT. The foundation of the Orchestre National de Jazz in 1986 thus came as the consecration of a jazz culture whose vitality is attested to by the existence of nearly 200 jazz festivals.

French pop music, needless to say, trails in a dismal third, and the best-attended pop concerts in France are given by American or British performers. The long tradition of CHANSON, exemplified by Édith PIAF or Georges BRASSENS, who could without difficulty fill Paris's large OLYMPIA music-hall, seems to have ground to a halt. Yet figures as divergent as Claude Nougaro and Michel Sardou remain highly popular, and the new Bercy concert-hall provides artists visiting Paris with a venue of world class. (**Keith Reader**)

Consumerism   MODERNIZATION in the years following the Second World War (often referred to as *LES TRENTE GLORIEUSES*) brought about the transformation of France from a country based largely on the ECONOMY and values of AGRICULTURE to one that had caught up with the leading industrial nations of the western world. By the 1960s, a fast-growing and less protected economy was accompanied by a general increase in disposable income and an expansion in the availability of mass-produced consumer goods (for example, clothes, cosmetics, cars, televisions, and so on). France had become a consumer society (*la société de consommation*) with consumption rising rapidly among all classes. The cultural values of the new consumer society were analysed by a number of sociologists and cultural critics, including Roland BARTHES, Jean BAUDRILLARD, Cornelius Castoriadis, Guy Debord, Henri LEFEBVRE and Edgar MORIN. They were joined by creative writers and film-makers, including Georges PEREC in *Les Choses* (*Things*, 1965), Simone de BEAUVOIR in *Les Belles Images* (*Beautiful Images*, 1966), and Jean-Luc GODARD in *Weekend* (1968). They decried the way in which consumerism converted individuals into customers, society into a market-place and the world into a product to be consumed.

Since the 1960s, levels of consumption have continued to rise rapidly. Between 1960 and 1996 the average level of consumption in France more than tripled, while spending on culture and leisure in the same period rose even more rapidly. Accompanying this dramatic rise in consumption has been a diversification in the market (subject especially to the development of a more inter-connected and global economy) and consequently a diversification in consumer choice and forms of consumption. Today the idea of the consumer society has therefore moved into a new phase, one in which GLOBALIZATION has opened up the more limited national economy of the post-war years. Critics of this new consumerism frequently bemoan the fact that France has lost its sense of individuality by becoming subsumed into a uniform and global-market place, dominated by the values of American LIBERALISM. For these critics, this signals the end of the republic of citizens and the victory of the individualistic consumer. (**Max Silverman**)

Further reading

Debord (1967). An influential critique of the consumer society of the 1960s by the leader of the counter-cultural Situationist movement of that decade. Rochefort (1995). Overview of French consumer society at the end of the century.

Contraception   Official French policy on contraception has been shaped by national anxiety over a shrinking population, and an intractably low birth rate. The First World War intensified what was already perceived as a demographic weakness, and the 1920 law made all promotion of or dissemination of information about contraception illegal. Though this had little positive effect on the birth rate, the law remained in force until 1967. In the 1950s, when a more incentive-based policy of generous family allowances had in fact temporarily raised the birth rate, a group of pro-contraception campaigners formed the Mouvement Pour le Planning Familial (MPPF). The groundswell of opinion in favour of freely available contraception led to the passing of the Loi Neuwirth in 1967: contraception was now legal and the new contraceptive device of the Pill began to be prescribed in the same year.

The post-1968 FEMINIST movement made women's right to choose whether and when to have children a central demand. Campaigning emphasized both contraception as sexual freedom (women could enjoy hetero-sex without the risk of pregnancy) and contraception as producing fewer but happier children (one popular slogan read *C'est tout de même plus chouette de vivre quand on est désiré* ('Life's so much better when you're a wanted child'). In 1974, prescribed contraception became reimbursable in the same way as other medical prescriptions. The advertising of contraceptives remained illegal, however, until in 1991 the threat of AIDS (*le SIDA*) contributed at last to the repeal of this part of the 1920 law.

The CATHOLIC CHURCH remains opposed to contraception, as papal encyclicals against artificial birth control and ABORTION have made clear. In practice, however, it seems that the majority of French Catholics ignore the Church's teaching on this point. As in most other developed countries, women in France are choosing to have fewer children and to have them later in life. Between 1980 and 1993, for example, the annual number of births dropped by almost 100 000, and the average age at which women gave birth rose from 26.8 to 28.5. (**Diana Holmes**)

Further reading

Laubier (1990); Montreynaud (1992); Picq (1993); Service des Droits des Femmes (1995).

Copeau, Jacques   1879–1949. Theatre director. He set up the Théatre du Vieux Colombier (1913) and an associated theatre school (1920) which influenced many actors and directors. His austere style and disciplined approach were influential into the 1950s.

Corsica   The traditions of 'the beautiful island' are southern Mediterranean, with cultural roots in classical antiquity and political alliances with Genoa, Pisa and also England in the early modern era. Corsica became part of France in 1769 after a short period of full independence under Pasquali Paoli. The Corsican language is spoken by 10 per cent of the population.

Since 1900, 40 per cent of the population have emigrated. The deaths of young Corsicans in the First World War had a significant impact on the island's economy. The population (250 000) is concentrated along the coast and in the towns of Ajaccio and Bastia, while in the interior the population density compares with the Sahara Desert. The influx of 20 000 French Algerians after the independence of ALGERIA in 1962 triggered an intensification of the Corsican nationalism which had re–emerged in the 1920s.

In the face of demands for independence since the 1960s Corsica has been granted greater autonomy and receives more financial subsidy than any other region in France. Corsicans resent the imposition of an undivided French republican identity, although the 'colonial' domination of France protects a weak Corsican economy. Some 25 per cent of the population voted for autonomy in the regional elections in 1999 against a background of high profile political violence from minority nationalist factions, who disagree over the degree of independence that can safeguard the fragile economy and the Corsican IDENTITY which is tied to it.

During the same period, under-investment and corruption have hampered economic development and exacerbated the political and social problems. The autonomy granted by the JOSPIN government in 2000 could increase political stability.

Significant inward investment in poor internal communications, weak and unbalanced agricultural and industrial sectors, and the highly contentious tourist industry could then improve economic and social aspects of the 'Corsican problem'. However identity issues continue to undermine a political solution. (**Bill Brooks**)

Further reading

> Thomson (1971). Despite its age, the best geographical survey of the economy and society of the island in English. Giudici (1998). An engaged and committed survey of the political, social and economic issues that confront Corsica.

Coty, René   1882–1962. Centre-Left politician. He briefly held ministerial office and was elected President of the FOURTH REPUBLIC (1953–59).

Cousteau, Jacques   1910–97. Pioneer of underwater exploration. Diving from his ship, *Calypso*, he made many films and TELEVISION series, of which *Le monde du silence* (*The Silent World*, 1955) is the best known.

Couve de Murville, Maurice   1907–99. Gaullist politician. Long-serving Foreign Minister under DE GAULLE (1958–68) and briefly Prime Minister (1968–69).

Creole   Creole languages are spoken in various former French colonies or present-day overseas departments: islands in the Indian Ocean (Mauritius, Réunion, Seychelles) or the Caribbean (Haïti, Guadeloupe, Martinique); mainland territories like French Guyana (South America) or Louisiana (USA).

On seventeenth-century colonial plantations, African slaves and their masters communicated in simplified forms of French, and so did the slaves between themselves when, as was often the case, they had no other common language. These pidgins became the native speech of subsequent generations, rapidly evolving their own sophisticated grammatical systems. The term creole specifically denotes such 'ex-pidgins'. There were similar developments from Dutch, English, Portuguese and Spanish, but the French-based group has the most speakers – some 8 000 000 worldwide.

Long despised as degenerate PATOIS, even by their mother-tongue users, creoles are today increasingly respected as languages in their own right. In independent states like Haïti or the Seychelles Islands, the regional creole is an important symbol of national IDENTITY, and enjoys official-language status alongside FRENCH. In the French overseas departments (DOM–TOM) too, though lacking official recognition, creoles are developing significant written traditions (novels, poetry and drama especially), while continuing to be spoken by all those born locally.

Though creoles from different places may not be mutually comprehensible, they follow similar general patterns. A Mauritian Creole example reveals the French basis, and the divergences from it. *Zo'n aret vin get nu* means 'they've stopped coming to see us'. *Zo* ('they') is short for *zot* – from *eux autres*, or more exactly colloquial *eux z'aut'*, 'them/that lot'; *'n* is an abbreviation of *fin(i)*, 'finish(ed)', placed before verbs to mark the perfect tense; *aret* is from *arrêter*, 'stop'; *vin* from *venir*, 'come'; get from *guetter*, 'keep watch' in French, 'look' or 'see' in Creole; *nu* from nous, 'we/us'. (**Rodney Ball**)

Further reading

Chaudenson (1995). Especially for information about French creoles. Todd (1990). General introduction to creole studies.

Cresson, Edith   Born 1934. Socialist politician, close to President MITTERRAND, she served as Prime Minister (1991–92) and as EU Commissioner (1994–2000).

Critical theory   'Critical theory' is notoriously difficult to define. Although the term in its purest sense describes the work of a specific school of Western MARXISM, it is also applied more generally to the writings of a number of twentieth-century French INTELLECTUALS who have influenced cultural and literary criticism in the second half of the twentieth century. Although there are risks inherent in applying critical theory slavishly to the reading of texts or to the analysis of cultural phenomena, any serious student or scholar must now take into account its implications for the fields in which they work. An over-emphasis on the importance of the work of theorists can detract from the analysis of specific objects of literary and cultural study themselves, but judicious engagement with critical theory remains a rich and often pleasurable source of intellectual liberation.

Critical theory, which emerged in opposition to the staid and unadventurous brand of biblio-biographical literary criticism focusing on *l'homme et l'œuvre* (man and his work), was central to the post-war intellectual experimentation in 1950s' and 1960s' France. The emergence of critical theory was closely linked to the emergence of new literary forms such as the NOUVEAU ROMAN. It borrowed ideas from the social sciences and rejected the compartmentalization of academic fields in favour of interdisciplinary approaches. In literary studies, the varied strands of such approaches were often collected under the title of *la* NOUVELLE CRITIQUE. Although this was influenced by developments in Marxist thought, its greatest debt was to STRUCTURALISM. One of critical theory's initial and perhaps most stimulating practitioners was Roland BARTHES whose study *Sur Racine* (*On Racine*, 1963) led to a famous exchange with the SORBONNE professor Raymond Picard. The title of Picard's *Nouvelle critique ou nouvelle imposture* (*New Criticism or New Fraud*, 1965) encapsulates the rage of certain scholars at what they saw as the slipshod scholarship inherent in critical theory. After 1968, two of the most productive strands of theory were FEMINISM and PSYCHOANALYSIS. The principal French theorists – Barthes, DERRIDA, FOUCAULT, KRISTEVA, LACAN – came to prominence in the later twentieth century, especially on North American university campuses. Dismissed by its (often unadventurous) critics as modish, meaningless jargon, critical theory is challenging and not, as is often claimed, inherently difficult. In approaching critical theory, students of literature and culture must be intellectually rigorous and discerning. The potential insights critical theory can offer remain, however, invaluable. (**Charles Forsdick**)

Further reading

Barry (995). An intelligent, clear, concise introduction to the principal tendencies in contemporary critical theory. Sturrock (1998). A collection of entertaining and informative essays on a number of the principal

French critical theorists (Barthes, Althusser, Lacan, Foucault, Derrida and others). Payne (1996). An invaluable source for students interested in exploring the complete range of critical theory. Useful index and full bibliography.

Croix-de-Feu The *Croix-de-Feu* (*Cross of Fire*) originated in 1928 as a benevolent association whose mission was to honour war veterans. Within a decade and in evolved form, it became the largest proto-FASCIST movement in inter-war France. What set the *Croix-de-Feu* apart from similar groups after 1930 was its new president. François de la Rocque de Sévérac was a retired lieutenant-colonel who fashioned himself into a charismatic *chef* (leader) opposed to the French Left and what he saw as the imminent threat of international COMMUNISM. By 1934, the group's membership had doubled to 35 000, including 1500 or so shock troops known as *dispos* (from the French adjective *disponible* 'available') on call to parade in formation and disrupt left-wing rallies. While other right-wing groups threw rocks at the police and tried without success to storm government buildings during the 6 February 1934 riots in Paris, the *Croix-de-Feu* stood in order outside the Chamber of Deputies. This display of disciplined restraint boosted membership to an estimated 600 000 until the Popular Front (*FRONT POPULAIRE*) government banned it in 1936 as a paramilitary organization. A month later, the *Croix-de-Feu* regrouped as the French Social Party (*Parti Social Français*) purportedly committed to electoral politics. The 1939 membership estimates of 1.2 million were less than half of the 3 million the party claimed. The VICHY government dissolved the PSF in 1942 and the Gestapo arrested La Rocque a year later.

Was the *Croix-de-Feu* fascist? De la Rocque openly espoused paramilitarism and devotion to an authoritarian leader as necessary to ensure the future of an integral France. At the same time, the *Croix-de-Feu*'s and PSF's defence of the FAMILY and a strong national STATE upheld a conservative tradition that extends to the current NATIONAL FRONT movement. (**Steven Ungar**)

Further reading

Soucy (1995). Indispensable: a clear and balanced account of nationalist groups, movements and parties groundedly opposed to democratic and republican values; second of a two-volume study.

Crozier, Michel Born 1922. Sociologist, best known for his theory (1970) that France was a *société bloquée*. His analyses particularly focused on the structure of the French STATE and on its BUREAUCRATIC nature.

Cubism Cubism was one of the foremost artistic movements of cultural modernism of the late nineteenth and early twentieth centuries. Modernism in all the arts challenged the dominant movements of REALISM and NATURALISM by exploring the formal aspect of representation and positing new and more profound perceptions of the real. Although Cubism as a movement flourished mainly in the years leading up to the First World War, it has nevertheless continued to exert a major influence on the development of modern art to the present day.

The distinguishing feature of Cubism is the breakdown of the naturalistic illusion of three-dimensional reality into a flat surface of geometric shapes and colour.

The attempt to analyse the essential or underlying form of a subject, usually in terms of the cube or cone, was also a reaction against the play of light and colour that was characteristic of the impressionist movement of the late nineteenth century. Experimentation with abstract forms in painting had been carried out by Paul Cézanne and Henri MATISSE but it is principally the work of Pablo PICASSO and Georges BRAQUE prior to the First World War that marked out the distinctive nature of the movement. In *Les Demoiselles d'Avignon* (1907), Picasso depicted prostitutes in a brothel in such a way that character and background are subject to the same stylized formal composition of geometric shape and colour. The Cubist flattening of spatial depth and perspective through the simultaneous juxtaposition of different views and sides of an object are also characteristic of the avant-garde poetry of Guillaume Apollinaire and Blaise Cendrars prior to the First World War.

The Cubist influence was clearly visible in other movements (such as FUTURISM) but, after the war, Picasso and Braque themselves developed in different directions. Although the movement itself was fairly short-lived, Cubism was of fundamental importance in terms of the development of ABSTRACT PAINTING in the twentieth century. (**Max Silverman**)

Further reading

Roskill (1985). Comprehensive introduction to Cubism with specific reference to France. Green (1987). How Cubism was received by its critics.

Cuisine Known for culinary riches including Bresse chickens, Périgord pâtés, and Burgundy and Bordeaux wines, French gastronomy dates back to medieval times. *Le Viander* (*c*.1375), by Taillevent (Guillaume Tirel) is the first French cookbook completely preserved. La Varenne's *Le Cuisinier François* (1651) reflects a *nouvelle cuisine* style favouring natural food tastes. Porcelain and fork use after the death of Louis XIV (1715) contributed to culinary refinement, as did restaurants, which first appeared in late eighteenth-century Paris. Joseph Berchoux's poem, *La Gastronomie* (1801), introduced this term. Grimod de La Reynière's *Almanach des Gourmands* (1803–1812), the first restaurant guidebook, and Brillat-Savarin's *Physiology of Taste* (1825), a treatise on gastronomy as science, both helped launch modern foodwriting.

Delmonico's restaurant in New York (1833) marked the emergence of French cuisine internationally. In 1855, the *appellation contrôlée*, a legal classification system of place names for wines, was introduced. Urbain-Dubois popularized '*service russe*', bringing dishes to the table in sequence to be served while still hot, in contrast to the older groaning board '*service française*'. At the turn of the century, August Escoffier topped the French culinary firmament, while a popular dietary shift from carbohydrates to animal fats was facilitated by improvements in transport and refrigeration.

The automobile, the writing of Curnonsky (Maurice-Edmond Sailland, 1872–1956), and the Michelin restaurant rating system (1926), promoted French regional cuisine and helped put LYON on the map. During the 1930s and in *Gourmet Magazine* after 1941, André Simon, M. F. K. Fisher, and Samuel Chamberlain extolled French food. Another *nouvelle cuisine* wave emerged briefly in the 1970s. In the 1980s and after, American styles, from McDonald's to California cuisine, made inroads in France. Surveys indicated a French cultural decline internationally but terms such as 'cuisine' illustrated the continuing influence of French in the culinary world. **(Bertram M. Gordon)**

Further reading

Flandrin and Montanari (1999); Spang (2000); Gordon(1999).

Culture   One of the most commonly used critical terms, it has many different meanings, ranging from 'high culture', such as literature, philosophy, classical music, or fine art, through 'popular culture', such as entertainment, sport and leisure, to the ETHNO-GRAPHIC sense of the entire way of life of a society or a social group. What these all have in common is that they are 'signifying practices', that is, social activities whose *meaning* may be as important as their practical function. So, for example, the ANTHROPOLOGIST Claude LÉVI-STRAUSS showed that in all societies, offering and eating food carries messages far beyond its nutritional function.

   In French, the notion of *culture* has a number of particular associations. The idea of *culture générale* has always been important in educational terms. From the start of their school career, French children are taught to develop a wide knowledge of the world, and to speak and write confidently on many topics. This is reflected in the school-leaving examination (*BACCALAURÉAT*), which includes mathematics, history and geography, a language other than French, physical education and philosophy for all students. It is also reflected in the respect given to INTELLECTUALS, and the expectation that they (or indeed any well-educated French person) will be able to discuss with authority any matters of public interest, regardless of their professional specialization.

   During the 1950s, the importance of 'high' culture to French national IDENTITY was recognized officially by the STATE, and expressed in the creation of a Ministry of CULTURE, led for ten years by the novelist and art critic André MALRAUX. Built initially around the performing arts and the *MAISONS DE LA CULTURE*, which were to take them to the people, the remit of this Ministry has continually broadened, to include popular culture, the audiovisual media and sport, among other things. The huge investment of prestige in the *GRANDS TRAVAUX* of successive Presidents, served to anchor culture to the French state. The position was confirmed by the GATT negotiations of the 1990s, in which the French negotiators successfully resisted attempts to classify culture (particularly audio-visual culture) as purely a matter of trade and industry. In the last decade, the term *culture* has largely taken over the role previously played by *civilisation*. **(Michael Kelly)**

Culture, Ministry of   The government department responsible for the arts and heritage. Created by President DE GAULLE in 1959, the Ministry's first incumbent was the novelist André MALRAUX (1959–69), Minister of State for 'Cultural Affairs'. Starting virtually from scratch, Malraux drew up a mission statement still broadly applicable today: to make the major works of humanity accessible, to secure the greatest possible audience for the national heritage, and to encourage the creation of new works to enrich that heritage. As this implies, Malraux construed 'culture' as product not process; and making culture available to all became his abiding ambition, exemplified in the MAISONS DE LA CULTURE (regional arts centres). He also had the historic buildings of Paris cleaned and gave limited encouragement to living artists. A major constraint, however, was his budget, which never reached even 0.5 per cent of total state spending.

Since Malraux, the Ministry has widened its remit and been twinned with other departments, mostly Communication (press and broadcasting) as it is today. It was not until the election of a SOCIALIST president in 1981, François MITTERRAND, that it became a department of 'Culture' specifically, under another long-serving Minister, Jack LANG (1981–86, 1988–93). He rebranded the Ministry by adopting a dynamic, youthful image. Its budget also doubled, subsequently (if briefly) reaching 1 per cent of state spending. This manna was distributed with largesse, even to popular arts like circus, comic strips (*BANDE DESSINÉE*) and rap, though spending on the traditional areas still predominated. Lang's successors have broadly followed his example, albeit with less panache and less money. But public spending on culture is still substantial by British or American standards, especially as the Ministry's budget (around 16 billion francs in 2000) is outstripped by local authority spending, which has grown remarkably since a degree of cultural decentralization has been introduced. (**David Looseley**)

Further reading

Looseley (1995). Traces the history of the Ministry since 1959, with particular emphasis on the Lang years.

Curie, Marie   1867–1934. Scientist. First woman professor at the SORBONNE, she made major discoveries in radioactivity and won two Nobel Prizes: the first in Physics (1903) with her husband Pierre Curie (1859–1906), the second in CHEMISTRY (1911), after his death.

Cycling   The French word *vélo* derives from *vélocipède* or bone-shaker which was an early form of the bicycle or *bécane*. The modern pedal bicycle was invented in 1840 by a Scotsman, Kirkpatrick Macmillan of Dumfriesshire. Pneumatic as opposed to solid rubber tyres were first fitted in 1888, while gears were developed from around the same period. The first cycle race was held in Paris in 1868, and won by the Englishman James Moore. Cycling as a sport developed various popular forms, including *cyclocross, piste* or track, criterium (round-city), mountain biking (or VTT, *vélo tout terrain*), road and stage races. Cycling was an Olympic sport from 1896.

The most famous and toughest of all cycle races is the *Tour de France*, launched by Henri Desgrange, director of the magazine *L'Auto* in 1903. Teams of competitors cover 4800 km in various stages or *étapes* over approximately three weeks, mostly in France, but with occasional incursions into neighbouring countries. The practice of awarding the winner of each stage the honour of wearing the *maillot jaune* (yellow jersey) started in 1919. A central aspect of the drama of the race, over and above the vicissitudes of the long and gruelling itinerary, is the competition between the *rouleurs* and the *grimpeurs*, the former gaining advantage in the speed trials, the latter in the *grands cols* or mountainous stages in the Alps, Pyrenees and Massif Central.

The Tour, as well as being a huge popular event, has taken on a mythic status in the French cultural calendar, with memorable champion cyclists – whether Belgian, Dutch, French, Italian, Spanish or Swiss, being fêted as heroes. Among the greatest must be counted Anquetil, Hinault and Merckx, all of whom achieved the super-human feat of being five times overall victors. The growing competitiveness and commercialization of sport in the media age, together with the widespread use of drugs in endurance sports, have, however diminished somewhat the raw, heroic appeal of cycle racing. (**David Scott**)

Further reading

Barthes (1957); Sansot (1991).

Czechoslovakia Czechoslovakia only became a state in 1919, following the PARIS PEACE SETTLEMENT. Its establishment formed part of French foreign policy in Eastern and Central Europe to dismember the former Austro-Hungarian Empire and to con-struct a barrier between the new Soviet Union and Western Europe. France was strongly supportive of Czechoslovakia throughout the inter-war years, although she finally capitulated to Hitler at the MUNICH Agreement in 1938, which saw Czechoslovakia absorbed into the Reich. Throughout the inter-war years, there was considerable interaction between Czech and French artists and musicians, particularly in the field of the avant-garde.

After the Second World War, Czechoslavakia enjoyed a brief period of indepen-dance as a liberal democracy, before being consolidated into the Soviet bloc in 1948. Relations with the West were inevitably restricted throughout most of the period of communist rule, although in the 1960s there was considerable interest in France in young Czech film-makers, such as Milos Forman, as well as in the puppet-plays and animation films of Jiri Trnka. The Prague Spring of 1968, which saw a considerable liberalization of the regime under Alexander Dubcek, only to be snuffed out through massive Russian intervention, coincided with a similar process of revolt in France which culminated in the events of MAY '68.

Although the communist regime remained in power until 1989, there was con-siderably more openness towards the West and major Czech artistic figures were allowed to live in exile. One of the most notable of these exiles was the novelist Milan Kundera, who settled in Paris. (**Nicholas Hewitt**)

Further reading

Hewitt (2000). Contains two essays on France and Czech literature and music.

D

Dadaism An anarchic and subversive movement in ART and literature officially launched in Zürich in 1916 (as regards the name), although many of its prime movers were active in New York as early as 1913. It soon spread to Berlin, Paris and other major European centres. The leading names in the movement, Arp, TZARA, Ernst, Huelsenbeck, MAN RAY, Ball, Schwitters, came from many countries and it was internationalist in spirit, but Dada made an early impact in France, two of its leaders being Francis Picabia and Marcel DUCHAMP. A number of the latter's 'artworks', a urinal, a bicycle wheel and a bottle-rack, had in fact been exhibited before the official birth of the movement, and are archetypal works.

The Dadaists, taking as their label *dada*, the French for a child's hobbyhorse, at random from a dictionary, sought to shock the BOURGEOIS. Just as they denounced the bourgeois nationalism that engendered the First World War, so they derided the associated cultural paraphernalia: art galleries, critics, collectors, dealers, academics, INTELLECTUALS, arbiters of good taste and decorum in art and literature. The work of art, the masterpiece of literature – sublime, serene, permanent – was anathema as a concept, and replaced derisively by an ephemeral, utilitarian object, or by a 'poem' made up of words torn from a newspaper and rearranging themselves at random to be chanted at venues such as the *Cabaret Voltaire* in Zürich. This principle of randomness was a key tenet of the movement that developed from and superseded Dada in the early 1920s, SURREALISM. Although dada was 'officially' pronounced dead in Germany in 1922, its spirit lived on; Marcel Duchamp still has a powerful universal influence in art colleges at the end of the twentieth century. (**Ted Freeman**)

Further reading

Bigsby (1971). A succinct and helpful study. Dachy (1990). Illustrates key works.

Daladier, Édouard 1884–1970. Centrist politician. He was Prime Minister three times in the inter-war period. In particular, he was responsible for ending the POPULAR FRONT, for signing the MUNICH agreement, and for declaring war on GERMANY.

Darlan, François 1881–1942. Admiral and right-wing politician. Commander of French naval forces in 1940, he became navy minister and eventually head of government under the VICHY REGIME. Present in French North Africa during the Allied landings, he was appointed governor of the region by the USA in November 1942, and was assassinated on Christmas Eve of that year.

Darnand, Joseph 1897–1945. Right-wing politician. A supporter of DORIOT and the Extreme Right in the 1930s, he was an enthusiastic collaborator and held several offices under VICHY, including head of the para-military *MILICE*. He was tried and executed at the LIBERATION.

Dassault, Marcel 1892–1986. Industrialist. A successful aircraft designer in the 1930s, he survived deportation to Buchenwald. After the LIBERATION he formed his own company and built most of France's military aircraft, including the successful Mirage jet fighters and fighter-bombers. He entered politics as a GAULLIST from 1951, but later co-operated with the SOCIALISTS on NATIONALIZATION.

D-Day (le jour J) 6 June 1944. Allied landings on the beaches of Normandy, around Arromanches, north of Caen, began the LIBERATION of France from German occupation.

Déat, Marcel 1894–1955. Right-wing politician. A SOCIALIST *député* in 1925, he held ministerial posts and moved to the Right, embracing FASCISM during the OCCUPATION. He served briefly as minister for labour under LAVAL (1944), and spent the remainder of his life in hiding in Italy.

Debord, Guy 1931–94. Writer. Founder and leader of the SITUATIONIST International, he launched provocative actions of social criticism, and wrote a highly influential analaysis of modern ALIENATION in *La société du spectacle* (*Society of the Spectacle*, 1967).

Debray, Régis Born 1940. Writer and politician. He came to notice as a theorist of REVOLUTION, who was imprisoned in 1967 in Bolivia. He developed theories about the role of INTELLECTUALS and the MEDIA in society, and advised President MITTERRAND on the Third World.

Debré, Michel Born 1912. Gaullist politician. An active member of the RESISTANCE, he rallied to DE GAULLE and served in his office at the LIBERATION, helping to found the National Administration School (ENA). He was the first Prime Minister of the FIFTH REPUBLIC (1959–62), and is often credited with drafting its constitution.

Decentralization A policy undertaken with some success by post-war governments, to counter the tendency for industry and administration to be centred in PARIS. Since the 1980s, the main focus of the policy has been to develop the REGIONS, and to establish clusters of related industries in particular areas, for example, concentrating the aerospace industries in the vicinity of Toulouse.

Decolonization The process by which colonized peoples gained their independence. Most parts of the French colonial empire became independent between 1945 and 1962. In broad terms, this was achieved most rapidly in territories where French rule was comparatively recent, such as in parts of the Middle East. Decolonization took longer in regions where the French were more entrenched, as in ALGERIA. A few small territories dating back to the earliest phase of French overseas expansion, now known as the DOM-TOM, are still not independent.

Decolonization was driven by a rising tide of nationalism among colonized peoples and changes in the international environment which weakened France's position overseas. The Nazi OCCUPATION of France during the Second World War demonstrated this weakness and at the same time led French political ÉLITES to emphasize the importance of the colonial empire as a symbol of France's status on the world stage. While Britain withdrew from most of its empire relatively peacefully, the French were more inclined to resist calls for independence, using military means if necessary. INDO-CHINA was relinquished only after the French had suffered a humiliating defeat at DIEN BIEN PHU in 1954, following an eight-year guerrilla war. A few months later the ALGERIAN WAR began, plunging France into the most traumatic phase of its retreat from empire. Almost 3 million Frenchmen served with the armed forces in Algeria before independence was granted in 1962. In the meantime, France had quit Tunisia and Morocco in 1956 before doing the same in Sub-Saharan Africa and Madagascar in 1960. While granting political independence, France maintained close links with many former colonies, prompting charges of NEO-COLONIALISM. The FRANCOPHONIE movement has often been interpreted in this way. (**Alec Hargreaves**)

Further reading

Ageron (1991). A thorough study, including sample documents and detailed chronology.

Deconstruction   A philosophical strategy, most closely associated with the work of Jacques DERRIDA, which was highly influential in French INTELLECTUAL circles in the 1960s and 1970s. From the 1970s onwards, deconstruction has also been much discussed in the English-speaking world. Derrida argues that Western metaphysics has tended to be dominated by a series of conceptual oppositions such as good/evil, universal/particular, and transcendental/empirical. These oppositions are shown to be derived from a series of presuppositions or constructions which are determined by power and history. One term in the opposition is always excluded or denigrated, since the opposition itself relies upon a notion of centre or presence. Derrida shows that the privileged term is actually constituted by the term that it suppresses.

One of the consequences of the deconstructive approach is to remind us that forms of rhetorical and metaphorical analysis can be applied to philosophical as well as literary texts. In this way, one mode of deconstructive reading seeks to bring out the frequently latent contradictions that lie within a text. Deconstruction also reinforces that idea that meaning is never quite present to itself, which means that it escapes the conscious intentions of the author, and unfolds just ahead of the interpreter. Deconstruction can also be conceived of as a way of 'inhabiting' the work of an author, so as to bring out new tendencies in that work. Derrida's influential readings of Plato, Hegel, Nietzsche and Heidegger would fall into this category

Some critics, notably Michel FOUCAULT, have claimed that one of the drawbacks of 'deconstruction' is that it places too much emphasis on the text, while ignoring the forces which constitute the text from the outside. Derrida tends to reject the notion that deconstruction is an established 'method', and has written on a number of polit-ical matters, including nationalism, apartheid and the Holocaust. Deconstructive reading can help to tease out the unacknowledged presuppositions and suppressions which underpin established discourses. (**John Marks**)

Further reading

Norris (1982). A clearly written introduction, with particularly useful sections on Derrida. Silverman (1989). A series of essays dealing with Derrida's deconstructive readings of philosophers such as Plato, Kant and Hegel.

Deferre, Gaston 1910–86. Socialist politician and press baron. He served in several ministerial posts under the FOURTH REPUBLIC, and again under MITTERRAND. He stood unsuccessfully for President twice, and was Mayor of MARSEILLE for 33 years (1953–86).

De Gaulle, Charles 1890–1970. Politician and General. Dominant political figure of the mid-twentieth century. An advocate of modernizing the French ARMY, he escaped to London at the Fall of France, and led the Free French in exile during the Second World War. Head of the PROVISIONAL GOVERNMENT (1944–46), he resigned to form the conservative nationalist RPF opposition movement. He returned to lead the government in 1958 at the height of the ALGERIAN WAR, and was President of the FIFTH REPUBLIC, whose constitution he devised, from then until 1969. His memoirs, written while he was out of office, are extensive and influential.

Deixonne, loi 1951. Law allowing Breton, Basque, Catalan and Occitan languages to be taught in French schools. It is regarded as the first modest step towards recognition of regional diversity.

Deleuze, Gilles 1925–95. Philosopher. A leading figure in the POST-STRUCTURALIST movement, whose *Anti-Oedipus* (with F. Guattari, 1972) offered a radical critique of PSYCHOANALYSIS and capitalism. He also wrote on ART and CINEMA.

Delors, Jacques Born 1925. Socialist politician. He served as Finance Minister (1981–84) and was a long-serving President of the European Commission (1985–95).

Delphy, Christine Born 1941. Feminist writer and activist. Working in the tradition of Simone de BEAUVOIR, she has focused on social rather than psychological factors in the situation of women. She has been influential as editor of the journal *Questions féministes*.

Democracy Whereas in a number of Western industrialized countries democracy and LIBERALISM went hand in hand, in France the meaning of democracy developed predominantly within the specific context of the French republican tradition inherited from the REVOLUTION. In practice, and especially during the years of the THIRD REPUBLIC (1871–1940), this meant a formal concept of rights and duties defined by the STATE according to the abstract and universal principles of liberty and equality before the law.

This state-based and unitarian concept of democracy, in which universal rights are enshrined within the constitution, has not always ensured *de facto* equality. For example, workers' rights have only been won through political and trade union action, while women were only accorded the vote in 1945. Nor has it always managed to resist the claims of partisan factions and extremist IDEOLOGIES. In the 1930s, parliamentary democracy and the rule of law were consistently undermined by the polarization of politics brought about by the ideological clash of FASCISM and COMMUNISM. With the creation of the FIFTH REPUBLIC (1958 to the present day), DE GAULLE attempted to bolster the power of the executive and the institutions of the state over and above parliament and party factionalism. However, during the second half of the 1960s, the centre was rocked once again, this time by popular grass-roots demands for new freedoms, which culminated in the astonishing events of MAY '68.

Since then, civil society has continued to flex its muscles against a centralizing and overbearing state. Numerous groups (WOMEN, IMMIGRANTS and their children, HOMOSEXUALS, campaigners for the environment, and so on) demand a more pluralist concept of rights and democracy than that provided by the republican tradition. Today hard-line defenders of republicanism equate this concept of democracy with American LIBERALISM and view it as an individualistic concept of rights which is destructive of social and national cohesion. Yet many now concede that democracy in the twenty-first century will have to be founded on a compromise between the formal concept of equality before the law and the rights of the individual and the group. (**Max Silverman**)

Further reading

Lefort (1988). Collected translated essays covering key questions of democracy and politics in modern societies. Touraine (1994). Historical and contemporary overview of concepts of democracy in France by the celebrated sociologist.

Deneuve, Catherine   Born 1943. Film actor. Starred in numerous successful films made in France and Hollywood, by directors including TRUFFAUT, BUÑUEL and Polanski. She was adopted as the model for official busts of the Republican symbol MARIANNE (1985–99).

Depardieu, Gérard   Born 1948. Film actor. One of the most successful French actors internationally, starring in more than 80 French and American films.

Départements d'outre-mer   See DOM.

Derrida, Jacques   Born 1930. Philosopher. Since the 1960s he has become one of the most celebrated French INTELLECTUALS internationally. His notions of DECONSTRUCTION and *différance* have been widely adopted, and have been particularly influential in CRITICAL THEORY.

Désir, Harlem   Born 1959. Political activist. President of the anti-racist movement *SOS Racisme* from 1984, he led important campaigns, including *Touche pas à mon pote* (Hands off my mate), which fought against racist assaults. Later became an activist in the SOCIALIST PARTY.

Detective fiction The term detective fiction covers a broad range of writing from the mid-nineteenth century onwards in which the investigation of a crime, generally murder, is pivotal to the plot development of the story. Largely dismissed as a minor literary genre, since the 1980s detective fiction in France has known something of a revival as literary stars have adapted its conventions to great acclaim.

French detective fiction has long been influenced by British and American fashions and trends. In the 1920s and 1930s, the murder-mystery story associated with the novels of Agatha Christie was much admired and imitated with its emphasis on the superior intellect and reasoning process of a Miss Marple or Hercule Poirot. In the immediate post-war period, American and British hard-boiled crime writers such as Raymond Chandler exerted a strong hold over the French literary imagination, as the cynical private eye investigated not only murder but the corruption and excesses of urban society. The creation of a special collection, the SÉRIE NOIRE (Black Series), in 1945 become an important outlet for translations of such work in France and functioned as a springboard for new French talent. However, it was in the wake of the social, cultural and political upheavals of MAY '68 that a more clearly defined French tradition emerged. The *néo-polar,* as it came to be known (*polar* is a *roman policier*), dominated the 1970s and 1980s. The novels of Jean-Patrick Manchette became the model for this highly critical representation of (sub)urban France, alert to the causes of criminality in unemployment and other forms of social EXCLUSION. Throughout the 1990s, the international success of Daniel Pennac, a former *Série Noire* writer, indicates how the conventions of detective fiction have penetrated and transformed mainstream literary production in France. (**Claire Gorrara**)

Further reading

Evrard (1996). General survey of French detective fiction from its origins in the nineteenth century to the present day.

Deux Magots, les Restaurant on the Boulevard Saint-Germain in Paris, known as a meeting place for the EXISTENTIALISTS in the late 1940s, and now a popular tourist haunt.

Dictionaries The oldest, and in theory the most prestigious monolingual French dictionary is the *Dictionnaire de l'Académie française,* first published in the seventeenth century, when the Academy was founded as the official 'guardian of the language'. The ninth edition has been appearing volume by volume since 1986, but completion is not yet in sight. So, although the Academy dictionary remains the ultimate authority for SPELLING, it is not often consulted otherwise: ever since Louis XIV's time, better, 'non-official' alternatives have been available.

Pre-eminent among these in the nineteenth century, and still respected today, was Émile Littré's four-volume *Dictionnaire de la langue française* ('le Littré'). Its mid-twentieth successor was Paul Robert's *Dictionnaire analogique et alphabétique* (six volumes), a second edition of which was published in nine volumes in 1985 as *Le Grand Robert de la langue française.* The single-volume version, *Le Petit Robert,* has become a respected and regularly updated work of reference in its own right. Its main rival (and precursor), *Le Petit Larousse illustré* (the official dictionary for Scrabble), first appeared towards the end of the nineteenth century. It too was originally an abridgement – of the *Grand Larousse encyclopédique*. Hence the illustrations and the famous 'proper names' section (recently imitated in the *Petit Robert 2* mini-encyclopedia). Meanwhile the STATE has continued its contributions to lexicography with the government-sponsored *Trésor de la langue française* (sixteen volumes), noteworthy for its vast store of illustrative quotations.

Other publishers, notably Bordas and Hachette, have also produced good general dictionaries. However, Larousse and Le Robert are the most versatile, each offering a range of more specialized collections: dictionaries of synonyms, etymologies, FRANGLAIS, place-names, ARGOT, rare words, quotations, etc. But the flourishing French lexicographical tradition is perhaps best reflected in today's proliferation of dictionaries of 'youth talk' (*TCHATCHE* and *VERLAN*), fashionable slang, and media usage. (**Rodney Ball**)

Further reading

Merle (1999). Good example of an up-to-date collection of trendy items.

Dien Bien Phu   With the end of the Second World War in 1945 and the expulsion of the Japanese from continental Asia, France immediately reoccupied its former colonies in INDO-CHINA. The result was nine years of war against the independence movement led ideologically by Hô Chi Minh, and militarily by General Giap's Communist guerrillas (VIÊTMINH). This classic colonial war was soon internationalized and overshadowed by the Cold War once Mao Zedong's Communists had triumphed in neighbouring CHINA (1949). In 1953 the French commander General Navarre conceived the plan of establishing a large fortified base at Dien Bien Phu in North Vietnam from where, it was hoped, the Viêtminh could be prevented from infiltrating Laos. Dominated by mountains held by the Viêtminh artillery, and at the operational limit of French fighter and supply aircraft, the base was soon encircled and besieged. The two months of fierce and heroic fighting in the spring of 1954 assumed epic proportions, with considerable loss of life on both sides (many of the French troops were in fact African colonials and Foreign Legionnaires). The battle was widely reported throughout the world, taking on a symbolic importance in the global COLD WAR context. After surrendering at Dien Bien Phu on 7 May 1954, the French swiftly signed the Geneva Agreements and withdrew from Indo-China. A well-equipped European army could thus be beaten by totally committed guerrilla forces. The example did not go unnoticed: just a few months later, on 1 November 1954, rebellion broke out in ALGERIA. (**Ted Freeman**)

Further reading

Dalloz (1990). A sound, well-documented account of the war and the battle. Roy (1965). A passionate and vivid account, fiercely critical of French political and military leadership.

Dior, Christian   1905–57. Fashion designer. He launched his own fashion house in 1947 as a leading exponent of the NEW LOOK, which challenged the wartime utilitarian styles. His company subsequently became noted for its ready-to-wear fashions.

Dirigisme   A long-standing tendency in France for the state to take a strong role in planning the economy, particularly exemplified after the Second World War by the MONNET plans, and NATIONALIZATIONS.

Documentaries   Documentary is an important but undervalued strand in French film-making. Louis Lumière's early documentaries, such as *La sortie des usines Lumière* (*Workers Leaving the Lumière Factory*, 1895) are conventionally contrasted with the 'fantastic tradition' associated with Georges Méliès. The late 1920s saw a reaction against the formalist avant-garde in 'poetic documentaries' such as Jean Vigo's *A propos de Nice* (*About Nice*, 1930) prefiguring the 'poetic realism' of fiction films of the 1930s. That decade also saw the gradual politicization of cinema, exemplified in Jean Renoir's *La vie est à nous* (*Life is ours*, 1936). The VICHY government used documentary as propaganda as in *Images et paroles du Maréchal Pétain* (*Words and Images of Marshal Pétain*) while at the LIBERATION many films recorded the heroic struggle against the enemy, the best being René Clément's reconstruction *La Bataille du rail* (The Battle of the Rails, 1945). In 1953 documentary film-making received a boost with the introduction of selective subsidy for short films of artistic merit. The so-called Left Bank Group used a novel approach to documentary based on disjunctions – between sound and image, still and moving images and colour and black and white – as exemplified in Resnais's essay on the concentration camps *Nuit et brouillard* (*Night and Fog*, 1956). By eschewing a unitary 'message' in this way, filmmakers were able to circumvent the censorship imposed during the Algerian War.

Documentary film-making again became highly politicized during MAY '68, with the production of short films, 'cinétracts' intended to counter the official version of events put out by state-controlled television. Documentary subsequently became a means to provoke a thoroughgoing revision of official versions of French history, especially that of the OCCUPATION, with Marcel Ophuls's masterpiece *Le chagrin et la pitié* (*The Sorrow and the Pity*, 1971) which questioned the authority of all sounds and images, whatever their source. Though political urgency has disappeared from French documentaries since the 1970s the genre flourishes in the 'fly on the wall' films of former press photographer Raymond Depardon who has been influenced by the Americans Richard Leacock and Frederick Wiseman. (**Jill Forbes**)

Further Reading

Barsam (1992). Contains informative chapters on French cinema. Prédal (1987). Comprehensive account of French documentary from Lumière to the present day.

Doisneau, Robert   1912–94. Photographer. Best known for his sentimental and increasingly nostalgic photographs of PARIS and its inhabitants, taken from the 1930s to the 1950s, and including '(Baiser) place de l'Hôtel de Ville' ('The Kiss', 1950).

DOM   The DOM-TOM, *Départements et territoires d'outre-mer* (Overseas Departments and Territories) are the geographical remnants of French COLONIZATION, described by one critic as 'the confetti of Empire'. Of the two, the DOM – which have existed since 1946 – are more closely linked to metropolitan France. They are legally a part of France and are supposed to share its institutions and legal system. They have the same status as mainland *départements*, although, since 1982, each DOM has also been a REGION in its own right. This means that within a single geographical area, *une région monodépartementale*, two layers of administration co-exist. PARIS remains the ultimate source of legislation, with a prefect appointed as its representative in each DOM. ALGERIA itself was divided into three DOM until it became a state in 1962. But the remaining DOM, all of which were colonies whose economies depended on slavery, have not followed the same route towards independence, and may as a result seem increasingly anachronistic in a 'postcolonial' world. To their critics, they prove the failure of French DECOLONIZATION. To their supporters, they represent an innovative means for France to maintain its role in world affairs.

There are currently four overseas departments: Guadeloupe, Martinique and French Guyana in the Caribbean, and Réunion in the Indian Ocean. Insular and isolated, the DOM have very strong economic ties with France (on whom they depend for most of their imports) and are heavily subsidized. French Guyana's economy, for instance, depends almost entirely on the Ariane space programme which is based there.

However, most French people pay little attention to the DOM and treat them as little more than exotic TOURIST destinations. Although most main French political parties have connected groups locally, independence movements exist in each of the DOM. Major political change is unlikely, however, at least for the foreseeable future. These overseas possessions, with their markedly multicultural nature, have produced a rich and imaginative literature in French and in their various CREOLES since the 1930s. Often overlooked in studies of France, the DOM are outposts central to France's global strategy, and this strategic value perhaps explains the political eagerness to maintain them. (**Charles Forsdick**)

Further reading

Aldrich and Connell (1992). The only major English-language study of the DOM-TOM, including an excellent overview and individual chapters devoted to politics, economics and future status. Mathieu (1993). Provides a useful account of the emergence of the DOM in the context of French colonial history, and devotes a separate chapter to each of them. See also the website of the *Secrétariat d'État à l'Outre-mer*, which has comprehensive and regularly updated pages on each DOM: www.outre-mer.gouv.fr/domtom/

DOM-TOM *Départements et territoires d'outre-mer* (Overseas Departments and Territories). Former French colonies, they are administratively two separate categories, but are often referred to together. See DOM and TOM.

Doriot, Jacques 1898–1945. Right-wing politician. Initially a militant communist, and mayor of Saint-Denis, he was expelled from the PCF in 1934 and turned to FASCISM. Under the OCCUPATION he was a fervent COLLABORATOR, and twice served in the German army on the Russian front. He was killed when he came under aircraft fire.

Doumer, Paul 1857–1932. Centrist politician. He held several ministerial posts, and was elected President in 1931. He was assassinated by a Russian anarchist the following year.

Doumergue, Gaston 1863–1937. Centrist politician. A Radical-Socialist, he was President of the THIRD REPUBLIC (1924–31) and came out of retirement briefly during the STAVISKY AFFAIR to be Prime Minister in 1934.

Drieu la Rochelle, Pierre 1893–1945. Writer. His early essays and novels like *Le Feu follet* (*Will-o'-the-wisp*, 1931) reflect disillusionment after the First World War. He then turned to FASCISM, which he celebrated in *Gilles* (1939). A leading advocate of COLLABORATION during the Occupation, he committed suicide to escape arrest at the LIBERATION.

Drôle de guerre On 3 September 1939 France declared war on GERMANY, following the expiry of its ultimatum that German troops withdraw from POLAND. On 10 May 1940, the German offensive against Belgium and France began as its troops crossed into the Ardennes. Between those two dates was the *drôle de guerre* (phoney war), a term which Roland Dorgelès, author of the famous novel of the First World War *Les Croix de bois* (*Wooden Crosses*, 1919), claimed to have invented in October 1939. It sums up well the strange experience of these months, living a war which obstinately refused to happen, or so it seemed.

From the outset, France pursued a defensive strategy, convinced that this would be a long war of attrition. The general mobilization of the French, calling nearly 5 million men into active service, was ordered on 1 September 1939, and soldiers were deployed across the north, and at the key defensive structures of the MAGINOT LINE. Diplomatic manoeuvres, to ensure the friendly support of a neutral United States, to keep Italy from going onto the offensive, and to neutralize the Soviet Union, who had signed a pact of non-aggression with Germany in August 1939, assumed overriding importance. The boredom of the French soldiers during these months of inactivity formed a stark contrast with the shock of the surprise attack and the speed of the German advance when the real war started.

Internally, the government of Édouard DALADIER, succeeded by that of Paul REYNAUD in March 1940, was concerned to manage the ECONOMY to support the military effort, raising taxes, and trying to keep the soaring prices under control. The French COMMUNIST PARTY was banned, along with its publications. After the Soviet Union advanced into Poland, 40 communist members of Parliament were arrested for 'intelligence with the enemy', and in January 1940 they were stripped of their office and imprisoned. (**Margaret Atack**)

Further reading

Blatt (1998). Includes discussion of military, strategic, domestic, and cultural aspects of the period. Crémieux-Brilhac (1990). An extremely detailed and comprehensive account.

Duchamp, Marcel 1887–1968. Artist. A leading figure in DADAISM, and early member of the SURREALIST MOVEMENT, he made his name with *objets trouvés* (found objects) such as the urinal *Fontaine* (Fountain), and emphasized the conceptual basis of ART.

Duclos, Jacques 1896–1975. Communist politician. A member of the PCF leadership from the 1920s, he was an unconditional supporter of the Soviet Union, and twice took charge of the party in THOREZ's absence. Often regarded as the most powerful person in the party, he failed to win the leadership succession. He stood for President of the Republic in 1969, receiving 21 per cent of the vote.

Duhamel, Georges 1884–1966. Writer. He wrote many novels and was a regular contributor to Le FIGARO. As Secretary of the ACADÉMIE FRANÇAISE (1942–46) he assisted pro-Resistance literary publications.

Dullin, Charles 1885–1949. Actor and theatre director. He founded the Atelier (Workshop) company, which was influential between the wars.

Dumazedier, Joffre Born 1915. Sociologist. A founder of the Peuple et culture movement, he developed a theory of leisure, and advocated popular culture as a key factor in a democratic society.

Dunkirk A port in the Nord department of France, Dunkirk (Dunkerque in French) is most often remembered as the scene of a military evacuation that took place between 27 May and 4 June 1940, towards the end of the Battle of France. In the face of a crushing German offensive, Allied forces (including British, French and some Belgian troops) were pushed back to the coast. Under attack from the German airforce and artillery, soldiers from the British Expeditionary Force from the French and Belgian armies were embarked from the beaches around Dunkirk in an evacuation code-named 'Operation Dynamo'. Eventually some 200 000 British and 130 000 French and Belgian soldiers were transported across the Channel. The operation was fraught with risk since the British Navy did not at that time have appropriate beach landing craft, so the rescue was carried out using a flotilla of 'small boats', including pleasure craft and shallow draught ferries. This contributed to the operation passing almost immediately into public consciousness and popular memory as a feat symbolic of British resolve, of defiance in the face of adversity. It was certainly portrayed as such in British propaganda and newsreels of the period, and long after the war the 'Dunkirk spirit' is often alluded to in Britain. In France, during the OCCUPATION both German and VICHY propaganda alleged that the British had abandoned the French to their fate at Dunkirk. (**Martyn Cornick**)

Further reading

Barker (1977); Harman (1980); Ponting (1990); Turnbull (1978).

Duras, Marguerite 1914–96. Writer and film maker. Her early novels contributed to the success of the *nouveau roman*. She wrote several plays and directed a number of films. Her work drew strongly on AUTOBIOGRAPHICAL themes, and she became the most celebrated French woman writer of the late twentieth century.

Durkheim, Émile   1858–1917. One of the founders of sociology, which he attempted to put on a scientific basis. He developed many key concepts, including the distinction between mechanical and organic social organizations. His study on *Suicide* (1897) is a classic, and his influence has been profound.

E

***École nationale d'administration* (ENA)**   Founded 1945. Estabished by Michel Debré to provide high-level training for senior civil service positions, it has since become the main route into the French commercial and administrative ÉLITES. In recent years, there have been concerns that the influence of *énarques* (alumni of ENA) owes more to their close social network than to their personal merits.

***École Normale Supérieure* (ENS)**   The term *École Normale Supérieure* may refer to any one of five higher education institutions: ENS Ulm, Sèvres, St Cloud, Fontenay and ENSET. The oldest and most prestigious is Ulm, so called from its location in the rue d'Ulm in the LATIN QUARTER of Paris, which was founded in 1794 to train secondary school teachers by preparing them for the *agrégation* examination. In 1985 it merged with the *École de Sèvres* (*École Normale Supérieure de Jeunes Filles*) itself founded in 1881 to train women teachers, while St Cloud (1882) and Fontenay (1887) merged in 1987. ENSET (1912) concentrates on training specialists in technical education. Under the THIRD REPUBLIC, Ulm gradually became the home of political radicalism as well as a breeding ground for the most eminent French scientists, humanists, philosophers and writers. Among the famous alumni whose names are associated with the *École* are 'Nicolas Bourbaki' and René Thom, Simone de BEAUVOIR and SARTRE and MERLEAU-PONTY, Romain ROLLAND and Jules ROMAINS. Louis Pasteur, Louis ALTHUSSER and Jacques DERRIDA all taught at the *École*. Politician *archicubes* (as former students are called) include Prime Ministers Léon BLUM and Laurent FABIUS and President of the Republic Georges POMPIDOU. The *Écoles* are small – Ulm admits approximately 200 candidates a year on the basis of a fiercely competitive entrance examination (*concours d'entrée*). Although the primary purpose of the *Écoles* is to train secondary school teachers, *normaliens* invariably secure posts in the universities or proceed via ENA into the senior echelons of the civil service. Indeed, the *Écoles* form a tightly-knit, loyal community and a powerful old boy network. ENS Ulm is famous for its *esprit de canular* (student pranks) as well as its somewhat arcane slang, often based on puns such as *cothurne* (buskin) which refers to a 'roommate'. Although described as *la fille aînée de l'État* under the THIRD REPUBLIC, Ulm has, in recent years, seen its influence decline while that of ENA has risen. (**Jill Forbes**)

Further Reading

Bourdieu (1989). A discussion of the social origins of students in the *grandes écoles* and their relative influence in contemporary French society. Brasillach, (1941). A memoir of the author's own time as a student at Ulm, containing details of celebrated pranks and students songs. Jeannin (1964).

Ecologists An umbrella term to describe those who militate for protection of the physical environment against man-made pollution, *les écologistes* (ecologists) achieved popularity in France in the 1970s as a pressure group against nuclear power, forming alternative economic units of production, and conducting increasingly successful political electoral campaigns. Mainly PACIFISTS, Ecologists can be either individualistic or collectivist. Some are reformists who believe that pollution can be tackled beginning with local issues within the current capitalist system. Others are radicals who wish to overthrow capitalism to inaugurate a new era of a harmonic eco-system and in so doing abolishing inequalities of all kinds.

Ecologists targeted France as a nuclear power and attracted world condemnation of the country over the RAINBOW WARRIOR incident (1985), when a Greenpeace activist was killed as a result of sabotage by undercover French agents. French ecologists campaign internationally against globalization, and have, for example, been involved in disrupting international summit meetings in Seattle and Davos, and in undertaking symbolic sabotage against mass consumer multinational companies (as in Millau, 2000). Often seen as a rearguard action to defend French farming interests, ecologists reject traditional hierarchical party structures and divisions, favour regional decentralization and are in favour of European-wide policy-making. They have succeeded in building up from a protest vote in the 1970s to a governing partner in two socialist governments (Brice Lalonde in Rocard's government in 1988 and Dominique Voynet in Jospin's 1997 cabinet, both as Environment Ministers). Although internal divisions exist with at least two parties – *Les Verts* and *Génération Ecologie*, ecologists have done well at municipal, regional and European elections (led by Daniel COHN-BENDIT in 1999) where the electoral system favours small parties. Greater media attention on ecological disasters such as the *Erika* oil spillage of December 1999 has forced government action. (**Máire Cross**)

Further reading

Prendiville (1997). A summary of French ecologism. Proud (1995). A review of the relations between the different groupings.

Economic policies Economic policies have reflected changing government attachment to economic LIBERALISM and DIRIGISME (state planning), resulting in an *économie mixte* of co-existing public and private sectors. Policies have constantly targeted France's MODERNIZATION and INDUSTRIALIZATION, as well as macroeconomic objectives of a stable FRANC, INFLATION, unemployment and trade. External influences on economic policy have come from wars, world recessions and European integration. Between 1918 and 1945, governments reassessed the nineteenth-century *laissez-faire* (free market) economic policies, in the light of lessons learned from state industrial intervention during the war economy (1914–18), and from Keynesian economics.

Inflation, budget deficits and a weakening franc in the 1920s forced state action, and the POINCARÉ stabilization (1926). Although right-wing governments attempted to minimize the role of state policy, the recession of the 1930s led to the FRONT POPULAIRE's stimulation of activity through demand management, NATIONALIZATION of the *Banque de France* and other interventionism.

During the Vichy regime, France suffered German exploitation of resources and costs of paying for occupying troops. During the TRENTE GLORIEUSES (growth 1945–75), policy again combined *dirigisme* and liberalism. Post-war support for the Left and the need for organized reconstruction favoured an increased state role. This included nationalizations, national planning, and taxation and regulation, as tools of economic and social policy. Technocratic *planification* (planning) flexibly directed rebuilding and modernization. But inflation, fuelled by colonial wars, and a weak franc characterized much of the FOURTH REPUBLIC. The economy also became less protectionist as European integration and French industrialization proceeded. The 1970s' oil crises created unemployment and stagflation, which neo-liberal policies (under GISCARD D'ESTAING (1974–81)) and SOCIALIST approaches (MITTERRAND (1981–83)) both failed to resolve. Since the mid-1980s, Left and Right have converged over economic policies, agreeing that France's economy must integrate within EUROPE by adopting the neo-liberal consensus on competition, money supply and interest rates, and higher than previously acceptable unemployment. **(Hugh Dauncey)**

Further reading

Levy (1999). Shows the effects on civil society of planning, liberalism and economic policies.

Economy   The French economy ranks fourth in the world. After 1945, France transformed itself into a modern, dynamic, high-tech economy through INDUSTRIALIZATION and development of the tertiary (service) sector. DECOLONIZATION, European integration and international trade opened France's economy to competition. Growth begun during the *Belle époque* was interrupted by the First World War, and after 1918 reconstruction failed to modernize the economy before recession struck in the 1930s. France had industrialized late and incompletely in the nineteenth century and although the 'war economy' of 1914–18 had initiated STATE intervention and stimulated crucial industries, the economy in the 1930s was essentially agricultural and industrially backward. The Nazi OCCUPATION (1940–44) influenced economic activity as German exploitation stimulated (and distorted) industry. Vichy's attachment to AGRICULTURE bolstered its role, and *DIRIGISME* and technocracy were strengthened. The TRENTE GLORIEUSES of growth 1945–75 transformed France from a predominantly agricultural economy, whose industry was still archaically structured and financed, into a leading industrial nation. Modernized agriculture, industrialization, and tertiarization created modern French capitalism through a leading role for the state and mixed economy of private and public sectors. The 'economic miracle' overcame disadvantages of a largely stationary labour force and energy dependence. In 1949 agriculture and industry employed equal numbers. By the early 1950s agricultural and industrial production regained pre-war peaks, and reconstruction ended as the economy, profiting from the MARSHALL PLAN, state intervention, planning and IMMIGRATION industrialized rapidly, and commenced modernizing agriculture. During the FOURTH REPUBLIC, mechanization of farming, industrialization and urbanization reduced the agricultural workforce; in the FIFTH REPUBLIC, industry peaked as the major employer during 1965–74. Economic crisis in the 1970s hit industry hardest and services grew rapidly: by 1996 farming represented only 5 per cent of the working population, behind industry (26 per cent) and services (69 per cent). Her farming supported by the EU, France is the second agricultural exporter in the world, and her industrial and post-industrial economy is a European leader. (**Hugh Dauncey**)

Further reading

Crouzet (1993) On economic policy, economic conditions and change.

Écriture   The term *écriture* was coined by French STRUCTURALIST critics of the 1960s and is a concept which challenges the institution of literature, and traditional assumptions about WRITERS and their authority over texts.

Generally, critics had understood their object of study to be a literary 'work' which was the product of an AUTHOR's intellect and whose meaning was largely regulated by that individual's intentions and design. For French critics, such as Roland BARTHES, the literary object was no longer conceived of as a 'work' but rather as a 'text' which was but one form of a wider set of practices and institutions called *écriture* or writing. For Barthes and others, the author is considered to be an impersonal agent of writing whose role it is to organize pre-existing linguistic and literary forms and conventions into a particular text. The interpretation of this writing is brought about by an impersonal *lecture* (process of reading), which invests the text with what seems to be an inherent meaning, by way of expectations formed by previous reading experiences. However, many POST-STRUCTURALISTS oppose the notion that a text has pre-fixed meanings and see all *écriture* (writing) as open to multiple and sometimes contradictory meanings. To both STRUCTURALISTS and post-structuralists, the text's representation of a reality beyond writing is an illusion, since the world itself could be held in its turn to be a text, a set of signs, codes and conventions, whose meaning is constituted and shared by members of different cultural communities. Out of such thinking on the literary work as text has come the notion of INTERTEXTUALITY, developed by theorists such as BARTHES and Julia KRISTEVA, which conceives of the literary text as the site of the intersection of countless other texts. (**Claire Gorrara**)

Further Reading

Sturrock (1987). The classic study of structuralism as a cultural movement and literary practice.

Écriture féminine   *Écriture féminine*, a literary style associated particularly with authors such as Hélène CIXOUS or Chantal Chawaf, has its roots in the post-1968 FEMINIST movement and in philosophy. In 1975, in a collective volume devoted to *Simone de Beauvoir et la lutte des femmes* (*Beauvoir and the Women's Struggle*), Hélène Cixous published 'Le Rire de la méduse' (Medusa's Laugh), a ground-breaking essay opening up new perspectives on women and writing. In polemical, highly wrought language, she denounced the power of 'phallogocentrism' to control and destroy women. She drew on the philosophy of Jacques DERRIDA and his critique of 'logocentrism', namely the role of binary oppositions in Western thought, and the hierarchical structure they conceal. She also drew on the work of PSYCHOANALYST Jacques LACAN, particularly his analysis of the primacy of the signifier of the phallus in the constitution of the Symbolic order of human culture. From these she developed the concept of 'phallogocentrism', which crystallizes the argument that Western culture, including syntax, language, reason and rationality, is founded on the exclusion of women. Women are consigned to the boundaries, defining the limits of the rational order by their irrationality and disorder. To write, Cixous argued, women must develop their own writing, and celebrate their power of disruption. Cixous's own works break down generic oppositions between theory and fiction, and explore what she terms a new feminine economy.

Écriture féminine is often translated as 'writing the body'. Annie LECLERC wrote a best-selling essay, *Parole de femme* (*Woman's Word*, 1974), which brought many of these theories to a wide audience, arguing that literature is imbued with male metaphors and male symbolism claiming universal status. Women are in the 'blanks, gaps, margins, spaces, silences, holes in discourse', as Xavière Gauthier put it in the *TEL QUEL* special issue of 1974 on *Luttes de femmes* (Women's struggles). To write women into language and literature, women had to write differently. (**Margaret Atack**)

Further reading

Sellers (1994). A comprehensive introduction to the work of Cixous. Jones (1986). An important essay first published 1981 which has been frequently reprinted.

Education   The contemporary educational system in France is a product of the Republican tradition going back to the principles of the Revolution of 1789. There is a liberal regime allowing the coexistence of both public and private systems of education. The French STATE is obliged to provide free and secular (that is, non-religious) schooling for all children aged up to 16. The private system, consisting mainly of Catholic schools, also benefits from government money, and many of these schools have a contractual relationship with the state. Even after the Revolution, and especially following the Restoration in 1815, the Church continued to play a part in education since this was considered to be one of its missions. With the establishment of the THIRD REPUBLIC, however, a series of laws were passed designed increasingly to secularize education, especially the *loi Jules Ferry* of 1881 and 1882 which made education compulsory for all children aged 7 to 13. State education was decreed to be neutral (non-religious) and free. Religious instruction was limited and controlled. During the remaining years of the nineteenth century further legislation was passed to consolidate state control as well as to expand provision and access to all levels (primary, secondary and university-level). With the Separation of Church and state in 1905 the hold of religious orders over education was much diminished.

The curriculum followed in French secondary schools (*lycées*) is broad based. In the final year of study (*terminale*), a student working toward the BACCALAURÉAT and wishing to specialize in a science subject must still study mathematics, history and geography, a language other than French, physical education and philosophy.

In 1998, the French state spent 634.4 billion francs on education, shared between 71 000 schools and colleges and a total of 15 million pupils and students, including 12.2 million at primary and secondary level and 2.1 million university students. **(Martyn Cornick)**

Further reading

For more detailed information, see the excellent website of the Ministère de l'éducation nationale at www.education.gouv.fr/

Eiffel Tower   A 320-metre metal tower, built at one end of the Champ-de-Mars in Paris by the engineer Gustave Eiffel (1832–1923). A popular tourist attraction, it houses a restaurant, several viewing platforms and an array of radio and television antennae. Built, over two years, for the 1889 *exposition universelle* (World Fair), this tapering and somewhat phallic column of latticed girders has become an internationally recognized symbol of France in general and Paris in particular, and was the location of France's most spectacular firework display on Millennium night.

Élites   The role and selection of élites in a country with a revolutionary history and a highly politicized population is significantly different from what happens in countries where there is no revolutionary tradition. Robespierre signed the order instituting the *École Polytechnique* at the height of the Terror. Since the Revolution, élites (intellectual and bureaucratic) have played a crucial role in the government of France and the establishment of a secular republic.

Élites are mainly trained in France's GRANDES ÉCOLES, which include the *École Normale Supérieure* (humanities), the *École Polytechnique, Ponts et Chausées, École des Mines* (engineers). The five *grands corps* of the French civil service: the diplomatic *corps*, the prefectoral *corps*, *l'inspection des finances*, the court of auditors, and the *Conseil d'État* (the highest administrative court) recruit exclusively from the *grandes écoles* through selective competitive exams on the basis of merit. However, over time certain families succeeded in colonizing the different *corps*. In 1945, after the trauma of VICHY, the creation of the *École Nationale de l'Administration (ENA)* sought to reestablish the principle of meritocracy, while also recognizing that France lacked a training institution which focused on the particular problems of administration and the development of public policy in the post-war era.

All the *grandes écoles*, with the exception of *ESSEC* and *HEC* (two business schools) are run by the French government. Since the 1950s the alumni of ENA have come to dominate not only the French civil service but also top managerial positions in the nationalized banks and industries, and, since the 1980s, top positions in the private sector through a process called *pantouflage* (literally: putting on slippers). Since the 1980s, the sociologist Michel CROZIER in particular has argued that the prestige of ENA has little to do with the quality of its education, which is often inappropriate for problem solving at the highest levels of public service. Against a background of an international market place and capital flows, together with recent corruption scandals, the reputation and education of élites in France are still under intense scrutiny. **(Bill Brooks)**

Further reading

Suleiman (1978). A comprehensive analysis from an American perspective. Crozier (1987). A critical view from a distinguished dissident French sociologist.

Elle   Founded 1945, by Hélène Lazareff, it became one of France's most popular women's magazines, and is now published in numerous foreign editions.

Éluard, Paul   1885–1952. Poet. A leader of the SURREALIST movement in the 1920s, and a close friend of PICASSO, he is most celebrated for his wartime poems of RESISTANCE, including *Liberté*. He combined themes of love, vision, human relations and the struggle to improve society.

Emmanuel, Pierre   1916–84. Poet. His poetry, written from a CATHOLIC and prophetic stance, is often highly rhetorical, with a strongly mystical tendency.

Empire   See IMPERIALISM.

Employés (white-collar workers)   White-collar workers emerged as an important social group in France in the second half of the twentieth century. The official French Statistical Agency's socio-economic categories include the 'socio-professional group' called *employés*, grouping together all non-manual working-class jobs. They are distinguished on the one side from *ouvriers* (manual workers), not necessarily by their levels of income, but by their higher educational qualifications and the non-manual nature of their work. Above them in the social hierarchy, and probably exercising authority over them in their day-to-day employment, are *les CADRES*, distinguished by their supervisory or managerial functions (and by their higher income and qualifications). As a social group, the *employés* grew rapidly in numbers after the Second World War, during the TRENTE GLORIEUSES, the 30 years of expansion up to the 1972–74 oil crisis. Mainly in the tertiary or service sector of the economy, the jobs have been filled predominantly by women. Their entry into the work force has coincided with the growth of educational opportunity (particularly of pre-school and secondary EDUCATION), of the caring professions such as health and social services, and clerical and secretarial jobs, from banking through commerce to tourism. The only predominantly male sector of this group is the police.

What the group has in common, other than its femininity, is its educational level, its lack of militancy, and its political importance. Surveys have shown the *employés* to have attitudes and aspirations more in common with *cadres* than with industrial workers. However, following the economic downturns of the 1970s, *employés* became electoral targets of the SOCIALISTS in 1981, and were a key group of voters in the presidential and legislative election victories of MITTERRAND and the Left. In the 1990s they suffered from increasing precarity of EMPLOYMENT. **(Geoff Hare)**

Further reading

Mendras and Cole (1991).

Employment Employment reflects the ECONOMY, ECONOMIC POLICIES, MODERNIZATION, demography, and developments such as INDUSTRIALIZATION and tertiarization. France long suffered labour-shortages and welcomed IMMIGRATION, but since the TRENTE GLORIEUSES, endemic high unemployment has challenged the 'equality of opportunity' of access to work. Unemployment, female emancipation, ever-lengthening EDUCATION and problems of financing retirement create an older, better-educated and feminized workforce.

Near stationary demographics during the early twentieth century and the human losses in the First World War meant that inter-war employment was characterized by scarce labour rather than by excess supply, except in the worst years of depression, when economic LIBERALISM denied government's role in fighting unemployment. Incomplete industrialization gave a predominantly agricultural working population, but post-war reconstruction and growth created almost permanent full employment during the 1950s and 1960s, as industry and modernization transformed the distribution of employment in different sectors, through declining agriculture and fewer PAYSANS, and more industrial workers and new managerial classes typified by the CADRES. Full employment meant expanded production came through productivity from hard-pressed WORKERS, or IMMIGRATION, or female employment.

The post-war demographic boom impacted on employment during the 1960s as young people left school and UNIVERSITIES, increasing the active population, but revealing mismatches between training and employment skills required for high-skilled industrial work and the burgeoning service sector. MAY '68 was partly the expression of such antagonisms, but 1970s' stagflation (stagnation with inflation) created high, permanent unemployment, with over 1 million in 1975 rising to 2 and 3 million in the 1980s and 1990s. The cessation of immigration (1974) did nothing to help France 'integrate' existing immigrant communities.

Economic liberalism in the 1980s and 1990s focused on INFLATION and freeing the labour market through part-time employment, fixed-term contracts and reduced employee benefits. French employers bear high employment costs for full-time workers, so *petits boulots* (litle jobs) and *précarisation* (increase in part-time and temporary contracts) reduce unemployment, while undermining employment privileges won by TRADE UNIONS. (**Hugh Dauncey**)

Further reading

Hantrais (1999). A good overview.

ENA See *ÉCOLE NATIONALE D'ADMINISTRATION*.

Engineers French engineers belong not only to a prestigious profession, which has been influential in the social and economic transformation of France since the war, but to a distinctive intellectual and educational tradition. In France, engineers are trained at selective engineering schools which are often separate from universities. The top schools, like the *École Polytechnique* or the *École Centrale* are part of the GRANDES ÉCOLES system. The *École Polytechnique*, sometimes referred to as 'X', was founded at the time of the French Revolution to supply technical expertise for the STATE and the military.

Graduates (*polytechniciens*) traditionally went on to one of the specialized schools linked to *Polytechnique* (such as the *Ecole des Ponts et Chaussées* which trained civil engineers) in order to gain access to the relevant body of public sector engineers (*les corps d'état*). Although the *École Polytechnique* retains a strong public service tradition, today's graduates often prefer to take up appointments in the private sector, a practice known as *pantouflage*. To this extent the employment profile of *Polytechnique* graduates has moved closer to that of the graduates of the *École Centrale*, which was founded in the nineteenth century (along with the less prestigious *École des arts et métiers*) with the specific purpose of educating engineers for industry.

Engineers have become an increasingly important group of workers since the mid-twentieth century as hi-tech industries have overtaken traditional 'smokestack' industries, and technical knowledge has become an increasingly valuable commodity. Moreover, in France, senior engineers, and especially *polytechniciens*, have led many of the government agencies responsible for economic planning and renovation since the Second World War. (**Jackie Clarke**)

Further reading

Crawford (1989). A sociological study of French engineers in the 1980s, which also includes some historical background. Clarke (2001). Discusses the cultural politics of engineering and the role of engineers in relation to other élites in the 1930s.

ENS   See ÉCOLE NORMALE SUPÉRIEURE.

Entre-deux-guerres   The *entre-deux-guerres* refers to the period between 1919 and 1940. These were years dominated by the experience of the First World War, both politically and culturally. The memory of the loss of almost one and a half million French troops hung over the 1920s and 1930s like a dark shadow, and sustained many in their belief that France should never again engage in such a devastating conflict. The consequences of this attitude were far-reaching, because successive French governments did little to maintain the armed forces at sufficient levels. Politically, the period was increasingly marked by parliamentary instability, especially during the early 1930s, once the economic effects of the October 1929 Wall Street Crash had filtered through to a traditionally protectionist France. Street demonstrations, particularly those following the riots of 6 FEBRUARY 1934, showed that France risked political upheaval. The influences of FASCISM (in Italy) and Nazism (in Germany) were strongly felt in France, above all among certain right-wing groups and INTELLECTUALS. Whether or not 'fascism' existed in 1930s France is a subject still debated among historians. In the cultural domain, the First World War put a brutal end to prevailing certainties: younger generations of writers and intellectuals sought new modes of thought and expression, giving rise to a number of AVANT-GARDE movements such as DADAISM and SURREALISM. The inter-war period was especially rich in cultural production, not only in literature (for instance around the monthly NOUVELLE REVUE FRANÇAISE), but also in the relatively new art of CINEMA. The 1936 POPULAR FRONT government (a coalition of left-wing and centre parties) introduced a number of radical social reforms, including the right to paid HOLIDAYS. However, internal opposition to reform and the influence of international crises – especially the Spanish Civil War and Hitler's expansionist ambitions – undermined French confidence, and it was a weakened and demoralised France that went to war in September 1939. (**Martyn Cornick**)

Further reading

Adamthwaite (1995); Johnson and Johnson (1987); Martin (1999); Reynolds (1996); Soucy (1995); Weber (1995).

Épuration   The *Épuration* (Purge) refers to the period during and after the LIBERATION of France in 1944, in which those alleged to have collaborated with the German occupiers were punished. It had two different phases. In the first, the *Épuration sauvage* (wild, illegal purge), many people were executed by local vigilante groups during the Liberation itself. In this period, women who were accused of having had relationships with the Germans (horizontal collaboration) were often paraded through the streets with their heads shaved (*les tondues*).

In the second phase, after the military Liberation of France, the judicial authorities of the PROVISIONAL GOVERNMENT and the subsequent FOURTH REPUBLIC tried around 320 000 cases of collaboration, and pronounced 1500 death sentences, and 44 000 prison sentences. A special High Court of Justice tried the most prominent officials of the VICHY REGIME. Among these, Pierre LAVAL, the former Prime Minister, was executed, and Marshall PETAIN, who had led the Vichy Government, received a commuted death sentence. By 1947, the pace of the judicial purges was beginning to slow, and amnesty laws had been passed by the early 1950s. By the mid-1960s, there were no wartime collaborators still held in French prisons.

With hindsight, it is clear that the judicial purge of collaborators was highly partial, influenced by such factors as the timing and location of the trials, and the public visibility of the alleged acts of collaboration. For example, a disproportionate number of journalists were punished in comparison with business leaders whose economic relationships with the Germans had often been less public. The aftermath of the *Épuration* has continued to influence French political and cultural life, as illustrated by the national soul-searching around later trials of such personalities as Klaus BARBIE, Paul Touvier and Maurice Papon. (**Hilary Footitt**)

Further reading

Novick (1968). A general account of the Epuration in France, and the first to critically analyse its extent.

Ernaux, Annie   Born 1940. Writer. Her novels, like *La Place* (*The Square*, 1981) and *Une Femme* (*A Woman*, 1988) have a strongly AUTOBIOGRAPHICAL theme, exploring CLASS relations and the experience of WOMEN.

Esprit   Founded 1932. Monthly intellectual review of broadly left-leaning Catholic inspiration. Marked by its first editor, Emmanuel MOUNIER, it makes radical reappraisals of key issues in politics and culture.

État français   Official title used to designate the VICHY REGIME. See also OCCUPATION.

Etcherelli, Claire   Born 1934. Writer and journalist. A member of the editorial team of SARTRE's review, *LES TEMPS MODERNES*, she is best known for her novel *Élise ou la vraie vie* (*Elise or Real Life*, 1967), which deals with issues of race and class.

Ethnicity   See RACE AND ETHNICITY.

Ethnography   See ANTHROPOLOGY.

Étiemble, René   Born 1909. Writer. A professor of literature, he wrote several novels and volumes of essays, of which the most remembered is *Parlez-vous FRANGLAIS?* (*Do you speak Frenglish?*, 1964), a polemic against the invasion of the FRENCH LANGUAGE by English.

Eurocentrism   Eurocentrism is the tendency of European cultures to ignore the individual nature of non-European cultures. It assumes that what is European is innately superior, God-given, natural and, accordingly, universal. History is reduced to European history and ART to European art. As a result, the pre-colonial aspects of colonized cultures are dismissed as precivilizational savagery. In most European museums, African art becomes a series of ethnographic artefacts as opposed to objects with aesthetic value. Eurocentrism is often seen as a reflection of the colonizer's understanding of the world and, as a result, has attracted increasing scrutiny in the postcolonial era. French imperial IDEOLOGY itself was openly and profoundly Eurocentric. The claims of the *mission civilisatrice* (civilizing mission) depended on the assertion of France as a benchmark of CIVILIZATION compared to which the colonies were seriously lacking. The oppressive nature of colonial practices was ignored in the name of progress. The policy of ASSIMILATION ignored indigenous difference and absorbed the colonies into *la Plus Grande France* (Greater France), a geographical construct to which France itself was clearly central. French republican EDUCATION, with its imposition of standard French and emphasis on French history, literature and philosophy, was central to these processes. Colonial schoolchildren were routinely, and confusingly, taught about *nos ancêtres les Gaulois* (our ancestors, the Gauls); those who spoke local languages in class were humiliated or punished. As a result, African and Caribbean pupils were denied access to any local heritage and had a Eurocentric world-view imposed upon them.

In his *Cahier d'un retour au pays natal* (*Return to My Native Land*, 1939), the Martinican poet and politician Aimé CÉSAIRE claims that 'no race holds a monopoly of beauty, of intelligence, of strength'. But Eurocentrism, and the hierarchies which it develops, persists in a variety of forms even after the formal collapse of COLONIALISM. Despite the official status of the DOM-TOM, for example, their description as *outre-mer* reinforces an understanding of geography in which France is the centre of gravity and its former colonies still relegated to the overseas peripheries. In the late twentieth century, Eurocentric thinking was attacked by a number of Francophone Caribbean intellectuals. Édouard Glissant, in particular, described the world as an archipelago of different cultures, no longer dependent on a centre-periphery model of geography but interrelated in more complex, non-hierarchical relationships. (**Charles Forsdick**)

Further reading

Shohat and Stam (1994). A wide-ranging study of Eurocentrism which considers the history of the phenomenon and its persistence in contemporary culture. Contains numerous French and Francophone references.

Euro-Disney   The Euro-Disney theme park opened in April 1992 in Marne-la Vallée, a new town development in the outer north-east suburbs of PARIS. Significantly, its opening took place in the same year that the French narrowly voted 'Yes' in the referendum on the Maastricht Treaty since both events were held by many INTELLECTUALS, as well as by those on the extreme Left and Right, to signal a loss of national IDENTITY. Euro-Disney was described as a 'cultural Chernobyl' (by Alain FINKIELKRAUT) because it supposedly contaminated France with American values. However, it was a prize actively pursued by French governments of all political persuasions, in the conviction that cultural and economic development were intimately linked in the new ECONOMY. It could therefore be argued that Euro-Disney should be considered one of the MITTERRAND presidency's *GRANDS TRAVAUX* alongside the LOUVRE Pyramid or the Opéra de la Bastille. The French government fought off other European candidates, notably Spain, to ensure that the Disney Corporation's fourth theme park would be sited in France and offered tax breaks and subsidies to support its bid. Planned during the 1980s recession, the park was intended to bring jobs to a depressed area of the Paris region and was supported by infrastructural improvements such as a new Métro and high speed train link. Whatever intellectual reservations may have existed, French business supported the project, with RENAULT, France-Télécom and Aérospatiale all contributing to its exhibitions. In layout and content, Euro-Disney imitates its American models. It offers 'rides' which are fairground thrills, like the Runaway Train, which is set in an imitation American desert, together with others which, like Disney's Hollywood animation films, are inspired by classics of European children's literature – Barrie, Grimm, Perrault and Andersen – but are repackaged for contemporary consumption via Hollywood interpretations. Now renamed Disneyland Paris, it remains a major tourist attraction, despite the financial difficulties from which it has suffered. (**Jill Forbes**)

Further reading

Forbes and Kelly (1995). Places Euro-Disney in the context of the impact of globalization. Looseley (1995). Discusses Euro-Disney as part of French cultural policy.

Europe   Europe has been a project and a vision for élites in France at least since the Enlightenment. The reality, the European Union, born with the Treaty of Maastricht of 1992 as 'an unidentified political object', is haunted by the demons of European history: a thousand years of religious, dynastic, nationalist and ideological conflict. The moral, political and economic collapse of Europe in the Second World War meant that the past was no longer an option, even if, until 1989, Europe was divided between West and East.

Enlightenment INTELLECTUALS, such as the abbé de Saint Pierre, Voltaire and Jean-Jacques Rousseau, had elaborated various models of a system of collaboration and co-operation between European states, based on reason, tolerance and mutual self-interest where a perpetual peace would take the place of war. The construction of post-war Western Europe has been rather less ambitious, being based on a pragmatic compromise between ECONOMICS and politics, centred on the reconciliation of France and Western Germany. Its founding figure, Jean MONNET accepted the division of Europe into ideological blocs, but envisaged a federal political structure emerging in the West through economic integration. DE GAULLE refused the division of Europe and favoured a Europe of nation–states stretching from the Atlantic to the Urals. The visions have been difficult to reconcile, as DELORS and MITTERRAND discovered in the 1980s and 1990s.

Before the collapse of Communism in Eastern Europe, deeper economic integration through the project for the single European currency was designed to cement political union between European member states. The tension between the political and economic necessity of expansion triggered by 1989 and re-unification and deeper economic integration in the context of globalization has brought a new urgency and excitement to the European project. It has also put it under strain as national concerns about the pooling of sovereignty in an integrated European union are heightened. (**Bill Brookes**)

Further reading:

Story (1993). A series of essays situating each of the member states in the context of Europe since 1989.
Mazower (1998). A provocative investigation of the history of Europe.

Everyday life *(la vie quotidienne)* Daily life has existed for as long as humanity itself, and the term 'everyday life' and its various synonyms have probably always been common in everyday speech. The primary meaning of *quotidien* was to designate that which was daily routine, trivial, domestic, unremarkable and even unmentionable. Strongly associated with women, the family and private life, it has therefore appeared as a kind of social unconscious. It was first conceptualized by Henri LEFEBVRE in his *Critique de la vie quotidienne* (*Critique of Everyday Life*, 1947). He argued that any particular detail in the life of real people may spontaneously appear as an exotic piece of local colour, but can potentially be understood as part of an overall picture, by reference to a wider social context. It thus becomes a starting point for the critical analysis of society as a whole, and for the impulse to transform it. Lefebvre offered a Marxist analysis of the alienation of everyday life that included a critique of capitalist economic exploitation; a critique of the class-based, oppressive nature of the capitalist state; a critique of bourgeois morality, as a strategy for securing compliance in the established order; and a critique of ideological mystification, especially in the form of religion. He argued that the struggle against alienation in all its forms is vital to restore human wholeness.

The concept was developed by the Jesuit cultural historian Michel DE CERTEAU in his book *L'Invention du quotidien* (*The Practice of Everyday Life*, 1980) to show how ordinary people can resist the pressure to be passive consumers. He argued that they can deploy extraordinary inventiveness in adapting the world of objects to their own purposes and values.

The notion of everyday life has become a focus for cultural critics, particularly in the left-wing and feminist traditions, to legitimize the experience of the domestic sphere, and to show how the exercise of power in modern societies is embedded in every aspect of life, even the most apparently innocent. Conversely, working people, and women in particular, can be empowered by becoming conscious of this, and can develop effective strategies for resisting or opposing the dominant social forces even in the smallest details of their lives. (**Michael Kelly**)

Further reading

Lefebvre (1991); Certeau (1984); Kaplan and Ross (1987).

Évian Agreements   On 17 March 1962, the Évian agreements were signed between Algerian nationalists and French leaders, thus ending the ALGERIAN WAR, a bitter and undeclared conflict, fought between 1954 and 1962, over Algerian self-determination. In July 1962, ALGERIA gained independence from its colonial occupier, France.

Algeria had been a French overseas territory since 1830 and was considered by many of those living in metropolitan France to be an integral part of France. Yet during this *guerre sans nom* (nameless war), the brutality of the fighting, which included the widespread use of torture by French soldiers, resulted in much public anxiety and concern. Events in Algeria ultimately contributed to the downfall of the FOURTH REPUBLIC and the election of General DE GAULLE as the President of the FIFTH REPUBLIC in 1958.

The peace agreement at Évian was followed by a referendum in which 90 per cent of voters in metropolitan France and 99 per cent of voters in Algeria approved Algerian self-determination. As with the LIBERATION of France a generation earlier, the end of armed hostilities witnessed a period when old scores were settled. After independence, 150 000 *harkis*, those Algerians who had remained loyal to their French masters and fought with them, were killed by Algerian nationalists, as were up to 10 000 French settlers, known as *pieds noirs*. Indeed, the majority of *pied noir* families, fearful of Algerian retaliation and panicked by the guerrilla tactics of those who wanted to maintain an *Algérie française* (French Algeria), fled to France for a new future. While some veterans from the Algerian War have campaigned for a national day of commemoration on 17 March, many other French people feel such memories of war and defeat are too painful. (**Claire Gorrara**)

Further reading

Gildea (1996). An overview of French national identity since 1945.

Exclusion   Social exclusion as a term identifies the increasing number of people who have no social protection (see *SECURITÉ SOCIALE*) against sickness, unemployment and old age, and who are marginalized as a result. New forms of poverty appeared with the impact of long-term unemployment of over a million from the 1970s onwards. Certain categories, the YOUNG, WOMEN and IMMIGRANTS are the most vulnerable to unemployment and the most reliant on handouts. The fight against social exclusion in post-industrial society has become a rallying cry for politicians of the Right and

Left. In his 1995 presidential campaign the Gaullist leader Jacques CHIRAC claimed as his priority the need to end *la fracture sociale* (social fracture). The SOCIALIST PARTY uses solidarity as the contemporary principle of fraternity, and in government since 1997 has raised the minimum wage and the RMI (social income) rates. By prioritizing the 35-hour week it is attempting a redistribution of WORK to end long-term unemployment. The increase of exclusion has brought MEDIA attention on voluntary action by individuals and groups. These include COLUCHE, the founder of *RESTAU-RANTS DU CŒUR*; the Catholic priest l'*abbé* PIERRE, who has been fighting homelessness for five decades; *ATD-Quart Monde*, the associations to help the homeless known as the '*SDF*' (*sans domicile fixe*, no fixed abode); unemployed, undeclared immigrants' and anti-racist associations such as *le mouvement des chômeurs*, *les SANS PAPIERS*, and *SOS-Racisme*. Some of these have resorted to sit-ins in churches or government offices, in attempts to provoke a government response to their plight. (**Máire Cross**)

Further reading

Marlière (1997) and Moores (1997). Information on poverty, and on the homeless. Murard (1993). A succinct account of the CSG and RMI.

Existentialism   A philosophical and cultural movement which was especially influential in the decade after 1945. Its name reflects the idea that 'existence precedes essence': things only have meaning (essence) after they have happened, and events are not the expression of some pre-existing destiny. Its main theme was that people are free to make their own choices in life. This can be a cause of anguish because no one can make your choices for you, and you are responsible for who you are and for the results of your own actions, however dreadful. Completely honest and frank relationships with other people can also be difficult. As a result, the existentialists argued, many people engage in *mauvaise foi* (bad faith), trying to deceive themselves that things are not their fault. A more lucid and 'authentic' approach is to make conscious choices and stick with them, for example, by making a commitment to a cause, particularly one which aims to defend the lives and freedom of other people. The existentialists drew inspiration from earlier writers like Pascal, Kierkegaard, Nietzsche, Husserl and Heidegger. Their main exponents in France were Jean-Paul SARTRE and Simone de BEAUVOIR, who wrote novels, plays and philosophical works exemplifying their ideas. They were joined by many well-known writers and artists, who contributed to their monthly review, *LES TEMPS MODERNES*. There were also Christian existentialists, such as Gabriel MARCEL, who emphasized the importance of spiritual choices. The existentialist message fitted the mood of France in the aftermath of the war, and it was widely followed in Europe, North America and elsewhere. It was identified with the anti-establishment life of the SAINT-GERMAIN-DES-PRÉS district in Paris, with cafés, night-clubs and the semi-bohemian lifestyle of students and intellectuals. It also provided the basis for a robust individualism, which continues to be widely influential. (**Michael Kelly**)

Further reading

Poster (1975). A detailed survey, situating existentialism in the intellectual and social context of the period. Morris (1993). Catalogue of an important London exhibition, copiously illustrated, with background essays on social and cultural context.

Exode   When German troops swept into Belgium on 10 May 1940, they triggered a sudden, mass exodus of civilians fleeing before them. It is estimated that when the French surrendered six weeks later, about 6 million French people were displaced refugees. The searing memories of the German occupation of 1914–18 were the primary cause for the flight from their homes of the French in the North. The harshness of the occupying troops, the experience of deprivation, requisitioning, deportations, and executions for the French inhabitants, were painfully fresh memories. There was genuine astonishment when the Germans proved to be polite, disciplined, and cooperative, and the phrase *Ils sont corrects* (They are polite) passed into legend.

The mass exodus from PARIS began when the French government left on 10 June; 2 million Parisians set off for the south, and the first German troops entered a ghost town. Across the north, the Jewish communities of towns like Lille, and of Paris were reduced to a quarter of their size. Robert Paxton notes that Evreux in Normandy had 172 inhabitants remaining out of a population of 20 000; Beaune-la-Rolande, just north of the Loire, swelled from 1700 to 40 000. At the same time, the French Army was being overrun, with refugees hampering mobility on the roads; many were stuck at the Loire because all the bridges were destroyed.

It took time to get them home again once hostilities had ended, given the extent to which the road and rail infrastructure was damaged. The fact that France was divided, under the terms of the armistice, into seven zones, also complicated matters. Alsace and Lorraine were annexed into German territory. About three and a half million refugees were back in their homes by the beginning of January, but Jewish refugees were forbidden to return to the occupied zone, as were refugees from the *zone interdite* (forbidden zone) in the north. (**Margaret Atack**)

Further reading

Amouroux (1976). This includes a large section on the *Exode*.

Express, l'   France's first and still most highly selling weekly NEWS magazine. Founded by Jean-Jacques SERVAN-SCHREIBER and Françoise GIROUD in 1953, it moved from a left-leaning to a centrist persuasion during the 1970s.

Fabius, Laurent   Born 1946. Socialist politician. The youngest Prime Minister for over a century (1984–86), with liberal and technocratic credentials, he was seen as MITTERAND's preferred successor, but was prosecuted in 1994 for involvement in a medical scandal over blood contaminated with the AIDS virus. Eventually discharged in 1999, he was appointed Finance Minister in March 2000.

Family   The traditional notion of the French family as the basic unit of society was developed from Catholic values and the needs of rural communities. The stability of the extended family was challenged by growing demands for greater personal freedom for individuals. This produced many sharp criticisms of the family, expressed, for example in MAURIAC'S novels of the 1920s. After the Second World War, the 'nuclear' family, of two married parents and two or more children, was adopted as the main vehicle for national recovery and stability. From the 1960s, the increased mobility of the population and the emphasis on personal (rather than social) relationships within the family led to a succession of legal changes, aimed at facilitating divorce and recognizing other forms of relationship. In the past 30 years, the number of marriages has declined from around 400 000 to 280 000 per year, while the number of divorces has risen from 10 000 to 50 000. With the growing diversity of individual arrangements for living together and having and rearing children, French social policy and public attitudes are tending to focus more on the household (*ménage*) than the family as the basic unit. (**Michael Kelly**)

Further reading

Hantrais, (1982). A useful study in English, though now a little dated. *L'État de la France* (1998). Especially pp. 77–83. This is an annual digest of trends and statistics, covering many aspects of contemporary France. Segalen (1996). A detailed analysis of the social patterns and changes.

Fanon, Frantz   1925–61. Writer and political activist. He drew on EXISTENTIALISM and clinical psychology to analyse racist attitudes in *Peau noire, masques blancs* (*Black Skin, White Masks*, 1952), and attacked COLONIALISM in his classic *Les Damnés de la terre* (*The Wretched of the Earth*, 1961).

Fascism   The nature and extent of fascism in France have long been subjects of debate. Historians who adopt a narrow definition include only some of the anti-Marxist, anti-parliamentary, anti-liberal organizations operating during the interwar period (notably *Le Faisceau*, *Le Francisme*, the PARTI POPULAIRE FRANÇAIS and Marcel DÉAT's Neo-Socialists) as well as intellectuals such as Robert BRASILLACH, Lucien Rebatet and Pierre DRIEU LA ROCHELLE. They exclude ACTION FRANÇAISE or the *Jeunesses Patriotes* and CROIX-DE-FEU, for example, despite the fascistic style of their paramilitary wings, their parades and their aggressive posturing. They do so on the grounds that they represented forms of authoritarian conservatism, which lacked the anti-bourgeois, anti-capitalist radicalism and revolutionary drive characteristic of true fascism. Other historians argue for a broader definition acknowledging a spectrum of fascisms, because the borderlines between fascism and authoritarian conservatism were extremely blurred. On that view, fascism was anticipated in France by ideas and movements associated with the nationalist extreme right in the late nineteenth century.

The anti-parliamentary leagues were not a serious threat to the Republic during the 1920s but amid the economic depression and political uncertainties of the 1930s they became more menacing. They were banned in 1936, but several legalized themselves as political parties. These made little impact, although the *Parti Social Français* (ex-*Croix de Feu*), and Jacques Doriot's *Parti Populaire Français*, a new grouping, attracted significant memberships. During the OCCUPATION fascists did not react uniformly. A small minority joined the FREE FRENCH or the RESISTANCE. Others aligned themselves with Marshal PÉTAIN's authoritarian regime, while many of the most radical moved closer to Nazism, despising VICHY as backward-looking and insufficiently pro-German. In 1944, under German pressure, several of the most extreme COLLABORATIONISTS were included as ministers at Vichy, then in the exiled puppet government at Sigmaringen. The ignominy of the period left the extreme Right discredited after the war but a number of small groups were formed under the FOURTH and early FIFTH REPUBLICS, some of them feeding later into the *FRONT NATIONAL* which achieved relative electoral success in the 1980s and 1990s. **(Christopher Flood)**

Further reading

Soucy (1985) and (1995) and *French Fascism:* The standard works on the subject written in English. Winock (1998). Translation of a book which remains valuable on many aspects of the French extreme right.

Fashion   Fashion in clothes and behaviour was, from the Renaissance to the French Revolution, principally dictated by the royal courts of Europe, and was associated with extravagant display and conspicuous consumption. Fashion changes or, at least certain fads or crazes, were usually the result of foreign influence, touches of the exotic, such as *chinoiseries* of the eighteenth century, which stimulated the illusion of new or different possibilities of dress and behaviour. With the French and Industrial Revolutions at the end of the eighteenth century, fashion was increasingly inspired by self-appointed fashion leaders: dandies, courtesans, actresses, hostesses of 'fashionable' salons. Industrial mass production and the economic domination of an expanding middle class led to a relative democratization of fashion, with the establishment, in PARIS in particular, of couturier houses catering for a discriminating urban clientele. In twentieth-century modern urban mass society, fashion became an industry, with the couturier names being supplemented and then superseded by designer labels, and fashion becoming the prerogative of all inhabitants of the large cities. The extravagant dress of urban sub-groups such as mods, rockers and punks made London rather than Paris the capital of 'street fashion' trends.

If fashion is particularly associated with the French, this is because of the prestige of the French royal court during the reigns of Louis the XIV, XV and XVI and the presence in nineteenth-and twentieth-century Paris, a highly centralized capital city, of a rich urban aristocracy and middle class. The feature that above all assured the domination of French fashion in the period was the establishment of couturier houses that set the style in woman's clothing for most of the Western world in the period 1860–1960. The great Parisian fashion designers were not necessarily French: the first was the Englishman Worth who dominated from 1858 to 1895; the Spaniard Ballenciaga was a major influence in the 1950s; and in the 1980s the Japanese. Nevertheless, certain French names, most notably CHANEL and DIOR, have become synonymous with French fashion, the former establishing the simple, elegant easy-to-wear clothes loved by women around the world, the latter, her rival, providing the romantic extravaganza (such as the famous 'NEW LOOK' of 1947) that stimulated so much post-war fashion discussion. (**David Scott**)

Further reading

Barthes (1967). A provocative study of the discourse of fashion. Baudrillard (1970). Laver (1982) Chapters 9 and 10. A history of costume, setting French fashion in a wider context.

Faure, Edgar   1908–88. Centrist politician. He held several ministerial posts in the FOURTH REPUBLIC, including Prime Minister, twice (1952, 1955–56). He was then a GAULLIST minister, and was responsible for the important EDUCATION reforms of 1968–69.

6 February 1934   For a few hours on 6 February 1934, PARIS came dangerously close to a serious civil disturbance. On that day, in the wake of the STAVISKY AFFAIR of the previous two months, right-wing groups including the First World War veterans' movement, the *CROIX-DE-FEU*, led by Colonel François de la Rocque, and the *Camelots du roi*, the young and often violent supporters of the ACTION FRANÇAISE, demonstrated against corruption in government and financial circles. Permission for the demonstration was given by Jean CHIAPPE, right-wing prefect of Paris's police force. Having marched down the Champs-Elyseés, the protestors made for the National Assembly; some wished to occupy it. In the Place de la Concorde they met with left-wing groups staging their own protest and the republican guards. A violent confrontation left 15 people dead and between 1500 and 2000 injured. The following day the predominantly left-wing government of DALADIER resigned. On 9 February there was a further massive demonstration organized by the COMMUNIST PARTY and on 12 February a general strike was called. The events of 6 February were short-lived, but they reflected a deep, underlying *malaise* and potential instability. These were to remain a threat to French society not just during the years of the POPULAR FRONT but for the rest of the decade leading to France's capitulation to the Germans in 1940. (**John Flower**)

Feminism   From feminist movements and feminist campaigns to change the situation of women, to the powerfully influential analyses of feminist philosophers, sociologists, and creative writers, feminism in France has a rich, complex, and at times controversial history. The number of feminist organizations and feminist newspapers at the turn of the century was impressively high, campaigning for women's liberation across a broad range of issues, including HEALTH, CLASS, and SEXUALITY. Throughout the century, women have sought to overturn the repressive and restrictive laws and practices, resulting from the inferior status accorded to married women particularly in the Napoleonic Code of 1804, and to win elementary rights such as the right to vote and to stand for election.

Influenced by the Women's Liberation Movement in America, French feminists staged a demonstration in the summer of 1968 at the Tomb of the Unknown Soldier under the Arc de Triomphe, to enormous press controversy. Demands for legal, free, ABORTION and CONTRACEPTION were at the centre of the *MOUVEMENT DE LIBÉRATION DES*

FEMMES which tackled all forms of discrimation and sexism. In the 1980s, the establishment of a Ministry for Women's Rights brought many feminist demands into the mainstream political life. In 1999, the proposal to introduce LA PARITÉ, the requirement for equal representation of women and men in Parliament, was successfully voted through after quite bitter controversy which also divided feminists, although it is not clear how and when it will be implemented.

Contemporary feminist analysis of culture and society owes much to Simone de BEAUVOIR's major philosophical study of the situation of women, *Le Deuxième Sexe*, in which she argues that culture, not nature, created the values accorded to gender difference in society. It also draws on the post-1968 theoretical analysis of gendered SUBJECTIVITY put forward in the work of Julia KRISTEVA, Hélène CIXOUS, Luce IRIGARAY, and Christine DELPHY and the *Questions féministes* group. (**Margaret Atack**)

Further reading

Albistur and Armogathe (1978). A broad overview from medieval times onwards. Marks and Courtivron, (1981). An influential anthology of extracts from the post-68 period that is particularly strong on feminist theory and creative writing. Duchen (1986). An authoritative study. Duchen (1987). A well-chosen anthology. Klejman and Rochefort (1989). A substantial and detailed study. Moi (1987).

Fernandel   1903–71. Actor. Starting off in music hall, he became the most popular comedian in French cinema, acting in innumerable films over a forty-year career. He is particularly remembered for his roles in PAGNOL's films based in Marseille, and in the *Don Camillo* series.

Ferrat, Jean   Born 1930. Singer-songwriter. Popular in the 1950s and 1960s for his songs which combined romance with social criticism and political COMMITMENT (on the Left).

Ferré, Léo   1916–93. Singer-songwriter. He adopted the persona of a marginal figure with strongly poetic lyrics which brought together themes of love and anarchy.

Fifth Republic   1958–present. At the height of the ALGERIAN WAR, which the institutions of the postwar FOURTH REPUBLIC appeared incapable of resolving, General Charles DE GAULLE was invited to lead the country and draw up a new constitution. Approved in a referendum in September 1958, the Fifth Republic's constitution gave a strong role to the President, who was to hold office for a seven-year term. The President is Head of State, and Commander-in-Chief of the Armed Forces. He appoints the Prime Minister, and has the power to dissolve the National Assembly. The Assembly, now of 577 *députés* (deputies), is normally elected for a five-year term: the Prime Minister and government are answerable to it. They are also answerable to the Senate (upper house, currently with 321 members), of which one-third of the members are elected every three years, for a nine-year term. A nine-member Constitutional Council oversees elections and rules on the constitutionality of legislation.

De Gaulle stamped his personal authority on the presidency, and increased it further by introducing direct election to the office. He and his first two successors

(Georges POMPIDOU, 1969–74, Valéry GISCARD D'ESTAING, 1974–81) governed with a Centre-Right parliamentary majority. Both subsequent Presidents (François MITTERRAND, 1981–95, Jacques CHIRAC, from 1995) have had periods in which their political opponents have held the parliamentary majority, and therefore formed the government. The three resulting periods of COHABITATION have produced tensions in the respective roles and responsibilities of President and Prime Minister, and have raised questions about the need for constitutional change. This has been further encouraged by the reduction of the President's term to five years, agreed in a low-profile referendum in October 2000. Though the constitutional arrangements of the Fifth Republic have frequently been questioned, their survival was facilitated by Mitterrand's acceptance of them, in spite of his earlier criticism of them as a *coup d'état permanent*. They have now lasted over 40 years, and though they may give rise to intermittent malaise, talk of a possible Sixth Republic appears to be highly speculative. (**Michael Kelly**)

Further reading

Forbes, Hewlett and Nectoux (2000). A very useful textbook on many aspects of the Fifth Republic. Larkin, (1997). A standard history in English.

Figaro, le   Founded 1854. A daily newspaper which has always prided itself on a high quality of writing. Close to the GAULLISTS, it has attracted prominent conservative writers. Among its wide range of associated publications, *Le Figaro littéraire* is a respected cultural review.

Film festivals   The film festival idea probably originated in Italy where, in 1934, the FASCIST state encouraged the launch of the Venice Film Festival as a showcase for national cinema. It proved so successful that POPULAR FRONT Education Minister, Jean Zay, launched a film festival in Cannes, the first of which was scheduled for May 1939 but was postponed when Hitler invaded Czechoslovakia in March of that year. Relaunched in 1946, the Cannes Film Festival rapidly became not just a showcase for French cinema, especially for the NOUVELLE VAGUE when TRUFFAUT's *Les 400 coups* won the Director's Prize in 1959, but also the principal market for the buying and selling of feature films from all parts of the world. This was reflected in its various prizes and events such as the Golden Palm, the Directors' Prize and the Critics' Fortnight, as well as in other Cannes festivals such as MIP-COM (commercials) and MIP-TV (TV programmes).

In the 1950s and 1960s Cannes also became a preferred means to promote young, female 'starlets', the prototype of whom was Brigitte BARDOT, who would be advantageously photographed on the beach dressed in revealing swimwear. In this way the Cannes Festival also contributed to the expansion of TOURISM based on sea, sand and a different relationship to the body, whether male or female. This trend lasted until the 1970s when cheaper air travel meant that the south of France was superseded as a fashionable destination for the rich and famous. After the decentralization of legislation of the early1980s, film festivals proliferated in France as city mayors used them to promote tourism and their local economy. Today there are more than 150 French film festivals, some highly specialized such as Abbeville's Bird and Wildlife Film Festival. In addition to Cannes, the best known are perhaps Créteil's Women's Film Festival, Deauville's American Film Festival and Cognac's Thriller Film Festival. (**Jill Forbes**)

Further reading

Directory of European Film and Audiovisual Festivals/Annuaire européen des festivals de cinéma et audiovisuel, published annually. Contains details of all the film festivals held in France and the various prizes
they award. Harris (2000).

Film Studios   The world pre-eminence of French CINEMA pre-1914 is closely associated with the early development of film studios, most of which were built in the inner suburbs of Paris or on the south coast. In 1887, the director Georges Méliès built a small shed (7m × 10m) in his Montreuil garden which he called an *atelier de poses* (workshop for poses) after the still photographer's studio. A range of craft workshops developed on the same site to service film production. Before the Hollywood Majors, such vertical integration (combining different stages of a business process) was typical of Charles Pathé, who opened the Vincennes studios in 1902 and the Joinville studios in 1906, and of Léon Gaumont, who created the Buttes-Chaumont studios in 1905. The studios rapidly became associated with particular genres and styles, none more so than Albatros, created by Russian *émigrés* Joseph Ermolieff and Alexander Kamenka at the Montreuil studios they leased in 1920. Albatros launched the career of Ivan Mosjoukine and became the hub of a celebrated artistic community.

The advent of sound saw Paramount take over Joinville and Tobis-Klangfilm build studios at Epinay, in order to produce films in different language versions (hence Joinville's nickname of Babel-on-Seine). As the French film industry went from economic crisis to crisis throughout the 1930s, so calls were increasingly heard from film-makers such as Jean RENOIR and Marcel L'Herbier for the creation of a French Hollywood. This came closest to achievement at the outbreak of the war, when many film industry personnel migrated south to escape the German occupiers and worked in Marcel PAGNOL's studios in MARSEILLE or the Victorine studios in Nice. Marcel CARNÉ's ambitious *Les Enfants du paradis* was filmed there in 1943. The post-war preference for location filming all but killed off French film studios, a process evoked in François TRUFFAUT's nostalgic *La Nuit américaine* (*Day for Night*, 1973), but many like the Buttes-Chaumont converted to television and continue to flourish under a different guise. (**Jill Forbes**)

Further reading

Albera (1995). Beautifully illustrated account of history of the Albatros studios and their productions.
Sadoul (1973). Gives much detail of the economics and practices of French film studios in the silent and
early sound period.

Finkielkraut, Alain   Born 1949. Philosopher. A staunch defender of rationalism and of French cultural traditions. His *Défaite de la pensée* (*The Undoing of Thought*, 1988) was widely discussed.

FLN *Front de Libération Nationale*, the Algerian National Liberation Front. See
ALGERIAN WAR.

Flore, Le Café on the boulevard SAINT-GERMAIN-DES-PRÉS frequented by the
EXISTENTIALISTS in the late 1940s, and now a popular tourist *rendez-vous*.

Football (clubs) France was not judged a top-ranking football nation until her 1998
World Cup victory in the *Stade de France*, but football has long been the most popular participation sport in France. Imported from England in late nineteenth century
by the middle classes, it spread to the working classes in the First World War and
through the influence of Catholic boys' clubs, and was promoted by paternalistic
factory owners. French administrators and press were influential in internationalizing
football (setting up FIFA, inaugurating a World Cup and European club and nations
cups). But French club football professionalized 'late' and 'incompletely' in 1932,
remaining broadly semi-professional until the 1960s, with strong municipal involvement. Whereas there is a tradition of successful medium-size town clubs (Reims,
Sedan, Sochaux), the entry of businessmen with political ambitions into clubs in the
1970s and 1980s and TELEVISION rights money from 1984 (Canal Plus) have brought
big-city clubs to the fore (MARSEILLES, Bordeaux, LYON, PSG). After heroic runners-
up performances by Reims (1956, 1959) and Saint-Etienne (1976), France's first
European Cup victor was Marseille (1993). Their club chairman Bernard TAPIE was
not the first French club official to be subsequently convicted of corrupt business
practices. French clubs still do not have the financial weight to compete with English
or Italian clubs, who regularly poach their best players, increasingly from the French
youth coaching system. The national team won international admiration for their
'champagne' football (and sympathy as gallant losers) by reaching the World Cup
semi-finals (1958, 1982, 1986), and winning the European Nations Cup (1984, 2000).
The World Cup victory was used, internally, to promote values of tolerance and solidarity around its multi-coloured team, seen to reflect the multi-racial IDENTITY of the
new France. **(Geoff Hare)**

Further reading

Dauncey and Hare, (1999b). The organization and impact of the World Cup on French society.

Football (national team) Football has undoubtedly overtaken CYCLING as the most
popular French sport. There are 2.2 million registered players at all levels (over 50 per
cent under 21 and including 31 800 women) and 38 professional clubs, with 800 professionals. France's 1998 World Cup victory was the climax of 20 years of development.
As well as representing an ethnic mix typical of French society today, the winners combined classic French skills of passing and movement with a physical strength previously lacking ; they were thus even able to overcome France's failure to produce a
top-class goalscorer since the 1950s. *Les Bleus'* triumph reflected both sophisticated
coaching and rigorous dietary and physical preparation routines; consequently,
French managers are now among the most sought-after internationally. French success
is all the more remarkable given the weak infrastructure of the domestic game; crowds

are small and TV earnings much less than in England, Spain or Italy, where top French players are increasingly forced to earn their living (currently over 30 in the English leagues). Many clubs still depend on municipal help or the sometimes irregular financial methods of charismatic chairmen like Bernard Tapie at Marseille. But the youth training centres in which clubs invested decades ago continue to produce exciting talents like Eric Cantona (Manchester United) or David Ginola (Spurs), even if they are mostly destined to play before foreign audiences. Although the current world champions are probably the strongest squad in world football, many consider that the finest French team was that of the 1980s led by Michel Platini, a creative midfielder who numbers among the top ten players of the last century. His fluid and imaginative stylists won Euro 1984 ; but cynical play by Germany and indulgent refereeing robbed them of a deserved 1982 World Cup. (**David Hanley**)

Further reading

Dauncey and Hare (1996). Gives an up-to-date overview. The French Football Federation's website is www.fff.fr

Force de frappe   France's nuclear strike force. See Nuclear deterrent.

Force ouvrière   (Workers' Strength). Trade union congress, formed in 1948, when a socialist oriented group left the communist dominated CGT (*Confédération générale du travail*) to form the CGT-FO. It is now one of the three largest trade unions in France.

Fordism   The term *Fordism* refers to a form of economic organization based on the mass production and mass consumption of goods, a model pioneered by the American industrialist Henry Ford, of the Ford Motor Company. Ford realized that by manufacturing cars on a more massive scale than ever before, and by taking advantage of new technological developments to improve productivity, he could produce cars cheaply enough to tap into a whole new market of people on modest incomes. The ideal was that the worker who made the car should also be able to own one, but this increased access to consumer goods came at a price. Workers had to produce more cars more quickly, and this was made possible by the introduction of assembly lines and Taylorist techniques which often condemned workers to perform a single monotonous task, day in, day out.

It was during the inter-war years that Fordism began to be regarded as a model for French industry to follow. Many French industrialists and commentators undertook study trips to American factories in this period and published accounts of their amazement or horror at the scale and speed of American production. French automobile manufacturers were among the first to follow Ford's example by adopting innovations like the assembly line between the wars. But it was only after the Second World War, and particularly with the expansion of mass consumption in the 1950s and 1960s, that the French economy as a whole came closer to the Fordist model. This evolution provoked anxieties about the demise of small businesses and artisan producers, about Americanization and consumerism; élites criticized what they saw as a standardization of tastes and products to the lowest common denominator. Thus, Fordist AMERICA was the object of both fear and fascination in much of the cultural production of pre-war and post-war France. (**Jackie Clarke**)

Further reading

Gramsci (1971). A classic critique of Fordism written while the Italian intellectual was in prison in the 1920s. Duhamel (1931). A particularly virulent and sensational expression of French fears in the face of Fordist America. A best-seller in France in 1931.

Fourth Republic   The Fourth Republic (1946–58) rebuilt the ECONOMY, created a welfare state and anchored France firmly within EUROPE and NATO, but failed to provide durable institutions. After the collapse of the VICHY RÉGIME France was ruled by DE GAULLE's PROVISIONAL GOVERNMENTS; elected assemblies tried to draft a constitution. In October 1946 the second draft constitution scraped a bare majority in a referendum, with a third of voters abstaining. The new institutions proved alarmingly like those of the THIRD REPUBLIC. A multi-party system, with elections held on proportional representation, produced 23 coalition governments in 12 years. Initially, 'tripartite' governments (SFIO, PCF and MRP) had comfortable majorities; they revived the economy by indicative PLANNING, building an ambitious welfare state. The advent of the COLD WAR from spring 1947 destroyed this coalition, forcing the PCF into opposition. Simultaneously de Gaulle's RPF, rejecting party government for a presidential executive, threatened the system from the right. With a good third of the deputies unavailable for majorities, governments could only come from the remaining 'Third Force' parties – SFIO, RADICALS, MRP and conservatives. These unnatural bedfellows struggled to defend parliamentary democracy against internal and external threats. They took France decisively into the Atlantic Alliance and EEC. But DECOLONIZATION proved their Achilles' heel. In INDO-CHINA, French armies were defeated humiliatingly at DIEN BIEN PHU (1954). Shortly afterwards, the nationalist FLN launched an insurrection in ALGERIA. All French governments refused independence talks and sought an illusory military solution, at increasing cost and with fatal consequences. Governments progressively abandoned authority to the alliance of soldiers, settlers and bureaucrats in Algiers. On 13 May 1958 this group launched an insurrection; the Paris politicians caved in and summoned de Gaulle as Prime Minister to liquidate a republic which had done much to modernize France. (**David Hanley**)

Further reading

Williams (1964). This remains a masterpiece.

Foucault, Michel   1926–84. Writer. He analysed several areas of human activity, attempting to show the underlying discourses at work, including studies of madness (1961), punishment (*Surveiller et punir* (*Discipline and Punish*), 1975), and sexuality (1976–84). He has been enormously influential worldwide.

Franc   The franc has traditionally focused French pride (or concern) as a symbol of the strength of the French ECONOMY. Consistently under pressure of depreciation, regularly devalued, and most recently constrained by monetary requirements for EUROPEAN integration, the franc's identity is threatened by the Euro. Depreciation of the franc during the 1920s was caused by the INFLATION of the war and costly rebuilding. Economically liberal right-wing governments refused 'shameful' devaluation, but weak STATE finances saw hostile currency speculation (1923), conflict between left-wing governments and the conservative (private) *Banque de France* (1926) and the POINCARÉ stabilization (1928). During the 1930s' Depression, the franc remained overvalued as the economy sheltered behind protectionism, but the FRONT POPULAIRE, initially keen to preserve the franc, devalued (1936, 1937), faced by mistrust of its ECONOMIC POLICY. Exchange controls were avoided until the war, but the franc continued to depreciate. Post-war, in 1952, Korean War inflation and speculation led to Pinay's deflationary stemming of price rises and a bolstered franc, but the ALGERIAN crisis weakened the economy. After 1958, the *grandeur* of DE GAULLE called for a strong, stable convertible currency: reforms devalued the franc and, most visibly, created the 'new franc' worth 100 old francs (1960). During the 1960s, the franc remained strong and gold reserves high as DE GAULLE protested against 'dollar imperialism' until MAY '68, when shaken confidence in government provoked speculation necessitating massive reserve spending. De Gaulle's strong franc was corrected by devaluation under POMPIDOU. Abandon of Bretton Woods (1971) and the European monetary 'snake' (1972) saw the franc float in reflection of France's economic performance during the 1970s. Market wariness of MITTERRAND's SOCIALISM and economic mismanagement pressured the franc in 1981–83, until the socialists adopted neo-liberal economic policies, and Left and Right accepted convergence criteria for European integration in the 1990s. **(Hugh Dauncey)**

Further reading

Arthus. *et al.* (1998). France and the franc and the European Monetary System.

France 2000 – statistics   France is the largest country in Western Europe (550,000 sq. km). Some 55 per cent of the territory is farmland, 27 per cent is forest. The population is 60.4 million. PARIS accounts for 10.6m, and three other urban areas are larger than 1 million (LYON, MARSEILLE-Aix-en-Provence, Lille-Roubaix-Tourcoing). The annual birth rate is 12 per thousand, and the death rate is 9 per thousand. Life expectancy is 82 years for women, 74 years for men.

Twenty five per cent of the population is under 20 years of age, 20 per cent over 60 years. Some 81 per cent declare themselves CATHOLIC, 7 per cent Moslem, 1.6 per cent PROTESTANT, 1.3 per cent JEWISH.

In France 12.3 million children attend school, and there are 2.1 million students in higher education.

The total labour force is 26 million, of whom 62 per cent are men, 48 per cent women. Around 10 per cent are seeking employment. 25 per cent are white-collar workers, 23 per cent manual workers. Net average annual earnings are 130,790 francs. There is a statutory paid holiday entitlement of five weeks per year.

France has the fourth largest ECONOMY in the world, by Gross Domestic Product (8 833 billion francs), with an annual growth rate of 2.9 per cent and an inflation rate of 1.3 per cent. It is the second largest exporter of services and farm products, and the fourth largest exporter of manufactured goods. 63 per cent of its trade is with other EU countries.

France is a founder member of the European Union, and holds a permanent seat in the United Nations Security Council.

La Marseillaise (The Battle Hymn of the Rhine Army) was first declared the national anthem in 1795. The motto of the Republic is *Liberté, Égalité, Fraternité* (Liberty, Equality, Fraternity). The French flag is a blue, white and red tricolour, first adopted in 1789. (**Michael Kelly**)

Francophonie   Literally, the ability to speak French. More commonly, the term denotes French-speakers outside France and organized efforts to strengthen their numbers. Understood thus, *francophonie* is to a large extent a legacy of COLONIALISM, through which the French language was exported to the overseas empire. Efforts to strengthen the global community of French-speakers following DECOLONIZATION have often been criticized as a form of NEO-COLONIALISM. These efforts are also closely connected with French antagonism towards the international dominance of AMERICA, the world leader in anglophone (English-speaking) culture.

There are today more French speakers outside France than within France itself. The largest concentrations are in North and Sub-Saharan Africa. Smaller numbers are scattered across former colonial territories around the world. In most so-called French-speaking countries, only a minority of the population speaks French, but these tend to be the most educated and powerful classes. In many Sub-Saharan countries where the mass of the population knows little French, this nevertheless serves as the language of government.

The Canadian province of QUEBEC is one of the few areas outside France (and neighbouring parts of BELGIUM and SWITZERLAND) where French is spoken by most of the population. But the dominance of English in the rest of Canada, and the proximity of the United States, also illustrate the threatening environment within which *francophonie* is often felt to be operating. Since 1986, there have been summit meetings attended by heads of state or of government from mainly or partially francophone countries. These are similar in some ways to meetings of Commonwealth leaders, bringing together representatives of former British colonies, but are more focused on linguistic and cultural issues. (**Alec Hargreaves**)

Further reading

Haut Conseil de la Francophonie, *État de la Francophonie*, Paris, published every two years. Biennial compilation of official statistics and documents. Ager (1996). A well-documented critical analysis.

Franglais   This hybrid term (*français* + *anglais*) was popularized, though not actually invented, by René ÉTIEMBLE in his classic and outspokenly hostile *Parlez-vous franglais?* (1964). It denotes a style of French which makes 'excessive' or 'unnecessary' use of English words or expressions; alternatively, it can refer to the items themselves.

Long-established imports like *club, football* or *tramway* would not therefore count as *franglais*, whereas recent arrivals like *in* ('*à la mode*') or *loser* ('*perdant*') undoubtedly would. The position of *week-end* or *car-ferry* is intermediate, though they seem well on the way to being 'naturalized'. Also less clear-cut in status are abbreviations like *le foot* (football) or *le hand* (handball), or coinages like *recordman* (record-holder), *faire du forcing* (pile on the pressure) or *se relooker* (revamp one's appearance). In such cases French has in effect created a word of its own from English materials, and one for which there was no previous French equivalent. Moreover, many authentic Anglo-American words have a distinctive meaning in French usage. Thus *le shopping* denotes shopping for pleasure, not for groceries (that would be *faire ses courses*), and may therefore be a useful, not an unnecessary acquisition.

The Anglicisms found in French number many thousands. But in running texts the proportion is usually low (1 per cent in the average issue of a newspaper like *France-Soir*). However, concern – sometimes linked to political anti-Americanism – is caused by the higher percentages found in technical writing or on the Internet, as well as by insidious Anglicisms like *en charge de* for *chargé de* (in charge of). Government committees have proposed alternative terminology, but attempts to impose this by legislation (for example, the 1994 TOUBON law) have been largely unsuccessful in the face of widespread public indifference, or even enthusiasm for *franglais*. But there have been a few 'victories': *logiciel* and *matériel* have supplanted *software* and *hardware*, for instance. (**Rodney Ball**)

Further reading

Thody (1995). A detailed and readable account.

Free French   The Free French describes the movement of those outside France who wanted to continue the fight against the Germans after the defeat of 1940. It was headed by General DE GAULLE who broadcast from the BBC in London on 18 June 1940, calling on the French to continue resisting. At this time, the Free French were few in number, controlled no French territory, and were virtually unknown.

The Free French crucially depended on the support of BRITAIN and AMERICA, but their relationship with the Allies was characterized by uncertainty and mutual distrust. When the Americans landed in North Africa in November 1942 they tried to supplant de Gaulle as leader. The General, however, outmanoeuvred his opponents and established a French Committee of National Liberation in Algiers in which the Free French played a central part. With the help of the RESISTANCE hero, Jean MOULIN, de Gaulle brought together the disparate groups of the Resistance within France under his nominal leadership. Despite fears that the Allies might form a military government at the LIBERATION, the Free French established their control over liberated territory through political commissioners, and de Gaulle assumed power with a PROVISIONAL GOVERNMENT when PARIS was liberated in August 1944.

The Free French occupy an epic place in French history. They are inextricably linked with de Gaulle, the man of the 18th June. In the rich post-war history of political Gaullism, the companions of de Gaulle in London in 1940 were known as *résistants de la première heure* (Resisters of the First Hour). For many members of the Resistance in France, however, the Free French were a conservative grouping, which sought to marginalize the internal Resistance and promote the post-war legend of the Gaullists. (**HF**)

Further reading

De Gaulle (1980). Vol I, 'L'Appel' describes the beginning of the Free French. Michel (1980). A general introduction.

French language   French derives from the Latin spoken 2000 years ago in northern France, when France (then called *Gaul*) was a province of the Roman Empire. It is thus a 'sister language' of Italian and Spanish, sharing many features of grammar and vocabulary with them. However, in the years following the collapse of the Empire (*c.* AD 400 onwards), 'proto-French' was strongly influenced by the Germanic speech of the invading Franks, who established the first northern French monarchy and gave the territory its modern name. Consequently, French has evolved further away from Latin than the other Romance languages. For example, the Latin word *aqua* (water), easily recognizable in Italian *acqua* and Spanish *agua*, has in French been reduced to *eau* (a single vowel [o] in pronunciation). And many basic vocabulary items are of Germanic, not Latin origin, e.g. *bâtir* (build), *haïr* (hate), *guichet* (same word as English *wicket*: 'little gate'). Forerunners of FRANGLAIS, almost!

Today's standard French is based on the usage of the seventeenth-century Versailles aristocracy. The humbler colloquial language contrasts with it grammatically in many respects, and also lexically, with its rich store of ARGOT (slang): for example, *flotte* for *eau* (water), *roupiller* for *dormir* (sleep). Parisian-style French has largely supplanted REGIONAL LANGUAGES and dialects in France, though it does show some local variations, particularly in pronunciation.

Outside the Hexagon, French is the mother tongue of the inhabitants of southern BELGIUM, western SWITZERLAND, and Quebec province in CANADA (there are regional varieties here too). Because of overseas expansion, especially in the nineteenth century, it has official status in many parts of West Africa, the Caribbean, the Indian Ocean and the South Pacific. Worldwide, there are some 70 000 000 native speakers of French, and perhaps 150 000 000 proficient second-language users. (**Rodney Ball**)

Further reading

Giusti (1997). A concise and readable historical outline. Atlas de la langue française (1995). Informative collection of maps, charts and statistics.

Front National   The emergence of the *Front National* (FN) as a significant force in French politics coincided with the rise of the radical Right in several West European countries during the 1980s and 1990s. The FN was founded in 1972 from a group of neo-FASCIST and ultra-nationalist organizations, seeking to replace factionalism with unity and to offer a more acceptable face to the electorate. During its first ten years the party was prone to internal divisions, personal rivalries, expulsions and occasional self-inflicted violence: it made no electoral impact, never receiving even 1 per cent of the national vote. In 1981 its leader, Jean-Marie LE PEN, having scored a mere 0.74 per cent in the 1974 Presidential election, failed even to gain the necessary 500 signatures of public office holders to qualify as a candidate. Yet, three years later, with the Left in power, the FN had started its breakthrough. From then until the late 1990s, notwithstanding setbacks, it established itself as a significant political force with a small but active membership of about 40 000, a sophisticated communications apparatus and a populist, nationalistic programme centring on opposition to non-European immigration but not confined to that issue.

Before the disastrous electoral decline caused by the bitter split in the party during the winter of 1998–99, the FN had consolidated its support at roughly 15 per cent of the national vote, drawn from all CLASSES and age-groups, but particularly from the WORKING CLASSES and the unemployed. It had much stronger scores in particular regions and the prospect of further improvement. Its representation in the Assemblée Nationale stood at one or zero, except in 1986–88, when it exceeded 30 thanks to the proportional voting system used experimentally in 1986. It had not improved its very limited representation in the European Parliament since 1984, but the FN has gained many seats on municipal and regional councils. The party continues to exist but as a shadow of its former self. (**Christopher Flood**)

Further reading

DeClair (1999). A useful general study. Davies (1999). Gives particular attention to the party's ideology and political communication.

Front national   1941– 45. The largest of the RESISTANCE movements during the OCCUPATION, it was led by the COMMUNISTS, but included a wide political and ideological spectrum. It tried unsuccessfully to establish a broad political party at the LIBERATION.

Front populaire   See POPULAR FRONT.

Furet, François   1927–97. Historian. His work on the French Revolution of 1789 challenged the prevalent MARXIST interpretations.

Futurism   Futurism was the dominant avant-garde movement in the arts in Italy this century. Founded by the poet Marinetti in 1909, it sought to break with the past and to promote the modern and the new, in particular insofar as they manifested themselves in terms of speed, violence and the technological. Radically iconoclastic, the movement promoted itself with manifestos (the first was in Le FIGARO in 1909) and various staged events, including an exhibition in PARIS in 1912. Its leading exponents were principally painters and sculptors – Umberto Boccioni, Carlo Carrá, Giacomo Balla and Gino Severino – but the movement also included architects – Antonio Sant'Elia – and designers – Fortunato Depero (clothes, theatre décor, advertising).

Key aspects of the movement's aesthetics were the inherent dynamism of objects, which the artist or sculptor should try to bring out in his representation of them, the transforming effect of speed, and the independence of colour as a dynamic and expressive phenomenon. Cars, guns and locomotives are leitmotivs in Futurist art. Marinetti theorized a similar programme in terms of language, taking the page as an artistic unit, using words and typography as fragments, which interacted with each other through juxtaposition and analogy rather than logic. The Futurists' celebration of violence and war can thus be understood both as an expression of the desire to finish with the past and to unleash the dynamism of modern machinery and communications.

Futurism shared with CUBISM an interest in expressing the simultaneity of different aspects of objects and in formal values. Although as an aesthetic movement it did not survive long after the First World War, its influence on later movements (Rayonism and Constructivism in Russia; DADAISM; Vorticism in England) was considerable. But perhaps its most decisive impact was on advertising and graphic design: there were few major innovations in subject and style in French or British POSTER design in the inter-war period that did not owe something to Futurism. (**David Scott**)

Further reading

Apollonio (1973); Hulten (1987). The catalogue of an exhibition held in Venice 1986.

Gabin, Jean   1904–76. Actor. A popular film actor, he appeared in over a hundred films, often playing earthy WORKING-CLASS characters.

Gainsbourg, Serge   1928–91. Singer-songwriter. A non-conformist figure, he courted controversy politically with anti-militarist songs, and morally, with sexual explicitness, exemplified in 'Je t'aime, moi non plus' ('I love you, so do I', 1969) with his wife Jane Birkin.

Gall, France   Born 1947. Pop singer, who established her reputation by winning the Eurovision Song Contest with 'Poupée de cire poupée de son' (Wax doll, rag doll, 1965).

Gallimard, Éditions   Founded 1911. One of France's largest and most respected publishers, with a wide list, including the popular paperback 'Folio', the prestige hard back 'Pléiade' collections, and the literary review, *NOUVELLE REVUE FRANÇAISE*.

Gance, Abel   1889–1981. Film director. He directed numerous films between the wars, the most remarkable of which is the eight-hour historical epic, *Napoléon* (1926).

Garaudy, Roger   Born 1913. Writer. For thirty years after the war, he was the leading COMMUNIST PARTY philosopher. Expelled for his liberal views in 1970, he has since espoused radical versions of CATHOLICISM and then ISLAM.

GATT (General Agreement on Tariffs and Trade) 1947–95. GATT was a series of negotiations between the world's major trading countries, which started in 1947 and ended with the creation of the World Trade Organization (WTO) in 1995. As part of the general attempt to reconsider global co-operation on finance and trade in the aftermath of the Second World War, GATT initially consisted of negotiated reductions of customs tariffs, carried out through a series of 'rounds', each with specific agenda and targets. As in other areas of world politics, France was for a long time a reluctant but ultimately co-operative partner in these negotiations, as successive leaders realized that opening up to world trade was an important way of MODERNISING the French ECONOMY. In the context of European integration, trade policy was increasingly in the hands of the European Community where the French have attempted to impose their priorities.

Tariff negotiations having been highly successful, GATT evolved in two directions in the 1960s. First, negotiations shifted towards other obstacles to trade ('non-tariff barriers'), particularly the very sensitive question of government subsidies. Second, services and cultural products entered the negotiations. Since then, disputes between Europe and America have arisen in GATT and the WTO concerning subsidies in areas such as agriculture and aeronautics. France, promoting what has become known as *l'exception culturelle*, has led opposition to the principle that cultural products, notably films, should be subjected to the same free trade regime as other products. Both GATT and the WTO have come under attack both from the protectionist Right and the Left in France as the expression of an AMERICAN-led GLOBALIZATION of CAPITALISM. **(Bill Brooks)**

Further reading

Eck (1996). A general but detailed introduction to the role of France in world trade and finance. Watkins (1992). A critical introduction to the GATT negotiations.

Gauchisme *Gauchisme* refers to the new extreme left social and political movements which came to the fore in the 1960s, particularly in the explosion of MAY '68, ending what many saw as the dominant position in Left politics in France of the French COMMUNIST party. TROTSKYIST and MAOIST political movements criticized the Soviet Union as a bureaucratic, state capitalist, and revisionist system, rather than a truly communist one, and also the Stalinist views on the need to defend socialism in one country, namely the Soviet Union, which the French Communist Party supported. The Vietnam War, seen as pitting the military and economic might of AMERICA against small Third World country, in the name of freedom and ANTI-COMMUNISM, was another key factor in shaping the *gauchiste* criticism of imperialism.

Gauchisme brought a new set of themes to the fore. The political REVOLUTION to end the power of the BOURGEOISIE as a CLASS was to be accompanied by a cultural revolution in ideas and values, such as auto-gestion (workers' control), anti-psychiatry, ecology, sexual liberation, spontaneity, and direct action. Trotsky's arguments for a 'permanent revolution', and Mao's 'Cultural Revolution', specifically attacking the cultural and ideological power of the bourgeoisie, were particularly important. So were the critiques of CONSUMER society and culture, and the notion of a revolution in

EVERYDAY LIFE, drawn from the works of Guy Debord and the SITUATIONISTS, of Herbert Marcuse (the translation of his *One Dimensional Man* became the best-seller of 1968), and of Henri LEFEBVRE, the MARXIST sociologist.

The writings of Jean-Paul SARTRE became increasingly identified with *gauchiste* themes in the 1960s and 1970s, particularly the violence of the STATE and the IDEOLOGICAL control exerted through bourgeois culture. He famously protested against the banning of the Maoist newspaper *la Cause du peuple* by publicly selling it in person on the streets of PARIS. (**Margaret Atack**)

Further reading

Cohn-Bendit and Cohn-Bendit (1968). A good introduction to the themes, revolutionary aspirations, and virulent rejection of the Communist Party by the most famous of May '68's student leaders, nicknamed *Dany le rouge*, and his older brother. Hamon and Rotman (1987) and (1988). An oral history of the '68 generation and many of the *gauchiste* leaders.

Gaulle, Charles de   See DE GAULLE, CHARLES.

Gaullism   A political movement and IDEOLOGY taking its inspiration from Charles DE GAULLE, who was an Army officer, a Resistance and Liberation leader, Head of the government from August 1944 until January 1946, founder of the first Gaullist political party, the RPF (*Rassemblement du peuple français*) in 1947, founder and President of the FIFTH REPUBLIC from September 1958 until June 1969. His legacy is the belief in French supremacy in European politics, the mobilization of the electorate in a populist movement, and the importance of a strong executive government. His opportunity to found his ideal regime came not in 1945 (when the THIRD REPUBLIC constitution was replaced by a very similar parliamentary regime of the FOURTH REPUBLIC) but in 1958 during the colonial crisis of ALGERIA when he was recalled from self-imposed exile to restore confidence in the government. The Gaullist party ruled for the next decade, with an unprecedented overall parliamentary majority from 1958 until 1973.

De Gaulle also instigated election of the head of state by direct universal suffrage for the first time in 1965 since its introduction in 1848 when Napoleon's nephew had gained a massive majority and used the presidential power subsequently to establish an autocratic anti-parliamentarian regime. Since 1958 the President's special domain is the appointment of the Prime Minister to lead the government and foreign policy. De Gaulle's wish to have France act as a counter-balance to the two superpowers, AMERICA and the USSR, led him to withdraw France from NATO and initiate the construction of an independent NUCLEAR DETERRENT. Gaullist authoritarianism was challenged by the protest movement of MAY '68. The Gaullist movement has been steadily declining since the death of De Gaulle's successor, Georges POMPIDOU, in 1974, with an ageing electorate and challenges from the extreme and moderate Right. (**Máire Cross**)

Further reading

Morelle (1998); and Mazzuccheti and Fredj (1995). Both provide a clear synopsis. Charlot (1971); and Hartley (1972). Both give an analysis of Gaullism in its heyday.

Gender 'Gender' designates not the physical difference between men and women, but the identities attributed to each sex by a given society. Gender is about masculinity and femininity, rather than maleness and femaleness. The French language thus presents an immediate problem: not only is 'genre' – to mean gender in the sense of sex-based identity, rather than grammatical gender – only just creeping into the language, but *masculin* and *féminin* signify both male/female and masculine/feminine. Yet the distinction is important, for history shows that the characteristics ascribed to each sex vary according to needs, desires and power relations within societies.

The definition of gender has changed a great deal in France over the twentieth century, partly in accordance with ECONOMIC needs (e.g. the need for a female workforce during the 1914–18 war extended the notion of acceptable 'femininity'), and partly because gender has been the site of IDEOLOGICAL struggle. Conservative views on gender, inherited from the nineteenth century, represented MASCULINITY as intrinsically strong, protective, oriented towards the public world, and justified women's exclusion from political power and civic rights by defining them as naturally weak, irrational and domestic. Throughout the century, French FEMINISTS have contested the disempowering connotations of traditional 'femininity'. More recently some men (particularly gay men) have begun to re-think the meanings of 'masculinity'. French culture none the less displays a marked commitment to maintaining the 'différence' between the sexes.

Feminism in France has produced conflicting theories of the sex/gender relationship. Simone de BEAUVOIR's *The Second Sex* provided a radical deconstruction of the theory of gender as natural: her memorable maxim '*On ne naît pas femme, on le devient*' (implying that 'femininity' is learnt or imposed rather than innate) could be – and has been – logically extended to the relationship between men and masculinity. Some contemporary feminists follow Beauvoir's social constructionism (e.g. Christine DELPHY), arguing that gender difference has no foundation in nature and has been used primarily to oppress women. The 'differentialists' (IRIGARAY, CIXOUS) insist rather that gender difference has been misrepresented, to the disadvantage of women, but that 'femininity' can be redefined positively and used to contest, indeed to explode, an exclusively *masculine* culture. A post-feminist crisis in French masculinity has been the theme of some recent writing, whether this is viewed as a symptom of desperate anxiety, or as a positive move. (**Diana Holmes**)

Further reading

Badinter (1986). Gives a positive view of the convergence of gender identities in France. Beauvoir (1949). A brilliant and highly influential attack on the theory of 'feminine nature'. Delphy (1993); Ozouf (1995). Explains historically why the French have remained particularly committed to the notion of gender difference. Powrie (1997). Essays on several films connected by a sustained argument on gender anxiety in 1980s France.

Genet, Jean 1910–86. Writer. Relishing his record as a thief and a criminal, he wrote a series of AUTOBIOGRAPHICAL novels, which explored the experience of HOMOSEXUALITY and marginality. His plays address themes of race and violence, as in *Les Nègres* (*The Blacks*, 1959) and power in personal relations, as in *Les Bonnes* (*The Maids*, 1947).

Genette, Gérard   Born 1930. Literary critic. His analysis of narrative discourse has been highly influential in literary CRITICAL THEORY.

Genevoix, Maurice   1890–1980. Writer. His novels of military life in the First World War and post-war country life give vivid and highly detailed descriptions.

Germany   For more than a century and a half, French relations with Germany have been characterized by an ambiguous mixture of respect, rivalry and fear. During the nineteenth century, German philosophers and poets (for example, Goethe, Herder, Hegel and Schiller) both inspired their French counterparts (Michelet, Hugo and others) and were deemed to represent a romantic nationalism which was totally antithetical to the rationalist Enlightenment tradition of France. The expansionist aspirations of Germany after the Franco-Prussian war and German unification (1870–71), leading to the conflagration of the First World War, bred fear and a deep-seated desire for vengeance in France. Yet many were still in thrall to the power of the German military and ideological machine. Tentative steps towards peace between the two nations in the 1920s were shattered with the rise of FASCISM in Germany and the new expansionist aspirations of the Nazis after 1933. A number of French intellectuals of the period (including Pierre DRIEU LA ROCHELLE, Robert BRASILLACH, Louis-Ferdinand CÉLINE and Léon Daudet) looked to German fascism as the solution to the decadence of Western CIVILIZATION. The occupation of France by the invading German army in 1940 epitomized the ambiguous attitude of the French towards their neighbour: the French response was a mixture of willing COLLABORATION with fascism and ANTI-SEMITISM by some and heroic RESISTANCE against them by others. VERCORS' famous novel *Le Silence de la mer* (*The Silence of the Sea*, 1942) depicts both the power and attraction of Germany and the spirit of French resistance against its brutality.

From the ruins of Franco-German relations in 1945, an unprecedented economic and political collaboration has since been fostered within the context of the European Union. Both nations have embraced a new realism founded on the realization that co-operation between them could ensure peace and prosperity at the heart of Europe and put an end to the crises produced by past antagonisms. (**Max Silverman**)

Further reading

Poidevin and Bariéty (1977). Historical overview of Franco-German relations. McCarthy (1993). Collected essays defining different aspects of contemporary Franco-German relations.

Giacometti, Alberto   1901–66. Artist. Best known as a sculptor, his elongated human figures are associated with EXISTENTIALIST ideas on anguish and the solitary nature of human IDENTITY.

Gide, André   1869–1951. Writer. He was a dominant figure of French literature, playing a key role in the review *LA NOUVELLE REVUE FRANÇAISE*. His novels, like *Les Caves du Vatican* (*The Vatican Cellars*, 1914) and *Les Faux-monnayeurs* (*The Counterfeiters*, 1926), deal with problems of personal freedom and fulfilment, which are also central to his published diaries and AUTOBIOGRAPHICAL works. He spoke out on controversial issues, for example, defending HOMOSEXUALITY and denouncing injustice in the French COLONIES, and was awarded the Nobel Prize in 1947.

Giono, Jean   1895–1970. Writer. His many novels of country life established him as a popular 'regional' writer. His strongly PACIFIST views led to him being arrested at the beginning and end of the war. His later novels reflect a more pessimistic view of life.

Girard, René   Born 1923. Philosopher. His analysis of religious and MYTHOLOGICAL themes has focused on the uncomfortable link between desire and violence in human culture.

Giraud, General Henri   1878–1949. Prominent French General. Captured at the Fall of France, he made a daring escape from prison (1942). He was supported by AMERICA as an alternative leader to DE GAULLE, but lacked the political skills to sustain that role.

Giraud, Jean   Born 1938. Cartoonist. A prolific artist in many genres of BANDE DESSINÉE, he is best known, as 'Gir', for his Western series *Lieutenant Blueberry* (from 1963) and as 'Moebius' for his SCIENCE FICTION and fantasy strips.

Giraudoux, Jean   1882–1944. Writer. After writing several novels, his plays, like *La Guerre de Troie n'aura pas lieu* (*The Trojan War Will Not Happen*, 1935), were successful in the 1930s, often using classical stories to explore contemporary issues, about which he was pessimistic. He was briefly appointed Minister for Information (1939–40).

Giroud, Françoise   Born 1916. Journalist. Co-founder of *L'EXPRESS*, she was a noted MODERNIZER of public opinion through various reviews. She served in GISCARD D'ESTAING's government as Secretary for Women (1974) and for culture (1976–77).

Giscard d'Estaing, Valéry   Born 1926. Politician. Leader of the liberal wing of the conservative majority during the 1960s, he served as Finance Minister (1962–66) and was elected President of the Republic (1974–81).

Globalization   Globalization denotes with differing emphases in different cultures and languages an amalgamation of economic, political, social and cultural phenomena connected with the significant democratization or monopolization, depending on the point of view, of technology, finance, and information during the past 20 years. While American commentators generally tend to view the process as positive there is a significant body of INTELLECTUAL opinion in France which views globalization as the threat of a universalist neo-liberalism (*la pensée unique*). Most accept that globalization describes the change from the 'COLD WAR system' to a global market economy, but there is no consensus as to whether the change is good or bad.

French intellectuals argue that globalization is not new but the continuation of a long history. They reflect that during that history much, like American Indians, is destroyed, and they argue that, under the umbrella of globalization, new imperial forces threaten the nation-state and the specific DEMOCRATIC traditions that it has evolved. The idea that the nation-state was the assimilated or assimilating cultural community, the integrated socio-economic community and above all the territorially based sovereign political community is being questioned or undermined. But there is nothing to take its place at the global level. Moreover, globalized media and a global consumer culture impact on individuals and communities, atomizing notions of a general will deeply associated with the French concept of republican identity. Proponents of globalization argue that a global CONSUMER culture, focused on the individual, encourages diversity, multiplicity, hybridity and economic growth. Opponents in France argue that the hegemonic economic power, AMERICA, presides over an arbitrary process.

A crucial aspect the globalization debate centres on equality: access to and exploitation of natural resources, employment opportunities, migrations and the international division of labour, and the distribution of wealth and poverty. The record of nation-states on these matters before globalization tends to suggest that a return to the past is not an option. (**Bill Brooks**)

Further reading

Hirst and Thompson (1996). A critical analysis of the concept in historical perspective. Moreau Defarges (1999). An introduction from an academic who advises the French government on foreign policy.

Glucksmann, André   Born 1937. Philosopher. An activist in MAY '68, he subsequently developed a sharp critique of Left-wing thinkers, articulated in *Les Maître-penseurs* (*The Master Thinkers*, 1977). Identified as a NOUVEAU PHILOSOPHE, he has campaigned on numerous moral and political issues.

Godard, Jean-Luc   Born 1930. Film director. Probably France's best known filmmaker, he was a leader of the NOUVELLE VAGUE (New Wave) with *A bout de souffle* (*Breathless*, 1959). His films increasing combined AVANT-GARDE CINEMA with social and political criticism, and he has never ceased to be provocative and controversial.

Goldmann, Lucien   1913–70. Writer. Romanian-born, he developed a MARXIST form of literary theory, inspired by Georg Lukács, which combined historical and structural analysis. It is exemplified in *Le Dieu caché* (*The Hidden God*, 1955), which studies Pascal and Racine in their seventeeth century context.

Gorz, André   Born 1924. Philosopher. A disciple of SARTRE and long-time member of the editorial team of *LES TEMPS MODERNES*, he has challenged accepted ideas about work and leisure, and been influential in the ECOLOGY movement.

Goscinny, René   1926–77. Cartoonist. Co-author, with Uderzo, of the *Adventures of Astérix the Gaul*, which first appeared in 1959. In 1955, he also created (with Morris) the popular mock-Western character Lucky Luke, 'the man who could draw and shoot faster than his shadow'.

Grammar, grammarians   See STANDARDIZATION (of the French Language).

Grandes écoles   The *Grandes écoles* are ÉLITE higher educational institutions in France. Today there are many such establishments (over 150). The oldest, like *Ponts et chaussées* (civil engineering) and *Polytechnique* (military engineering), date back to the eighteenth century, as does the best-known school in the arts and humanities, the ÉCOLE NORMALE SUPÉRIEURE (ENS); (also known as *Normale sup*), situated in the Rue d'Ulm in Paris. This institution traces its origins back to 1794, during the French Revolution, but the ENS only assumed its name and occupied its current premises during the 1840s. It is renowned mostly for the writers, journalists, philosophers and university teachers that it produced over the years, particularly during the inter-war period, among the most famous being Jean-Paul SARTRE and Raymond ARON, scientists Paul LANGEVIN and Jean Perrin, and writers Paul NIZAN and Robert BRASILLACH. Well-known contemporary intellectuals such as Pierre BOURDIEU, Alain TOURAINE, Régis DEBRAY and Bernard-Henri LÉVY are also all graduates of the ENS. In 1882 Jules Ferry founded another *École normale* at Saint Cloud, just outside Paris, in order to establish a new class of educators, teachers, inspectors and other educational administrators, who would lay the foundations for the secularized Republican educational system conceived at the time. Thus Saint Cloud produced teachers for the primary and secondary system, while the Rue d'Ulm catered more for the élite *lycées* and universities. A further *École normale*, for young women students, was created in 1881 at Sèvres, to provide teachers for the new girls' schools created during this period. After the First World War Sèvres gradually established a research base, most notably for the work of Marie Curie.

   In the twentieth century, there has been a big expansion of the *grandes écoles*. The ÉCOLE *nationale d'administration* was created in 1945 to provide cohorts of high-level civil servants and diplomats. Though the best-known schools are based in Paris, there are networks of institutions in major cities, specializing in particular disciplines or career paths, such as the nine *Instituts d'études politiques* (political sciences) and the growing number of *Écoles supérieures de commerce* (business studies). Admission into all the *grandes écoles* is via highly competitive entrance examinations, but there is also a system of support for candidates from poorer backgrounds (*boursiers*). (**Martyn Cornick**)

Further reading

Bourdieu (1989); Hallmark (1998); Luc and Barbé (1982).

Grands travaux   Although this term is used to refer to major programmes of public works such as the construction of the Channel Tunnel or the TGV (high speed train) network, it has been more closely associated since the 1980s with François MITTERRAND'S programme of architectural projects, the most well known of which are in PARIS. Three of the projects were inherited from his predecessor Valéry GISCARD D'ESTAING:

the *Institut du Monde Arabe* (IMA), a centre for Arab culture situated in a building designed by Jean Nouvel and associates; the *Musée d'Orsay*, a museum of nineteenth-century art housed in the renovated Orsay railway station opposite the LOUVRE; and the *Cité des Sciences*, a modern science museum occupying a transformed building which had originally been designed as a major new abattoir on the outskirts of Paris at La Villette. Mitterrand added several new cultural projects of his own: the *Opéra-Bastille*, the *Cité de la Musique* and the Parc at la Villette, the *Arche de la Défense*, the *Grand Louvre* (necessitating the building of a new Finance Ministry at Bercy), and in his second presidency, the *Bibliothèque de France*. A number of smaller projects were also included, most notably the renovation of the *Galerie de l'Évolution* at the *Muséum National d'Histoire Naturelle*. The president's personal role in the *grands travaux* was widely attacked as being 'monarchical', and opponents criticize his alleged obsession with inscribing his political legacy in stone. Nevertheless, the projects constituted a response to well-established demands in terms of cultural facilities, even though their future running costs will continue to cause problems for the authorities concerned. Responding to criticisms that resources were being concentrated into Paris, the STATE also sponsored a number of projects in the provinces, but these were not so closely identified with Mitterrand. (**Susan Collard**)

Further reading

Collard (1996); Collard (1998). See also the website of the Ministry of Culture: www.culture.fr/culture/historique/index.htm

Grappelli, Stéphane   1908–97. Musician. He was the leading JAZZ violinist from the 1930s, when he partnered the jazz guitarist Django REINHARDT, and during his long career played with most leading musicians internationally, including classical violinist Yehudi Menuhin.

Gréco, Juliette   Born 1926. Singer. Came to fame as an icon of the EXISTENTIALIST movement, her songs and stage persona convey the image of an independent woman.

Greimas, A.J.   1917–92. Linguist. His studies in SEMIOTICS have been particularly influential with cultural critics.

Guattari, Félix   1930–92. Writer. Best known for his work with DELEUZE, their *Anti-Oedipe* (*Anti-Oedipus*, 1972) offered a radical critique of PSYCHOANALYSIS and capitalism.

Guibert, Hervé   1955–91. Novelist. He wrote numerous works before coming to widespread public attention with AUTOBIOGRAPHICAL works exploring the effects of AIDS on the human body and relationships, for example in *A l'ami qui ne m'a pas sauvé la vie* (*For the Friend who did not Save my Life*, 1990).

Guillevic, Eugène   Born 1907. Poet. A lifelong communist, his poems are short and dense, and deal with the experience of art as well as personal and social issues.

Guitry, Sacha 1885–1957. Playwright. Prolific writer of light and entertaining plays, in which he and his wife often took leading roles. He was compromised by his links with COLLABORATIONIST circles during the OCCUPATION. He also directed several films.

Hallyday, Johnny Born 1943. Singer. He established his reputation as a French exponent of rock music, covering American and British songs and introducing their styles of performance into France.

Happiness *(le bonheur)* In France, as in the entire developed world, twentieth-century culture has placed increasing emphasis on the happiness and fulfilment (*épanouissement*) of the individual. The shift of emphasis from the collective good to personal fulfilment is most visible in the case of marriage and the FAMILY. From a practical and economic partnership that integrated the new couple into the wider community and reproduced the next generation, marriage has gradually been transformed into a relationship motivated by sexual love, and evaluated according to its capacity to provide emotional and sexual satisfaction. A study of *petites annonces* (lonely hearts columns) between 1930 and 1977 revealed a significant shift of emphasis from the advertisers' earning capacity and respectability, to their physical attributes and personality.

Both the material austerity of the OCCUPATION (1940–44) and the moralizing, anti-individualist policies of VICHY subordinated personal happiness to collective survival. However, with the economic boom of the 1950s and the development of the CONSUMER society, the pursuit of happiness became both a central theme of modern self-affirmation (see, for example, the immense popularity of Brigitte BARDOT's hedonistic heroine in Roger Vadim's 1956 film *Et Dieu créa la femme*) and a primary means of marketing products. Christiane ROCHEFORT's novels of the 1960s satirize what she presents as the imposition, by the STATE and capitalist industry, of a standardized, repressive model of Happiness (*le bonheur*) designed to divert potentially subversive energies into material consumption and safely privatized pleasures. The counter-culture of the late 1960s and 1970s attempted to reclaim the right to happiness as an insurrectionary demand: *la Révolution doit s'arrêter à la perfection du bonheur* ('the Revolution will stop when perfect happiness is achieved'), as the epigraph for the MAY '68-inspired play *1789* neatly put it. The principle of the individual right to happiness continues to be invoked both for commercial purposes (advertising) and in the cause of political protest (the 1996 defence of the *sans-papiers*; the campaign for the 35-hour week). **(Diana Holmes)**

Further reading

Ariès and Duby (1999); Rochefort (1961); (1963); (1966).

Hardy, Françoise   Born 1944. Singer-songwriter. She established her reputation with 'Tous les garçons et les filles de mon âge' (All the boys and girls of my age, 1962) and has specialized in introspective ballads.

Health   Third in terms of health expenditure among the OECD countries, France has a complex system of health provision which is both public and private. Traditionally, there has been a fierce defence of private practice with freedom of choice for patients and direct access to general practitioners and specialists, medical confidentiality, a fee for service paid directly, and freedom of prescription. Rates of payment per visit and refunds for prescription are settled by the SÉCURITÉ SOCIALE regime, with 99 per cent of doctors affiliated to it, as are the 75 per cent of public sector hospitals and the remaining private clinics. Reform is difficult as the medical and pharmaceutical lobby is strong. There are health inequalities as the minimum life expectancy is higher in some areas, the high expenditure does not result in third best performance – the road accident rate, death from alcohol, tobacco, AIDS and infant mortality figures are higher than rates in comparable countries. Apart from soaring costs due to demographic changes and increased specialization and use of TECHNOLOGY in hospitals, one of the greatest problems is a lack of co-ordination and management of information between different health bodies needed to improve planning in the health service. This is increasingly evident from the political scandals over public health issues which revealed misinformation and inadequate regulation at national and European levels, concerning two modern diseases, AIDS (the case of haemophiliacs infected with contaminated blood in the 1980s) and BSE of the late 1990s and 2000s. The JOSPIN government has attempted to reform the health service by introducing deterrents for patients to curb spending (*tickets modérateurs*) and encouraging the use of generic medicines, by limiting the numbers of students studying medicine and by introducing a *carnet de santé* (health folio) for each citizen to give incentives to share medical information for a more transparent system. (**Máire Cross**)

Further reading

Hirsch (1994). For information on health cost coverage under the *Sécurité sociale* system. Immergut, (1992). For some comparative historical background on the medical lobby in politics.

Henriot, Philippe   1899–1944. Politician and journalist. An extreme right-wing *député* during the 1930s, he became a leading advocate of COLLABORATION, with a regular programme on Radio-Vichy. A close ally of DARNAND, he served as Minister of Propaganda in 1944, before being shot by the RESISTANCE.

Hergé (Georges Rémi)   1907–83. Cartoonist. Belgian-born author of the best-selling *Adventures of Tintin* (from 1929). Drawing on traditional CATHOLIC values, he initially sought to challenge the dominance of American cartoons in Europe, and later used Tintin's travels to encourage better understanding of other peoples. See also BANDE DESSINÉE.

Herriot, Édouard 1872–1955. Politician. Leader of the RADICAL PARTY between the wars, he held several ministerial posts including Prime Minister three times. He was mayor of LYON for 50 years.

Hersant, Robert 1920–96. Publisher. France's biggest press baron during the 1980s and 1990s. He was known for his conservative views and ruthless business methods.

Hocquenghem, Guy 1946–88. Writer. A leading gay activist, he became prominent as a spokesman for the gay rights movement during the 1970s. As well as novels, he has written essays, such as Le Désir homosexuel (Homosexual Desire, 1972).

Holidays Until 1936, annual holidays remained a luxury for those in paid employment, who were reluctant to forego their wages for the time not worked. The turning point in popular holidays came then, with the introduction of congés payés (paid holidays) by the POPULAR FRONT government. This led to the first mass vacations, with emphasis on open-air activities in the mountains or by the sea: walking, cycling, camping and caravanning. The war and post-war hardship delayed the rapid growth of holidays until the 1950s, when the years of prosperity (TRENTE GLORIEUSES) made the means available for many more people to take advantage of their increased leisure opportunities. The 2 million people who went on holiday in 1947 rose to 8 million in 1951, 20 million by 1966, and has now reached a plateau of around 30 million, more than half the population.

Like most other developed countries, France has taken advantage of commercialization and cheap travel (especially by rail and air) to create a holiday industry. The CLUB MÉDITERRANÉE was an early French post-war venture, creating a network of holiday villages, and has been followed by many other companies offering organized holidays. In recent years, perhaps owing to economic difficulties in the 1990s, the number of days people spend on holiday has tended to decline, falling from an average of 27 days per year in 1970 to around 22 days now. However, the variety of holidays has grown, both in France and abroad. Summer holidays have been joined by winter holidays, half-term holidays, and long weekends. And the range of activities available is now virtually limitless as GLOBALIZATION has opened up holidays to international competition. The fermeture annuelle (annual closing) is still a French institution, with the month of August making ghost towns of the larger cities. The numbers in the seaside resorts and countryside swell in proportion, and make the ebb and flow of sortie and rentrée at the beginning and end of the holiday season an annually renewed source of hilarity and indignation on the country's road and rail networks. (**Michael Kelly**)

Further reading

Bodier and Crenner (1996); Donnat (1998a); Rauch (1996).

Holocaust   The Holocaust is the term deployed for the attempted destruction of European JEWS by the Nazis during the Second World War. Within France, it is calculated that 75 721 Jews, mostly foreign-born, were deported; all but 2567 perished. Apologists claim these deaths resulted from German demands. Certainly, in occupied France the Nazis quickly implemented racist measures, but Berlin did not press VICHY to do the same. Under its own volition, the PÉTAIN government passed policies, notably through two *Statut des juifs* (October 1940, June 1941), to seize Jewish property, deprive Jews of French citizenship, and debar Jews from public office. In March 1941, it created a *Commissariat Général aux Questions Juives* (Commision on Jewish Matters) to watch over Jewish affairs. It is sometimes said these measures were designed to resist German meddling and ensure French autonomy. This is partially true, but only meant that the French were doing Hitler's job for him. It is also said these policies reflected a traditional cultural chauvinism distinct from biological racism. Yet historians have emphasized that Vichy's definition of a Jew was indeed racial. Eventually, Vichy colluded in the Holocaust. In 1942, Laval agreed to hand over foreign-born Jews before French ones, a sordid policy that led to the infamous VÉL D'HIV round-up of 16 July when some 16 000 Jews, nearly a quarter of them children, were packed in a Paris sports stadium before being sent to Auschwitz. After 1944, few were prepared to acknowledge the help French authorities had given the Germans but, thanks to the pressure of RESISTANCE organizations and Jewish historians, in the 1980s and 1990s several Vichy officials (Paul Touvier, Maurice Papon, and the Gestapo Klaus BARBIE) were charged with 'crimes against humanity'. In 1992, President MITTERRAND declared 16 July a day of commemoration but, tellingly, refused to accept responsibility for the deportations on behalf of the French state. (**Nicholas Atkin**)

Further reading

Marrus and Paxton (1981).

Homosexuality   For most of the early twentieth century, homosexuality was the 'love that dare not speak its name', generally agreed to be morally and socially unacceptable. Its existence was a well-known secret, recognized and tolerated in private. Many readers might know, for example, that COCTEAU's or PROUST's female protagonists (Gilberte, Albertine) were thinly disguised male lovers. And though Proust depicted homosexual activity in some detail, in *Sodome et Gomorrhe* (*Cities of the Plain*, 1921), only Gide, in *Corydon* (1911) dared to present an open justification of 'pederasty', at the price of widespread disapproval and scandal. The conservative VICHY REGIME brought in legislation to repress homosexual activity, making it illegal for anyone under the age of 21, and banning its public expression. Studies of SEXUALITY in the 1940s, such as the Kinsey Report (1948–53) and BEAUVOIR's *Le deuxième sexe* (*The Second Sex*, 1949), began to open the topic for debate. The provocative novels and plays of Jean GENET and Cocteau's films also helped to legitimize male homosexuality in high culture.

The emergence of gay activism and openly gay popular culture was sparked by the upheavals of MAY '68. These gave rise to a number of militant 'homosexual liberation' groups, initially associated with the small GAUCHISTE groupings of the Far Left, but increasingly spreading to mainstream political and religious movements. During the 1970s, support grew for gay and lesbian rights, often echoing developments in BRITAIN and AMERICA. Prominent writers and intellectuals, including BARTHES and FOUCAULT, publicly revealed their own homosexuality, and explored it in literary and philosophical terms. The first MITTERRAND government repealed the Vichy legislation in 1981, and set the age of consent at 15. Since that time, gay and lesbian currents have been a dynamic component of both high and popular culture, with a thriving press and entertainment scene, as well as writers, such as Hervé GUIBERT, Guy HOCQUENGHEM and Yves NAVARRE, and film-makers, such as Cyril Collard, whose *Les nuits fauves* (Savage Nights, 1992) is widely studied. The industries directed at gay lifestyles (including leisure, fashion and tourism) make the 'pink franc' a significant part of the consumer economy. (**Michael Kelly**)

Further reading

Darier (1987). A useful survey. Martel (1996). A view of gay and lesbian culture. Robinson (1995). An overview of male and female homosexuality in twentieth-century French literature.

Honegger, Arthur 1892–1955. Composer. Co-founder of the 'Group of Six' (1920), he is best remembered for his religious works, including the oratio *Le roi David* (King David, 1924).

Humanism A belief in the importance of human values and human rights. Humanism is often associated with the Renaissance, when human life became accepted as a legitimate and important subject of ART and philosophy in EUROPE, alongside spiritual matters. From the time of the French Revolution (1789), the idea of *les droits de l'Homme* (human rights) has been an important part of the Republican tradition in France. Initially, human rights were seen as a challenge to divine rights, defended by the Monarchy and the Church. But for much of the twentieth century CATHOLICS have also accepted that they can think of themselves as humanists, defending the rights of the human person, which has taken over from the 'human soul' as a focus of concern.

After the conspicuous inhumanities of the Second World War, almost all sections of French opinion were agreed in accepting humanism as a common frame of reference, and this approach became the consensus in international organizations such as the United Nations. During the 1960s, philosophers such as FOUCAULT and ALTHUSSER challenged the prevailing humanist assumptions, arguing that they were purely ideological, and that when they were spelled out, they were too vague and general to have any theoretical value. FEMINIST thinkers challenged humanist ideas on the grounds that they assumed 'Mankind' to be essentially male. Women could only enjoy *les droits de l'Homme* if they modelled themselves on men. More recently, fundamentalist religious groups, especially Catholic and Islamic groups, have argued that humanism undermines spiritual values and the respect due to God. Alongside the broad humanism of the French Republic, there is also a current of secular humanism, which stems from eighteenth- and nineteenth-century philosophers, and which France shares with other European countries. This current presents itself as an alternative to Christianity and often adopts religious practices. Humanist weddings and funerals have achieved some popularity among atheists and agnostics. (**Michael Kelly**)

Humanité, l'   Founded 1904 by Jean Jaurès, it became the official organ of the French COMMUNIST PARTY in 1923, promulgating the party's view on all aspects of life and current affairs. It sponsors an annual festival, which is still a big cultural event.

Hungary   Cultural relations between France and Hungary were particularly important during the inter-war years and in the field of the visual arts: PAINTING, CINEMA and PHOTOGRAPHY. Hungarian artists were deeply influenced by French Fauvism and developed their own national style. Similarly, at the end of the 1930s, they belatedly discovered SURREALISM, which became a powerful influence on Hungarian art. It was after the short-lived Hungarian Soviet led by Bela Kun in 1919, followed by a right-wing dictatorship under Admiral Horthy, that many Hungarian artists and intellectuals left for Western Europe, including Berlin and PARIS. Amongst these émigrés was the painter Lajos Tihanyi and, in his wake, the photographers André Kertesz and BRASSAÏ. Both of these figures helped to pioneer the development of photography as an art-form. In particular, Brassaï specialized in pictures of the capital at night: the districts and activities which were unknown to the population as a whole. Often accompanied by his friends Henry Miller or Raymond QUENEAU, he photographed criminals and prostitutes, all-night bars and brothels, and noctural workers such as sewer-men and market porters.

Hungarians also played a part in the development of French cinema. The Korda brothers worked in Paris briefly, but it was the set-designer Alexander Trauner who was the most influential figure, working particularly with the director Marcel CARNÉ and the script-writer Jacques PRÉVERT. Exiled Hungarians also had an important role in the interwar years as art dealers and literary agents, such as Feri Dobó.

After the Second World War there was a further brief interaction between Hungarian artists and the French before the establishment of the Communist regime in 1947 and the imposition of the Iron Curtain. Further waves of *émigrés* did reach France, both in the period 1945–47 and after the 1956 uprising. (**Nicholas Atkin**)

Further reading:

Hewitt (2000). Includes three important contributions on Hungarian painting and photography.

Hussards, Les   A group of young, right-wing writers, who came to prominence in the period immedately following the LIBERATION. Composed essentially of Roger Nimier, Jacques LAURENT and Antoine Blondin, they derived their name from Nimier's novel of 1948, *Le Hussard bleu* (*The Blue Hussar*).

The Hussards were both politically and aesthetically opposed to the post-war regime which stemmed from the RESISTANCE and Liberation. Politically, they questioned the legitimacy of the claims of the Resistance to be the only authentic voice of France during the OCCUPATION and in their fiction portrayed the period as one of extreme ambiguity, in which genuine believers in the Extreme Right were the moral equals of Resisters. In particular, they denounced the way in which the

Resistance came to dominate the successive governments of the FOURTH REPUBLIC, and, in particular, the process of purges (*ÉPURATION*) which continued until the early 1950s.

Aesthetically, they saw the political dominance of the Resistance as being enshrined in the doctrine of EXISTENTIALISM, with its emphasis on a politically committed literature with a clear moral purpose. Their novels, when not, as in Nimier's *Le Hussard bleu*, specifically questioning the orthodox view of the Occupation, turned deliberately to a challenge to the dominance of history, as in Blondin's *L'Europe buissonnière* (*Truants in Europe*, 1949), or to a literature which was deliberately un-historical and concerned with purely structural issues, as in Laurent's monumental *Les Corps tranquilles* (*Quiet Bodies*, 1949).

The medium to which they had natural recourse was humour, used as both satire against the prevailing political system and as a counter-weight to the high seriousness of the Existentialists. At the same time, they progressively retreated from the immediate post-war world in their fiction into an evocation of the 1920s. Significantly, their increasing alienation from the world of post-war France was embodied in their repeated evocation of the image of childhood. (**Nicholas Hewitt**)

Further reading

Hewitt (1996). A comprehensive account of the 'Hussards'.

Hyppolite, Jean   1907–68. Philosopher. He translated and commented on Hegel's *Phenomenology of Mind*, promoting neo-Hegelian ideas in France. Close to the EXISTENTIALISTS, he became a powerful figure in higher education, and influenced important STRUCTURALIST and POST-STRUCTURALIST writers.

Identity   A French citizen's identity is in the first place supposed to be defined by his or her citizenship of the *république seule et indivisible* (one and indivisible Republic), the proud heritage of the 1789 Revolution. Republican citizenship is predicated on equality before the law and before the STATE, that allegedly makes issues of GENDER and ethnicity of secondary importance. The fact that WOMEN did not get the vote in France until 1944 may suggest that this model is less universal and far-reaching than it proclaims itself to be. Nevertheless it exercises an influence in France without precedent in other Western countries, accounting at least in part for the continuing importance of the state in economic affairs and the comparative lack of headway made by regional autonomist groups. Louis XIV's assertion *L'État, c'est moi!* (I *am* the state) can in principle be uttered by any and every French citizen.

Geography, gender and ethnicity have combined to make this Republican view less monolithic now than at any time before. A sense of attachment to one's native or adopted province is an important factor in many French people's identity, illustrated by the fact that it is almost *de rigueur* for a President of the Republic to have a provincial as well as a Parisian base. (MITTERRAND, geographically as well as domestically bigamous, had two – in Charente and Burgundy). One of the SOCIAL-IST government's first actions in 1981 was to recognize the strength of this attachment and drain a degree of power away from PARIS by the setting-up of elected regional assemblies. The increasingly vocal activities of gay and lesbian as well as women's groups – often necessary to secure in practice that equality to which the Republican constitution entitles them in principle – have served in recent years to focus the debate between Republicanism and *communautarisme*, the latter overlapping in many respects with Anglo-American 'identity politics'. Finally, the powerfully affirmed cultural identities of IMMIGRANT and BEUR groups have mounted a significant challenge to the homogeneity of the state, instanced by the continuing debates over whether Muslim girls should be allowed to wear the veil at school. *Seule* the Republic may remain, but its indivisibility has latterly been much called into question. (**Keith Reader**)

Ideology   Among the most debated and contested of contemporary cultural keywords, especially in France whose revolutionary political legacy and concomitant preoccupation with ideas have placed it consistently at the centre of the stage. Thus. 1789 was an ideological revolution, inspired by Enlightenment thinkers such as Rousseau and proclaiming through the slogan 'Liberty, Equality, Fraternity' what was to become the cornerstone of republican ideology.

Debates over the sense(s) of the term have been particularly acute in the post-Second World War period. This was in the first instance due to the intellectual dominance of MARXISM, for which ideology has always been an important concept. Classically, as in Marx and Engels' *The German Ideology*, it was used to suggest a degree of error. Ideology in this sense was close to false consciousness – a misleading but historically necessary phase which would be supplanted by the correct revolutionary insights of science. Louis ALTHUSSER revised the use of the concept, retaining elements of the earlier sense but drawing on the work of LACAN to see it at the same time as an inescapable condition of human consciousness. Ideology for Althusser is in the first instance a social practice through which the STATE wields symbolic power; but it is also, like the Lacanian IMAGINARY, a necessary part of human beings' apprehension of their existence in society. The 'ideological state apparatuses' that are the school or the law courts are thus sites of struggle rather than straightforwardly repressive encumbrances to be swept away by the revolutionary tide.

The intense debate that surrounded these views in the 1960s and 1970s might now seem to belong to another epoch. The hegemony of electoral DEMOCRACY and the market economy, visible in the trajectory of the *Parti Socialiste* over the past 20 years, has led commentators in France, as elsewhere, to proclaim the 'end of ideology' – by which they generally mean the end of left-wing socialism. Yet DERRIDA's (1993) *Spectres de Marx* and the recent revival of interest in SARTRE – an ideologue of a distinctly non-Althusserian hue – suggest that reports of ideology's demise may still be greatly exaggerated. (**Keith Reader**)

Further reading

Althusser (1971). The most influential of Althusser's texts.

Imaginary   A crucial term in the LACANIAN variant of PSYCHOANALYSIS, whose ramifications have been important in film and cultural studies as much as in clinical practice. The imaginary, for Lacan, is the phase during which the (male) child experiences a fullness of bonding with the mother prior to the access to language and recognition of sexual difference, that come with the access to the symbolic order. This access begins when the child recognizes itself in a mirror as a bodily entity distinct from the mother (who in an optic clearly drawn from artistic representations of the Madonna and child is seen as holding the infant up to the mirror). Yet there is not, and never can be, a once-and-for-all passage from the imaginary to the symbolic. The mirror-image is 'a mirage of the "I"', promising as it does a co-ordination and autonomy which can only ever remain, precisely, imaginary.

What this means in practical terms is that some illusion of plenitude and the overcoming, or even non-existence, of difference in all its manifestations is an inescapable component of human psychic activity, even when we are aware that it can only ever be illusory. The stress on the importance of vision in the passage from imaginary to symbolic largely accounts for the prominence of the concept (less pronounced now than in the 1970s and 1980s) in film studies in particular. It has also found wider use in a sense in many ways cognate with the term 'IDEOLOGY', going beyond the individual psyche to relate to the ways in which human collectivities represent to themselves the conditions of their social existence. Thus, it would be possible to speak of the OCCUPATION as a defining period of the contemporary French imaginary – a sense a long way from Lacan, but much broader in its influence. (**Keith Reader**)

Further reading

Bowie (1991). An excellent short account of Lacan's work.

Immigration   The process by which people move from one country to another and settle there. France experienced relatively high rates of inward migration during much of the nineteenth and twentieth centuries, mainly to compensate for labour shortages arising from low rates of natural population growth and heavy losses suffered in military conflicts. Smaller numbers of international migrants were also admitted as political refugees

During times of economic difficulty, such as the 1930s' slump and the period of globally conditioned restructuring seen since the mid-1970s, immigrants have tended to become targets of popular and political hostility. Labour migration from non-European countries was officially halted in 1974, but family settlement, political refugees and flows of illegal immigrants continued to swell the minority ethnic population. Immigration controls were frequently tightened, particularly by Centre-Right governments, resulting in the SANS-PAPIERS crisis of the mid-1990s.

Until the post-war period, the overwhelming majority of immigrants were of European origin. Today, most immigrants are from Third World countries, foremost among which are former French colonies in North and Sub-Saharan Africa. The largest group originates in the region known as the Maghreb, i.e. ALGERIA, Morocco and Tunisia. Their children, born and raised in France, have fashioned hybrid cultural practices often referred to as BEUR culture. These minorities have been at the centre of public debate over RACE AND ETHNICITY in contemporary France. It is often suggested that the role of ISLAM in the cultural heritage of the countries where they originate makes ASSIMILATION into mainstream French society difficult, but this ignores the generally rapid cultural adaptation of minority ethnic groups. (**Alex Hargreaves**)

Further reading

Hargreaves (1995). A wide-ranging study covering social, cultural and political aspects. Dewitte (1999). A state-of-the art survey of specialist topics.

Imperialism and Empire The distinction between imperialism and COLONIALISM is not always strictly defined, but in its customary and more general usage, imperialism refers to the political, economic and ideological aspects related to the creation and maintenance of an Empire. The word only acquired this meaning from the 1880s onwards, when Franco-British rivalry over territorial expansion in AFRICA led to a period of 'New Imperialism'. The 'scramble for Africa' and expansion elsewhere were justified ideologically by belief in the superiority of Western culture and CIVILIZATION. This led to the *mission civilisatrice* (civilizing mission), which is one of the principal IDEOLOGICAL justifications of French imperialism. By the early twentieth century, the word 'imperialism' had begun to acquire pejorative overtones as a result of its critique by Lenin as the 'highest stage of capitalism'. French imperialism of this period was certainly accelerated by economic considerations and the desire to control markets and raw materials overseas. More recent studies suggest, however, that the flow of capital from the colonies to metropolitan France was not as substantial as was often supposed at the time. Some postcolonial historians have claimed that the rapid expansion of Empire after the annexation of Tunis by the French in 1881 was instead a matter of political strategy in relation to other European countries and of national pride. The encouragement in metropolitan France itself of the idea of an Empire was accordingly very important. Imperial rhetoric and propaganda were common in literature, journalism and popular culture, and the ideological foundations of Empire can be found in notions of cultural and racial superiority. Although before the First World War, the attitude of the French public towards their overseas possessions was largely indifferent, this situation changed after 1918 when it was hoped that the Empire would become a source of national renewal. A previous policy of 'assimilation' of the colonies into the Greater France evolved into 'association', which supposedly permitted greater respect of indigenous institutions. Propaganda in favour of Empire reached a peak in France in 1931 with the Colonial Exhibition in Paris. However, by this time, ANTI-COLONIALISM had already begun to emerge both in the colonies and in France itself, and most of the French Empire was rapidly – and often violently – dismantled in the two decades following the Second World War. (**Charles Forsdick**)

Further reading

Girardet (1972). A comprehensive account of the ideological underpinnings of the French Empire in the period of New Imperialism.

Indo-China In 1887 France consolidated its interests in south-east Asia through the creation of the Indo-Chinese Union (essentially Laos, Kampuchea and Vietnam). French CIVILIZATION was propagated, yet little economic development was permitted other than that which benefited France. In the 1930s, nationalist groups emerged led by Phuc Quoc, a republican, and Hô Chi Minh, founder of the Vietnamese Communist Party (1929) and later leader of the VIÊTMINH (Vietnam Independence League, 1941). Real problems for France arrived after its defeat by Germany (1940), which encouraged Japan's imperial ambitions. Whereas France's AFRICAN possessions rallied to DE GAULLE, in Indo-China VICHYite officials under Admiral Decoux co-operated with the Japanese, crushing nationalists in south Vietnam, leaving rebels in northern strongholds. In March 1945, fearing Indo-China might turn GAULLIST, Japan granted 'independence' to Vietnam under Emperor Boa Dai and to Cambodia under Prince Sihanouk. Boa Dai subsequently made way for Hô Chi Minh (September 1945), who asserted true autonomy. Paradoxically, French sovereignty was reimposed by its colonial adversary, Britain, which was eager to discourage US plans for DECOLONIZATION. Negotiations between Paris and the Viêtminh ensued; it was even agreed Vietnam would remain within the new French Union. Compromise was scuppered by the intransigence of PARIS and local administrators. In 1946 Thierry d'Argenlieu, High Commissioner for the area, claimed Cochin-China in the south and bombed Haiphong. Conflict followed in which France initially triumphed, reinstating Boa Dai as a figurehead (1949).

Circumstances changed thanks to the COLD WAR, which saw the USSR, Communist CHINA (1949) and the PCF recognize the Vietnamese guerrillas. America, once supportive of Asian nationalism, now backed France; yet French forces succumbed to the Maoist tactics of the Viêtnimh, suffering terrible losses at DIEN BIEN PHU (May 1954). The Geneva peace conference (June 1954) divided Vietnam into two: the north under the Viêtminh, the south under US protection. No side accepted these terms, plunging the region into a war that ended in 1975; Cambodia endured fraticidal bloodshed until 1991. France might have withdrawn from Indo-China (1954–55) yet, ominously, its army and colonial officials distrusted metropolitan politicians and were determined not to make concessions to Algerian nationalists. **(Nicholas Atkin)**

Further reading

Clayton (1994); Norindr (1996).

Industrialization Industrialization drove French economic MODERNIZATION after 1945. Until the 1970s' oil crises and beginnings of deindustrialization, industrialization and urbanization characterized France's transformation from overdependence on AGRICULTURE to a modern economy of agricultural, industrial and developed service sectors. Inter-war industrialization was slow, as industrial 'take off' was held back by the agricultural bias of the economy and by outdated business practices and financing, which, with rare exceptions (e.g. in the AUTOMOBILE industry) kept companies small. Business within France and the EMPIRE sustained this level of industrialization and France was largely isolated from international trade. Recession in the 1930s further slowed industrial growth, and government instability and *laissez-faire* economics gave no real support for industrialization despite the gap between France, on the one hand, and Britain and Germany, on the other. Industrialization started properly with economic reconstruction after 1945, as government identified priority sectors (such as steel, chemicals and transport) through PLANNING. Agriculture modernized through mechanization, fertilizers and land redistribution, and rural depopulation accelerated as workers migrated to towns and industry. Growth in the period 1945–65 was essentially industrial, state-led and spurred by DECOLONIZATION and entry into the Common Market. From 1958, GAULLIST industrial policy helped guarantee France's independence commercially in the Common Market and militarily: in the 1960s the miltary-industrial complex developed around the nuclear industry, aerospace, electronics and armaments. DE GAULLE realized that France needed strategic industries and supported struggling sectors (computing, shipbuilding, steel). Under POMPIDOU, industrialization remained a priority as France still lacked large industrial companies capable of European and world competition, and under GISCARD D'ESTAING France identified niche sectors and 'national champion' firms. Since the mid-1970s, recession has hit traditional industries hard, leading to deindustrialization in certain regions and sectors. The primacy of services in the economy suggests France may be entering a post-industrial era. (**Hugh Dauncey**)

Further reading

Lane (1995). A comparative treatment of industrial organization.

Industry Ministry   The Industry Ministry has occupied a precarious position in governments. INDUSTRIALIZATION has been a state priority since 1945, becoming an imperative under DE GAULLE and POMPIDOU, and although during economic crises government has attempted to facilitate restructuring of French industry, the industry portfolio has been undermined by national PLANNING, nationalized industries and the pre-eminence of the Economics and Finance Ministry in ECONOMIC POLICY. Post-1945, industrial reconstruction and industrialisation were led essentially by the national Plan; the Industry Ministry was responsible more for technical control of industry and for managing the energy sector. Nationalized industries and the public sector found their natural contact was the Finance ministry, and the industry portfolio only occasionally acquired priority, for instance under MENDÈS-FRANCE (1954–55). De Gaulle's return in 1958 stimulated national programmes of technological and industrial development in the space, nuclear and defence sectors but these were led by sectoral agencies rather than the Industry Ministry. As industries such as iron, steel and coal suffered in the recession of the 1970s and early 1980s the industry ministry managed their decline, although under Pompidou and GISCARD D'ESTAING the portfolio had expanded to cover industrial and scientific development.

In 1981 the Industry Ministry became infamous for the 'battle of Poitiers', where Japanese videoplayers were stockpiled in an attempt to limit imports. Links between industry and TECHNOLOGY were reflected by the creation of the *Ministère de l'industrie et de la recherche* under CHEVÈNEMENT in 1982, but the industry portfolio remained ill-defined. The industry portfolio has rarely been the sole concern of a ministry: during the 1980s and 1990s industry was combined frequently with responsibility for PTT, tourism, and trade. In 1997 the industry portfolio was subsumed within the *Ministère de l'économie et des finances*, reflecting its dependence on government spending. **(Hugh Dauncey)**

Further reading

Green (1981). Government policies in the 1970s to help industry adapt to the oil crisis.

Inflation   Inter-war and post-war France suffered periodically from serious inflation provoked by internal or external causes. Reconstruction in 1919 and 1945 fuelled price rises, as did rapid growth and INDUSTRIALIZATION, a stationary working population, war in Korea and DECOLONIZATION during the 1940s and 1950s. During the 1960s moderate inflation was accepted amid general prosperity but minor rises in unemployment and social discontent led to the economically inflationary events of MAY '68. Oil price rises in the 1970s provoked rapid inflation. Between 1973 and 1974 inflation doubled, reaching almost 20 per cent, through oil price increases and wage hikes. By mid-July 1975, recession had raised unemployment to over 1 million after almost full EMPLOYMENT in the post-war period and triggered austerity measures including price freezes and reduced public spending. Stagflation in the 1970s broke with the growth and prosperity of the *TRENTE GLORIEUSES* (1945–75) and stymied GISCARD D'ESTAING's social reformism, helping elect MITTERRAND in 1981. The ECONOMY's exposure to external pressure through oil prices emphasized the importance of nuclear energy. In 1981 the SOCIALIST administration adopted different ECONOMIC policies to resolve low growth and high unemployment, but stimulation of demand only encouraged continued inflation and affected employment little, leading to a programme of 'austerity' in mid-1982. This change of policy, motivated by inflation and at the cost of jobs, was experienced by some socialist voters as a betrayal. Since 1983, Left and right-wing governments have followed very similar anti-inflation policies. Within the context of 1990s European economic and monetary integration France chose to 'shadow' the German economy, maintaining a strong FRANC and low inflation in a strategy of competitive deflation. The *franc fort* has had serious social costs as France has tried to foster productivity, and unemployment has remained higher than in the UK and Germany. **(Hugh Dauncey)**

Further reading

Eck (1988). The French economy since the Second World War, covering government policy, inflation, industrialization.

Information technology   France realized the backwardness of her computing and information technology in the mid-1960s, and since then has stimulated information technology to protect the continuing MODERNIZATION of French industry, business, bureaucracy and society, and to develop French expertise in strategic technologies. During the 1960s, DE GAULLE's volontarist modernization of industry and business revealed the weakness of French computing, and created the *Plan Calcul*, a state-run programme fostering French (super)computing capacity to compete with American domination of emerging information management technologies. The Nora-Minc report on *The Computerisation of Society* (1977), predicted the convergence of computing and telecommunications, and the government stimulated state-led programmes of technological development such as the MINITEL. The Minitel French telematics system, available from the mid-1980s, provided commercial, municipal, administrative and other information services via telephone networks. The French public's experience of Minitel facilitated the rising importance of information technology at work, although home-use of the Minitel inhibited household personal computer ownership in the 1990s. It also slowed the take-off in France of the Internet. French bureaucracy has been modernized partly by information technology, although the state has been embarrassed (after the failed *Plan Calcul*) by the lack of French hardware, and by domination of software by English-language US programming giants. POST-MODERN perspectives on information technology suggest that it changes power relationships between government and governed, and between the STATE and corporations. In France's centralized political and cultural system, information technology in general, but in particular use of the Internet, can facilitate democracy and transparency, as evidenced by the importance of websites in the strikes of November 1995. But the French state itself has also fostered the French public's information maturity by launching ambitious plans for information superhighways. (**Hugh Dauncey**)

Further reading

Durand and Taylor (1990). Discusses how new technology changes traditional structures of work.

Institut de France   The *Institut de France* is a national institution comprising five separate academies known as 'classes': the ACADÉMIE FRANÇAISE, the *École National Supérieure des Beaux Arts*, the *Académie des Inscriptions et Belles Lettres*, the *Académie des Sciences* and the *Académie des Sciences Morales et Politiques*. (see ACADÉMIES). Founded in 1795 by the *Convention*, its purpose was to replace the role of the royal academies in encouraging scientific and cultural activity for 'the glory of the Republic'.

Members are elected by their peers and all belong both to the *Institut* and to one or more of the academies, the most well-known and influential of which is the *Académie Française*, because of its role as official guardian of the French language. Created by Cardinal Richelieu in 1635, it is also responsible for the permanent revision of the *Dictionnaire de l'Académie française*, now in its 9th edition. Members are not all literary figures, some represent the Church, the Army, the diplomatic service, medecine and journalism, but it was not until 1980 that the first woman, Marguerite YOURCENAR, was elected to the *Académie Française*, since when only two more women have been thus honoured. Members are known as *les immortels* because of the motto which figures on the seal given to the academy by Richelieu: *À l'immortalité* (To Immortality).

The *Institut* is located in the Palais de l'Institut situated opposite the LOUVRE facing the Pont des Arts on the Quai Conti. This palace was originally built for the Collège des Quatre Nations as Mazarin's legacy to Louis XIV, and included his personal library, now known as the Bibliothèque Mazarine. After Napoleon decided in 1805 to use the college building for the *Institut de France*, the chapel was converted into the main meeting chamber under the dome where members of all five academies gather together formally once a year, wearing the distinctive green ceremonial clothing that dates back to the Consulate. (**Susan Collard**)

Further reading

See the website of the Académie française: www.académie-française.fr

Integration   The participation of different members of society in shared institutions and processes. In current usage, it refers particularly to the social incorporation of minority ethnic groups. This meaning came to the fore during the late 1980s and early 1990s following the politicization of IMMIGRATION, RACE AND ETHNICITY. Many on the Right and extreme Right of the political spectrum questioned the willingness or ability of immigrant minorities of Third World origin to adapt to French norms. These anxieties were closely connected with fears of ISLAM. In 1989 the SOCIALIST-led government of Michel ROCARD responded to these fears by announcing the creation of the *Haut Conseil à l'Intégration* (High Council for Integration) to advise on policy measures aimed at improving the integration of minority groups. Since then, there has been a broad consensus among all the main political parties except for the Extreme Right *FRONT NATIONAL* on the desirability of integration as a policy goal in the field of ethnic relations. At the same time, there has been a growing emphasis on the need to combat social disadvantage and racial discrimination if this goal is to be achieved.

Considerable ambiguity and ambivalence surround the question of cultural differences. Conservative politicians often use 'integration' as a euphemism for 'ASSIM-ILATION', implying that minorities must abandon distinctive cultural traditions and adopt the cultural norms dominant in France. Leftward-leaning political actors are more inclined to argue for a model of integration in which social participation goes hand in hand with respect for minority cultures. Some see integration as a process of mutual adaptation between minority and majority ethnic groups in which two-way cultural exchanges are a normal part of social interaction. (**Alec Hargreaves**)

Further reading

Dewitte (1999). An in-depth survey by expert contributors.

Integrism   The term *intégrisme* refers to fundamentalist CATHOLIC traditionalism, particularly as represented by the Society of St Pius X and its followers. The Society was founded by Archbishop Marcel Lefebvre (1905–91) in 1970 with the creation of a seminary at Ecône in Switzerland. It rejects the liturgical and other reforms introduced by the Second Vatican Council (1962–64). The Society trains priests to exercise their functions in the most traditional way, including retention of the Latin Mass. It also defines itself as a provider of traditional Christian education. Its stance has led to conflict with the Catholic hierarchy. The seminary was officially suppressed in 1975 and attempts were made to prevent the ordination of priests there. In 1976 Mgr Lefebvre was forbidden to administer the sacraments. Later, he was interrogated in Rome several times. This did not prevent him from consecrating four bishops in 1988, as a result of which the movement was, in effect, pronounced schismatic and its members excommunicated (although the Society denies that it is schismatic or that it has been excluded from the Church). Nevertheless, it has established itself on four continents. It has six seminaries (one in France), 130 priories (37 in France), 50 primary schools (18 in France), about 20 secondary schools (19 in France), and three universities (two in France). There are links with other traditionalist communities within several monastic and conventual orders. It also organizes various charitable and professional associations. It claims that the Church has lost its way, whereas the Society has remained true. It is resolutely anti-ecumenical. It detests the modern world for its acquisitive materialism, its licentiousness and its desertion of the faith. Although the Society's objectives are not political, its traditionalism extends to the reactionary politics of many of its members. There are ties with extreme right-wing organizations ranging from small monarchist groups – Mgr Lefebvre himself was prone to dwell nostalgically on the traditional link between the Cross and the Crown in France – to the much larger Front National, within which the Catholic tradition-alist wing has considerable influence. (**Christopher Flood**)

Further reading

Very little is available in English, but useful information, not dealing specifically with France, can be found in the following partisan sources:
Lefebvre and Laisney (1998). Nemeth, (1994).

Intellectuals   The noun *intellectuel* has existed in French for slightly more than a century. It entered general use in the 1890s in order to designate those who supported Dreyfus and claimed to defend the rights of the individual against the institutions and vested interests of the state – the judicial system, the army, and the Catholic Church. Within 30 years in the aftermath of the First World War, the meaning of the word began to broaden quickly. For the majority, the *intellectuels* became those who willingly participated in the socio-political, religious, and philosophical debates of their time. Frequently WRITERS, their theories were developed and debates conducted in essays and the pages of newspapers and periodicals, many of which ran to a hand-ful of issues only. All shades of opinion were represented, notable participants being BARRÈS and DRIEU LA ROCHELLE for the Right, NIZAN and BARBUSSE for the Left, MASSIS and BERNANOS for conservative CATHOLICISM. Some remained entrenched in extreme views but increasingly the *intellectuels* became associated with left-wing, liberal values especially as FASCISM threatened to sweep across EUROPE. During the second half of the century this pattern continued, but with developments in areas such as philosophy, LINGUISTICS, psychology, and ANTHROPOLOGY, and as the debates around EXISTENTIALISM and STRUCTURALISM, for example, amply demonstrate, the *intellectuels* were frequently – but by no means always – less narrowly partisan. In this way they were closer to the view of the *intellectuels* as independent, critical spirits already outlined by Julien BENDA in his essay *La Trahison des Clercs* (*Treason of the Clerks*, 1927). Benda had argued that intellectuals could only participate in public debate if guided by absolute, Platonic values, and that to enter the arena of politics directly was a betrayal of their true role. (**John Flower**)

Further reading

Goetschel and Loyer (1995); A useful general survey. Forbes and Kelly (1995); Reader (1987). A detailed study of the post-1968 situation.

Internet   France realized the importance of the Internet later than the US and UK. The MINITEL complicated France's espousal of the Internet, but government initiatives to accelerate use of the Web have helped convert the public, although the Internet is sometimes considered another 'Anglo-Saxon' threat to FRENCH LANGUAGE, culture and business. The Minitel telematics system, which made France a world leader in household use of telematics in the 1980s paradoxically slowed France's acceptance of the Internet. Although French citizens were aware of electronic information services and more accustomed to their use, Minitel's success meant that people saw little use for on-line services through home computers, especially since the terminal was initially distributed free. In the mid-1990s government reports on the Information Superhighway highlighted France's need to catch up in using the Internet, and the state initiated ambitious plans to equip schools and universities with computers, and targeted wiring every French home by 2015. A major difficulty for domestic use of the Internet was that home-ownership of PCs was significantly lower than in the UK and USA, and service providers and services were relatively slow to appear. Minitel and the Internet initially cohabited uneasily, but in the late 1990s Internet use accelerated, after support from governments of Right (JUPPÉ, 1993–97) and Left (JOSPIN, from 1997), and after major strikes in 1995 had publicized the Internet by communicating via websites. A prime political concern was that French republican equality could be broken by dividing society into information-rich and information-poor. Thus among other initiatives to introduce a wider public to the web, in 2000 *La Poste* launched the *Cyberposte* project, allowing value-for-money web-access in selected post offices. The French STATE has also been worried by the difficulty of regulating the Internet and by issues of encryption. (**Hugh Dauncey**)

Further reading

OECD (1998). On French videotext, Internet and electronic commerce.

Intertextuality   The concept of intertextuality emerged in France in the late 1960s and has become an important way of thinking about how a literary work is produced and takes on meanings. Roland BARTHES can be credited with first developing the concept with his view of a 'text' as a network of intersecting writings which are drawn from a variety of sources, already familiar to reader and AUTHOR. The author is no longer the sole arbiter of a text's meaning but rather a figure who draws together and arranges materials from elsewhere. In this way, literature becomes a form of repetition where influential narratives or myths from the past are recycled in later texts in a modified version. Such recycling can be more or less deliberate, with writers and film-makers highlighting, sometimes in a playful manner, how we borrow and rework texts from the past. One good example from popular culture could be the adaptation of Edouard Rostand's successful play *Cyrano de Bergerac* (1897) as a Hollywood comedy, *Roxanne* (1987), starring Steve Martin.

It is through such combinations and juxtapositions that new relations are created between literary texts and cultural narratives. This can lead to a richer reading experience as allusions and references to an eclectic range of literary and non-literary texts are identified. Critics who engaged in intertextual analysis of literary works reveal how we consciously and unconsciously bring our own cultural experiences and knowledge to bear on the reading process. Reading contexts change over time and what a reader of the 1930s and a reader of the 1990s make of the same text can be radically different. In a sense, attention to intertextuality emphasizes how texts are constantly 're-written' as they are re-read, re-produced and re-interpreted by subsequent communities of readers. (**Claire Gorrara**)

Further reading

Webster (1990). An introduction to some aspects of literary theory.

Ionesco, Eugène   1912–94. Playwright. Romanian-born pioneer of the Theatre of the Absurd (*NOUVEAU THÉÂTRE*), with *La cantatrice chauve* (*The Bald Prima-donna*, 1950), which is still running in PARIS. His often grotesque and SURREAL plays are still widely performed.

IRCAM – *Institut de Recherche et de Coordination Acoustique/Musique*   Workshop for experimental music research in PARIS, founded by Pierre BOULEZ in 1975.

Irigaray, Luce   Born 1932. Philosopher. Leading exponent of WOMEN's writing, inspired by Freud and LACAN. Her books, including *Speculum de l'autre femme* (*Speculum of the Other Woman*, 1974), explore the links between BODY, mind and spiritual dimensions.

Islam   Dominant religion in the Arab world and surrounding regions, now practised by a significant minority in France. In Islamic countries ruled by France during the colonial era, Islam often served as an emblem of resistance to French domination, notably in ALGERIA. Since DECOLONIZATION, IMMIGRATION from North and Sub-Saharan Africa, together with other mainly or partially Islamic countries, has led to the settlement of a growing Muslim minority in France. Roughly 4 million strong, Muslims now constitute the country's second largest religious faith, smaller than the Catholic population, but significantly larger in number than PROTESTANTS, JEWS and Buddhists.

Compared with adherents of other religious faiths, Muslims in France are organizationally weak. This is partly due to the relatively recent growth of the Muslim minority and the generally low socio-economic and educational backgrounds of the labour migrants who formed its initial core. In addition, Muslims are divided by doctrinal, national and other differences, which have often given rise to organizational rivalries. Militant and sometimes violent Islamist (Islamic fundamentalist) political movements in a number of predominantly Muslim countries have helped to generate negative stereotypes of Islam among France's majority ethnic population, placing the Muslim minority at a further disadvantage.

Muslims have often been perceived as a threat to the legal code of LAÏCITÉ, but these fears are largely misplaced. Very few Muslims in France have any sympathy with Islamist movements. Most respect the prevailing norms in France, including those associated with *laïcité*, but they have yet to share in the benefits enjoyed by other religious faiths, such as state funding for religious schools. (**Alec Hargreaves**)

Further reading

Boyer (1998). A thorough, well-documented study. Cesari (1998). Focuses on the evolution of Islam among second- and third-generation members of minority ethnic groups.

Jacob, François　Born 1920. Scientist. He made important discoveries in biochemistry and genetics, popularised in *La Logique du vivant* (*Living Logic*, 1970). He was awarded the Nobel Prize in 1965.

Jarre, Jean-Michel　Born 1948. Musician and composer. He has successfully mixed popular and classical styles, using technology with ingenuity. His best-known album remains the innovative *Oxygène*, 1976, which was a world-wide hit.

Jazz　This musical genre, developed in AMERICA, was introduced into France after the First World War. Initially seen as big band music with an element of improvisation, it developed towards freer 'hot' small-group music, inspired by Louis Armstrong and popularized for example by Django REINHARDT and Stéphane GRAPPELLI. Considered decadent by VICHY and the Nazi occupying forces, jazz returned with great vigour in 1945, in the form of 'swing' and 'bebop', championed by EXISTENTIALISTS and LEFT BANK enthusiasts like Boris VIAN.

In the libertarian 1960s, 'free jazz' was embraced, in the style of Miles Davis. Despite its American associations, jazz began to attract public subsidies, recognized as a performance art as well as commercial entertainment. A National Jazz Orchestra was founded in 1986. There is a growing body of music criticism and scholarship dealing with jazz in France.

Jeanmaire, Zizi   Born 1924. Dancer and singer. After beginning in opera, she appeared as a dancer in several Hollywood films and had a successful MUSIC-HALL career in the 1950s and 1960s. She took over the Casino de Paris venue with her husband Roland Petit.

Jeanne d'Arc   Jeanne d'Arc (1412–31), also known as 'la Pucelle', was a girl in a medieval man's world whose inspirational if unorthodox leadership contributed decisively to the ending of English dominion in France and the country's ultimate unification. The events of her short life – Domrémy and the 'voices', raising the siege of Orleans, crowning Charles VII at Reims, wounded at Compiègne, tried and burned at the stake at Rouen – are both national history lesson and *image d'Epinal* where fact becomes myth. Rehabilitated by the Church in the 1450s, variously represented thereafter as peasant, mystic, warrior and cross-dressing iconoclast, Jeanne was an object of popular piety long before her canonization (1920), especially in Lorraine where her likeness vies with traditional roadside *calvaires*. She acquired greater national prominence between 1871 and 1914 in lithographic or bronze reductions of works representing her *en sublime*, holding the royal standard, eyes raised heavenward (Ingres, 1854), or triumphantly equestrian (Frémiet 1874).

A patriotic rallying-point in 1914–18, her ideological polyvalence re-emerged during the Second World War. To the Joan of PÉTAINIST rural Catholic orthodoxy, COMMUNISTS and GAULLISTS opposed the RESISTANCE heroine who would drive out the foreign invader, while a pro-German collaborationist poster superimposed her martyrdom on the Allied bombing of Rouen. More recently, the Rue Jeanne d'Arc in PARIS's thirteenth *arrondissement*, complete with statue and buildings picked out in royalist motifs, housed the local offices of the extreme Right *FRONT NATIONAL*. The object of international consecration by writers and musicians as varied as Schiller and Shaw, Tschaikovsky and HONEGGER, Péguy, CLAUDEL and ANOUILH, Joan is also an ionic cultural product, a star of stage and screen. Over 20 film-makers, from Meliès (1900) and Cecil B. de Mille (1917) via Dreyer (1928) and Premminger (1957) to Rivette (1997) and BESSON (1999) have recreated her life, while reflecting their own age. A 'site' of problematic sexual 'Otherness', Joan offers a more compellingly contemporary mirror than France's republican MARIANNE. **(Bill Kidd)**

Further reading

Warner (1981).

Jews   See JUDAISM AND JEWISHNESS.

Joan of Arc   See JEANNE D'ARC.

Joliot-Curie, Irène and Frédéric   1897–1956, 1900–58. Scientists. Irène, daughter of Marie and Pierre CURIE, married Frédéric Joliot, and together they made important discoveries in atomic physics. Both played important roles in developing France's atomic energy industry, and were active in the COMMUNIST PARTY and the World Peace Movement. They were jointly awarded the Nobel Prize for Chemistry in 1935.

Jospin, Lionel   Born 1937. Socialist politician. A university lecturer by profession, he served as Minister for Education (1988–92) and stood unsuccessfully for President in 1995. He was appointed Prime Minister in 1997.

Jouissance   *Jouissance* is one of those words that cannot be fully and adequately translated. It means extreme pleasure, enjoyment (as in *jouissance de la vie*, enjoyment of life) and it also means sexual orgasm. Roland BARTHES in *Le Plaisir du texte* (*Pleasure of the Text*, 1973) plays on the word's ambiguity to distinguish between two kinds of reading. On the one hand, for Barthes, there is the *pleasurable* text (*texte de plaisir*) that conforms to familiar patterns, reassures and contents the reader by, for example, telling a story of a recognizable kind. On the other hand, the more formally adventurous *texte de jouissance* upsets the reader's expectations, demands total, close attention, produces a shock of pleasure that is (Barthes implies) erotic in its intensity. The text's formal qualities, rather than its subject, create a quasi-sexual reading experience, a challenging, subversive encounter different not just in degree but in kind from (what Barthes implies is) mere comfortable enjoyment of a book.

The second major use of the word in French culture has been within feminist theory. Both Hélène CIXOUS and Luce IRIGARAY have argued that sexual pleasure (*jouissance*) is differently structured for each sex, and that in cultures monopolized by men, the more genitally located, single-climax male experience of orgasm has determined not only the representation of sexuality, but also the whole shape of relationships, cultural forms and language itself. For Irigaray, women's multiplicity of erogenous zones stands metaphorically for their potential to relate differently (more openly, less proprietorially) to other people, and to create new, less linear forms of language and writing. Cixous also connects women's *jouissance* to what she terms the 'feminine IMAGINARY' and 'women's libidinal economy', though she also insists on the availability to men of 'feminine' ways of relating and creating. Both writers use *jouissance,* as Barthes does, to signify not orgasm in the narrow sense but a way of apprehending the world intensely, actively, erotically. (**Diana Holmes**)

Further reading

Barthes (1973a); Cixous (1974). Reproduced in several anthologies of feminist writing. Irigaray (1977). Sellars (1991). An excellent introduction to Cixous and Irigaray.

Journalism   Initially the collective term for newspapers, since the mid-nineteenth century 'journalism' refers more generally to the professional activities of journalists. In parallel with the development of the MEDIA, its meaning broadened to embrace not only print media, but also news reporting on RADIO, TELEVISION and other electronic media. As a result of technological, cultural and commercial change in the communications industry, it has become increasingly difficult to draw the dividing line between journalism, information science, public relations and advertising.

From its beginnings, journalism lacked prestige in France. In the eyes of impoverished nineteenth-century writers aspiring to literary fame, it was a source of income, but a second-rate occupation. Incorporating all manner of activity, from typesetting and printing to PHOTOGRAPHY and reporting, yet requiring no specific qualification, journalism lacked status. With INDUSTRIALIZATION however, it became a regular form of employment for increasing numbers of WORKERS who developed a sense of professional identity and purpose: to inform the citizens of a DEMOCRACY. The increased economic and political power of the industry made the profession more attractive, but employment and intellectual property rights were not secured until 1935, when the first union (the *Syndicat National des Journalistes*) achieved its goal of formal establishment of a card-carrying profession with legal entitlements.

Television has brought to a few, highly visible journalists, such as Christine Ockrent, Anne Sinclair and Patrick Poivre d'Arvor, immense influence and celebrity status. However, at the close of the twentieth century, surveys revealed that the French public have a poor opinion of journalists. Television journalists in particular are criticized for lacking independence, for collusion with politicians, and being susceptible to corruption. The French envy the AMERICAN reputation for investigative journalism and challenging the establishment. Significantly they do not have their own terms for reporter and interview. (**Pam Moores**)

Further reading

Feyel (1999). Historical textbook.

Journal officiel   The paper in which all French official texts and decisions are recorded.

Judaism and Jewishness   The emancipation of the Jews in 1791 was on the condition that they renounce their status as a separate community and accept their position as individual citizens. During the nineteenth century, the majority of Jews in France were eager to embrace this path of acculturation and ASSIMILATION within the framework of Jacobin republicanism. Hence Franco-Judaism, as it developed during the years of the THIRD REPUBLIC (1871–1940), was a distinctive attempt to dovetail a concept of Judaism with the demands of integration in the republic. The result was a largely secularized form of Judaism.

The arrival of Jewish immigrants from Central and Eastern Europe following the pogroms in the last decades of the nineteenth century and the beginning of the twentieth century – poorer, more 'oriental' in appearance, more overtly religious and often speaking Yiddish – was seen by many established Jews in France as antithetical to the model of Franco-Judaism. Yet this influx of Ashkenazi Jews reinvigorated a Judaism which was becoming increasingly secularized. The rise in ANTI-SEMITISM in the same period (marked especially by the Dreyfus Affair at the end of the nineteenth century and then later by virulent campaigns against prominent Jews such as Léon BLUM during the 1930s) was a more significant threat to the secularised model of Franco-Judaism, while collaboration with the Germans by the VICHY state during the Second World War broke with the republican contract completely.

Since 1945 a different version of Franco-Judaism has emerged. It has been influenced partly by the influx of Sephardi Jews from North Africa, who have been far less reticent about manifesting their Jewishness in the public sphere than preceding generations of Jews. But it has also been shaped by the need to come to terms with memories of the HOLOCAUST (now commonly known as the Shoah since the appearance of the epic film of the same name by Claude Lanzmann in 1985) and by the desire among many younger Jews to incorporate a sense of Jewish culture and history into a more multi-dimensional concept of identity. Attachment to France amongst present-day Jews has not necessarily been dimmed but, for many, blind faith in the republican brand of assimilation and equality is now viewed more sceptically. (**Max Silverman**)

Further reading

Benbassa (1999). Comprehensive historical overview of the situation of Jews and Judaism in France. Birnbaum (1992). Detailed survey of French anti-Semitism from the 1930s to the present.

Juppé, Alain   Born 1945. GAULLIST politician. He held several government positions, including Foreign Minister (1993–95) and was Prime Minister (1995–97).

Kojève, Alexandre   1902–68. Philosopher. His seminars on Hegel in the 1930s were influential in several post-war INTELLECTUAL circles, especially in his analysis of the master–slave relationship. For most of the post-war period, he held a senior post in the civil service.

Kristeva, Julia   Born 1941. Writer. A leading literary theorist in the 1970s, she examined the relations between language and human SUBJECTIVITY. She trained as a PSYCHOANALYST, and has most recently presented influential studies of national and ethnic identity, including *Étrangers à nous-mêmes* (*Strangers to ourselves*, 1988) which draws on her experience as Bulgarian émigré.

Lacan, Jacques 1901–81. Psychoanalyst. An early exponent of Freud in France, he developed a difficult and provocative account of mental development, and the unconscious, using the insights of Hegelian philosophy and linguistic analysis.

Lacroix, Christian Born 1951. Fashion designer. Best known for his spectacular and luxurious presentations.

Lagrange, Léo 1900–40. Socialist politician. Affectionately remembered for his role as Under-Secretary of State for Sport and Leisure in the FRONT POPULAIRE government (1936–37, 1938), when he introduced reforms in sport and popular tourism, particularly Ski Schools and a Sports Certificate.

Laguiller, Arlette Born 1940. Far Left politician. A TROTSKYIST activist and leader of the *Lutte ouvrière* movement, she has stood for President four times, receiving up to 5.3 per cent of the votes.

Laïcité The separation of the STATE from religious institutions and a policy of neutrality towards them. After a century of rivalry and instability in relations between the French state and the CATHOLIC church, dating from the revolution of 1789, their separation was legally codified in 1905.

This formal separation is in practice less watertight than it may appear. Although religious organizations have no official standing within the institutions of the state, which in turn plays no role in organized religious bodies, public subsidies help to pay the running costs of a substantial number of Catholic and JEWISH schools on condition that they agree to teach the national curriculum. When, during MITTERRAND's presidency, the Left attempted to end these arrangements in 1984, it was forced by huge public demonstrations to retain them. Even the formal separation of church and state does not apply in ALSACE and Lorraine, which were under German administration when the 1905 law was passed. When these regions, lost in 1871, were reunited with France in 1918, institutional and financial links between the French state and the Catholic, Protestant and Jewish religions were reinstated and they remain in force today.

IMMIGRATION from countries where ISLAM is the main religion has now brought a large Muslim minority to France. Girls wearing Islamic headscarves have sometimes been excluded from state schools on the grounds that they are breaching the code of *laïcité*, but the courts have consistently ruled that this is a faulty interpretation of the law. Religious believers have the right to express their faith in schools and other public places, but they are not allowed to proselytize there, that is, they must not attempt to convert others to share their beliefs. (**Alec Hargreaves**)

Further reading

Bauberot (1995). This sets the contemporary debate over *laïcité* in historical context.

Lalonde, Brice Born 1946. Politician. A leading figure of the Green movement, he stood for President in 1981, and was appointed Minister for the environment in 1988.

Lang, Jack Born 1939. Socialist politician. After a career in the theatre, he entered politics and became a long-serving and successful Minister of CULTURE (1981–86, 1988–93) under MITTERRAND. Appointed Minister of Education in 2000.

Langevin, Paul 1872–1946. Scientist. An early pioneer of the physics of relativity, he made important discoveries in electromagnetism and ultra-sound. He supported a number of left-wing campaigns in the 1930s and was active in the RESISTANCE.

Language See FRENCH LANGUAGE

La Roque, colonel François 1885–1946. Right-wing politician. On retiring from the army, he joined the *CROIX-DE-FEU* (Cross of Fire) war veterans association which, as its President from 1931, he transformed into a mass political movement of the Extreme Right, with a paramilitary organization, which became the collaborationist *Parti social français*.

Latin Quarter The 5th and 6th *arrondissements* (districts) of Paris, on the LEFT BANK of the River Seine, particularly the area around the SORBONNE, where in medieval times, Latin was widely spoken by students. Traditionally the centre of INTELLECTUAL life, it is now more focused on TOURISM.

Laurent, Jacques 1919–2000. Writer. A member of the right-wing HUSSARDS movement, he wrote both novels and polemical essays, and was founding editor of the magazine *La Parisienne* (from 1953). Under the name Cécil Saint-Laurent, he wrote the erotic best-seller *Caroline chérie* (*Darling Caroline*, 1958).

Laval, Pierre 1883–1945. Right-wing politician. He was a minister and three times Prime minister during the inter-war period. After the Fall of France, he was a determined advocate of COLLABORATION, and was twice head of government under PÉTAIN (1940, 1942–44). He was tried and executed at the LIBERATION.

Lebrun, Albert 1871–1950. Centrist politician. Last President of the THIRD REPUBLIC (1932–39).

Lecanuet, Jean Born 1920. Centrist politician. Leader of the CHRISTIAN DEMOCRATIC movement since the 1960s and long-standing Mayor of Rouen.

Leclerc, Annie Born 1940. Feminist writer. Best known for her *Parole de femme* (*Woman's Word*, 1974), which celebrates psychological and physical characteristics specific to women.

Le Clézio, Jean-Marie   Born 1940. Writer. Author of numerous popular novels, often set in exotic locations, and dealing with the contrast between life in remote Third world environments and the alienation of urban industrial society.

Le Corbusier   1887–1965. Architect. Swiss-born pioneer of avant-garde design in ARCHITECTURE and urban planning. He was particularly known for his challenging ideas, his plans for large-scale developments, and his mass high-rise housing schemes.

Lefebvre, Henri   1901–91. The leading Marxist philosopher of his generation, his *Critique de la vie quotidienne* (*Critique of Everyday Life*, 1947–81) analysed forms of human alienation in work and LEISURE, and in the physical environment of the CITY and countryside.

Left Bank   The central districts of Paris on the southern bank of the River Seine, on the left when moving downstream, where literary and intellectual life has traditionally been concentrated.

Léger, Fernand   1881–1955. Painter. Inspired by CUBISM, his work features geometrical shapes and bright colours. He often focused on industrial scenes and the social life of working people.

***Légion des volontaires français contre le bolchévisme* (LVF)**   1941–44. French military unit formed by DORIOT and DÉAT to fight in the German army, against COMMUNISM, on the Eastern Front.

Leiris, Michel   1901–90. Writer. A professional ethnographer, he was close to the SURREALISTS and EXISTENTIALISTS, and is best known for personal and AUTOBIOGRAPHICAL writings such as *L'Age d'homme* (*Manhood*, 1939).

Leisure   Leisure first became a major political issue in 1936, with the election of the POPULAR FRONT government. This government, controversially, recognized the importance of leisure for the population as a whole by appointing Léo Lagrange as a junior minister in charge of the *Secrétariat d'État aux Loisirs* (State Department for Leisure), by reducing the working week, and by instituting paid holidays (*congés payés*). The government's concern was that both the moral and physical health of the population at large could be improved through increased and productive leisure. The policy was to wean WORKERS away from the CITIES, with their bars and CAFÉS, into healthy activity such as SPORT, cycling and hiking. At the same time, the Popular Front was concerned with leisure as a means of enriching people's lives culturally: it promoted MUSEUMS, popular THEATRES, cultural centres (*Maisons de la Culture*) and drew up a blueprint for edifying RADIO schedules.

This policy was continued both under the VICHY regime, which shared the concerns of the Popular Front about the corrupting aspects of city life, and in the immediate post-war period. It was not until the advent of the FIFTH REPUBLIC in 1958, however, that a new comprehensive policy towards culture and leisure was implemented under the first Minister of Culture, André MALRAUX. Once again, the emphasis was on developing the enriching use of leisure time.

However, even in the 1930s, the government had been struggling against a strong current of commercial leisure activities, involving spectator sports and popular entertainment. With the creation of an increasingly urban and affluent mass society in the late 1950s and 1960s, leisure activity became associated more and more with the MASS MEDIA, CINEMA and POPULAR MUSIC. (**Nicholas Hewitt**)

Further reading

Ory (1994). An exhaustive analysis of the Popular Front's leisure policy. Looseley (1995). A discussion of twentieth-century French cultural policy.

Le Pen, Jean-Marie   Born 1928. Extreme right-wing politician. A populist in the style of POUJADE and an ultra-nationalist with openly racist policies, he amalgamated various factions to found the *FRONT NATIONAL*, which gained electoral successes from the late 1980s.

Le Roy Ladurie, Emmanuel   Born 1929. Historian. A leading exponent of the *ANNALES* approach to history, focusing on long-term social changes, his study of a French village, *Montaillou* (1975) became a best seller. He was Director of the French National Library (1987–94).

Lettres françaises, les   1942–72. Left wing literary journal. Founded by the Comité national de la Résistance (National Resistance committee), it was the leading organ of literary RESISTANCE, publishing many major writers. After the war it was taken over by the PCF and became a weekly magazine of the arts with a sharp political focus. Edited 1953–72 by Louis ARAGON, it reappeared briefly in 1989–93, edited by Jean Ristat.

Lévinas, Emmanuel   1906–95. Philosopher. Developing the JEWISH intellectual tradition, his work reintroduced ethical concerns in to contemporary French philosophy, emphasizing the respect due to Others, including God.

Lévi-Strauss, Claude   Born 1908. Anthropologist. He explored the underlying patterns in the life of pre-industrial communities, in such things as kinship, rituals, art and stories, and showed their affinities with life in developed societies. The key figure in STRUCTURALISM, his AUTOBIOGRAPHY, *Tristes tropiques* (1955) is widely read.

Lévy, Bernard-Henri   Born 1948. Writer and broadcaster. Particularly concerned to promote the role of the INTELLECTUAL in society, he has often aroused controversy in reappraising the life and work of prominent French intellectuals.

Liberalism   French liberalism is multifaceted, referring to complexes of judgements on economics, politics and society. Much twentieth-century French history concerned conflict between 'illiberal extremes' in politics, and only with the decline of COMMUNISM and the discredit of FASCISM did France approach a true liberal 'consensus' during the mature FIFTH REPUBLIC. Anglo-Saxon 'Liberal democracy' is often contrasted unfavourably with French 'Republican traditions', understood to add the best of 1789 – such as *laïcité* – to the 'basic' democratic freedoms of simple 'liberalism'.

Economically, liberalism and 'neo-liberalism' in France have represented free-market approaches to the ECONOMY and ECONOMIC POLICIES, where the STATE acts as mere ring-holder for market forces. Such thinking has mainly characterized the Right and Centre Right, although the MRP and radicalism combined free-market economics with progressive social policy. 1980s' and 1990s' PRIVATIZATION by right-wing governments followed Reaganite and Thatcherite supply-side economics, reversing earlier SOCIALIST (or other interventionist) NATIONALIZATION. Since 1984, when MITTERRAND bowed to dominant free-market economics in Europe, and France's espousal of EU convergence in the 1990s, governments have followed prevailing neo-liberal economics, focusing on INFLATION rather than EMPLOYMENT.

Politically – the VICHY RÉGIME excepted – France has always been 'liberal', in that essential freedoms and more have been guaranteed, although GAULLISM's strangle-hold on politics during the 1960s and concerns over the democratic deficit of DE GAULLE's presidency raised questions – in MAY '68 – over the liberalism of the new Republic. Under POMPIDOU, GISCARD D'ESTAING and Mitterrand, France moved towards a liberal political synthesis, as the COMMUNIST PARTY abandoned revolutionary leanings and the Left acceded peacefully to power in 1981. Giscard, in particular, through a neo-liberal fusion of the mixed economy and greater personal freedoms in ABORTION, GENDER, SEXUALITY, MARRIAGE, REGIONALISM and justice, symbolized France's new interpretation of a liberal Republican state. (**Hugh Dauncey**)

Further reading

Fysh (1997). Political, economic and social liberalism in 1960–90.

Liberation   Liberation refers to the ending of German and VICHY authority in France at the end of the Second World War, and the passing of power to the PROVISIONAL GOVERNMENT of General DE GAULLE.

The military liberation of France began with the Allied landings in Normandy on 'D-Day' (6 June, 1944, in French *le jour J*). The majority of France was liberated between June and October 1944, although the last German troops did not surrender until May 1945. There was not one Liberation of France, but many, as local circumstances on the ground varied enormously according to the military or political context, and depending on which groups liberated territory.

In French history and culture, the Liberation has assumed a mythical status far beyond its military implications. For many it means the period in which the Germans withdrew from an area, and the local RESISTANCE forces took control, a time of extraordinary scenes in many of the towns and villages of France. For some, it suggests frightening images relating to wildcat executions (*ÉPURATION*), and the public humiliation of women collaborators.

The Liberation has also come to mean the transitional period between war and peace, between the accession of the Provisional Government of General de Gaulle (August 1944), and the establishment of a new FOURTH REPUBLIC (January 1947).

Some writers regard the Liberation as a missed opportunity, a failure to take advantage of the revolutionary potential of the situation to create an entirely new France. In fact, the achievements of the Liberation were substantial. An independent, democratic French STATE, recognized by the Allies, was born from the ashes of the 1940 defeat and the dishonour of collaboration. **(Hilary Footitt)**

Further reading

Footitt and Simmonds (1988). Accounts of the relationship between the Allied and French liberators 'on the ground'. Kedward and Wood (1995). Essays on the images of Liberation held by different groups within France.

Libération   Daily newspaper. It began as a clandestine paper published by a RESISTANCE movement of the same name, and continued as a left-wing daily paper until it closed in 1964. Relaunched in 1973 by Serge July, it has since been a racy and informative paper of the left-wing intelligentsia.

Libraries   French libraries were originally private, church-based or belonging to the early universities. The oldest public library in France is the Bibliothèque Mazarine, now situated among the buildings of the *INSTITUT DE FRANCE* and originally opened to all in 1644.

There are now well over 8000 libraries in France. Many are small municipal institutions with just a few thousand volumes, but there are also regional libraries and those of UNIVERSITIES, *GRANDES ÉCOLES* and other specialized institutions (for example, the *BANDE DESSINÉE* library in the national centre in Angoulême). To these should be added a network of *médiathèques* (multi-media reference institutions), cultural centres and *bibliobus* (local travelling libraries). Since 1906 the *Association des Bibliothécaires Français* (Association of French Librarians) has been the main professional body in the field.

The French library has not, however, always been 'user friendly'. Main libraries are traditionally non-lending, with closed access stacks, often overcrowded and slow. Research libraries are highly centralized, there being no legal deposit library outside of Paris. The training of librarians is similarly centralized, with the majority of top-ranked *conservateurs* inevitably passing through the École des Chartes.

The flagship of French libraries is undoubtedly the new Bibliothèque nationale de France, whose Tolbiac site in eastern Paris opened in 1996. The library consists of an upper section open to all adults, and a *rez-de-jardin*, the research library on the ground level of the exotic garden that the buildings surround. The complex includes over 400 000 open-access works. Research readers have abundant access to internet, CD-ROM and audio-visual facilities, a well as to a large number of digitized volumes via the on-line Gallica database. These facilities supplement the more traditional holdings of some 13 million volumes.

Despite the exorbitant luxury of architect Dominique Perrault's buildings and the high-tech installations, the library has encountered frequent teething problems:

computer malfunctions, strikes and even nostalgia for the previous seventeenth- to nineteenth-century buildings, where the manuscripts and prints sections are still held. (**Laurence Grove**)

Further reading

See the Bibliothèque nationale de France's extensive website, which includes links to other library-based pages, and is available in an English version: www.BnF.fr

Linguistics   There are three main areas in which French scholars have made important contributions to linguistics. First, they have explored the origins and development of French, with investigations like those of Arsène Darmesteter (1846–88) into word history, or Jules Gilliéron (1854–1926) into dialect geography, and culminating in the monumental *Histoire de la langue française* by Ferdinand Brunot (1860–1938).

Second, they have contributed to general linguistic theory. The renowned francophone Swiss scholar, Ferdinand de Saussure (1857–1913) taught that languages are not just lists of items, but systems of interlocking units, analysable independently of their history. Saussure's approach was taken further by the 'functionalist' school, the most prominent French functionalist being André MARTINET (1908–99). Functionalism investigates how differences between linguistic units (e.g. the four standard French nasal vowels) are exploited for communication (the *un* of *brun* occurs less often than the other three, so many speakers dispense with it altogether, replacing it with the *in* of *brin*). An independent tradition of 'language psychomechanics', founded by Gustave Guillaume (1883–1960), focuses on the links between the various uses of a tense like the imperfect, or on the relationship between negatively and positively polarized expressions (*il boit peu*, 'he drinks little' vs. *il boit un peu*, 'he drinks a little'). And the 'dependency' and 'valency' grammars of Lucien Tesnière (1893–1954) foreshadow aspects of Chomsky's recent work on government and binding.

The third aspect of French linguistics is the 'descriptivist' analysis of colloquial French as a coherent system in its own right, not as a collection of regrettable deviations from the standard. Launched in the 1920s by another Swiss scholar, Henri Frei, this approach continued with Martinet and with present-day linguists like Françoise Gadet, Claude Hagège or Henriette Walter, whose television appearances and popular books are beginning perhaps to change public perceptions about 'correctness' in language. (**Rodney Ball**)

Further reading

Ducrot *et al.* (1995). Includes accounts of the work of many eminent French linguists. Leeman-Bouix, (1994). Presents and defends the descriptivist approach.

Literary History   This term refers to the ways in which we select, order and understand literary texts in relation to historical periods and national cultures. From the nineteenth century onwards, such a project has been linked to explaining how literature is related to the social, political and intellectual life of a NATION. Literary history is aimed at stimulating discussion of why certain literary works, called classics, still affect us and remain the staple of school or university syllabuses, while others do not survive. Assembling a collection of such classics forms a CANON of literary works identified as the great works of a country.

However, attempts at providing overarching frameworks for studying literature have come under attack since the 1960s as a number of writers and critics have resisted the notion that literature can be compartmentalized in this way. Writers have claimed that such a totalizing analysis of literature reduces literary genius and creativity to a prescriptive catalogue of key works and misses out the vital role of the individual writer. And writers associated with recent developments in CRITICAL THEORY, PSYCHOANALYSIS and POST-STRUCTURALISM, have challenged the view that a literary text and its meanings can be evaluated in such a chronological and rationalizing fashion. Selecting texts for a national canon inevitably involves impressionistic and subjective judgements about individual works and their authors, which can leave aside writers who do not fit the tastes of the day. WOMEN writers are one group whose contribution to Western culture has been rendered largely invisible by male canon compilers of the past. Today, literary critics are more sceptical about the possibility of establishing a canon of great works. They have come to focus increasingly on popular and more marginal forms of writing as well as the reading process itself and how we interpret texts as communities of readers. (**Claire Gorrara**)

Further reading

Eagleton (1983). A polemical but stimulating general introduction to aspects of literary theory.

Livre de poche   France's first cheap paperback series, launched in 1953 by Hachette with a consortium of publishers. Its enormous popularity has led some participating companies, like Gallimard, to withdraw and publish their own paperback collections.

Louvre   Claiming to be 'the world's greatest museum', the Louvre is the result of over eight centuries of evolution from royal palace to crowning glory of MITTERRAND'S GRANDS TRAVAUX. Its present role is centrepiece of the network of *musées nationaux*, a museum whose 60 000 m² of exhibition space display artefacts and paintings from eleven millennia of civilization up to the mid-nineteenth century.

The Louvre started life as a fortified royal tower in the 1190s, to be expanded in the reigns of Charles V (1364–80) and Henri IV (1589–1610). On the death of Louis XIV (1715) the eastern courtyard (*Cour carrée*) was complete and the south wing bordering the Seine had reached the Tuileries. The period following 1789 saw the first public visitors and, in the nineteenth century, the addition of the north wing. In 1989 a new entrance was created via Pei's central glass pyramid and four years later the newly modelled north wing, hitherto occupied by the Finance Ministry offices, opened.

The Louvre now operates through three main sections each branching off from the central reception area under the pyramid. 'Denon', named after the museum's first administrator, occupies the south wing including the *Grande Galerie*, the central passage of sky-lit elegance created from 1595–1610. 'Richelieu' occupies the north wing, dominated by two sculpture courts. The *Cour carrée*, including the new chronological displays of French PAINTING, is the 'Sully' section. Beneath it visitors can view the remains of the medieval palace that were unearthed during the 1983 building works.

Many of the Louvre's most famous treasures are now popular icons: Delacroix's *Liberty Guiding the People*, Gericault's *Raft of the Medusa*, the Venus de Milo and of course the *Mona Lisa* (in French *La Joconde*). Fittingly perhaps for a Mitterrand-esque people's palace, it has been expanded into an underground shopping mall with Virgin mega-store and food court around an inverted pyramid. Ironically the affiliated *École du Louvre* is unashamedly ÉLITIST and steep admission prices mean the museum is often the domain of the TOURIST or the BOURGEOIS. **(Laurence Grove)**

Further reading

See the extensive website, which includes a virtual visit of the museum and provides an English version: www.louvre.fr

Love   Love, in its romantic and erotic form, is a central preoccupation of novels, films, songs throughout the western world, and is probably the most pervasive theme in twentieth-century French culture. The SURREALIST writer André BRETON invented the term *l'amour fou* to designate the experience of passionate, life-enhancing desire provoked by a chance encounter, and disruptive of normal routine. While the majority of French people organize their lives around a more durable, domesticated form of love (though the number of marriages has reduced, for example by 100 000 between 1971 and 1981, there has been a considerable rise in the number of couples in long-term cohabitation), *l'amour fou* drives the plots of many popular fictions, including for example, in the cinema, TRUFFAUT's *La Femme d'à côté* (*The Woman Next Door*, 1981) and Beineix's *37.2 le matin* (*Betty Blue*, 1986).

Love stories have long been assumed to be the staple diet of woman readers, and WOMEN's material and social dependence on men did, until recently, make the possibility of happy love a key female preoccupation. Romance has been an immensely popular genre throughout the last century: Delly – pen-name of husband and wife co-authors – produced best-selling romances regularly from 1907 to 1941; women's magazines provided a regular supply of love stories and in 1978 American Harlequin romances began publication in French. More 'serious' women writers have used the love story to explore the meanings of love, and its compatibility (or not) with women's freedom. Examples of this are COLETTE's novels, such as *Chéri* (1920) and *La Naissance du jour* (*Break of Day*, 1928), Christiane Rochefort's novel *Le Repos du guerrier* (*The Warrior's Rest*, 1958), and Julia Kristeva's essay *Histoires d'amour* (*Love Stories*, 1983). **(Diana Holmes)**

Further reading

Holmes (1996). For more on the women writers mentioned above. Wilson (1999). Includes discussion of films that represent *l'amour fou*. Zeldin (1983). Includes sections on how the French see love.

Lyon   France's third CITY in terms of population, and the second when the agglomeration is taken into account. Situated at the meeting of the Rhône and the Saône, Lyon occupies an important crossroads, close to Italy, Switzerland and the South of France. This situation accounts for its long-lasting mercantile role and reputation as a financial centre, instanced by the *Crédit Lyonnais* bank. Its range of cultural amenities is rivalled only by PARIS, but it is less popular with tourists than its rivals MARSEILLE, Nice and Toulouse, largely because of the cold winters brought about by its continental climate. Yet *le vieux Lyon*, a beautifully-restored *quartier* by the Saône, and the city's range of museums, notably the *Musée des Tissus* (Museum of Textiles) and the *Musée des Beaux-Arts* (Art Gallery), provide a rich diet for the visitor.

So too, notoriously, do the restaurants and *bouchons* (originally more modestly priced wine-shops selling food) of this most self-consciously gastronomic of cities. The *mères* or woman chefs of Lyon have long been famous worldwide (La Mère Brazier's eponymous restaurant has served an identical menu for more than half a century), and more recently Paul Bocuse's restaurant in his native village of Collonges-au-Mont-d'Or has achieved a worldwide reputation. Local specialities include *quenelles* of pike, *tablier de sapeur* (grilled breadcrumbed tripe) and an intimidating range of *charcuterie*, washed down with local wines such as Beaujolais or Saint-Joseph. *Lyonnais* cooking is solid, bourgeois, inclined to the conservative but capable of unexpected moments of lightness and innovation – much like the city itself. (**Keith Reader**)

Lyotard, Jean-François   1924–98. Philosopher. He explored MARXIST and PSYCHO-ANALYTICAL ideas before concluding that no overall theory of human life was possible. He expounded the absence of coherence and certainty in *La Condition postmoderne* (*The Post-Modern Condition*, 1979), which launched the idea of POST-MODERNISM.

Madelin, Alain   Born 1948. Conservative politician. On the right wing of the Republican parties, he espoused policies of PRIVATIZATION and liberalization, inspired by the example of Margaret Thatcher in Britain. He was briefly Minister for Finance (1995).

Maginot Line   The Maginot Line was built as a series of defensive fortifications at a cost five billion francs by the French during the 1930s to protect against the kind of German invasion and huge population losses that had occurred in the First World War. Named after War Minister André Maginot, the Line extended from the Swiss border through northeastern France but was never extended from the Ardennes forest to the North Sea, which helped ensure that a German attack would occur in Belgium rather than France. The Line signalled that the French would hunker down to face a German invasion rather than launch offensive operations to protect their allies in Central Europe against the threat of growing German power.

When the German attack came in May 1940, the Maginot Line proved useless as armoured German divisions swept through the Ardennes, around the Line, while most of the French army tried vainly to defend Belgium. French soldiers manning the fortresses were forced to surrender without having been defeated in battle. 'Maginot mentality' came to mean a psychology of retreat behind a supposedly impregnable and highly expensive wall, incapable, however, of keeping out disaster.

Following the 1940 campaign, the Maginot Line became a tourist site for the victorious Germans, who tried unsuccessfully to turn its guns around against the advancing Allies in 1944. Following the war, the French army regained control of the fortifications but ceased maintaining them after 1964 when France, no longer feeling threatened by Germany, turned to nuclear defence. Beginning in the 1970s, local communities began acquiring and restoring the fortifications, opening them to tourists. By 1988, of twenty-five fortifications, ten had opened to public touring, attracting some 200 000 visitors annually. (**Bertram M. Gordon**)

Further reading

Kemp (1981); Pallud (1988). For the fortifications since the war.

Maisons de la culture   The *Maisons de la culture* (Houses of Culture) were originally multidisciplinary arts centres (stage, library, exhibition space, and so on) in a number of French CITIES. They were the brainchild of France's first Minister of CULTURE, André MALRAUX, in the 1960s and were to take highbrow culture from PARIS into the 'provinces', which were deemed to be culturally barren. This aim met with only limited success, but there remains a potent myth of the *Maisons*, deriving from the idealism of the cultural democratization movement, the FRONT POPULAIRE and the LIBERATION.

Malraux's initial plan was to have a *Maison* in each of France's 96 *départements*, funded equally by central and local government. But his budget was inadequate to so massive an undertaking, and only a handful were ever operational at one time. Another aim was to widen the social composition of audiences for the arts. This too proved over-ambitious at a time when appreciating the arts usually meant being educated and middle-class; some even viewed the *Maisons* as bastions of BOURGEOIS IDEOLOGY. A more practical problem was finding the polymath directors to run them. A common expedient was to base them on existing theatre companies, though this sometimes contradicted the multidisciplinary ambition.

Malraux and his *Maisons* were a target in the uprising of MAY '68. His resignation the following year marked the end of the policy in its full-blooded form. Smaller, cheaper establishments were set up instead, while the existing *Maisons* struggled to survive the 1970s and 1980s, confronted with high operating costs and official indifference. In 1990, the remaining eight, and around 50 of the smaller establishments, were assembled in one network, called *Scènes nationales* (National Stages), of which there are now 65, all focused on the performing arts. The name *Maisons de la culture* has largely been abandoned or supplemented. (**David Looseley**)

Further reading

Looseley (1995). A history of cultural policy which includes discussion of the *Maisons*.

Malle, Louis 1932–95. Film director. Working in France and Hollywood, he often focused on personal motivations and moral issues. His *Lacombe Lucien* (1973) and *Au revoir les enfants* (1987) were influential in the reappraisal of France's wartime history.

Mallet, Serge 1927–73. Sociologist. Theorist of the New Left, he argued in *La nouvelle classe ouvrière* (*The New Working Class*, 1963) that the WORKING CLASS was undergoing profound changes.

Malraux, André 1901–76. Writer and politician. The most prominent left-wing writer of the 1930s, his novels, such as *La condition humaine* (*Man's Estate*, 1933), were often set in revolutionary movements. He had a distinguished record of military action in the Spanish Civil War, and then in the RESISTANCE. He was a staunch supporter of General DE GAULLE and became the first Minister for Cultural Affairs (1959–69). His art criticism and AUTOBIOGRAPHICAL works are also widely read.

Man Ray 1890–1976. Artist and photographer. A member of the DADA and SURREALIST movements, he is best known for his photographs, like *Larmes* (Tears, 1930), with unusual lighting effects to create highly stylized artistic images.

Maoism An extreme left-wing political movement, active in the 1960s and early 1970s. Its members were inspired by the writings of Mao Tse-tung (or Mao Zedong, 1893–1976), Chairman of the Chinese Communist Party, whose thoughts were given mass circulation in the 'little red book' of quotations at the time of the 'Cultural Revolution' (1966–76). These offered a version of Marxism–Leninism in slogan form. They called for the thoroughgoing destruction of BOURGEOIS society in all its aspects (economic, political, cultural) and its replacement by a radical different communist society. They looked to a highly disciplined party organization to lead a revolution of WORKERS and PAYSANS. Maoism was attractive to a number of students and young INTELLECTUALS, who looked to developments in CHINA to provide an alternative model of society, different from capitalist France and different from the alternatives offered by traditional left-wing movements. They particularly valued its simple messages, its emphasis on struggle, its demands for wholehearted dedication, and its uncompromising discipline in action.

Les maos were active during the events of MAY '68 and its aftermath, and received limited support, mainly propaganda material, from China. They briefly gained support from established intellectuals, notably ALTHUSSER, who legitimated the study of Mao's form of Marxism, and SARTRE, who admired their radicalism and the purity of their commitment. The movement was always hostile towards the SOCIALISTS and COMMUNISTS, who amply reciprocated, and it increasingly focused on fighting against other Left groupings, including bitter conflicts between factions that emerged within Maoism itself. The in-fighting intensified as the Cultural Revolution disintegrated, often reflecting divisions within the Chinese leadership, and the movement largely collapsed by the time of Mao's death in 1976. French Maoism was influential in producing high-profile intellectuals who later rejected all left-wing ideas, like some of the *NOUVEAUX PHILOSOPHES* (from 1976). It also influenced a number of Third World intellectuals studying in PARIS, including the Cambodian dictator Pol Pot.

Further reading

Hamon and Rotman (1987); Reader (1987).

Marcel, Gabriel   1898–1973. Philosopher and playwright. A Catholic thinker, often described as EXISTENTIALIST, though hostile to SARTRE, his best known book *Etre et avoir* (*Being and Having*, 1935) popularized the distinction between being and having as representing conflicting ethical stances.

Marcellin, Raymond   Born 1914. Gaullist politician. He was appointed Minister of the Interior after MAY '68, with the mission of repressing the dissident movements. His draconian *loi anti-casseurs* (Anti-vandalism Act, 1970) facilitated the breaking up of demonstrations.

Marchais, Georges   1920–97. Communist politician. As General Secretary of the French COMMUNIST PARTY (1970–94), he was noted for his tight grip on the party apparatus, and his blunt manner in public debate. He stood unsuccessfully for President in 1981.

Marianne   Although from the Renaissance, female allegorical forms had been used to represent France, it was with the disappearance of the monarchy during the revolutionary period of the late eighteenth century that Liberty in the form of a woman began to assert her dominance, first as a symbol of the French Republic, and later of France as a nation. The name Marianne, initially pejorative, only became generally accepted as a positive term at the time of the THIRD REPUBLIC (1870) from which time, in the form of statues and busts, she was instated in *mairies* and town squares all over France.

The iconographic attributes of Marianne are various and unstable. The forms she has taken on the French definitive postage stamps, of which she has become the principal national icon from 1945 to the present day, provide a representative overview. Conventionally, she takes the form of a stately female, with prominent maternal breasts, of which one is often bared. She wears a red Phrygian bonnet (originally worn by liberated Roman slaves), a revolutionary rosette (in blue, white and red) and either carries the tricolour flag or supports herself on the *fascies*, another symbol of Roman origin, which within the French Republic symbolizes the magistracy rather than the military. In addition, she often wears on her head, with or without Phrygian bonnet, a wreath of olive, vine or oak leaves, symbolizing respectively Peace, the fertility of France and civic virtues.

Marianne's semiotic adaptability and flexibility have enabled her to survive in France where equivalent national deities in other countries have faded from public consciousness (Britannia, Helvetia, Germania, Hibernia). The fact that living female icons, such as Brigitte BARDOT and other film stars, have often lent their form to representations of her, has assured her vitality and contemporary relevance, ensuring her status as an object of fantasy and desire as well as national and political significance. (**David Scott**)

Further reading

Agulhon (1979); Agulhon (1989); Agulhon and Bonte (1992). Pastoureau (1998).

Marie-Claire   First launched in 1937 and again, after a ban for its wartime publication, in 1954. It is a leading women's magazine, with an up-market profile and a reputation for high quality photography and feature writing.

Maritain, Jacques   1882–1973. Philosopher. Converted to CATHOLICISM in 1906, he became a leading exponent of the philosophy of St Thomas Aquinas. After ACTION FRANÇAISE was denounced by the Pope, he developed a new social philosophy, in *Primauté du spirituel* (*Primacy of the Spiritual*, 1927) and *Humanisme intégral* (*True Humanism*, 1936), which redefined the relations between faith and politics.

Marseille   Traditionally vying with LYON for the status of France's second city, Marseille's cultural, linguistic, political and economic identity has more often been defined, resentfully, in contradistinction to that of the French capital. It is well ahead of both PARIS and Lyon in terms of age (founded by the Greeks as Massilia in the sixth century BC). The Mediterranean warmth of its southern climate and public greetings, shown in Marcel PAGNOL's films and books, is often contrasted to northern, Parisian coolness. Marseillais's urban Provençal accent contrasts with the Parisian standard. Rivalries (often violent) have grown up recently between football fans. Their equivalent of the local derby being OM vs. PSG. The SOCIALIST traditions of the Marseille municipality are opposed to GAULLIST Paris. Importantly, since the 1980s, the *Marseillais* feel the economic and industrial decline of the once thriving Mediterranean port, and contrast their situation to the pull exerted by the Paris–Ile de France region in terms of post-industrial employment opportunity. As capital of the Bouches-du-Rhône *département* and the centre of a conurbation of over a million inhabitants, Marseille is still France's principal port and a major petro-chemical centre. As a natural point of entry for immigrants from the southern shores of the Mediterranean, the city has a significant Maghrebi minority. In the context of extensive youth unemployment and summer riots in the *BANLIEUES* (poor suburbs), a white backlash has been seen in some surrounding boroughs that have voted in strength for *FRONT NATIONAL* candidates. Its cultural icons include author and film-maker Marcel Pagnol, Mayor Gaston DEFFERRE, disgraced entrepreneur and politician Bernard TAPIE, and footballer Zinedine ZIDANE. (**Geoff Hare**)

Further reading

Ardagh (2000).

Marshall Plan   Increasingly persuaded that the Soviet government intended to spread COMMUNISM in a 'defenceless Europe', Secretary of State George Marshall announced on 5 June 1947 the intention of the US government to furnish economic aid for the post-war reconstruction of EUROPE, with the exception of Franco's Spain. The resulting 'European Recovery Plan' is more commonly known as the Marshall Plan. From 1948 to 1951, the United States infused 14 million dollars (the equivalent of 170 million dollars today) into various strategic and highly visible sectors such as energy, public works, and transportation, and into the generation of a consumer economy, with the expansion of intra-European commerce foremost in mind.

While funnelling dollars into Europe was a strategy to combat anti-Americanism, in France the Marshall Plan actually heightened Franco-American tensions. France needed American money for food staples and raw materials in the continuing material difficulty of the early post-war years. But aid came paternalistically, in the form of a monthly allowance. French ministries had to file requests for funds to the American 'Mission' that oversaw how francs as well as dollars were spent, in order to curb inflation and shape French investment. Moreover, while in favour of the Western alliance on political grounds, France was reluctant to embrace the American vision of a European economic community, largely because GERMANY was being groomed as its centre.

By 1950, however, the American combat against communist infiltration in Europe took a back seat to fighting communist regimes elsewhere in the world. France's rearmament was deemed more important than rebuilding its infrastructure. American funds never went into housing, but instead financed the war in INDO-CHINA and the French arms industry.

Despite French resistance to American paternalism, the various organs that implemented the Marshall Plan in France, along with vast sums of money, had a tremendous socioeconomic influence, and were instrumental in inaugurating LES TRENTE GLORIEUSES, the three decades during which France underwent a most dramatic process of transformative MODERNIZATION. (**Susan Weiner**)

Further reading

Wall (1991). An accessible historical study, that was the first in English to use American and French archival sources.

Martin du Gard, Roger 1881–1958. Writer. He wrote many novels, including the epic series *Les Thibault* (1922–40), which aims at faithfully detailing the life of the period. His diaries and letters are still read, especially his voluminous correspondence with André GIDE. He was awarded the Nobel Prize in 1937.

Martin, Henri Born 1927. Sailor. Imprisoned in 1950 for agitating against the French war in INDO-CHINA, he became a *cause célèbre* among left-wing INTELLECTUALS, including SARTRE, until he was released in 1953.

Martinet, André 1908–99. Linguist. A leading theorist of pronunciation and communication, he developed an influential method for language learning.

Marty, André 1886–1956. Communist politician. Leader of the mutiny of the French Black Sea fleet in 1919, he became a high-profile COMMUNIST militant. He was expelled from the party in 1953 amid bitter controversy.

Marxism   A set of ideas initially developed by Karl Marx (1818–83) and adopted by many French INTELLECTUALS and political parties during the late nineteenth and twentieth centuries. Marxists hold that human societies are ultimately dominated by their ECONOMY, the way in which they produce what people need in order to live, flourish and reproduce themselves. Other aspects of society, such as property relations, social CLASSES, and the STATE, are developed in response to economic forces. So too, though less directly, are the ideas, images and stories which people use to try to understand their world. They suggest that modern societies are dominated by capital, the wealth required to invest in economic development, and that this tends to make everything into a commodity, whose value comes from being bought or sold. They argue that in capitalist societies, wealth becomes concentrated in the hands of an ever smaller ÉLITE, who cannot easily be held accountable by the majority of the people, whose lives are increasingly affected by them. Marxists propose that capital should be taken out of private ownership and used for the benefit of the whole of society. They recognize that this will involve a struggle, amounting to a social REVOLUTION. These DEMOCRATIC and egalitarian ideas proved especially attractive to French WORKERS, and were influential in sections of the TRADE UNION movement. The political parties of the Left adopted them for most of the twentieth century, though they usually disagreed, often bitterly, over how Marxism should be interpreted and how it should be put into practice. Among the larger parties, the French COMMUNISTS looked to the Soviet Union for a model, while the SOCIALISTS looked to social-democratic models developed in Central and Western Europe. Smaller groups advocated the views of TROTSKY, MAO or other leaders. After the Second World War, many French intellectuals espoused Marxist ideas, using them to shed light on long-running philosophical and cultural debates, and adapting them for use in the social and human sciences. Marxism was sharply criticized for its association with authoritarian communist regimes, and fell out of favour during the 1980s as those regimes collapsed. (**Michael Kelly**)

Further reading

Kelly (1982). Looks mainly at the philosophical issues, focusing on debates among communist intellectuals. Judt (1986). Focuses on the political implications. Poster (1975). Shows the influence of Marxism on a wide range of post-war intellectuals.

Masculinity   As problematic and fraught an area in France nowadays as in any other Western culture. Centuries of male dominance have been undermined (though emphatically not done away with) by the ever-increasing numbers of women in the work force, the easier availability of CONTRACEPTION and ABORTION, and equal opportunities legislation, much of which was introduced by the MAUROY SOCIALIST government in the early 1980s. Elizabeth Badinter went so far as to diagnose the 1980s' French male as a 'sick man', repressing his femininity at the behest of patriarchy and his masculinity in the wake of FEMINISM.

France's position as the most northernly of the Mediterranean countries, traditional bulwarks of machismo, has perhaps made her particularly susceptible to the kind of 'sickness' Badinter diagnoses. The shift in her major cinematic icons of masculinity, from Jean GABIN before the Second World War or Jean-Paul BELMONDO in the late 1950s and 1960s to the hulking 'suffering macho' (to quote Ginette Vincendeau) Gérard DEPARDIEU, is indicative of this. The 'sickness' indeed seems to go back to well before the 1980s, to judge by Marco Ferreri's 1976 film *La Dernière Femme* (*The Last Woman*), in which Depardieu plays a working-class man, deserted by his wife, who castrates himself with an electric carving-knife. Nor can 'masculinity' any longer be assumed to operate entirely within a heteronormative optic; the increasing volubility and visibility of gay groups, often demanding no more than the equality of treatment supposedly guaranteed by the Republic, are proof enough of that.

Yet all the leading French political figures at the time of writing are male and, despite the brief and ill-starred premiership of Édith CRESSON (1991–92), this long-standing gender stranglehold shows little sign of changing. When CHIRAC's first Prime Minister, Alain JUPPÉ, included a scattering of woman ministers in his first cabinet, they were immediately nicknamed 'les jupettes' (a pun on 'short skirts'), and a number of them had only fleeting careers. The French STATE remains, in its still powerful essence, fundamentally a masculine preserve. (**Keith Reader**)

Further reading

Badinter (1992). On masculine identity.

Maspéro, François   Born 1932. Publisher and novelist. His bookshop, 'La Joie de Lire' (Joy of Reading) in the LATIN QUARTER, and the associated publishing company, spread left-wing ideas from round the world during the 1960s and 1970s.

Mass media   See MEDIA.

Massis, Henri   1886–1970. Writer. An essayist and journalist, he edited the conservative literary review *La revue universelle* from 1920. Noted for his acerbic polemical style, he supported ACTION FRANÇAISE, the VICHY REGIME and a range of Far Right causes in France and internationally.

Masson, Loys   1915–69. Writer. Born in Mauritius, he wrote novels, poems and essays which combined a passion for social justice with a mystical version of CATHOLIC spiritualism.

Massu, General Jacques   Born 1908. He led French troops during the Battle of Algiers (1957) and became military commander of Algiers (1958–60).

Matisse, Henri   1869–1954. Artist. Leader of the Fauves before the First World War, he continued to be influential and innovative. His paper cut-outs and stencils, such as *Jazz* (1947) and *Blue Nudes* (1952) are widely reproduced on cards and book covers.

Mauriac, François   1885–1970. Writer. The leading CATHOLIC novelist of the interwar period, his novels, including *Génitrix* (1923) and *Thérèse Desqueyroux* (1927), explore tense family relations in provincial France. Moving away from the conservative Right, he played a key role in the literary RESISTANCE, and supported Left and liberal causes after the war, rallying again to DE GAULLE in 1958. His *Bloc-notes* column in *L'EXPRESS*, and later in *LE FIGARO littéraire*, were influential in forming public opinion.

Mauroy, Pierre Born 1926. Socialist politician. The first socialist Prime Minister of the FIFTH REPUBLIC (1981–84), he is also credited with the regeneration of Lille, where he has been mayor since 1973.

Maurras, Charles 1868–1952. Writer. A founder of ACTION FRANÇAISE in 1899, he was the leading political journalist of the Far Right for the first half of the twentieth century, advocating ANTI-SEMITISM, xenophobia and royalism. An ardent COLLABORATIONIST, he was imprisoned at the LIBERATION.

Mauss, Marcel 1873–1950. Sociologist and ethnographer. His work on sociology of religion focused on issues like sacrifice and magic. His major work, *Essai sur le don* (*The Gift*, 1932–34) was influential on LÉVI-STRAUSS, LEIRIS and others.

MAY '68 The extraordinary events of May '68 are a landmark in French cultural and political history, even though the nature and extent of their influence remain a controversial question. A series of student protests leading to the occupation of the SORBONNE quickly escalated to large and increasingly violent demonstrations, widespread occupations of universities and factories, and a general strike. The first 'night of the barricades', with pitched street battles between students and police in the LATIN QUARTER, took place on 11 May, and by 20 May 10 million people, in both public and private sectors, were on strike. It even appeared that the French President, Général DE GAULLE and his government led by Prime Minister Georges POMPIDOU, would be brought down.

The causes were complex. Political protest against the Vietnam War, and simmering discontent at the poor conditions in the overcrowded universities were important triggers, as were the scenes of police actions against student demonstrators. Many point to the explosive effect of a rapidly modernizing economy and the individualism associated with the culture and values of CONSUMER society, developing in a country dominated by authoritarian and conservative political and social attitudes. Alongside the denunciations of CAPITALISM and IMPERIALISM from the GAUCHISTES and other extreme Left groups, tracts, banners, graffiti, and slogans called for complete cultural freedom: *Il est interdit d'interdire* (Prohibiting is prohibited), *l'imagination au pouvoir* (all power to the imagination), and *sous les pavés, la plage* (beneath the cobble-stones the beach) epitomized May's libertarian spirit and the ''68 generation'.

The mass social protest ended as abruptly as it had begun, with the holiday weekend of 1 June. A landslide victory for the right-wing GAULLIST party in elections later that month confirmed that France had turned its back on REVOLUTION. Whether May marked a profound shift in attitudes, values, and practices, or whether its effects were at best superficial, is still debated. But it remains an important historical reference: the mass celebrations over France's victory in the 1998 World Cup, and the assertion of a new multicultural identity associated with it, were memorably described as 'the May '68 of the 2000 generation'. (**Margaret Atack**)

Further reading

Atack (1999). An analysis of the themes, ideas, and impact of May '68 through eight selected texts. Hanley and Kerr (1989). Contains articles on many aspects of the protests and their social and political impact. Reader with Khursheed (1993). Focuses on the cultural and ideological complexity of the events and their interpretations.

MC Solaar   Born 1969. Leading black rap artist of the 1990s, his style is more lyrical than aggressive.

Médecins sans frontières   Voluntary association, founded by a group of French doctors in 1971 to provide medical assistance in international emergencies. It is now an important aid agency supported by worldwide donations, and was awarded the Nobel Peace Prize in 1999.

Media and mass media   The mass media are means of communication such as PRESS, CINEMA, RADIO and TELEVISION, which permit transmission of information and entertainment to the public on a wide scale.

Mass circulation newspapers were the first such French examples during the golden era of the press, from 1870 to 1914. *Le Petit Parisien*, with a circulation of 1.5 million copies in 1914, was the best-selling paper in the world at the time. Radio reached a mass audience during the following decades, and rallied the NATION during the 1940s. At the end of the war, awareness of the political potential of the media led to establishment of STATE control over BROADCASTING. French television of the 1960s and 1970s was truly a mass medium uniting a national audience. However, in the 1980s, the end of the state broadcasting monopoly, the PRIVATIZATION of the first television channel and launch of new rivals, together with the introduction of cable, SATELLITE, and the video recorder, multiplied viewing possibilities and fragmented the audience. Media consumption was expanding rapidly, but on a more individualized and diverse basis.

The media represent a major cultural influence, especially considering that, at the end of the twentieth century, the average French family was using media equipment for more hours per week than they spent at school or work. The French are especially concerned to protect their language and national IDENTITY, and so anxiety over 'invasion' by American media production has led to protectionist cultural policies. Quotas are used to boost the scheduling of French films and television programmes, and promote playing of francophone songs on the radio. Legislation also promotes use of the French language in the media, but may have limited impact in the face of Anglo-Saxon domination of the INTERNET. (**Pam Moores**)

Further reading

Bertrand (1995). Introduction to press, radio and television. Kuhn (1995). Historical overview.

Melville, Jean-Pierre 1917–73. Film director. Noted for his thrillers, like *Le Samouraï* (1967) and for his film adaptation of Vercors' wartime classic *Le Silence de la mer* (*The Silence of the Sea*, 1949).

Memory In France as in Britain and America, the modern cult of memory is inseparable from conflict. The *Souvenir Français*, the national War Graves Association, was created in 1887 in the aftermath of the Franco-Prussian war (1870–71). The First World War (1914–18) created paradigmatic forms of collective remembrance, which include Armistice Day, the unknown soldier's tomb at the Arc de Triomphe, and ceremonies at local war memorials. The commemoration of the military dead of the Second World War (1939–45) was subsumed into these patterns. In France however, four years of German OCCUPATION, civil war between RESISTANCE and COLLABORATION, and STATE complicity in the persecution of the JEWS problematised and fractured wartime memory and added further dates to the commemorative calendar, as did bitter colonial conflict in INDO-CHINA (1947–54) and ALGERIA (1954–62). For half a century, therefore, France's relationship with its past was a 'broken mirror' in which more recent events such as the 1990s' Papon and Touvier cases were refracted and distorted. Memory is also subject to generational change. With the erosion of real memories has come greater awareness of memory as a 'site', theorized by the historian Pierre Nora, where history and imagination, cultural IDENTITY and *patrimoine* (heritage) intersect. With the support of the *Ministère des Anciens Combattants et des victimes de guerre* (Ministry for War Veterans and Victims), which confers a degree of national political recognition on official and voluntary agencies, memorials were inaugurated in the 1990s to hitherto unacknowledged individuals and groups, including women, ethnic minorities and the civilian victims of wartime repression. New types of commemorative museum such as the *Historial de Peronne* and the *Mémorial de Caen* have been established, and memory tourism has added D-DAY beaches and MAGINOT LINE fortifications to the 1914–18 battlefield circuit. Recurrent anniversary celebrations (of 1914, 1918, 1940, 1945, 1962, etc.), proliferating oral history groups, and local web sites underline France's contemporary fascination for things memorial. (**Bill Kidd**)

Further reading

Nora (1997). A multi-volume collection of essays on many aspects of French memory. Barcellini and Wieviorka (1995). On the memory of the Second World War.

Mendès-France, Pierre 1907–82. Centre-Left politician. Known for his commitment to MODERNIZATION, he is often seen as a 'lost leader', whose vision and integrity were much respected, but who lacked the opportunity to implement his economic ideas. He was briefly Prime Minister (1954–55).

Merleau-Ponty, Maurice 1908–61. Philosopher. His *Phénoménologie de la perception* (*Phenomenology of Perception*, 1945) inspired the post-war EXISTENTIALIST movement, especially in analysing how people experience their BODIES. As political editor of *Les TEMPS MODERNES* (from 1945), he was an influential commentator on moral and political issues of the day.

Messiaen, Olivier   1908–92. Composer. He is particularly noted for his many organ compositions, and for his orchestral works. His *Quattuor pour la fin des temps* (*Quartet for the End of Time*, 1941), written and first performed in a concentration camp, is often included in compilations.

Messmer, Pierre   Born 1916. Gaullist politician. He served as a minister under DE GAULLE, and as Prime Minister under POMPIDOU (1972–74).

Metz, Christian   1931–93. Film theorist. He adapted the theories of structural linguistics to develop a 'grammar' to analyse the meaning of film. He later extended this, drawing on PSYCHOANALYSIS in *Le Signifiant imaginaire* (*The Imaginary Signifier*, 1977).

Michaux, Henri   1899–1984. Poet and artist. Inspired by the SURREALISTS, his dense poems and austere paintings explore the limits of meaning and the anguish of existence.

Milhaud, Darius   1892–1974. Composer. A co-founder of the 'Group of Six' composers, he specialized in dramatic music, including theatre, opera, ballet, and film soundtracks, combining classical, popular and jazz styles.

Milice   The *Milice* (militia) was created by the LAVAL government in January 1943 with the stated purpose of contributing to the political, social, economic, intellectual and moral renewal of the country. Many of its members had previously served under Joseph DARNAND in the paramilitary Service d'Ordre of VICHY's *Légion des Combattants*. In practice the *Milice* functioned as a paramilitary police force operating primarily against the RESISTANCE and other internal enemies of the Vichy state. It was headed by Darnand, who had served with distinction in the First World War. A former member of *ACTION FRANÇAISE*, then of the *Cagoule* conspiracy, then of DORIOT's fascist *PARTI POPULAIRE FRANÇAIS* during the inter-war years, Darnand followed the logic of his political trajectory during the OCCUPATION. Though personally loyal to PÉTAIN, he swore allegiance to Hitler and held the rank of *Sturmbannführer* from October 1943 onwards. Ideologically, the *Milice* was FASCIST ultra-right, anti-democratic, anti-Marxist, ANTI-SEMITIC, anti-masonic, anti-bourgeois, anti-capitalist, authoritarian, ÉLITIST, corporatist, and hypernationalistic. It had a school for training and political indoctrination, a youth organization and a periodical publication, *Combats*. With a membership of around 20 000, it became, in effect, an auxiliary of the Gestapo, committing assassinations, reprisals, arbitrary incarcerations, interrogations and summary executions on decisions of its own court martials. By 1944 it had considerable influence at Vichy. Darnand became Secretary General for the Maintenance of Order in January 1944, and Secretary of State for the Interior in June. One of his confederates, Philippe HENRIOT, served as Secretary of State for Information and Propaganda from January 1944 until his assassination in June. After the war, Darnand and many of his senior staff were executed. Large numbers of regional officials and ordinary militiamen were also killed or imprisoned. A macabre coda was provided in 1994 by the trial and imprisonment of Paul Touvier, the *Milice*'s former intelligence chief for the Rhône region, on grounds of crimes against humanity. (**Christopher Flood**)

Further reading

Gordon (1980). A classic study of the collaboration system. Paxton (1982). A classic study of the Vichy regime as a whole. Burrin (1996). A useful recent study.

Minitel   The Minitel was a remarkable success for French industry and INFORMATION TECHNOLOGY in the 1980s, providing France with advanced mass-use telematics and an evolving industry of telematic services. STATE development of the Minitel represented INDUSTRY MINISTRY activity typical of French *DIRIGISME* before France's conversion to the neoliberal European consensus. Curiously, the Minitel complicated France's adoption of the INTERNET. The Nora-Minc report on *The Computerisation of Society* (1977) forewarned government to prepare France for the information age. The Industry Ministry and powerful state telephone company (the DGT) collaborated to develop the Minitel. Launched in 1980, the Minitel is a small terminal which connects via the telephone network to a range of commercial and administrative services. The first service (provided by the DGT) was phone numbers, immediately provoking dissatisfaction amongst phone users as paper phone books in post offices were rapidly withdrawn. Such high-handedness symbolized the supply-led Minitel project, in which consumers received free terminals developed by a state programme and, apart from administrative services provided by the state, commercial services were expected to be subsequently developed by private enterprise. Commercial services did develop. Alongside SNCF timetables and booking, the Minitel soon allowed telematic banking, pizza delivery and a host of commercial activities paid for by connection time. Services that state regulators were unhappy to recognize were various chatting, dating and sexual-encounter businesses of the '*Minitel rose*' (Pink Minitel), which led to accusations that government had created an uncontrollable instrument of immorality. In general, the Minitel industry is a commercial success for the private sector prepared by public-sector finance. By the early 1990s, after ten years of the Minitel, French home-computer ownership was low and take-up of the Internet was slowed by the persisting success of the second generation of Minitel terminals and a mature portfolio of services. Minitel and Internet now coexist. (**Hugh Dauncey**)

Further reading

Abadie (1988). The inside story of the setting up of the Minitel.

Minuit, Éditions de   Founded in 1942 by VERCORS and Pierre de Lescure, it was a clandestine imprint for RESISTANCE literature, which published 25 texts during the Occupation. After the war, under Jérôme Linden, it then became one of the leading publishers of AVANT-GARDE literary and philosophical works.

Mistinguett   1873–1956. Singer and dancer. A popular and versatile MUSIC-HALL performer, she exemplified the persona of a witty and sexy Parisian woman, and starred in many shows internationally.

Mitchell, Eddy Born 1942. Singer. He was a popular rock n' roll star in the 1960s, singing mainly American songs, but later wrote his own lyrics in a wide range of popular genres.

Mitterrand, François 1916–96. Centre-Left politician. He started his career under the VICHY REGIME, and held numerous ministerial posts in FOURTH REPUBLIC governments. After 1958 he became DE GAULLE's leading opponent, standing for President unsuccessfully in 1965. He joined and then led the SOCIALIST PARTY, and became France's longest-serving President (1981–95).

MLAC *(Mouvement pour la libération de l'avortement et de la contraception)* The MLAC (Movement for the Right to Abortion and Contraception) was founded in 1973 by some members of the so-called second wave FEMINIST movement, the MLF (*MOUVEMENT DE LIBÉRATION DES FEMMES*). It was initially an extension of the previous movement for the right to abortion (*Mouvement pour la libération de l'avortement*) founded in 1971. Its aim was to have ABORTION and CONTRACEPTION made more freely available. From the outset the MLF had focused its struggle on what had been previously dismissed in political circles as personal issues: abortion (illegal in France since 1920), contraception, pornography, violence and crimes against women. The MLAC was committed to improving WOMEN's public and private lives by raising public awareness of women's oppression through many forms of public protest and solidarity with victims of oppression. These included the 1973 publication in Le NOUVEL OBSERVATEUR of a Manifesto signed by 343 prominent women, including Simone de BEAUVOIR and Gisèle Halimi, who claimed to have had an abortion, and demonstrations outside the courtroom of a trial at Bobigny in support of two women on trial for involvement in abortion for a minor.

After the 1920 Act was repealed (by the newly elected President GISCARD D'ESTAING's Minister of Health, Simone VEIL), MLAC directed a further campaign against the law's shortcomings. They argued that it was CLASS biased, as it did not allow for free abortion on demand, and many women could not afford to travel to neighbouring European countries where the legal time limit was more generous than the French ten-week period. In 1976 another trial at Aix was publicized when five militants of MLAC were charged with attempting to procure an abortion for a minor, victim of a rape. This pressure group was successful in the way it encouraged politicians such as Giscard and MITTERRAND to recognize women's concerns, it mobilized women to publicly demonstrate throughout the 1970s to have recognized as fundamental, the right of women to control their own BODIES. Like many other feminist causes it also divided the MLF over the way to address the more general struggle against patriarchy. (**Máire Cross**)

Further reading

Duchen (1986). Good on explaining how abortion came to be a critical issue for feminists of the 1970s. Laubier (1990). A documentary anthology containing key texts on MLAC with historical contextualization.

MLF (*Mouvement de libération des femmes*) FEMINIST movement, formed after MAY '68, with an agenda of radical change to end the oppression of WOMEN. It was influential in the 1970s, and provided the impetus for several campaigns, particularly on issues of abortion and contraception, such as the MLAC. It was a loose coalition of different political and ideological tendencies. The differing strategies ultimately became irreconcilable, and the MLF ceased to be a broad grouping in 1979, when one of its components, the *PSYCH ET PO* group won a legal battle to secure sole right to use the title MLF.

Mnouchkine, Ariane Born 1934. Theatre director. Founder of the *Théâtre du Soleil* (Sun Theatre) in 1964, she directed many important plays, of which *1789* (1970) telling the story of the French Revolution, remains the best known.

Mode rétro In the 1970s France seemed to rediscover the period of the German OCCUPATION from 1940 to 1944, as films, novels, memoirs, and historical works appeared in greater and greater numbers, often challenging what was presented as a falsely reassuring picture of French behaviour and attitudes at this time. It became generally agreed that France had colluded in the creation of a 'RESISTANCE myth', which both DE GAULLE and the French COMMUNIST PARTY had actively created.

This *mode rétro*, as it was quickly dubbed, was ushered in by several important works: *Le Chagrin et la pitié* (*The Sorrow and the Pity*, 1969) Marcel OPHULS'S 4-hour-long documentary on Clermont-Ferrand under the Occupation, which French television refused to show until 1981; novels by Patrick MODIANO, including *La Place de l'Étoile* (*Star Square*, 1968), and *La Ronde de nuit* (*Night Round*, 1969), and Louis Malle's film, *Lacombe Lucien* (1974), with a screenplay by Modiano. All these works focused upon the ambiguities and compromises of these years. They stressed the extent to which French people supported Nazism, collaborated with the Germans, and displayed ANTI-SEMITIC attitudes. The American historian Robert Paxton demonstrated, in *La France de Vichy*, the political continuities between the anti-Republican, anti-democratic Right and the ideology of VICHY, as well as the fact that Vichy had willingly met, or even exceeded German demands in relation to handing over Jewish refugees. While the 1970s and 1980s were primarily concerned with investigations of COLLABORATION, the emphasis shifted in the 1990s to French complicity in the HOLOCAUST and the deportation of JEWS from France to the death camps.

Recent work has begun to question the extent to which the Resistance myth dominated the post-war period, seeing it rather as a creation of the FIFTH REPUBLIC in the aftermath of the bitter divisions of the ALGERIAN WAR. The extent to which this obsession with the history of the Second World War was in fact continuing to prevent discussion of the more recent Algerian war has also been an important topic in the 1990s. **(Margaret Atack)**

Further reading

Rousso (1987). A comprehensive and highly influential analysis of the differing phases of Vichy in scholarly works, political debates, and popular culture. Conan and Rousso (1994). A more polemical but equally important investigation arguing that France's continuing obsession with Vichy is paradoxically a way of avoiding it. Morris (1989). A helpful analysis of the work of a group of young writers, including Modiano, coming to terms with their parents' complicated history.

Modernization The *term* 'modernization' is frequently used to describe France's rapid socio-economic development post-1945, but the *process* of modernization has generally been taken as a fundamental objective of government policy, particularly during the 1960s. The STATE has fostered France's modernization, in efforts to maintain French prestige and economic competitiveness.

Changes in industrial organization and undermining of old certainties caused by the Great War brought realization that France's late and slow INDUSTRIALIZATION during the nineteenth century had weakened her as a major European power. Still predominantly rural and AGRICULTURAL in the 1930s, France modernized slowly, as new industrial and business practices such as FORDISM were introduced from AMERICA, and as the state investigated technocratic management of policies. DE GAULLE's appeal in the 1930s to modernize the ARMY through mechanization was ignored, but VICHY's interventionist technocracy facilitated the post-war reassessment of France's position and the will to modernize.

Economic reconstruction and growth during the FOURTH REPUBLIC, encouraged by the modernizing zeal of national PLANNING accelerated industrialization and urbanization, and as the economic importance of EMPIRE declined, French protectionism opened to international competition after the Treaty of Rome (1957). Post-war demographic buoyancy required modernization of schooling, as secondary and then tertiary EDUCATION (in the 1960s) massified to provide an educated workforce. TECHNOLOGY also contributed to modernization, and GAULLISM during the 1960s emphasized France's need to be technologically as well as socio-economically 'modern' through ATOMIC WEAPONS, the SPACE PROGRAMME and TRANSPORT. During the 1970s, 1980s and 1990s, France's continuing modernization was inextricably linked to economic GLOBALIZATION and European integration, as the economy aligned with EU financial convergence criteria and as trade increasingly reflected European transport axes.

Post-war modernization had positive and negative effects, making France an industrial heavyweight, but arguably neglecting the interests of PAYSANS, *petits commercants* (small traders), IMMIGRANTS and others left behind in her economic development. (**Hugh Dauncey**)

Further reading

Gaffney (1988). Debates and analyses.

Modiano, Patrick Born 1945. Writer. His novels explore memories of the past and their continuing influence, particularly where memories of the German OCCUPATION are concerned, as in *La Place de l'Étoile* (*Star Square*, 1968). He helped to popularize the MODE RÉTRO.

Mollet, Guy 1905–75. Socialist politician. He led the SOCIALIST PARTY (1946–69) and held several ministerial posts, including Prime Minister (1956–57).

Monde, le Daily newspaper, founded in 1944 by Hubert BEUVE-MÉRY, it became France's most respected national newspaper, with a Centre-Left ethos and a reputation for independence and impartiality. It has a number of associated weekly magazines, including *Le monde de l'éducation* and *Le monde diplomatique*.

Monnet, Jean   1888–1979. Economist and politician. Head of the first French economic reconstruction plan (1945–52), he became a leading figure in founding the European Economic Community (1957).

Montand, Yves   1922–91. Actor and singer. Successful in the 1950s and 1960s as a singer of popular songs, including a repertoire of traditional folk songs, he also supported various left-wing causes, with his actress wife Simone SIGNORET. He appeared in numerous films, including *Jean de Florette-Manon des sources* (1986).

Montherlant, Henri de   1895–1972. Writer. A successful novelist in the inter-war period, his novels like *Les Jeunes Filles* (*The Girls*, 1936–9) used experimental narrative techniques. He began writing for the theatre with *La Reine morte* (*The Dead Queen*, 1942) and became a prolific playwright, admired even by critics who did not share his conservative values and bleak outlook.

Montoire   October 1940. Two meetings were held between Hitler and PÉTAIN at this small town in the Loire Valley. The photograph of their handshake there became a symbol of COLLABORATION for both its supporters and opponents.

Morality   The French THIRD REPUBLIC (1870–1940) separated morality from religion, insisting on the secular nature of the STATE and teaching, through the state EDUCATION system, a new republican morality that emphasized patriotism, civic pride, hard work and self-control. The belief that the republican school must be a haven of secular rationality persists today, as the *affaire des foulards* (1989–95) demonstrated: Muslim girls were sent home from school for wearing the *foulard* or headscarf that visibly proclaimed their religious beliefs.

At one level, the last century has seen the erosion of collective belief in any shared national morality. The First World War, when an initially optimistic, patriotic war led to hitherto unimaginable levels of suffering and carnage (1.3 million French soldiers dead, a further 1.1 million wounded), undermined faith in the moral authority of governments. The Second World War, and the OCCUPATION, revealed the profound conflict between alternative political moralities in France. In the 1950s, Jean-Paul Sartre's EXISTENTIALIST philosophy (disseminated well beyond academic circles) defined any acceptance of an externally conceived moral code as 'bad faith' (*mauvaise foi*): the individual could only achieve 'authenticity' by deciding and living by his/her own system of values. In a POST-MODERN age, moralities are widely recognized as relative, constructed and culturally specific, rather than absolute.

At the same time, French people (of whom in a 1994 poll 83 per cent declared individual conscience to be their main moral guide) continue to behave in many instances as though they subscribed to a shared moral system. Protest movements from MAY '68 to the 1990s' *SANS-PAPIERS* movement, for example, acted in the name of justice, human rights, a vision of what national morality ought to be. The French appear less concerned than the English or Americans, for example, with questions of *sexual* morality, as the appearance of Mitterrand's mistress and illegitimate daughter at his funeral (January 1996) demonstrated. But the more culturally and ethnically diverse society that France has become does not exclude a majority consensus on a certain core morality. (**Diana Holmes**)

Further reading

Cook and Davie (1999). See Chapter 10 'Religion and *Laïcité*'. Forbes and Kelly (1995). See Chapter 1 for a discussion of Republican morality.

Morin, Edgar   Born 1921. Sociologist and philosopher. He was active in post-war left-wing intellectual circles, described in his *Autocritique* (1959). He analysed cultural phenomena, including film stars and the spreading of rumours, and developed a philosophy of science, set out in his four-volume work *La Méthode* (*Method*, 1977–91).

Moulin, Jean   1899–1943. Resistance hero. A senior civil servant and *préfet* before the war, he joined the RESISTANCE and was appointed by DE GAULLE to co-ordinate the internal French Resistance movements. He established the COMITÉ NATIONAL DE LA RÉSISTANCE (CNR), but was captured and tortured to death by the Gestapo.

Mounier, Emmanuel   1905–50. Philosopher and journalist. Editor of the monthly review ESPRIT, he developed a philosophy of the human person (PERSONALISM), which called for full engagement in political and social affairs, and was influential in CATHOLIC social thought.

Moustaki, Georges   Born 1934. Singer and songwriter. He wrote popular hits for other artists, including Édith PIAF's *Milord*, before establishing himself as a singer with songs like *Le Métèque* (The dirty foreigner).

MRP (*Mouvement Républicain Populaire*)   1944–67. The MRP (Popular Republican Movement) was the first serious Christian-democrat party in France but faltered badly. During the inter-war period, CATHOLICS were divided between right-wing miniparties and Christian-democrat minnows. The MRP's launch in 1944 offered them a mass party with satellite organizations (women, youth, farmers, etc.), led by ÉLITES formed in the inter-war Catholic Action social movements and the RESISTANCE. Initially the party claimed a quarter of the vote; it was a key member of post-war governments which rebuilt the economy and the welfare state. It accepted a market economy with STATE intervention in the name of social justice. It differed from LIBERALISM in basing its politics on the *person* (co-operative and community-inclined) rather than on the competitive *individual*. It has always been the most EUROPEAN-integrationist and Atlanticist party. The MRP's progressive policies, devised by urban élites, proved too advanced for many rural voters, who drifted back to the old Right or the new rival, GAULLISM. The MRP was nevertheless a pivotal member of majorities after 1947, providing premiers like BIDAULT and SCHUMAN. It was blamed for the end of the FOURTH REPUBLIC, but served briefly under DE

GAULLE, before breaking with him over European integration. Since then French Christian democracy has struggled. The MRP was formally wound up in 1967, but survived under various names – LECANUET's *Centre démocrate*, the *Centre des Démocrates Sociaux*, now *Force Démocrate* – but only as an ally of the Right, via the UDF. Today perhaps 8 or 10 per cent of voters are Christian democrats, concentrated as ever in the Catholic heartlands – BRITTANY, ALSACE-LORRAINE, below the Massif Central. This rump testifies both to the general decline of religion and to the inability of the MRP and its avatars to secure monopoly representation of the Catholic vote when there still was one to speak of. (**David Hanley**)

Further reading

Hanley (1994). See Introduction and Chapter 9. Letamendia (1995). An exhaustive treatment.

Munich   On 29 September 1938, the British and French Prime Ministers, Chamberlain and DALADIER, met Hitler and Mussolini at Munich to resolve the crisis in CZECHOSLOVAKIA. Heartened by *Anschluss* (union) with Austria, March 1938, Nazi sympathizers and agents in the Czech Sudetenland pressed for this area to become part of Hitler's Reich. Earlier meetings between Chamberlain and Hitler in September proved inconclusive and war seemed inevitable for France because of its 1924 alliance with Czechoslovakia. At Munich, it was agreed that the Sudetenland should indeed become German, with plebiscites to decide the fate of ethnically mixed regions. The Conference was thus the high point of the diplomacy of appeasement which the liberal democracies had been pursuing towards the *Führer*. For some historians appeasement was a morally enfeebled policy, yet at least it is understandable why France chose the path of conciliation. There remained a strong public distaste for war after the 1914–18 conflict; there remained a Depression that refused to go away; rearmament was in its infancy; General Gamelin was undertaking an overhaul of military strategy; political divisions were fierce since the POPULAR FRONT; and Paris was inclined to follow London's lead. Whereas Munich encouraged Hitler to become more daring in his foreign policy, in France it was greeted with acclamation. Daladier was fêted as a hero. In truth, opinion was split into two, a division that cut across traditional political loyalties. The *Munichois* (supporters of the agreements) included pacifists among the SOCIALIST PARTY, much of the Centre Right, which wished to extricate France from eastern Europe and rely on the EMPIRE, and several members of the extreme right who later collaborated with the Nazi occupier. The *anti-Munichois* believed no more ground should be given to Hitler. Among this number was Daladier himself who, over the next few months, readied France for war by speeding up rearmament, ending economic problems, and strengthening government. (**Nicholas Atkin**)

Further reading

Young (1996).

Musée de l'homme   Opened 1937. Anthropological museum (Museum of Man) in the Palais de Chaillot, founded by Paul Rivet (1876–1958). Its staff formed the first concerted RESISTANCE movement (1940–1), which was destroyed by German military intelligence.

Musée d'Orsay   A top visitor attraction in Paris, the Orsay museum (*Musée d'Orsay*) began life as the terminus of the Paris–Orléans railway company. Since its principal collections cover the period 1848–1914, the heroic age of the RAILWAYS, the synergy between its past and present functions is intrinsic to its wider cultural significance. Designed by Victor Laloux and inaugurated for the Paris Exhibition of 1900, it boasted electric traction and lifts to the departure platforms below ground level, now used to exhibit sculpture. Original features retained include prominent ornate clocks and the iron *marquise* sheltering the former taxi rank. Its turn-of-the-century elegance and LEFT BANK location amidst the *beaux quartiers* close to the centres of political power (*Assemblée nationale*, ministries, Presidential Élysée Palace) distinguished it from the Gare du Nord (1859) with its cathedral-like façade or the equally cavernous Gare de L'Est. Decommissioned in 1939, it served as a reception centre for returning wartime deportees in 1945, becoming a 'site' of memory for RESISTANCE writers such as VERCORS and DURAS. It also enjoyed brief cinematic notoriety in Orson Welles's film of Kafka's *The Trial* (1963).

The museum conversion, proposed by President Valéry GISCARD D'ESTAING in 1977 and completed in 1986, is now firmly associated with his successor President MITTERRAND's GRANDS TRAVAUX. Exhibits are grouped on three floors (*Rez-de-chaussée, niveau médian, niveau supérieur*) by genre, by themed collection, individual artist (Courbet, Van Gogh, the Impressionists, Gauguin, etc.) and movement (Symbolism, NATURALISM, Art Nouveau including furniture and jewellery). There are major works by Manet, Daumier, Puvis de Chavannes, Moreau and Renoir. Sculpture is well if somewhat eclectically represented (Carpeaux, Rodin, Falguière, Bourdelle), and there are *marbres* of statues now destroyed. The museum space is well lit, showing works to advantage; sculptures are viewable in the round as they would be in an outside location, and the open-plan 'terraces' are easily navigable. These qualities are replicated on the museum's excellent 'virtual visit', CD-ROMs, and its website. (**Bill Kidd**)

Further reading

Consult any good Paris guide–book (such as the Eyewitness series), and the Museum website: www.musée-orsay.fr

Museums   The opening of the LOUVRE to all in 1793 signalled France's first public museum, of which there are now over one thousand. The museums of 15 provincial cities owe a large part of their original collections to the 1801 law whereby the Louvre's excess stock was transferred to regional institutions. France's public museums now come under the auspices of the Ministry of CULTURE and/or the Regional Councils (*Conseils régionaux*) concerned.

At the centre of the network is the *Réunion des Musées Nationaux* (Confederation of National Museums) consisting of 33 museums spearheaded by the Louvre, the world's largest. Others include the *Musée Cluny*, the museum of the Middle Ages in a fifteenth-century abbatial Parisian palace, the *MUSÉE D'ORSAY* (nineteenth-century art including an extensive Impressionist collection) and the prehistoric painted caves at Lascaux. On a smaller scale the *Réunion* includes the *Musée de la Maison Bonaparte*

(Napoleon's birthplace) in Ajaccio, Corsica, and the *Musée Fernand Léger* in Biot, Provence. Twenty-one of the national museums are in or around PARIS.

Some of France's most unexpected treasures are to be found in non-national museums. Examples include the Goyas in the newly-refurbished *Palais des Beaux Arts de Lille*, or the collection of seventeenth-century paintings in the *Musée de Nantes*. In some cases the setting is outstanding: Toulouse's *Musée des Augustins* displays gothic sculpture and religious art in the fourteenth-century cloisters and chapel of the former Augustinian priory.

France also boasts a wealth of private museums, from the *Musée Grévin* waxworks to castle treasure-houses (such as the collection of sixteenth-century paintings in the Château de Chenonceau). Although many remain unashamedly traditional, others promote learning through the latest gadgetry, such as the 'virtual' visit of the Impressionists' haunts at the *Musée des Impressionistes* (Auvers, Picardy) or the high-tech Futuroscope theme park near Poitiers.

The *Conservateurs de musée* (Curators) are generally trained through highly specialized and élite schools such as the *École des Chartes*, *École du Louvre* and *École des Beaux Arts*. Organization in art galleries tends to be chronological. Labelling is clear, but often brief. Museums in France are rarely free, although reduced rates often apply for teachers or the under-26s (but not students *per se*). (**Laurence Grove**)

Further reading

The *Réunion des Musées Nationaux*'s website on www.rmn.fr offers information on all of their national museums with many links to other pages. Includes an English-language version. Many non-national museums such as Lille or Toulouse also have web sites.

Music, classical   French music in the 1920s and 1930s was dominated by the group of composers known collectively as *Les Six*, including notably POULENC, HONEGGER, and MILHAUD. However, after the scandal of the first performance of *Le Sacre du Printemps* (*The Rite of Spring*) in 1913, the Russian-born Stravinsky remained more influential, especially through his development of the neo-classical style. Nadia Boulanger (1887–1979), the distinguished teacher of composition, presented him to her students at the 'American Conservatoire' as an ideal model.

With the publication of his *Quatuor pour la Fin du temps* (*Quartet for the End of Time*), written during the Second World War, Olivier MESSIAEN revealed himself as the most individual composer of the immediate post war years. Highly respected as a professor of musical analysis at the Paris Conservatoire, he was able to integrate in his music the natural complexity of birdsong, oriental exotism, and the passionate religiosity of his late opera *Saint François d'Assise* (*St Francis of Assisi*, 1975).

His near-contemporary Henri Dutilleux (born 1916), a professor at the *École Normale de musique*, first acquired celebrity with his 2nd symphony (1959); he has since written concertos for the cellist Rostropovich (*Tout un Monde Lointain*), and the violinist I. Stern. Another full-scale symphony (*The Shadows of Time*, 1999) was written for the Boston Symphony orchestra under Ozawa.

Pierre BOULEZ has acquired an international reputation. A former student of Messiaen, but also influenced by modern German techniques, he adopted from the outset a style of uncompromising post-serialism, notably in *Le Marteau sans Maître* (*The Hammer without a Master*). Seen in France as an *enfant terrible,* he made a career abroad, as a distinguished conductor, before being invited back to France as founding director of the IRCAM research institute and the *Ensemble Intercontemporain.* The new generation of French composers includes M. Levinas (born 1949), T. Murail (born 1947), and P. Dusapin (born 1955). (**Bill Brooks**)

Music, popular   Popular music includes folk, band and dance musics, blues, pop and JAZZ. Theoretically, it is made by or accessible to ordinary people irrespective of cultural competence. Until the twentieth century, French popular song (*CHANSON*) largely retained the oral, participatory character it had had since medieval times. But the record industry, BROADCASTING and the global market transformed it into a commercial product.

Early in the century, the advent of MUSIC-HALL, revue and RADIO turned singing into showbiz and France's first international recording stars were born (Maurice CHEVALIER, Édith PIAF). Imported music from AMERICA (jazz, blues, tango) also introduced dance crazes. In the 1930–40s, American influences were audible in the songs of Charles TRENET, the guitar of Django REINHARDT, and bands like Ray Ventura's *Collégiens.* A second wave of Americanization after the LIBERATION then brought swing and bebop, though during the 1950s a more European style of 'poetic' song (BREL, BRASSENS) developed, in PARIS's LEFT-BANK cabarets.

By 1960, radio stations like *Europe 1* were bringing yet another US influence: rock'n'roll. During the next decade, an 'Anglo-Saxon' pop invasion spawned numerous French imitators like Johnny HALLYDAY. But from the folk-rock boom of the late 1960s emerged new singer-songwriters (Maxime Le Forestier, RENAUD, Francis Cabrel) who responded to Anglo-American influences more creatively. Even more ambitious experiments in cross-fertilization followed in the 1980–90s, as French pop seemed finally to reach maturity. Less derivative rock, punk and rap performers proliferated, while influences from North Africa and elsewhere created an even richer multicultural mix. Today, this eclecticism thrives, some of it, chiefly techno, such as Air, or Daft Punk, even reaching 'Anglo-Saxon' audiences.

Nevertheless, for many, the burning issue is still how to preserve Francophone song given young people's insatiable demand for pop in English. One legislative ploy in 1994 was a quota of French-language music on radio stations. Ironically, however, France has broken into the English-speaking market with techno, a genre which is largely instrumental. (**David Looseley**)

Further reading

Rioux (1994). A substantial historical introduction.

Music-Hall   Music-hall evolved at the end of the nineteenth century from café-concerts and from popular dance halls by providing a more sophisticated and lavish form of popular entertainment, including professional dancers, comedians and, particularly, singers. It rapidly became one of the most significant forms of popular entertainment. Its golden age, however, was undoubtedly the inter-war years, which saw the establishment of a stable of major stars playing in PARIS, at venues such as *L'OLYMPIA* and *BOBINO'S*, and the music-halls of the provinces. These stars, whose careers often spanned the OCCUPATION, included singers and dancers like MISTINGUETT, Josephine BAKER, Maurice CHEVALIER, Jean GABIN, Édith PIAF and Charles TRENET, as well as comedians such as FERNANDEL. So popular was music-hall at the time that its stars also often had highly successful careers in the cinema.

After the Second World War, music-hall continued, with a new generation of singers who came to prominence after the OCCUPATION, mainly originating from the LEFT BANK, and often specializing in more a meaningful, poetic repertoire, sometimes with explicit political content. This new generation included Juliette GRÉCO, Léo FERRÉ, Mouloudji, Georges BRASSENS, Jacques BREL, Yves MONTAND and BARBARA, all of whom achieved a mass popular audience, as did comedians such as Guy Bedos and Raymond Devos.

By the 1970s, traditional music-hall was in decline, challenged by TELEVISION, the growth of the suburbs, and the rise of American-dominated popular music. All the provincial music-halls closed, and even in Paris the tradition was virtually at an end, with the permanent closure of *Bobino's* and the temporary closure of *L'Olympia*. A more durable survivor of the music-hall tradition, fuelled by tourism, is to be found in shows featuring by female dancers: *Les Folies-Bergère*, *Le Moulin Rouge* and *Le Casino de Paris*. (**Nicholas Hewitt**)

Further reading

Behr (1993). A biography of Maurice Chevalier as music-hall star.

Myth   An idea, image or story that carries widely shared symbolic meanings. Initially, myths were associated with the stories of gods and heroes from the ancient world, so often repeated and reformulated that they became a shorthand language for thinking about human affairs. Classical myths were popular in the 1930s and 1940s, and used by dramatists like GIRAUDOUX and ANOUILH, or CAMUS, who used the myth of Sisyphus, condemned to keep rolling a rock up a mountain, to analyse the ABSURDITY of human life.

Myths, such as that of Oedipus, who killed his father and married his mother, were used by PSYCHOANALYSTS like Freud and LACAN to explain human psychological development from childhood. They were also analysed by the ANTHROPOLOGIST Claude LÉVI-STRAUSS to reveal conceptions of kinship and the relationship between nature and culture. He showed that these and many other stories enabled societies to establish and maintain a common understanding of relationships and values.

Roland BARTHES extended this to the EVERYDAY images or stories found in the MEDIA, which persuade people how to think or feel. In *Mythologies* (1957), he showed, for example, that a car like the CITROËN DS was not just a motor vehicle, but was advertised so as to bear *connotations* or associations, which included modernity, elegance, lightness, and divinity (DS, *déesse*, goddess). In a series of similar analyses, he showed that these modern myths are usually mystifications, aimed to encourage consumers to buy products, or intended to gain support for a political position.

The idea of myth is now used to criticize any widely held idea or account of events, by pointing to a discrepancy between 'myth' and 'reality', usually with a view to uncovering an attempt to deceive the general public. (**Michael Kelly**)

Further reading

Barthes (1973b). Lévi-Strauss (1977). Strenski (1987).

N

Nancy, Jean-Luc   Born 1942. Philosopher. A student of DERRIDA, his work discusses Kant, Hegel, LACAN, and other thinkers, exploring the boundaries of meaning and identity, with an awareness of spiritual dimensions which may not be amenable to analysis.

Nation   In its modern juridical and political sense, nation dates from the French Revolution. When, on 17 June 1789, the Third Estate called itself *l'assemblée nationale,* it asserted the existence of a sovereign entity defined by collective equality under laws freely accepted. Distinct both from the nation-state and the régime as enshrined successively in monarchy, empire and republic (though most attuned to the latter's professed universalism), the concept of nation(hood) based on consent and not race, language or culture was re-articulated by the historian Fustel de Coulanges (1871). It acquired historic contemporary credence from the fact that as late as the 1860s, as many as 40 per cent of the population in some areas did not speak FRENCH as their mother tongue: the nation existed, Frenchness would need to be created. In that sense, nation is also a socio-cultural construct as well as a legal concept, and a vector of other political values. It is synonymous with the progressive forces of *pays* and *peuple, patrie* and *république*: foreign invasion in 1792 and regicide in 1793 accreted the latter. And it belongs inside the vocabulary, physical geography (*Place de la Nation*) and iconography of revolutionary republicanism, while the primacy of popular (national) sovereignty was incorporated in successive republican constitutions before and since the First World War.

However, nation as inclusive citizenship has been periodically displaced or appropriated, on the Left by militant secularism and CLASS-based movements, and on the Right by exacerbated forms of nationalism such as that generated by the Dreyfus affair and theorized by writers such as BARRÈS and MAURRAS. The latter's rejection of 'alien' spiritual and political communities, and the CATHOLIC nation, acquired a late lease of life under VICHY's *État français* (1940–44). This still finds an echo on the Extreme Right, as the nation-state loses ground to the European Community and as multiculturalism challenges the 'one and indivisible Republic's' historic compromise between public and private rights and duties. (**Bill Kidd**)

Further reading

Hobsbawm (1992). Jenkins (1990).

National Front   See FRONT NATIONAL.

Nationalization   The taking into state ownership, on behalf of the NATION, of privately owned companies. There are two traditions in France of state intervention in the economy. The oldest dates back to the seventeenth century, when Louis XIV's minister, Colbert, financed important new manufacturing enterprises. *Colbertisme* involves state funding and control to ensure the success of industries which are seen as strategic assets for the country, particularly where private industry lacks the means to develop them. The more recent tradition stems from nineteenth-century social-ism, which argued that the major means of production and sources of wealth should be organized for the benefit of all the people, owned and managed by the collectivity.

The SOCIALISTS made some initial nationalizations in 1936, as part of the POPULAR FRONT programme, taking over some arms manufacturers and extending state involvement in the RAILWAYS. The major programme of nationalizations was carried out at the LIBERATION by the PROVISIONAL GOVERNMENT, where DE GAULLE's instinctive *colbertisme* converged with the left-wing programme favoured by the socialists and COMMUNISTS. Over an 18-month period (1944–46), strategic industries were nation-alized, including the energy utilities, major transport companies (air and rail), some major manufacturers (SNECMA aircraft and Renault motors), the *Banque de France* (French national bank) and large parts of the financial services (four main high street banks and most insurance companies). This created a dynamic state sector, which played an important role in post-war prosperity (*LES TRENTE GLORIEUSES*).

A further wave of nationalizations was undertaken on the election to President of François MITTERRAND (1981). His Prime Minister, Pierre MAUROY, nationalized nearly all the remaining financial services and several large industrial groups, includ-ing Pechiney, Thomson, and Rhône-Poulenc.

Since the mid-1980s, a series of PRIVATIZATIONS has reduced the extent of nation-alized industry, though the state remains an important force in the French national economy. (**Michael Kelly**)

Further reading

Ross, Hoffmann, and Malzachert (1987). Andrieu, Le Van and Prost (1987).

NATO (North Atlantic Treaty Organization)   In French, OTAN (*Organisation du Traité de l'Atlantique du Nord*). France's relationship with NATO has evolved considerably over the years since its creation. In the context of the COLD WAR, the perceived enemy of Western European states was the USSR, and together with Great BRITAIN, France was instrumental in persuading the American government to sign the North Atlantic Treaty in Washington in 1949, which represented a political commitment from signatory states to consider an armed attack against one or more of them as an attack against them all. An integrated command structure was then set up as the military arm of the treaty. Although political opinion in France was divided in its attitude towards AMERICA, French governments first welcomed American bases on their territory and the NATO headquarters was located in Paris until the 1960s, when President de Gaulle began to assert the doctrine of national independence. After gradually withdrawing parts of the French army and navy from the integrated NATO command, in 1966 he ordered the departure of all American troops based in France, and the headquarters consequently moved to Brussels. Nevertheless, France has always remained politically a committed member of the Atlantic Alliance.

In the 1980s, a change of attitude became obvious on the part of the French government of François MITTERRAND, who broke with the GAULLIST doctrine of official neutrality between the USA and the USSR, to support NATO policy. He made an unprecedented speech in the German Bundestag in 1983 urging German acceptance of Cruise and Pershing missiles. Since then, given the increasing implausibility of claims to independence, France has moved gradually closer back into the NATO orbit, particularly since the Gulf War, without actually officially re-establishing full membership. This has been facilitated by the changing role of NATO since the end of the Cold War. (**Susan Collard**)

Naturalism   Naturalism was one of the most influential literary movements of the late nineteenth century. Its theorist and chief practitioner was the novelist Émile Zola. Like the Realists before him, such as Balzac, Zola believed in the mimetic power of the novel, that is, its capacity to capture, accurately, both the material reality and the spirit of the novelist's society. A man of his age, Zola took these aims further: the novel would harness scientific theories (evolution, heredity), be encyclopaedic in scope and fully researched in documentary style, bringing all CLASSES and social groups into the huge reflecting mirror of fiction. In his application of these principles, Zola's epic imagination brought his theories and researches to life: his 20-novel *Rougon-Macquart* cycle, still widely read, depicts the society of the Second Empire (1852–70) in sweeping narratives and colourful imagery, persuasively mimetic and immensely readable. Modernist writers of the twentieth century have reacted against Naturalism's pretension to reproduce reality in the novel, arguing that narrative conventions (linear plot, closure, unified characters) construct, rather than reflect, a coherent reality, and that the novel may as well recognize and celebrate its own artificiality. Yet Naturalism in fiction has remained popular and resistant to criticism: many popular novels and films broadly espouse Zola's mimetic aims.

In the visual arts too, naturalism means the accurate reproduction of reality (as opposed to idealization, stylization, ABSTRACT art). The invention of PHOTOGRAPHY in the late nineteenth century, then of CINEMA (1895 in France), seemed to liberate art from any need to record and document – the camera did it better. However, neither photography nor film has finally chosen to go fully down the Naturalist route. As Zola's work had already revealed, the inevitable mediation of the creator's subjectivity, the structuring function of the medium itself (in the case of the camera, type and quality of film, selection and angle of shot, editing) mean that the innocent transparency assumed by the theory of naturalism could only ever be partial. (**Diana Holmes**)

Further reading

Mitterand (1986). Concise, clear introduction to Naturalism.

Navarre, Yves 1940–94. Writer. His novels, plays, poems and essays deal particularly with homosexual relationships and rights. His novel, *Le jardin d'acclimatation* (*Zoological Gardens*, 1980) won the Goncourt Prize.

Négritude The cultural and political concept of *négritude* emerged from the meeting, in 1930s' Paris, of a number of black students from colonies in Francophone AFRICA and the Caribbean. The term was coined by the Martinican poet and politician Aimé CÉSAIRE as a means of reclaiming the racist word *nègre*. Brought to metropolitan France to complete their ASSIMILATION into the French EDUCATION system, these writers linked to *négritude* were instead exposed to the influence of the Harlem Renaissance as well as COMMUNISM and SURREALISM. They began to question the effects of COLONIALISM on their respective cultures and, as a result, developed a theory of the distinctive nature of African culture and psychology. This foregrounded the grandeur of pre-colonial CIVILIZATION while turning superficially racial and colonial interpretations of blackness into a more complex understanding of the 'African personality'. Despite their origins on either side of the Atlantic, the négritudinists celebrated their common blackness as a potential means of unification. Works in French by black African and Caribbean authors had appeared before the 1930s. They tended, however, to ignore issues of RACE and social injustice, and were on the whole imitative of exoticist literature written for a metropolitan readership. Literature emerging from the *négritude* movement was radically different, for it encouraged pride in a vast and complex African heritage (rooted in Africa, but spread as a result of diaspora) while serving as a trigger for political action.

Négritude has been hijacked by a number of individuals for divergent political purposes, and even its principal exponents (Césaire and SENGHOR) differed over its precise meaning. The term came under increasing criticism from the 1950s onwards when it was seen to erase political and cultural differences between distinct peoples (and particularly between Africa and the Caribbean). The late twentieth-century *créolité* movement has, for instance, proposed a more complex notion of Caribbean unity in which the ethnic and cultural diversity of the region is recognized and African origins play a less dominant role. *Négritude* represented nevertheless an essential stage both in the awakening of political consciousness in Africa and the Caribbean and in the discovery of a distinctive francophone literary voice. (**Charles Forsdick**)

Further reading

Césaire (1995). A parallel text edition, with full introductory notes, of Césaire's seminal text. The poem, in which the word '*négritude*' appears for the first time (in relation to the Haitian revolution), remains central to francophone Black literature. Jack (1996). A comprehensive account of the emergence of *négritude* and of its significance in the history of francophone Black literature.

Neo-colonialism   Neo-colonialism is the situation wherein a former colonial power exerts control over its former colonies, or a stronger STATE exerts control similar to colonial control over another independent state. Although European IMPERIALISM had always been based on differing degrees of control, not always taking the form of direct COLONIZATION, the idea of neo-colonialism can be traced to the end of the European empires after the Second World War. At a time when standards of living for the WORKING CLASSES were generally improving, the concept of neo-colonialism attracted the interest of the French left who wished to condemn both the role of the CAPITALIST system in the continued poverty of countries of the South, and the specific role of France in the former colonies of Sub-Saharan Africa.

The first sense of neo-colonialism is the direct role of ex-colonial powers in the politics of former colonies, through political influence or military intervention. The second sense is a cultural one, that the West retains power over countries of the South through things such as LANGUAGE and CONSUMER products. The third sense is economic. Analysts have pointed to both the direct role of companies and to the general working of the world economy in the exploitation of the South.

Interest in the concept of neo-colonialism has declined in the past twenty years. It is often felt that the concept does not take enough account of the complexity of societies in the South, nor of the independent actions of their political leaders. The political insight that the idea undoubtedly brings in some cases had been partly lost in the desire to fit complex interactions into all-encompassing economic concepts. **(Bill Brooks)**

Further reading

Two highly critical texts on the role of France in Sub-Saharan Africa:
Mende (1979). Beti (1972).

New Look   A movement in women's fashion, led in 1947 by young male designers. Rejecting the utilitarian wartime styles which prioritized comfort and economy, they re-introduced full swinging skirts, wasp waists and high-heeled shoes which emphasized feminity.

News   News is recently received, noteworthy information of general interest, usually published or broadcast. Traditionally the French relied on newspapers, but as the media developed, the population turned increasingly to RADIO and subsequently TELEVISION as their preferred source of news. Radio news coverage is especially good in the morning, and regular bulletins are provided throughout the day. The main time slots for television news are lunchtime and, above all, 8.00 p.m. in the evening for the principal news broadcast: *le vingt heures*.

From 1945 onwards, news was provided by the STATE BROADCASTING corporation, and private stations were banned. Coverage was heavily censored, especially during the DE GAULLE presidency. However, many people listened to the news broadcast on long-wave from beyond France's borders by independent stations such as *RTL* (*Radiodiffusion-Télévision-Luxembourg*), *Europe 1*, and *RMC* (*Radio-Monte-Carlo*). Since the deregulation of the 1980s, and proliferation of MEDIA sources, the French have access to a wide range of news programmes. At 8.00 p.m. competition is intense between the independent television channel *TF1* and the state-owned *France 2*, which both provide national and international coverage, while *France 3*'s specialism is its coverage of regional news. For news in brief, the independent channel *M6* broadcasts news images accompanied by voice-over commentary. On radio, state-owned *France-Inter* has a reputation for quality news coverage, while its sister station *France-Info*, created in 1987, was the first in Europe to provide non-stop news. Cable and SATELLITE have also extended choice, with non-stop news on *LCI* (*La Chaîne info*) and *Euronews*, and extensive coverage on *TV5 Europe*, which all figure among the most popular cable and satellite channels. *CNN* is also available on many networks.

France also prides itself on possessing one of the leading world news agencies, *AFP* (*Agence France Presse*). (**Pam Moores**)

Further reading

Charon (1991). Wide-ranging collection of brief contributions with useful bibliographies.

Night-clubs Night-clubs come in various shapes and sizes, but they are generally distinguished from other kinds of entertainment by their restrictive entry: in terms of cost, membership or special interest. On one level, there is little to distinguish establishments like the *Crazy Horse Saloon* from those types of MUSIC-HALL which specialize in lavish spectacles centred largely on female dancers. Yet, into this category would fall those clubs, often to be found in Montmartre, which form part of the capital's sex industry.

At the same time, throughout the twentieth century, night-clubs have provided congenial surroundings, often including drinking and dancing, for a privileged CLASS or social group. In PARIS, such establishments are often found in the 16th *arrondissement*, on or near the Champs-Élysées and, in the 1960s, they became the basis for sophisticated discotheques. At the same time, night-clubs became the focus for cultural and intellectual activity. One interesting example of this was *Le Bœuf sur le Toit*, in the Rue Boissy d'Anglas, just off the Place de la Concorde. Founded by the artist, poet and film-maker Jean COCTEAU just after the First World War, it played host throughout the 1920s to a dazzling mixture of socialites and writers, such as François MAURIAC, DRIEU LA ROCHELLE and Louis ARAGON.

A final category of night-club would be those devoted to comedy, such as the traditional home of *chansonniers* (comic artists), the *Caveau de la République*, the more recent *Bistro de la Gare*, or jazz clubs. The latter became extremely important in the years following the OCCUPATION on the LEFT BANK and were closely associated with the EXISTENTIALIST movement. Establishments such as *Le Tabou*, run by the writer and jazz trumpeter Boris VIAN, saw the début of young music-hall artists like Juliette GRÉCO as well as the introduction of modern JAZZ from AMERICA. (**Nicholas Hewitt**)

Further reading

Hammond and O'Connor (1988). Contains rich material on the night-club as spectacle.

Nimier, Roger 1925–61. Writer. Leader of the conservative HUSSARD group, named after his novel *Le Hussard bleu* (*The Blue Hussar*, 1950), he celebrated the heroic virtues and criticized the post-war Centre-Left consensus. He was also an influential journalist and editor.

Nizan, Paul 1905–40. Writer. A militant COMMUNIST, his novels, like *La Conspiration* (*The Conspiracy*, 1938), cast an ironic glance over the efforts of BOURGEOIS young people to work out their personal relationships and political beliefs. His journalism and polemical essays were rediscovered, under SARTRE's impetus, in the 1960s.

***Nouveau roman* (New Novel)** The New Novel was the main phenomenon dominating French literature in the 1950s and 1960s. Experimental in nature and revolutionary in intention, the New Novel aimed to break with an earlier, nineteenth-century tradition of fiction and to create a literature that reflected the uncertainties of twentieth-century experience. A product of the period immediately following the Second World War, this attempt to reinvent the novel and to encourage new ways of reading literature was a response to growing CONSUMERISM and the rise of new MEDIA (cinema, RADIO, TELEVISION). The term *nouveau roman* was one of a number imposed by critics on a loosely associated grouping of authors who shared similar objectives despite the often differing appearances of their individual works. Its practitioners adopted the title once it had become common critical currency, largely for the sake of convenience.

The New Novelists never constituted a unified literary school or produced a shared manifesto, though most of them were published by *Les Éditions de Minuit*. What linked them, in particular, was a shared commitment to the experimental potentials of a literature which should present the reader (in the terms of the New Novel's principal theorist, Jean Ricardou) with the 'adventures of writing' as opposed to the more traditional 'writing of adventures'. Acknowledging the inevitable artificiality of literature, this loose grouping of authors debunked conventional understandings of plot, character, description and narrative viewpoint; their novels are often described as metafictional since they foreground the role of the AUTHOR and reader in creating fiction and making sense of it. Contemporary critics accused the New Novelists of being excessively formalistic, insensitive to contemporary socio-political concerns and even unreadable. The prominence of their work was increased, however, by the publication of collections of critical essays by two of its principal practitioners, Nathalie SARRAUTE and Alain ROBBE-GRILLET. The New Novel went into decline after the mid-1960s, although the New Novelists continued their individual projects in different media and other literary forms. Although dismissed by some contemporary critics as an outmoded phenomenon of literary history, the New Novel remains important as it explored many of the theoretical and philosophical issues central to twentieth-century thought and had lasting implications for literature in France. (**Charles Forsdick**)

Further reading

Britton (1992). A comprehensive discussion of the interrelationship of theory and practice in the New Novel. Robbe-Grillet (1988). Robbe-Grillet's vigorously argued and influential collection of essays (first published in French in 1963) on French fiction and the impact of the New Novel.

***Nouveau théâtre* (New theatre)**   A radically innovative type of theatre at its peak in the 1950s. Geneviève Serreau gave it this title (generally now preferred by theatre historians to Martin Esslin's 'Theatre of the ABSURD') by analogy with the NOUVEAU ROMAN, whose authors similarly discarded traditional (Cartesian or Aristotelian) notions of plot, character and language, which were meant to be logical, human and 'realistic'. This 'new theatre' had a difficult birth because it was regarded as a hoax, but it was championed by directors such as Roger BLIN and Jean-Marie Serreau, and soon became international, followed, for example by Harold Pinter, Edward Albee, and N. F. Simpson. It began, often in front of minute audiences, in the small LEFT BANK theatres of PARIS. The *Théâtre de la Huchette* has survived, still putting on an unbroken run of the Romanian exile Eugène IONESCO's plays. His *La Cantatrice Chauve* (*The Bald Prima Donna*, 1950) is still performed worldwide, and the best example of that author's 'antitheatre': mocking an audience's expectations of a suspenseful plot, developed via comprehensible dialogue, in which all will become clear by the final curtain. Two other leading exponents are also exiles writing in French, the Russian Arthur ADAMOV and the Irishman Samuel BECKETT; they are superficially as playful ('ludic') as Ionesco but embody a profounder metaphysical anguish. Beckett's *En attendant Godot* (*Waiting for Godot*, 1953) will survive as one of the literary masterpieces of the century.

The greatest French dramatist of the movement, Jean GENET, creates a similar world of ironic fantasy in which alienated and humiliated outcasts succumb to the existential nightmares of the twentieth century, as in *Les Bonnes* (*The Maids*, 1947) and *Les Nègres* (*The Blacks*, 1959). (**Ted Freeman**)

Further reading

Serreau (1966). An excellent study of the movement in France. Esslin (1991). Situates the phenomenon from a wide perspective.

***Nouveaux philosophes* (New philosophers)**   The term *nouveaux philosophes*, came into being during the 1970s at a time when old-style, COMMITTED INTELLECTUALS appeared for many to have disappeared. The *nouveaux philosophes* (prominent among them being Bernard-Henri LÉVY, Alain FINKIELKRAUT and Jean-Paul Dollé) consider, in general terms, that during the twentieth century, by allowing themselves to be caught up in the socio-political debates of their time and by espousing specific causes, intellectuals wittingly abandoned or lost their ability to remain independent. This charge is directed especially at all forms of connivance with totalitarianism, not simply of a political nature but of a cultural one too. They are critical of STATE intervention and of instant mass culture which they see resulting in intolerance and a loss of quality and critical judgement. In a period when the written word is losing or has lost much of its power, they warn against the instant and shallow appeal of technical innovation. Paradoxically, however, just as the committed intellectual of the twentieth century relied on the essay and the book, the *nouveaux philosophes* rely on and promote themselves through newspaper articles, and RADIO and TELEVISION programmes. In rejecting narrow socio-political affiliation they often look back to Julien BENDA and his belief (expressed in *La Trahison des clercs* (*Treason of the Clerks*, 1927) that intellectuals should be guided instead by absolute, Platonic values in any intervention in public debate, and should remain essentially and critically aloof. The designation of them as *philosophes* (which they sometimes reject) rather than intellectuals also suggests a return to the kind of disinterested inquiry that was characteristic of their eighteenth-century forebears. Whether by their actions they differ substantially from their twentieth-century predecessors is doubtful; but so too is whether they will have the same impact on the intellectual history of France. (**John Flower**)

Nouvel Observateur, le Founded and edited by Jean Daniel in 1964, it is a leading weekly magazine of ideas and current affairs, on the non-communist Left. It took over from the earlier *Observateur* (1950–54) and *France-Observateur* (1954–64), maintaining an independent critical position, and participating in numerous political campaigns.

Nouvelle critique (New criticism) In the post-war period, new kinds of theoretical work on literature and the arts emerged, accompanying the renewal of fiction in the NOUVEAU ROMAN, and there was a great deal of dialogue and cross-fertilization between novelists and critics on the question of the formal properties of a literary work. SARTRE's *Qu'est-ce que la littérature?* (*What is Literature?*, 1948) was a magnificent overture to these new investigations, rejecting utterly the conventions of academic criticism as well as arguing for COMMITTED literature. BARTHES famously described his first major work, *Le Degré zéro de l'écriture* (*Writing Degree Zero*, 1953) as seeking to continue Sartre's argument, but at the level of literary forms.

The *nouvelle critique* exploded into public consciousness with the publication in 1965 of Raymond Picard's polemical pamphlet, *Nouvelle Critique ou nouvelle imposture* (*New Criticism, New Fraud*) attacking Barthes's *Sur Racine* (*On Racine*, 1963). A new Quarrel of the Ancients and Moderns was born as arguments raged in the national press and literary magazines about the new critical 'jargon' as opposed to the values of LITERARY HISTORY (the author, the background, and the literary value of the work). Picard, the author of a notable study of Racine's youth, attacked an interpretation which drew on Freud, SEMIOLOGY, and ANTHROPOLOGY. Barthes had already, in one of his *Mythologies* (1957), dissected most cruelly what he saw as the tautological banalities of traditional academic literary criticism, which proved the greatness of the works by reference to the greatness of the author, and vice versa.

Other notable schools of criticism associated with *la nouvelle critique* were the phenomenological school (BACHELARD, Richard, Poulet), studying the structuring role of consciousness and SUBJECTIVITY in literary works; psychocriticism (Mauron), revealing unconscious structures in the work and relating them to the AUTHOR; STRUCTURALIST analysis of narrative (GENETTE, GREIMAS) and the 'genetic structuralism' of the Marxist Lucien GOLDMANN, drawing strongly on the work of Lukács to illuminate the political structures and class interests underpinning an author's *vision du monde*. (**Margaret Atack**)

Further reading

Barthes (1966). Barthes's reply to Picard, and a good introduction to the methods and values of the *nouvelle critique* by one of its leading exponents.

Nouvelle critique 1948–80. Monthly intellectual and cultural review of the COMMUNIST PARTY. Initially militant in COLD WAR polemics, it moved in the 1970s to include a broader range of debates on AVANT-GARDE literary and philosophical issues.

Nouvelle revue française Founded 1909. The pre-eminent literary review up to the Second World War, it published many leading writers and set literary trends. Taken over briefly during the OCCUPATION by a pro-German team under DRIEU LA ROCHELLE (1940–43), it re-appeared in 1953 as a respectable, but rather conservative publication.

Nouvelle vague (New wave cinema) The epithet *nouvelle vague* (New Wave) was coined by journalist Françoise GIROUD to describe the generation of young people coming to maturity in the 1950s. However, when François TRUFFAUT's first feature film *Les 400 coups* (*The Four Hundred Blows*) won the director's prize at Cannes in 1959, the name quickly became attached to a group of young film-makers whose first feature films were released in the late 1950s. They include Jean-Luc GODARD *A bout de souffle* (*Breathless*, 1959), Claude Chabrol *Les Cousins* (*The Cousins*, 1958), Jacques Rivette *Paris nous appartient* (*Paris Belongs to Us*, 1961), Eric Rohmer *Le Signe du lion* (*The Sign of the Lion*, 1959). These directors were not trained through traditional apprenticeships but by their activity as film critics for the journal CAHIERS DU CINÉMA, their assiduous frequentation of the Paris *Cinémathèque*, and their admiration for an idiosyncratic CANON. This included American directors such as Alfred Hitchcock, Howard Hawks, Nicholas Ray and Samuel Fuller; the Italian neo-realists; and selected French directors like Jean RENOIR and Jean-Pierre MELVILLE. *Nouvelle vague* films were revolutionary in their reliance on low budgets, small crews, location shooting, natural lighting, and the use of then unknown actors such as Jean-Paul BELMONDO and Jean-Claude Brialy. They were assisted by cameramen, such as Raoul Coutard and Henry Decaë who had trained in newsreels and who gave *nouvelle vague* films the documentary look which is part of their appeal today. Most *nouvelle vague* films focus on the intimate concerns of young people, usually the heterosexual couple, and engage more or less explicitly with questions of MODERNIZATION, especially France's relationship with AMERICA which is often expressed as a relationship between Hollywood and French cinema. But these films are also characterized by complex narrative structures, an elliptical narrative style, a self-reflexivity, and a refusal of narrative closure, which has continued to ensure their international influence. (**Jill Forbes**)

Further reading

Graham (1968). A collection of translations of key texts relating to the *nouvelle vague*. Marie (1997). A short guide, intended for university students, which outlines the main characteristics of the *nouvelle vague*. Monaco (1976). A history of the movement with analysis of key films.

Novel The twentieth century has emphasized the novel as the pre-eminent literary genre in France, encompassing both the popular genre-based best-sellers and highly intellectual works reflecting on the nature of language, narrative, and creativity. It is sustained by a large and very active PUBLISHING industry, extensive literary JOURNALISM, and literary PRIZES. Hundreds of novels are published every September at *la rentrée littéraire* (beginning of the literary year), as the literary world gets back to work after the summer break and gears itself for the season of prestigious literary prize-lists triggering lucrative sales.

The novel has been marked by the major events of the century. The First and Second World Wars, the revolutionary social and political upheavals of the 1930s, the bewildering pace of MODERNIZATION and change in French society, have all inspired great novels. So have the contradictions and tensions of the human condition in the modern world, from both religious and non-religious perspectives. The novel has recorded the experiences of those who have burst on the scene as new voices, from the margins: WOMEN's writing, BEUR fiction, novels recalling the suppressed memories of HOLOCAUST and war.

REALISM has been the dominant form, but it has also been challenged, by the New Novel (*NOUVEAU ROMAN*), by *ÉCRITURE FÉMININE*, or the novelists of OULIPO (*Ouvroir de littérature potentielle*) who exploited mathematical formulae and complex abstract patterning to generate surprisingly powerful narratives. But the fact that realists and anti-realists alike hail Flaubert as their master reveals the extent to which literary and social dimensions overlap in the modern novel. PROUST, CAMUS, SARTRE, CÉLINE, GIDE, BEAUVOIR, PEREC, or DURAS all offer strong material for learning about the experiences, beliefs, attitudes and values of French society, as well as making the reader think about the literary nature of the enterprise, the structures of literary narrative and language, and their relationship to the unstructured formlessness of EVERYDAY life. The recent renewal of realism associated with Daniel Pennac combines powerful story-telling with self-reflexive narratives. (**Margaret Atack**)

Further reading

Unwin (1997). Essays covering a wide range of philosophical, social and literary aspects of both popular and canonical fiction from the nineteenth century to the present.

Nuclear deterrent   France's nuclear deterrent has since the 1960s constituted the central theme of defence policy, and of much French diplomacy. Presidential authority over deterrence strengthened the presidency early in the FIFTH REPUBLIC. The collapse of the USSR left the *force de frappe* (strike force) and strategy largely unchanged. ATOMIC WEAPONS owed much to DE GAULLE both through the *Commissariat à l'énergie atomique* (Atomic Energy Commission, 1945) and through his acceleration, in 1958, of FOURTH REPUBLIC work on nuclear technology. Strategists suspected, after Hiroshima, that France's independence ultimately required nuclear capability. US and Soviet threats during the SUEZ CRISIS (1956) proved to them that France should develop a nuclear deterrent. Deterrence became reality in 1964. Under sole control of the President, whose new office in the Fifth Republic thus gained in visibility and power, the deterrent was used by de Gaulle to guarantee France's place in the bipolar COLD WAR system. French strategic thinking argued that atomic weapons played an equalizing role in possible conflict, by allowing the weak to deter the strong, given the consequences of retaliatory strikes. Insistence on complete independence for the deterrent strained relations with AMERICA, as de Gaulle navigated foreign policy between the superpowers, avoiding military collaboration within NATO and allowing suggestions (in 1968) that French missiles should target sites all around the world. The nuclear deterrent is thus as much concerned with France's independence as with the security of France: even French tactical nuclear weapons in EUROPE were considered as 'final warning' of deployment of the French strategic deterrent. The durability of France's strategic position defined by GAULLISM has been such that successive presidents have not sought to change, despite closer relations with the US, and with the former USSR. Franco-German co-operation and European integration may suggest possible European deterrence, but France's *force de frappe* is still the guarantor of her national independence. (**Hugh Dauncey**)

Further reading

Posner (1991). Defence policy and deterrent strategy in the nuclear era.

OAS (*Organisation de l'armée secrète*)   The OAS (Secret Army Organisation) was active in ALGERIA and France during the closing years of the Algerian struggle for independence. In 1958 General DE GAULLE had come to power with massive support from European colonists and others who believed that he would keep Algeria for France. In September 1959, however, de Gaulle had declared that the Algerian people should be offered self-determination, including the option of independence. Agitation by European-Algerian activists in favour of *Algérie française* continued during the autumn of 1959 and throughout 1960, in parallel with riots and demonstrations by FLN supporters. The referendum on the issue of Algerian self-determination having received support from a large majority of French voters in January 1961, an attempt was made by a group of generals to organize a PUTSCH to seize power in Algeria.

The OAS became active after the failure of the putsch. Whereas Generals Challe and Zeller surrendered to the French authorities, generals SALAN, Jouhaud and Gardy, as well as a number of other officers, went underground. With Jean-Jacques Susini, Jean-Claude Pérez and other activists, they formed a terrorist organization pledged to resist Algerian independence by making the country ungovernable, to force a military putsch or/and to provoke a mass uprising by the European population. Besides recruiting dissident military personnel, the OAS drew support from a number of extreme right-wing groups in Algeria and France. Its instruments were bombings and murders (including 553 victims in February 1962 alone), distribution of propaganda tracts and pirate radio broadcasts. It made a number of attempts to assassinate de Gaulle. The OAS failed to achieve its objectives. Its leaders suffered imprisonment or exile and some of its killers were executed, while Algerian independence was achieved in July 1962. Its activity contributed to the bitterness which subsequently led to savage reprisals in Algeria against European settlers and against Arabs who had served France. (**Christopher Flood**)

Further reading

Harrison (1989). One of very few books to have been written on the subject in English. Henissart (1973); Horne (1985). Both of these include useful discussions of the OAS.

Occupation   At war with Germany since September 1939, France was invaded in May 1940 and remained occupied until August 1944. The THIRD REPUBLIC was replaced by the *ÉTAT FRANÇAIS* with Marshal PÉTAIN as its head. During the first two years, France was divided into two main zones; occupied to the north, unoccupied to the south. In November 1942, the Germans moved into the southern zone in direct response to the arrival of allied forces in North Africa. In 1940, after a few weeks in Bordeaux, the French government was installed in VICHY, but control was essentially exercised by the Nazi authorities from PARIS. The initial policy of division set French against French, and rapidly weakened the country economically, psychologically, and morally. Pétain claimed that his policy of COLLABORATION protected France against more oppressive measures and that it gave the country time to recover its strength. Although the Nazi presence was initially seen by some to be tolerable, the situation rapidly worsened. While for most what mattered was mere survival, more than a few actively collaborated with the Nazis. They believed that only by so doing would a regeneration of France within EUROPE be possible and they enthusiastically pursued policies of ANTI-COMMUNISM, anti-republicanism, and ANTI-SEMITISM. Some fought with the Nazis on the Eastern front; others joined the FASCIST *MILICE*, created in January 1943, and were frequently more vicious in their oppression than their Nazi mentors. Active RESISTANCE was slow to form, despite appeals to resist in June 1940 from DE GAULLE, who had exiled himself in London and had assumed the leadership of the FREE FRENCH. Gradually RESISTANCE grew, with the French COMMUNIST PARTY being particularly active, though at no time would more than about 5 per cent of the population be involved. Acts of resistance often led to severe retaliation by the Nazis. At the LIBERATION, reprisals against collaborators by those who had resisted were often brutal. (**John Flower**)

Octobre, le groupe   1932–36. Theatre group. Specializing in 'Agit-prop' (from agitation and propaganda) performances with a direct political message, it was close to the COMMUNIST PARTY, and attracted numerous prominent writers and artists.

Oeuvre, l'   1904–44. Launched as a Centre-Left magazine, it became a daily paper in 1915, priding itself on its serious intellectual content. Taken over by Marcel DÉAT in 1940, it became an organ of the COLLABORATIONIST circles, and was closed at the LIBERATION.

Olympia, l'   Large Right Bank concert hall in Paris, Boulevard de Capucines, it is a major venue for popular music concerts.

Olympic Games   The French FIFTH REPUBLIC has used the Olympics as a tool of international self-aggrandisement. The modern Olympics were originally associated with Frenchman Baron Pierre de Coubertin's philosophy of the promotion of physical and moral development of young people through participation in SPORT. His initiatives led to the creation of an International Olympic Committee and the organization of the first modern Games (Athens, 1896). PARIS hosted the Olympics in 1900 and 1924 and is a candidate for 2008. France also hosted the first Winter Games at Chamonix (1924), then at Grenoble (1968) and Albertville (1992), but has never hosted the Paralympics for handicapped athletes. The French National Olympic Committee (CNOSF) plays a major role in the centralized and hierarchical organization of French sports administration in the regions and departments, acting as a link to government funding for the 80 or so national sports governing bodies (*fédérations*). Since President DE GAULLE's fury at the failure of the French team in 1960 (Rome), the four-yearly Olympics have been a privileged focus of state policy for maintaining and enhancing French *grandeur*. This has allowed Presidents to bask in French medallists' reflected glory, as in 1996 (Atlanta) with 37 medals (15 gold), and 2000 (Sydney) with 38 (13 gold), across a wide range of sports. This success was attributed to French coaching investment and expertise, as best exemplified at the National Sports Institute (INSEP). Olympic heroes include skier Jean-Claude Killy, cyclists Daniel Morelon, Jeannie Longo and Florian Rousseau, runners Colette Besson and Marie-Jo Pérec, hurdler Guy Drut, fencer Laura Flessel, and judokas David Douillet and Djamel Bouras. Recently the French Sports Ministry has taken a lead in combating the scourge of drugs in sport, which they attribute partly to the hyper-commercialization of events like the Olympics. **(Geoff Hare)**

Further reading

Dine (1998).

Ophuls, Marcel   Born 1921. Film director. His documentary *Le Chagrin et la pitié* (*The Sorrow and the Pity*, 1971) was banned from French TELEVISION, but when shown in cinemas, it launched a reappraisal of France's wartime record.

Orientalism   Edward Said's study *Orientalism* (1978), suggested that literary studies were reticent to address the relations between IMPERIALISM and culture. The subsequent proliferation of postcolonial studies can rightly be viewed as a response to Said's challenge. Defining 'Orientalism' from multiple perspectives, he insisted upon the particular imbrication of insititutional scholarship, imaginary representations, material interests and political domination that give the idea of Orientalism such force. Besides the overlap between the personal and political in his choice of this specific domain, Said explains that the Orient's proximity to Europe, the fact that its oldest colonies were there, and the fact that it is the source of its civilizations and languages, were contributory elements to the fact that the Orient has played a crucial role in EUROPE's definition of itself.

Whether in regard to the nature of its personality, modes of thought or idea of itself, the 'Orient' has functioned for the West as one of its most recurrent images of the OTHER. Its effects have been to foster certain actions and to strengthen a sense of internal IDENTITY. Indeed, in accordance with FOUCAULT, a discursive formation such as Orientalism is viewed as *enabling* rather than restrictive: it generates modes of behaviour as well as mentalities, producing strategies of domination as well as representations. The fashion for Japanese art and artefacts in the nineteenth century exemplified this in supporting the emergence of a strong impressionist movement in French painting. But one of the clearest examples is the Colonial Exhibition of 1931, which included a full-scale replica of the temple of Angkor Wat (Cambodia) and specimen 'native villages' from French colonies. Its careful presentation of the exotic 'other' was designed to emphasize the grandeur of France's imperial role. In a different register, French ethnologists, such as LEIRIS and LÉVI-STRAUSS, studied the art and customs of colonized peoples to identify universal human characteristics, theorized and promulgated in the UNIVERSALIST context of French culture. The fascination with China by the *TEL QUEL* group during the 1970s has also been seen as a French 'orientalist' strategy.

The concept of orientalism implies a criticism of its underlying tendency, which is to 'essentialize' the Orient as a stereotype, and thus promote French or Western superiority. It may be argued that it implies an essential 'West' or a tacit idealization of the Orient, and that it is no different from mechanisms for the construction of otherness within any cultural formation. At all events, the concept serves to focus on the responsibilities incumbent upon any mode of representation of foreign cultures and peoples. (**Michèle Richman**)

Further reading

Said (1993). Clifford (1988) Chapter 'On Orientalism'.

Orsay museum   See *MUSEE D'ORSAY*.

ORTF, *Office de Radiodiffusion-Télévision Française*   1964–74. French national broadcasting agency, which replaced RTF. It was broken up into seven independent companies as part of GISCARD D'ESTAING's liberalization programme. See also BROADCASTING, RADIO, STATE, and TELEVISION.

Other *(l'Autre)*   The highly ambiguous concept of the Other/other is central to much twentieth-century French thought, and in particular to the work of EXISTENTIALIST Jean-Paul SARTRE, PSYCHOANALYST Jacques LACAN and philosopher Emmanuel LEVINAS. In a more general sense, the 'other' is anyone separate or different from the self. The recognition of others allows an individual or a group to define and situate what is deemed 'normal' or mainstream. In twentieth-century France, a number of groups have been defined as internal others, their otherness seen in terms of benchmarks which are often artificially constructed and arbitrarily imposed: such groups include WOMEN, JEWS, HOMOSEXUALS, provincials and IMMIGRANTS. Processes of 'othering' depend on stereotypes and on the homogenization of differences; they allow at the same time the marginalization or control of groups or individuals perceived as a threat to established institutions or cultural hierarchies. It is in relation to COLONIALISM and exoticism that some of the recent major debates relating to the Other have occurred. During the period of colonial expansion, the colonial other served as a means of defining the colonizer and of creating a unified sense of national and collective identity, which ignored divisions of CLASS and wealth. Recognition of the colonial subject as 'other' allowed the establishment of binary relationships and the assertion of the sense of superiority on which the French colonial worldview depended. IDEOLOGICAL assimilation and EUROCENTRISM are extreme versions of such a process, since they aim at the absorption of the 'other' into the 'same'. In a colonial context, othering is the process by which others are created and controlled, often in literary representations or in specific stage management of events, such as the 1931 Colonial Exhibition. In a postcolonial era, there is a need to recognize the cultural diversity of France itself and to accept that a colonial understanding of otherness is increasingly redundant. This is particularly true of the second-generation North African community in France, often known as BEURS or 'arabo-French', who are neither entirely French nor simply North African. As a result, there is an urgent need to renegotiate what is understood by both 'French' and 'the other'. (**Charles Forsdick**)

Further reading

Todorov (1994). This account of French reflections on otherness provides a historical overview on the subject, while exploring the late twentieth-century consideration of this area. Hargreaves and McKinney (1997). A collection of 15 essays which consider the implications of postcolonial culture for the mass media, music, the visual arts and literature in contemporary France.

OULIPO (also OuLiPo) Founded 1960. The *Ouvroir de littérature potentielle* (*Circle for Potential Literature*) is a literary movement founded by QUENEAU and others to encourage innovation by the use of strict rules to provide a creative constraint or a generative device for literary writing. George PEREC's novel *La Disparition* (*A Void*, 1969), written without the letter 'e', is a well-known example.

P

Pacific French influence in the Pacific is currently concentrated in French Polynesia, New Caledonia and Wallis-and-Futuna. However, the scattered islands and atolls of the South Pacific have been central to France's overseas history since they were first visited and described by French travellers in the eighteenth century. The nature of Polynesian society, and in particular the island of Tahiti, attracted French artists, writers and scholars to the South Seas, where they hoped to find an earthly paradise peopled by 'noble savages'. In the French popular imagination, New Caledonia (a group of islands in Melanesia) has always been contrasted with Tahiti, and a number of Melanesians were even displayed as living relics of 'savage' societies at the 1931 Colonial Exhibition in Paris. Throughout the Pacific, Westernization triggered what subsequent scholars have described as a 'fatal impact'. This has led to wide-ranging demographic shifts and to the decline of pre-contact Oceanic cultural forms. The work of artist Paul Gauguin, who spent long periods in the Pacific , focused on these changes and heralded a series of twentieth-century authors, such as Victor Segalen (1878–1919), who wrote about the disastrous consequences of colonialism, evangelism and other forms of Western intervention. Yet it was the Second World War which had the greatest impact on New Caledonia and French Polynesia. Not only were large numbers of American troops based there, but also post-war reforms in the French colonies led to progressive political change. France refused to envisage total independence for its Pacific territories, and their links with EUROPE were strengthened from the 1960s onwards. An international airport opened on Tahiti in 1961 and France's nuclear testing site was transferred to French Polynesia in 1963. Although this situation led to rapid economic growth, France was accused in the 1980s of economic exploitation, environmental pollution and the perpetuation of colonialism. There were fierce arguments over nuclear testing on the Mururoa atoll; ecological concerns were weighed against the area's economic situation, since tourism and the experimental station were the major sources of income for French Polynesia at the time. At the same time, in the ethnically complex islands of New Caledonia, Melanesian nationalists, known as *Kanak,* began a period of active resistance to French control which triggered nearly a decade of political turmoil and led to the eventual rejection of their status as a TOM. (**Charles Forsdick**)

Further reading

Aldrich (1993). The most comprehensive study in English of twentieth-century French activity in the Pacific.

Pacifism   Political desire for peace and moral opposition to war. While the nineteenth century was a relatively peaceful period after the violent revolutionary era (1793–99) and Napoleonic wars (1799–1815), the twentieth century saw France's involvement in international and colonial conflicts with heavy numbers of casualties, material damage and the psychological trauma of defeat and occupation. Small peace movements developed around those wars. While pacifists have organized into formal international organizations they have also protested individually, for instance, becoming conscientious objectors to military service, which was compulsory for all men until recently abolished during Jacques CHIRAC's presidency. Wartime governments have always treated pacifists harshly, such as the primary school teacher Hélène Brion, arrested in 1917 and tried by military court for treason. As a reaction to the horrors of the trench warfare and the seemingly unresolved diplomatic tension in EUROPE, thousands joined peace movements in the 1920s, in particular WOMEN, and campaigned through international conferences for a regulation of international diplomacy. French people were bitterly divided over the armistice signed with

GERMANY in June 1940 by PÉTAIN, which brought a cessation of hostilities. Many COLLABORATORS including Pierre LAVAL justified their acceptance of Nazi rule by their desire for peace. Pacifists, many of whom were in the COMMUNIST PARTY or were well known INTELLECTUALS, demanded an end to the colonial conflicts in INDO-CHINA and ALGERIA during the 1950s, which implicated the French Army in torture, civilian repression and violations of human rights. France's involvement in the Gulf War brought little space in the press for condemnation, as pacifists are in a very small minority on the Left and Right. (**Máire Cross**)

Further reading

Hazareesingh (1994). Contains a chapter on 'Why no peace movement in France' (pp. 178–206) explaining the weakness of French peace movements. Gordon and Cross (1996). Contains the account of Hélène Brion's trial translated into English. Evans (1987). Describes the importance of pacifism as a mobilizing force for suffragettes in France before and after the First World War.

Pagnol, Marcel   1895–1974. Writer and film director. His plays and comic novels were popular between the wars, particularly the trilogy *Marius* (1929), *Fanny* (1931) and *César* (1936), which gently satirize the provincial manners of Marseilles. He made several films, which have been rediscovered after Claude BERRI's remakes of his *Manon des sources* (1952).

Painting   If language is one of the defining attributes of humanity, so also is the art of visual representation, the history of which, as the caves of Lascaux and other prehistoric sites show, long antedates linguistic records. In France, as in most of EUROPE, the visual arts over the last two millennia have predominantly reflected the ideology of spiritual (religious) or political (monarchical) power. With the French Revolution, however, painting, without losing its political potential, began progressively to release itself from specific social or religious functions, and to express the temperament of individuals or like-minded groups.

In France since the Renaissance, two fundamental attitudes to painting seem to have predominated. The one, usually associated with mastery of the line, tends to recuperate or rejuvenate the energies of the classical tradition (Nicolas Poussin, 1594–1665, Claude Lorrain, 1600–82, Louis David, 1748–1825, Dominique Ingres, 1780–1867). The other, orientated rather towards colour and light, is concerned to express the vitality of the contemporary (Antoine Watteau, 1684–1721, Eugène Delacroix, 1798–1863, the Impressionists, from 1874). In the modern period (1850–1950), in which the influence of Paris as the artistic capital of Europe was decisive, both traditions, but particularly the latter, were explored with increasing intensity by the various AVANT-GARDES (post-impressionism, fauvism, CUBISM).

The presence in France, and especially PARIS, from the late nineteenth into the first half of the twentieth century, of major artists from other European countries (Van Gogh, PICASSO, GIACOMETTI, Kandinsky, Mondrian, Miró, Dali), along with the discovery of African and Pacific art, provided an important stimulus both for modern French painting (BRAQUE, LÉGER, MATISSE) and for the wider, international movements in art (SURREALISM, ABSTRACT PAINTING). In the current, post-modern period, painting's links with pre-avant-garde art (classicism, even academicism) have been rehabilitated in a spirit of inclusiveness that has come more widely to characterize the contemporary cultural scene. **(David Scott)**

Further reading

Francastel (1977 and 1984). Leppert (1996).

Paris   Few capital cities, if any, in Western Europe exert the kind of political, social, cultural, and intellectual influence over their countries as does Paris over France. Its centripetal force is immense; people 'go up' to Paris from Calais or Strasbourg as well as from Nice or Bordeaux. A resident population of around 2.1 million increases substantially each day as people arrive to work by a network of motorways and a complex but efficient system of public transport. Paris also attracts millions of tourists each year. True Parisians, whose families have lived in the capital for three generations or more, are increasingly hard to find, however, as the cost of living rises. Those who remain live inside the *boulevards extérieurs* in the central core of Paris made up of 20 *arrondissements*, which curl out clockwise from the centre in the forms of a snail's shell. Many of these have barely changed in 100 years, for example, the student area of the LATIN QUARTER and the PUBLISHING and intellectual centre of Montparnasse on the LEFT BANK; Montmartre, the *quartier* for artists and Bohemians, and that of the great jewellers and the *haute couture* around the Place Vendôme on the Right Bank. Some *arrondissements* also have a strong ethnic identity, from the Jewish Marais in the 4th to the Chinese communities in the 13th.

CAFÉ life and regular street markets remain an important characteristic of Parisian society, contributing to an intimate village-like quality to the life of many areas. Majestic historic monuments and buildings like the Arc de Triomphe, the LOUVRE, or the Grand Palais, the Champs-Élyseés, and the magnificent boulevards, the hallmark of the nineteenth-century town-planner, Haussmann, and the elegant curve of the Seine have long been attractions. But modern architecture has also made its mark, for example, to the west, in the business area of the Défense, and to the east, the Bercy sports stadium and the Ministry of Finance, or the new opera house at the Bastille. Several poor and unfashionable areas (Belleville and the Canal St. Martin, for example) especially in the northern *arrondissements* are benefiting from investment and restoration though not always without significant social consequences. Despite some moves towards DECENTRALIZATION (educational establishments, big business and administration) and the growing challenge from important provincial centres such as LYON, it is unlikely that Paris's dominance will lesson in the foreseeable future. **(John Flower)**

Paris-Match   Founded 1949. A successful illustrated weekly magazine, with a reputation for high quality photographic reporting of current affairs and of the private lives of celebrities.

Paris Peace Settlement   Amid economic chaos, revolution and the break-up of empires in Turkey, Russia and Central Europe, in 1919 the victorious powers –

BRITAIN, France, Italy and AMERICA – gathered in Paris to finalize peace. The French capital was an unsuitable place to conduct such business, as wartime had aroused plenty of Germanophobia, but left few practical amenities such as hotels and offices. In this difficult environment, the French sought lasting security against Germany, possibly through the takeover of the left bank of the Rhine. Such plans were scuppered by the British, eager to resurrect a continental balance of power, and Wilson, the US President, who was guided by his idealistic 'Fourteen Points'. Reassured by Anglo-American defensive guarantees, the French signed the Versailles settlement of 28 June 1919. This insisted on GERMANY accepting 'war guilt', paying reparations and undertaking disarmament. Among territorial changes, Berlin lost its colonies; ALSACE-LORRAINE was returned to France; the Saar coalmines likewise became French for 15 years; the Saarland itself was placed under the newly created League of Nations; the Rhineland was demilitarized; and a Polish corridor separated Germany from East Prussia. The Treaty was considered harsh in Berlin, giving rise to extreme nationalism, but could have been worse and, overall, was a setback for France. The Treaty Annexe of Guarantees became worthless when the US Senate failed to ratify Versailles; the amount of reparations could not be agreed upon or easily extracted; and France had failed to secure the Rhine. In truth, it was not so much Versailles that caused France future problems, but the other treaties signed in Paris during 1919–20: Sèvres (with Turkey), Saint Germain-en-Laye (Austria), Neuilly (Bulgaria), and Trianon (Hungary). These created independent nations in eastern Europe, a number of which signed military agreements with Paris. Yet these states were fragile, and never compensated for a Russian alliance as France had hoped. (**Nicholas Atkin**)

Further reading

Boyce (1998). Contains several helpful essays.

Parité The 1990s' campaign to ensure equal representation of WOMEN and men in all political organizations, in particular, decision-making bodies. It succeeded partially when a law was passed in 1999 to insert in the Constitution the principle that there should be parity (equal numbers) of both sexes in politics. France holds the worst record in Europe, with the persistence of low percentages of women in parliament and government in the 50 years since women were granted the vote. Several attempts by women's groups to have modest positive discrimination measures introduced to increase women electoral candidates led to nothing. After the refusal in 1992 by the Supreme Court (*conseil constitutionnel*) to accept Yvette ROUDY's proposal for quotas for women candidates on the grounds that this went against the UNIVERSALIST principles of the Republic, the movement for *parité* gained enough momentum to be accepted as an electoral issue by Lionel JOSPIN in 1997. The strategy to have the principle accepted in the constitution rather than legislating for political parties to change was declared as inadequate by some feminists such as Françoise Gaspard, and bitterly opposed as too partisan by others such as Elizabeth and Robert Badinter. Since the constitutional changes, it is now up to the government to determine which sanctions to impose on political parties that refuse to adhere to the principle of parity. (**Máire Cross**)

Further reading

Reynolds (1998). Gives an account of the paucity of women in government. Cross (2000). A recent assessment of the role of French women in politics and the debate over gender and republicanism. Mossuz-Lavau (1998). An excellent summary of the historical context of women's suffrage in France, their electoral participation and the arguments over *parité*.

Parti communiste français   See COMMUNIST PARTY.

Parti populaire français   See PPF.

Parti radical   See RADICALISM.

Parti socialiste unifié   See PSU.

Pasqua, Charles   Born 1927. GAULLIST politician. Known for his right-wing views on social issues, like IMMIGRATION, and his tough line on law and order. He served as Minister of the Interior in 1986–88 and 1993–95.

Patois   The term *patois* is much misused and misunderstood. It is most properly used to refer to non-standard dialect forms of French, standard French being that version of the language which, championed by the *Académie française*, is taught in schools and used in the MEDIA. A *patois* might be considered to be an extremely localized dialect. For example, a region might have its dialect, whereas a particular *patois* might be limited to a few villages, or even, in some instances, specific words might vary from one village to next.

However, for many years the term *patois* was used pejoratively in France to refer to any non-standard variety of French as well as to France's regional languages. *Patois* was, principally the language of the rural poor and as such was considered by speakers of standard French – mostly middle-class town dwellers – an unsophisticated, inferior language variety, lacking any real grammar or as merely badly learnt standard French. Consequently, efforts were made to eradicate the use of *patois* in much the same way as regional languages. However, this view of *patois* as 'bad French' is in no way true. France's various *patois* have, in fact, all evolved from Latin in much the same way as standard French. In fact, in the words of French linguist Henriette Walter, French is 'merely a successful *patois*'. However, these prejudices ensured the low prestige of *patois*.

Today *patois* enjoys greater prestige and popularity. In many parts of France it is possible to find literary works and newspapers written in *patois* as well as recordings of *patois* songs, even *patois* dictionaries and grammars. Nevertheless, as a result of education, the mass media, a more mobile population and other socio-economic factors, numbers of *patois* speakers continue to fall, particularly among young people. (**James Minney**)

Further reading

Lodge (1993). Traces the development of the French language. Walter (1988). General introduction to language issues in contemporary France.

Paulhan, Jean 1884–1968. Writer. Influential in literary circles as editor of *La Nouvelle revue française* (1925–40, 1953–68) and as adviser to the publishers Gallimard. He wrote stories, essays and art criticism.

Paysans The *paysans* – self-employed small farmers – long represented French society in general, such was their preponderance in a mainly rural and agricultural country. Long-term decline in EMPLOYMENT in AGRICULTURE and the rise of industry and services transformed rural classes into a vocal minority, destabilized by MODERNIZATION, defensive of France's traditions, and courted by politicians.

The First World War accelerated the THIRD REPUBLIC's transformation of 'peasants into Frenchmen' through geographical mobility and education by mobilizing *paysans* from all France. Rural war memorials show their losses, and inter-war INDUSTRIALIZATION and URBANIZATION further undermined the stability of practices that Fourastié (1979), considering 1945 (when 25 per cent of the workforce was agricultural), described as 'humanity stagnant for a thousand years'. By 1930, France was predominantly urban, but VICHY supported *paysans* by emphasizing the nobility of farmwork. Food rationing during the OCCUPATION and afterwards was aggravated by *paysans*' tendency towards self-sufficiency. During post-war modernization, mechanization transformed agriculture, particularly during the 1960s, as the STATE and farmers' organizations rationalized land ownership and updated cultivation. Rural depopulation (*exode rural*) further weakened rural society, and new foodstuff retailing through supermarkets competed with traditional product distribution.

Political activism has characterized the *paysans*, ever-ready to defend their status. Self-employed, they generally support Centre-Right and right-wing parties, and specialize in direct action (dumping produce, or worse, outside town halls or hypermarkets), when competition undermines profitability, underwritten by France's leadership of EU agricultural policy. Militancy extends also to GLOBALIZATION exemplified by US fast food: in 1999 a French McDonald's was destroyed by farmers protesting against industrialized food. *Paysans* are fundamental to France's myths about her past, and, given the dangers of agribusiness, crucial to the French countryside's future. (**Hugh Dauncey**)

Further reading

Cleary (1989). Gives a good overview. Fourastié (1979). Focuses on modernization, 1946–75. Mendras (1970). A classic analysis.

PCF *Parti communiste français.* See COMMUNIST PARTY.

Pensée, la Founded 1939. Philosophical quarterly review, sponsored by the COMMUNIST PARTY. It was particularly noted for its rationalist ethos and its attention to the philosophical implications of science and technology.

Perec, Georges 1936–82. Writer. An energetic technical innovator, and leading figure in the OULIPO movement, his novels include *Les Choses* (*Things*, 1965), a study of ALIENATION in CONSUMER society, and *La Vie mode d'emploi* (*Life: A User's Manual*, 1978) which describes an entire apartment block at a single instant.

Péri, Gabriel   1902–41. Communist politician. A journalist and *député* (1932–39), he was an early member of the RESISTANCE. Captured and executed by the Gestapo, he was regarded as a martyr and became a symbol of Resistance.

Personalism   Personalism is a philosophical tradition which was particularly influential before and after the Second World War, and which engaged significantly with the social and political issues of that period. It is perhaps best understood as a critique of individualism. Personalists believed that an individualistic view of human nature, which they traced back to the Renaissance, was responsible for creating a society based on the pursuit of individual gain rather than the pursuit of the collective good. The Renaissance philosopher René Descartes had summed up the basis of the idea of human beings as essentially rational individuals with the words 'I think, therefore I am'. Personalists sought to replace this concept of the individual with their concept of the 'person', which emphasized the spiritual qualities which drew people towards others, towards social action, and towards religious faith. These values led personalists to criticise CAPITALISM and CONSUMERISM and to envisage a communitarian social order which valued the community over the individual.

The major intellectual figure behind personalism was the Catholic philosopher, Emmanuel MOUNIER. He was one of a number of young personalist INTELLECTUALS who emerged in the 1930s and gathered around new reviews like *ESPRIT* and *Ordre nouveau*. These intellectuals are often referred to as *les non-conformistes* (the non-conformists), because they attempted to cut across traditional political divisions in France, criticizing (but sometimes borrowing from) both the conservative Right and the MARXIST Left. Personalists were vociferous critics of Americanization, TAYLORISM and FORDISM. It has been argued, somewhat controversially, that their philosophy was close to FASCISM and was the inspiration for policies adopted by the VICHY government, which collaborated with Nazi Germany during the Second World War. In fact, the influence of personalism was much more diffuse and had as much impact on the French RESISTANCE and on the post-war anti-Americanism of newspapers like *LE MONDE*, as it did on Vichy. (**Jackie Clarke**)

Further reading

Kelly (1979). One of relatively few books on this subject in English, this study offers further details on the philosophy and politics of personalism and locates it particularly in relation to Catholic politics. Loubet del Bayle (1969). The classic study of the new generation of intellectuals for whom personalism was so central in the 1930s.

Pétain, Philippe   1856–1951. Soldier and conservative politician. A hero of the First World War for his important victory at Verdun (1916), he was appointed Marshal of France in 1918. After retirement, he served in several ministerial posts. He became *Chef d'état* (head of state) at the Fall of France, embraced COLLABORATION with Hitler, and led the VICHY régime (*État français*, 1940–44). He was imprisoned at the LIBERATION.

Petit Parisien, le   1876–1944. France's top-selling daily newspaper in the first half of the twentieth century, known for its investigative reporting and its human interest features.

Pflimlin, Pierre 1907–2000. Centre-Right politician. Leader of the CHRISTIAN DEMOCRATS, he was the last Prime Minister of the FOURTH REPUBLIC (1958), long-serving mayor of Strasbourg (1959–83) and President of the European Parliament (1984–87).

Philippe, Gérard 1922–59. Actor. With his striking good looks and graceful presence, he was a popular and respected leading actor of French classical theatre, and the star of several films, greatly mourned at his early death from cancer.

Philosophy The study of ideas and thinking, philosophy is an important component of the French education system, compulsory for all students at the BACCALAU-RÉAT. France has produced many influential philosophers and intellectual movements. See, for example, ABSURD, COMMITMENT, CRITICAL THEORY, DECONSTRUCTION, INTELLECTUALS, *ÉCRITURE FÉMININE*, EXISTENTIALISM, FEMINISM, HUMANISM, MARXISM, *NOUVEAUX PHILOSOPHES*, PERSONALISM, POST-MODERNISM, POST-STRUCTURALISM, STRUCTURALISM.

Photography The work of Eugène ATGET marks a watershed, inasmuch as it directly inspired the agenda responsible for the very backbone of French photographic modernism. This agenda required the photographer to co-ordinate documentary goals and artistic ambitions in the service of an essentially urban project. PARIS was conveniently at hand. In the 1920s and 1930s, Henri CARTIER-BRESSON incorporated both formalist and surrealist principles into his vision of Paris. André Kertész used high-angle shots to add an analytical dimension to his celebration of the city. In BRASSAÏ's famous photographs of night-time Paris, the *flâneur* (stroller) turns voyeur, and the private and public dimensions of city life overlap to disquieting effect. After the horrors of the Second World War, a more distinctly HUMANIST mood prevailed, as expressed in the urban WORKING-CLASS themes of Willy Ronis and Izis, and in the genial lyricism of Édouard Boubat and Pierre DOISNEAU. Many of the best photographers working in and on Paris, especially between the wars (Kertész, Brassaï, Florence Henri, Germaine Krull), were both foreigners and JEWS. The photographer as nomadic *émigré*, rather than mere *flâneur*, helped ensure that the most powerful images of the city were those that not only recovered the familiar but also discovered the unusual, whether as a source of pleasure, concern, or anxiety.

As a photographed object, Paris has lost ground since the 1960s, The reasons for this include the physical shift provoked in the 1980s by offers of commissions to work on state-sponsored photographic surveys of the contemporary French landscape; and the aesthetic shift towards the new agendas of conceptual art. This saw deliberately 'un-arty' photographs being used in multi-media installations (for example, the work of Christian Boltanski, Sophie Calle and Annette Messager). More positively, during the 1980s and 1990s, Paris has reasserted itself as an important centre for photography exhibition spaces (such as the *Maison Européenne de la Photographie*) and photographic theory (exemplified in Roland BARTHES's *La chambre claire*). (**Johnnie Gratton**)

Further reading

Barthes (1980), A hugely influential study of photography, written in the wake of Barthes's mother's death. Clark (1997). An excellent general study reflecting recent critical developments and contemporary cultural issues. Frizot (1998). A wide-ranging set of essays written from a French perspective.

Physics French physics has always had a high reputation, although France is concerned that pure research and industrial research are falling behind international competitors such as GERMANY and BRITAIN, and that French Nobel Prize winners are less frequent than they should be. In the inter-war period, physicists Jean Perrin (1926) and Louis Victor de Broglie (1929) were awarded Nobel Prizes, but French physics was marked most by Irène Curie and Frédéric JOLIOT, who won Nobel Prizes in 1934 for work on radioactivity. After 1945, scientific research and industrial and technological development became priorities to which pure and applied physics could contribute, and public sector research was encouraged in GRANDES ÉCOLES devoted to CHEMISTRY and physics, in public sector companies, and within *grands programmes* of technological and industrial development. The major *grands programmes* stimulating physics were in the nuclear and space sectors, where influential state agencies the *Commissariat à l'énergie atomique* (the Atomic Energy Commission, 1945) and the *Centre national d'études spatiales* (National Centre for Space Studies, 1961) employed directly and indirectly large numbers of researchers to create France's ATOMIC WEAPONS, nuclear energy, and space capability. Physics has been a priority of the *Conseil national de la recherche scientifique* (CNRS, National Council for Scientific Research), whose laboratories and research programmes have complemented those of public and private sector industry, and France has been active in international collaboration in physics, for example, within CERN. Science and mathematics have always been prestigious in France, and the importance of mathematics in the BACCALAURÉAT has arguably facilitated the development of physics, although in the 1960s, French lack of home-produced supercomputers was a complication for the space and nuclear programmes. Since the 1970s, France has garnered three Nobel Prizes (Néel, 1970; Charpak, 1992; de Gennes, 1994) but concerns are still voiced about the strength of French physics, and about departures of French scientists to the USA. **(Hugh Dauncey)**

Further reading

Barré and Papon (1993). On science and technology policy in France.

Piaf, Édith 1915–63. Singer. With a powerful voice, the persona of a PARIS street girl, and associations of personal tragedy and suffering, which were echoed in her songs, she was internationally acclaimed for songs like *Milord* (1958) and *Non, je ne regrette rien* (No, no regrets, 1961).

Picasso, Pablo 1881–1973. Artist. Born in Spain, he was the most famous artist of his day, especially in PAINTING, drawing, sculpture and ceramics. He lived most of his life in France, launching CUBISM and then inspiring SURREALISM. After *Guernica*, his first politically committed painting, shown at the Paris World Fair of 1937, he became active in left-wing INTELLECTUAL circles, especially supporting the peace movement, for which he drew and painted many doves.

Pierre, Abbé Born 1910. Capuchin priest and social worker. Initially a socialist, he founded the Emmaüs Communities in 1947 to help homeless people, and led a successful media campaign on their behalf in the 1950s. A passionate and long-lived advocate for this cause, he has recently been associated with right-wing nationalism.

Pilote Founded 1959. Popular *bande dessinée* magazine founded by René Goscinny. Best known for its *Astérix* stories, it aimed at an adult audience as well as children.

Planchon, Roger Born 1931. Director and playwright. Inspired particularly by Brecht, he directed many contemporary and classical plays from the 1950s onwards, founding his own company, based at Villeurbanne, in 1957. From the 1960s he also wrote his own plays.

Planning Economic planning was a distinctive feature of French post-war development. At the LIBERATION, General DE GAULLE's economic adviser, Jean MONNET introduced a framework of state planning for the reconstruction of the country, formalized by the establishment of the *Commissariat Général au Plan* (Commission for the National Plan), which he directed (1947–52). Loosely inspired by the Soviet Five-Year Plans, it provided a model of 'indicative planning', in which the state built a consensus around social and political objectives, in consultation with business interests and TRADE UNIONS. The *Commissariat* was a unit of experts, independent of the civil service, which consulted widely and reported directly to the Prime Minister. The first Plans set detailed targets for production and development in key industries, along with targets for state and private investment. They were led by a strong public sector, including government departments and nationalized industries, and were an important component of the economic prosperity of *les TRENTE GLORIEUSES*. After the mid-1960s, Plans became increasingly flexible, to accommodate the growing importance of European integration, international trade and free markets, over which the French state had decreasing influence. MITTERRAND's first socialist government, in 1981, tried to restore the role of the state in planning, but was forced to abandon the attempt in the face of short-term economic difficulties. As a result, the tenth and eleventh Plans set modest objectives without specific quantified targets, and the role of the *Commissariat* thereafter become one of preparing expert studies on long-term social and economic trends. **(Michael Kelly)**

Further reading

Cerny and Schain (1985); Forbes, Hewlett and Nectoux (2001).

Poincaré, Raymond 1860–1934. Centrist politician. President of the Republic (1913–20) and subsequently holder of several ministerial posts including Finance, where he is remembered for stabilizing the FRANC.

Poinso-Chapuis, Germaine   1901–81. Centrist politician. A CHRISTIAN DEMOCRAT, she was the first woman to be appointed to hold a full ministerial post, as Minister for Health (1947–48).

Point, le   Founded 1972. Weekly magazine of current affairs, edited by Claude Imbert. Known for its sober and impartial stance, it is widely read in business and professional circles.

Poland   There is a long history of Franco-Polish diplomatic and cultural relations, going back to the seventeenth century and the establishment of the Polish Prince Stanislas as King of Lorraine. With Poland dominated throughout most of its history by its powerful neighbours Prussia and Russia, it traditionally looked towards France as a symbol of freedom and liberalism, and throughout the nineteenth century PARIS was a regular choice of exile for political and cultural dissidents. At the VERSAILLES Peace Conference in 1919, France supported the establishment of an independent Polish state, as part of its foreign policy of maintaining a ring of independent Eastern and Central European countries around the fledgling Soviet Union, and reducing the power of GERMANY, although its loyalty was strained by the Polish invasion of the Ukraine. Nevertheless, France remained a natural cultural ally in the inter-war years and there was considerable interaction between French and Polish cultural figures, in particular in the field of the plastic arts.

   This collaboration was extinguished by the outbreak of the Second World War and the invasion and occupation of Poland by Germany. Before the war, French right-wing opinion had opposed France's treaty obligations to Poland, refusing to 'die for Danzig', but France nevertheless went to war in defence of its ally. After the war, Poland was absorbed into the Soviet bloc under a communist regime and, apart from COMMUNIST PARTIES like the *Parti Communiste Français* and their organizations, contact with the West remained slight until the 1980s. The French were, however, impressed by young Polish film-makers, like Roman Polanski, Andrzej Wajda and Andrzej Munk. The Solidarity campaign of the 1980s, led by Lech Walensa, which resulted in the overthrow of the communist regime in 1989, was warmly applauded in France. (**Nicholas Hewitt**)

Further reading

Hewitt (2000). Contains an essay on France and Eastern European painting.

Pompidou, Georges   1911–74. Gaullist politician. He served as Prime Minister under DE GAULLE (1962–68), and followed him as President of the FIFTH REPUBLIC (1969–74). He was an active patron of the arts, and launched the modern Arts Centre at Beaubourg which was named after him. See POMPIDOU CENTRE.

Pompidou Centre, *Centre Georges Pompidou*   The Pompidou Centre takes its official name from its initiator, the GAULLIST President Georges POMPIDOU, who was a keen amateur of modern ART. Taking advantage of the renovation of the old market area in central PARIS known as Les Halles, and with encouragement from LE

CORBUSIER and MALRAUX, he took the bold decision of creating a new museum of modern art at the heart of the capital. The building was designed by architects Renzo Piano and Richard Rogers, the winners of France's first international architectural competition, and it was not Pompidou's personal choice. Much controversy was aroused by the juxtaposition of their very radical design against the adjacent buildings dating back to the Middle Ages. Indeed, Pompidou's successor, Valéry GISCARD D'ESTAING, tried to prevent its completion, and its inauguration in 1977 was largely due to the determination of his Gaullist Prime Minister Jacques CHIRAC, Pompidou's political *dauphin* (crown prince). This project set a precedent for presidential intervention in the field of culture.

The Pompidou Centre contains the *Musée National d'Art Moderne* (National Gallery of Modern Art, MNAM), which covers the period 1905 to the present, and the *Centre de Création Industrielle* (Centre for Industrial Creation, CCI), concerned with ARCHITECTURE, urbanism and design. It also houses two other major cultural institutions: the BPI (*Bibliothèque Publique d'Information*, Public Information Library), and an experimental music centre, IRCAM: (*Institut de Recherche et Coordination Acoustique / Musique*, Institute for Acoustic and Musical Research and Coordination) directed by the composer Pierre BOULEZ until 1992.

Often referred to simply as Beaubourg, the name of the *plateau* on which it is situated, it surpassed original estimates of visitor numbers. Cynics may argue that this was largely due to the crowds of tourists flocking up the external escalators for the free view from the top rather than for what was inside. Nevertheless, frequentation of the BPI, designed for use by 7000 people per day, was in fact up to 25 000. By the mid-1990s a major renovation programme had become necessary, and the whole site was closed for over two years, re-opening again on 1 January 2000 with vastly improved facilities. (**Susan Collard**)

Further reading

See the websites for the Centre, and for its component institutions:
www.centrepompidou.fr
www.bpi.fr
www.ircam.fr

Ponge, Francis 1899–1988. Poet. With a strong awareness of the visual arts, his poems typically deal with objects, described with wit and ingenuity to reveal their importance in human life and to show the process of poetic creation.

Popular Front Government of France between May 1936 and April 1938 elected as a coalition among COMMUNIST, SOCIALIST and RADICAL Parties under the leadership of Léon BLUM. The electoral victory resulted from a fragile alliance formed two years earlier in response to the perceived threat to republican and parliamentary values on the part of militant right-wing elements such as those that tried to storm the Chamber of Deputies on 6 FEBRUARY 1934. As partisan tensions yielded to the shared vision of a government of the people true to the egalitarian principles of the French Republic, the political Left organized its efforts to extend politics as far as possible into social policies affecting individuals and groups on an everyday basis. In October 1934, French COMMUNIST PARTY leader Maurice THOREZ called openly for the formation of a Popular Front movement. By mid-July of the next year, mass rallies solidified a broad movement supporting peace and freedom throughout the world.

Beset with strikes and labour disputes almost as soon as the elections ended, Blum succeeded none the less in legislating significant domestic reforms including the 40-hour working week, paid annual vacations, and compulsory schooling until the age of 14 years. Foreign policy issues also beset the coalition as pressure from conservative and reactionary government lobbies prevented Blum from intervening officially to aid the Republican cause in the Spanish Civil War. Blum's first cabinet dissolved in June 1937 after failing to resolve domestic budgetary and labour crises. His second cabinet, created in March 1938, lasted less than a month. Despite a number of significant failures, the Popular Front remains the model of a democratic regime driven by social and cultural concerns. (**Steven Ungar**)

Further reading

Weber (1995). Astute study organized by topics and attuned to the breadth of social issues beyond politics. Reynolds (1996). A superb mix of concerns with class and gender makes this a singular contribution to work on the period.

Popular music   See MUSIC, POPULAR.

Postage stamp   Postage stamps are icons of the countries that issue them, a fact that has guaranteed their survival well into the era of electronic communications. The stamp has a dual SEMIOTIC function, which is reflected in the two forms it takes: definitive (indexical) and commemorative (iconic). Definitive stamps are generally small and squarish, and provide the minimal indexical information about the post to which they are attached: the name of their country of origin and the price of postage paid. In addition, most countries add a distinctive icon, usually a monarch's head, allegorical figure or other national symbol. Since 1945, the figure of MARIANNE has regularly appeared on French definitive stamps. Commemorative stamps are usually larger and rectangular, adopting a horizontal (landscape) or vertical (portrait) format. In addition to providing basic indexical information, they commemorate specific historical or contemporary figures and events, usually providing a pictorial icon of them. Such stamps are of particular interest to young collectors, with small princi-palities, such as Monaco, producing a disproportionate number of issues. The famous French *Monuments et sites* series, initiated in 1929–30 to promote TOURISM and continuing to the present day, with their fine engraved images of *lieux de mémoire* (sites of memory), provide a comprehensive record of France's cultural heritage.

French stamps, since their introduction in 1849 (the first definitives showed Ceres, Roman goddess of agriculture) offer a faithful record of the country's history over the last 150 years, reflecting the ideological orientation of successive republics as well as the Second Empire (1852–70) and the *État français* (1940–44). The stamp's potential as a medium of political propaganda has been realized since its inception, with a change as minimal as the use of the word *France* instead of *République française* (as during the presidency of GISCARD D'ESTAING, 1975–81) marking an ideological shift. Similarly, François MITTERRAND's presidency was able to claim the bi-centenary of the French Revolution for the SOCIALISTS by issuing in 1989 a year-long series of stamps commemorating the event. (**David Scott**)

Further reading

Scott (1995).

Posters   The public display of royal edicts and other notices became widespread in France from the Renaissance, with occasional illustrative devices, mostly formulaic or derivative, being used from the eighteenth century. It was following the invention of the lithographic method of printing in 1798, a technique by which text and image could be produced by a single process, that the possibilities of the poster became fully realised. From the beginning of the nineteenth century, there followed a plethora of posters, advertising first literary and then theatrical and other entertainment productions. The perfecting of techniques of colour lithography, in the second half of the nineteenth century, launched a golden age of poster production, with artists as accomplished as Jules Chéret (1836–1932) and Henri de Toulouse-Lautrec (1864–1901) producing the MUSIC-HALL and café-concert images that defined their epoch.

In the twentieth century the scope of the poster for political propaganda and for commercial advertising was quickly explored, stimulated by two world wars and the massive development of CONSUMER spending. The establishment of the advertising hoarding and other prominent displays resulted in the poster becoming an integral part of the modern urban landscape, and thus in turn stimulating artistic representation of the modern scene (especially in FUTURIST art). The increasing sophistication of poster art from the 1920s meant that it was taken increasingly seriously as an aesthetic medium, artists such as Cassandre producing images that captured the spirit of the inter-war period. The profound concern of the various international AVANT-GARDE movements (Bauhaus, De Stijl, Constructivism) with questions of typography and communication further stimulated poster development. With the consumer boom after the Second World War and the subsequent post-industrial/ capitalist focus on marketing the image, the poster reached new heights of originality and aesthetic sophistication. Today posters are collected as art objects and the development of computer-generated and multi-media images, far from threatening the poster, has further stimulated the poster's post-modern development. (**David Scott**)

Further reading

Ades (1984); Bargiel (1991); Mouron (1985).

Post-modernism   A general term for the cultural and philosophical consequences of the gradual shift away from the established values and parameters of modernity. Jean-François LYOTARD argues that, in the light of events such as the HOLOCAUST, the Enlightenment 'project' can no longer be legitimated by 'meta-narratives' of progress and human emancipation. In *The Postmodern Condition* (1979), Lyotard argues that the unified and totalizing project of modernity will be replaced by multiple 'language games' and plural forms of legitimation.

Jean BAUDRILLARD goes even further, claiming that we now live in world of 'simulation', or 'hyper-reality', in which signs refer simply to other signs, rather than a 'real' referent. Baudrillard argues that philosophy and theory can no longer make easy assumptions concerning the unproblematic status of reality. Baudrillard's mode of writing may justifiably be described as 'post-modern', in that he has largely rejected the possibility of representation. Writing should be a way of transforming and inventing reality, a 'fatal strategy', which seeks to push things to their limit.

Historically, France has been particularly closely associated with the 'project' of the Enlightenment, and in recent times some French cultural critics have seen post-modernism as a destructive rejection of universal values in favour of a naïve and relativistic celebration of the particular. Debates of this kind have been intensified by the rapid technological and social changes which have taken place in France since the Second World War. FINKIELKRAUT, for example, talks of a general blurring of the boundaries between high and low culture, an eclectic, 'self-service', 'anything-goes' attitude, which undermines universal republican values. For Finkielkraut, the post-modern era is dominated by CONSUMERISM, which gives rise to the 'idolatry of juvenile values'. In contrast, Gilles Lipovetsky argues that post-modernism is essentially a liberating DEMOCRATIZATION of the exploration of individual freedom and self-expression associated with modernism. For Lipovetsky, post-modernism is an indicator of an increasingly open and democratic society. (**John Marks**)

Further reading

Lyotard (1993). A detailed and accessible explanation of Lyotard's conception of the post-modern. Gane (2000). A comprehensive and lively guide to Baudrillard's work.

Post-structuralism   A philosophical tendency, which developed in the 1960s in France. For the generation of INTELLECTUALS that followed SARTRE in post-war France, the triumvirate of Marx, Freud and Nietzsche formed a philosophical framework which fed directly into STRUCTURALISM and post-structuralism. These three major European thinkers, combined with the French epistemological tradition of Cavaillès, BACHELARD and Caguilhem, provided the inspiration for a 'philosophy of suspicion', which sought to locate the unconscious or latent signifying systems that structure manifest meanings. Behind the *doxa* of received opinion and conventional wisdom lie structures of signification which undermine HUMANIST notions of intentionality and selfhood.

Structuralism and post-structuralism are inextricably linked as two forms of this 'philosophy of suspicion', with the latter movement effectively representing an intensification of earlier structuralist ideas. DERRIDA finds in structuralism the tendency towards a science of signs, which elevates the notion of structure to the very 'transcendental' status that it seeks to undermine. For Derrida, the crucial blind spot, or *aporia*, of Saussure's structuralism is the rigorous distinction between signifier and signified, which implies the possibility of a pure concept that is not mediated through language. This 'DECONSTRUCTIONIST' reading of Saussure is itself an example of a post-structuralist approach, in that Derrida seeks out the points at which a text reveals or suggests the ways in which the structure of signification, which apparently underpins the text, is not closed or stable. The earlier work of Michel FOUCAULT is arguably structuralist, since he attempts to uncover the unspoken or unconscious rules which govern discourse. The structuralist phase of his work develops into a later post-structuralist approach which is concerned with tracing the multiple links between power and knowledge. Some commentators have distinguished between the 'textualist' post-structuralism of Derrida and the 'worldly' post-structuralism of the later Foucault. Although this distinction contains an implicit critique of the 'textualist' approach, it does highlight the important differences which pertain to the impor-tance attributed to language in post-structuralism. (**John Marks**)

Further reading

Harland (1987). A clear guide to the philosophical development of post-structuralism. Williams (1999). Situates post-structuralism within the development of a distinctively French form of discourse analysis.

Poujade, Pierre   Born 1920. Right-wing politician. Leader of a shopkeepers' protest movement in 1953, he founded a populist conservative party which gained 11.6 per cent of the vote in 1956, but then declined rapidly.

Poujadism   Poujadism was named after its founder, Pierre Poujade, owner of a newsagent's shop in Saint-Céré (Lot). It started in 1953 as a local protest by small shopkeepers and artisans against the prospect of tax inspections. They came at a time when government policy had curbed inflation and cut into the narrow profit margins of a sector which was under threat from MODERNIZATION, including population movement away from villages and small towns, and changes in the retail sector. Local protest rapidly became regional then national. Poujade was a tireless speaker at public meetings. Under the title of *Union de Défense des Commerçants et des Artisans* (UDCA), the movement captured the anxieties of an entire section of the lower mid-dle classes. Having flirted for a time with the COMMUNISTS, by 1955 the UDCA was tacking towards the extreme right. Nicknamed Poujadolf by hostile commentators, Poujade became the object of a leadership cult within the movement. He and others developed an increasingly virulent, ultra-nationalist and populist rhetoric, some-times larded with anti-Semitism. Denouncing the power of the STATE, they accused France's governmental, economic and intellectual ÉLITES of corruptly betraying the people. In the parliamentary election of 1956, the UDCA organized candidacies in every seat and won over 11 per cent of the national vote, which translated into 53 seats. However, the rapid triumph of the movement was followed by rapid decline. Besides being deprived of 11 of its seats for electoral irregularities, the parliamentary group proved directionless, ineffectual and ill-disciplined. Within a year it had disin-tegrated. The movement had lost its momentum as its political ineptitude became increasingly evident and governmental policies took the sting out of the grievances of its members. Despite its transience, the Poujadist episode was important as a response to profound socio-economic change, as an example of rapid mobilization of anti-state protest, and as a vehicle for the Extreme Right to return to national politics (Jean-Marie LE PEN, future leader of the FRONT NATIONAL, was one of the spokesmen and *députés* for the UDCA), preparing the way for its agitation over the DECOLONIZATION of ALGERIA. (**Christopher Flood**)

Further reading

Shields (2000). Gives a useful discussion of the nature of the movement.

Poulenc, Francis   1899–1963. Composer. Member of 'Les Six', the influential group of modern French composers who sought to renew French classical music between the wars.

PPF *(Parti populaire français)*   The PPF (French People's Party) was a FASCIST party formed in June 1936 by Jacques DORIOT, formerly a leading member of the French COMMUNIST PARTY until his expulsion in 1934 for advocating tactical co-operation with the SOCIALISTS. At the time of founding the PPF, he was mayor of Saint-Denis and a *député* (member of parliament). Doriot's aim in creating the PPF was above all to fight the Communists using similar means and forms of organization to theirs. The party attracted powerful financial backers at the outset, but these tended to drop away as the POPULAR FRONT government crumbled and the perception of a revolutionary threat from the left receded. While its leadership included a number of former Communists and others from the extreme Left, the PPF also drew ex-members of extreme right-wing groups such as the CROIX-DE-FEU, and fascist intellectuals including Pierre DRIEU LA ROCHELLE, Alfred Fabre-Luce and Paul Marion. By 1938 the party was claiming a membership of 300 000, but the real total was probably much less than 100 000. In its early days nearly half of the membership was WORKING CLASS, although the balance shifted in favour of the lower middle classes over the following years. Its programme emphasized strong government, corporatist economic and political organization, defence of small business and peasant interests, and development of the empire. The rhetoric was virulently ANTI-COMMUNIST, anti-parliamentary, nationalistic and increasingly ANTI-SEMITIC. The cult of the leader was fostered in fascist style, although the party did not have a paramilitary apparatus and did not describe itself as fascist until the wartime period. Doriot was not an effective strategist or policy-maker. His steering of the party was inconsistent and erratic, his attempts to forge alliances with other parties were unsuccessful. Many of his most able helpers had dropped away by the end of 1930s. During the OCCUPATION he was among the extremists who despised Marshal PÉTAIN's régime. He committed the PPF to wholehearted COLLABORATIONISM, and himself served on the Eastern Front. Still, he was unable to impose himself as French Führer. He was among the exiles at Sigmaringen and was killed in 1945. Many of his party members were executed or imprisoned in the post-war purges. (**Christopher Flood**)

Further reading

Soucy (1995). The PPF figures as part of the wider fascist picture.

Press, daily   The French read few daily newspapers compared to nations of equivalent industrial and cultural development: half as many as the British, and a quarter of the number in Scandinavian countries. Although a leading world economy, France is not even in the first twenty in terms of circulation of daily papers, whereas at the beginning of the twentieth century it was world leader, selling twice as many dailies as its British counterparts.

Moreover, in contrast to the centralization of much of French intellectual production, provincial newspapers account for more than 70 per cent of the total circulation of 10 million dailies. The best-selling title is *Ouest-France*, based in Rennes (BRITTANY), which sells almost 800 000 copies. That is roughly twice as many as leading PARIS-based national dailies: influential newspapers Le MONDE and Le FIGARO, popular metropolitan title *Le Parisien*, and sports daily *L'Équipe*. Only six Parisian titles regularly figure among the top twenty dailies.

Regional papers are less political and more consensual. They often enjoy a virtual monopoly within their distribution zone, whereas national titles are in direct competition. Local papers also provide a better complement to RADIO and TELEVISION which focus primarily on national and international NEWS. *Ouest-France*, for example, prints around 40 different editions so as to provide focused local coverage.

There are various explanations for the difficulties of the daily press: the historical disruption caused by two world wars and German OCCUPATION; lack of confidence in journalists, particularly those based in Paris; uneconomic distribution systems; the downward spiral induced by high cover prices and falling circulation; and the success of weekly news magazines. Significantly, ownership of the latter is concentrated in commercial groups, whereas dailies are, for the most part, owned by independent operators. Although good for French pluralism, this may limit commercial dynamism and investment capacity. (**Pam Moores**)

Further reading

Charon (1996). A systematic guide.

Press, weekly   There are around 1300 weekly titles in France, the vast majority of them from the prosperous and dynamic magazine sector. Among the most popular publications are television guide *Télé 7 Jours*, women's magazine *Femme actuelle*, internationally renowned glossy PARIS-MATCH, sentimental *Nous Deux*, and the children's paper *Journal de Mickey*. The wide range of special interest magazines covers cars, fashion, sport, finance, the economy among other things. Many are not just French successes: ELLE and MARIE-CLAIRE print around 20 different editions in various languages and countries. Conversely, the sector offers access to JOURNALISM from around the world, collected together in a magazine such as *Courrier International*. What characterizes the weekly press is the sheer diversity and originality of the publications on offer. There are satirical rags such as CHARLIE HEBDO alongside the notoriously iconoclastic yet respected Le CANARD ENCHAÎNÉ, famed for investigative journalism and exposure of scandal. This is also the home of the gutter press, conspicuous by its absence from French dailies, for example, sensationalist *France-Dimanche*, and infamous titles *Le Nouveau Détective*, *Ici Paris* and *Spécial-Dernière*.

Extreme right-wing papers too, such as *Minute* and *National Hebdo*, which do not have sufficient readers to sustain daily publication, find here the audience necessary for survival.

In France, weekly magazines fulfil the news function assumed by daily newspapers in many countries. There is no tradition of Sunday papers, *Le Journal du dimanche* being the only serious title of note. Right-wing broadsheet *Le FIGARO* sells a special weekend edition on Saturdays, together with its own *Figaro-Magazine*. In addition, there is a whole series of news magazines like *L'EXPRESS, Le POINT* and *Le NOUVEL OBSERVATEUR*, synthesizing the week's events, illustrated in colour and presented in a convenient format, which appeal to busy professionals and undermine the circulation of daily titles. (**Pam Moores**)

Further reading

Albert (1990). A comprehensive survey.

Prévert, Jacques   1900–77. Writer. With a combination of surrealism and socialism, his poetry used humour and satire to strike against authority, injustice and exploitation, and the collection *Paroles* (*Words*, 1946) remains a best-seller. He wrote the lyrics of popular songs, including *Feuilles mortes* (*Autumn leaves*, 1946), as well as film scripts.

Privatization   Privatization became controversial in France in the 1990s as right- and left-wing governments sold off nationalized companies, reversing some of the socialist NATIONALIZATIONS of the early 1980s. 'Denationalization' symbolized state economic disengagement, reflecting France's acceptance of neo-liberal economics, but measures to safeguard French industrial sovereignty over privatized companies indicated hesitancy about abandoning STATE control. The first privatizations were launched by Prime Minister CHIRAC during COHABITATION (1986–88). Their rationale was to free companies from government regulation, to facilitate the free market, and to widen share ownership. This represented the objective of 'modernizing' French CAPITALISM to align it with other EU economies, with smaller public sectors and individual investors already active in stock markets. The privatization law of July 1986 authorized the sale of 31 banks and companies, of which 13 were floated on the *Bourse* (Paris Stock Exchange). The major flotations were Saint-Gobain (chemicals), Paribas, Société Générale, CCF (finance), Matra and CGE (technology) and television channel TF1. SOCIALIST governments (1988–93) maintained a policy of 'neither privatization nor nationalization', nevertheless permitting publicly-owned companies to acquire and sell subsidiaries as a means of restructuring the public sector. Under the second MITTERRAND cohabitation, the BALLADUR government privatized another 21 companies, nine of which entered the *Bourse*: BNP, AGF (banking,insurance), Elf, Renault, Rhône-Poulenc, Seita, Usinor-Sacilor, Péchiney (industry) and UAP. In 1997, the left-wing JOSPIN government allowed private investors to acquire shares in France-Telecom and Air France, continuing to open flagship state companies to market forces. Privatization is controversial because some companies may have been sold cheaply, giving shareholders large capital gains and suggesting public wealth has been squandered. Additionally, the issue of who controls privatized companies ('hard cores' of stable shareholders have been created and foreign control is discouraged) implies that France is not unreservedly wedded to the free market. (**Hugh Dauncey**)

Further reading

Zahariadis (1995). A comparative study of 1990s' privatization.

Prizes, literary There are currently several thousand literary prizes awarded annually in France. This phenomenon is of great importance for anyone interested in the French corporate PUBLISHING industry or in wider issues of the sociology of contemporary literature. Perhaps the most famous is the Goncourt, a prize of 50F awarded annually in early November for the year's best work of literary prose (usually a novel). It was first awarded in 1903 under the terms of the will of the nineteenth-century novelist Edmond de Goncourt who inaugurated the prize in memory of his brother Jules. The selection is made by the *Académie Goncourt*, a national institution, known usually as *les Dix* (The Ten). The other major annual prizes are: the Renaudot (novel), the Interallié (literary journalism), and the Fémina, whose all-female jury rewards the best French novel of the year, and the best foreign novel appearing in French translation. Other prizes are awarded for various categories of author, target audience, subject matter, and genre.

Literary prizes are attacked by their critics for encouraging patronage and an excessive emphasis on commerce, advertising and the media. An imaginary publishing house called 'Galligrassiseuil', an amalgamation of the principal French publishers: Gallimard, Grasset and Seuil, is often accused of having a stranglehold over literary production. The stakes remain extremely high, however, as a Goncourt-winning novel sells on average 350 000 copies and is almost guaranteed an immediate paper-back edition as well as foreign translations. Marguerite DURAS's *L'Amant* (*The Lover*, Goncourt, 1984) sold 1.3 million copies and Jean Rouaud's *Les Champs d'Honneur* (*Fields of Glory*, Goncourt, 1990) sold 600 000. Recent winners of the Goncourt include a number of non-metropolitan and postcolonial authors: e.g. Moroccan Tahar Ben Jelloun, with *La Nuit sacrée* (*The Sacred Night*, 1987) and Martinican Patrick Chamoiseau with *Texaco* (1992). Their recognition can be seen as a positive development since the awarding of such major prizes has introduced French readers to a wider understanding of their own language, and allowed the important shift from an exclusive notion of French literature to a more inclusive idea of literature in French. (**Charles Forsdick**)

Further reading

Caffier (1994). In the 'Que sais-je?' series. A concise but very useful guide to the history of the Prix Goncourt; also gives a clear insight into the culture of French literary prizes.

Programme commun 1972–76. A manifesto agreed between the COMMUNIST and SOCIALIST parties as the basis for a coalition government. It was abandoned amid disagreements on updating it, but many of its ideas were taken up by the left-wing government elected in 1981.

Protestantism   There are around 1 million Protestants in France, with perhaps as many more who consider themselves close to Protestantism. The 400th anniversary of the Edict of Nantes (1598), granting religious tolerance (revoked a century later by Louis XIV), was an occasion to recall the Religious Wars which ended with Protestants driven out of large areas of France. They are still mainly grouped in the south and east of the country, with concentrations in a number of larger cities (PARIS, MARSEILLE, Montpellier, Nîmes, La Rochelle, Strasbourg and Mulhouse).

The two main Protestant churches are the *Église réformée de France* (Reformed Church), with a Calvinist tradition, strongest in the south; and the *Église de la confession d'Augsbourg d'Alsace et de Lorraine* (Church of the Confession of Augsburg), a Lutheran church based in the eastern provinces. In addition, there are many smaller groups, including representatives of most Western Protestant denominations.

Despite their small numbers, Protestants are not usually referred to as a 'minority', since they are not generally socially disadvantaged, and despite some lingering tensions with the dominant Catholic population, they are well represented in professional and business circles. Many Protestants have served in government, including Michel ROCARD as Prime Minister (1988–91). (**Michael Kelly**)

Further reading

Willaime (1998); Flower (1993a).

Proust, Marcel   1871–1922. Novelist. His 3000-page novel *A la recherche du temps perdu* (*Remembrance of Things Past*, 1913–27) is much read and studied. Dealing with universal issues including time, memory, identity, love, death and art, it lovingly and intricately recreates a social world that was swept away by the First World War. It has attracted several film adaptations.

Provence   Forming part of the administrative region of Provence-Alpes-Côte d'Azur, Provence is a self-contained area between the Rhone to the west, the Baronnies mountains to the north, and a less easily defined eastern boundary just west of Nice. Access by motorway, rail (TGV to MARSEILLE and Nice) and air is easy, and results each summer in the highest number of tourists (3–4 million) received by any part of France, more than doubling the resident population. The incidence of second homes for French and foreigners is high, especially in the coastal resorts and in the Luberon hills north of Aix. After TOURISM, AGRICULTURE is the main source of revenue, with fruit, market-gardening and wine featuring prominently, though competition, often subsidized, from the rest of EUROPE is a growing threat. While Aix can claim to be the cultural capital of Provence, Marseille is the largest, most industrial and racially mixed city. With the gradual reduction in its port activities, it faces a major unemployment problem bringing in its wake serious social and political unrest, and is now a long way behind LYON as France's second city. There is, of course, a popular, stereotyped image of Provence as a land of sun, sea and sand, but the reality is more complex. The weather can be unstable with long periods of drought, violent storms, hail and severe frosts. Dense forests (threatened by fires), sparse often rugged uplands (*garrigue*), deep gorges, waterfalls, hidden valleys are all within a short distance of each other. The architectural magnificence of the Roman remains at Arles or Fréjus, of the Papal Palace at Avignon, or the elegant eighteenth-century town houses in Aix are matched by the many fine chateaux and by the small-scale delights of a host of hill-top, often walled, medieval villages with their narrow streets, tiny houses and fortified churches. Major international music, film and theatre FESTIVALS in and around Aix, Arles and Avignon are paralleled by the celebrations of regional traditions stretching back centuries. Unlike the coastal strip, inland Provence, even at the height of summer, can be surprisingly peaceful and seem remote and even inward-looking. This is where the true Provence is to be found. (**John Flower**)

Provisional Government   The Provisional Government (GPRF, *Gouvernement Provisoire de la République Française*) was a transition regime which took power when PARIS was liberated in August 1944, and continued in office until January 1947 when the first government of the new FOURTH REPUBLIC took over. It was headed until January 1946 by General DE GAULLE, and included representatives of the main political parties and RESISTANCE groups who had opposed the German occupiers and the COLLABORA-TIONIST VICHY government. In the early months of the LIBERATION, it had fended off possible American threats of an Allied Military Government in France (AMGOT), and ensured that local Resistance groups were brought under central control.

The Provisional Government had to contend with national traumas like the purge (*ÉPURATION*) of suspected collaborators and the return from GERMANY of political deportees and prisoners of war. It was faced with rebuilding a national economy which had been devastated by war and by the demands of the German occupiers. In addition, it sought to assert French influence abroad, defending the French EMPIRE and insisting on France's status as an occupying power of defeated Germany.

In economic terms the Provisional Government carried through a large-scale programme of reforms, NATIONALIZING industries, and renovating social welfare provisions. In a process of democratic renewal, it accorded WOMEN the right to vote for the first time in France and submitted proposals for constitutional reform to the French electorate. For some French people who had wanted the Liberation to bring radical change to France, the Provisional Government was a disappointment. Nevertheless, the reforming agenda of this period undoubtedly laid the foundations for the remarkable post-war recovery of France in the FOURTH REPUBLIC. Most importantly, the Provisional Government provided the means by which an independent and democratic French state could be restored after the national nightmare of defeat and occupation. (**Hilary Footitt**)

Further reading

Rioux (1980). Covers the political, social and economic history of the Provisional Government.

PSU *(Parti socialiste unifié)*   Founded in 1960, it brought together members of three groups: the PSA (*Parti Socialiste Autonome*) including future Prime Minister Michel ROCARD (which had broken away from the SFIO in 1958 in protest at Guy MOLLET's Algerian policy), the UGS (*Union de la Gauche socialiste*) led by Claude Bourdet and Gilles Martinet, and *Tribune de communisme*, made up of dissident communists.

Its initial aim was to secure the independence of ALGERIA, after which the party lost a clear sense of direction, but managed to achieve a modest electoral showing (4 per cent) in the elections following the events of MAY '68. Michel Rocard was then a candidate in the presidential election of 1969, winning just under 4 per cent of the vote, and subsequently won a seat in the National Assembly in a by-election in 1969. Rocard's main aim was the fundamental transformation of society through the application of *autogestion* (self-management) but this was seen by many in the party as a dangerous opening towards social democracy (as opposed to socialism). When Rocard decided in 1974 to support the policy of the Union of the Left and join the PARTI SOCIALISTE transformed by François MITTERRAND, the PSU continued its existence without him.

By the late 1970s a new leader, Huguette Bouchardeau, had emerged, but she only obtained 1.11 per cent of the vote when she stood in the presidential election of 1981. The party adopted a position of 'critical support' of the socialist government, until Bouchardeau became Minister for the Environment in March 1983, causing a rift in the party, which continued to strive to become a socialist 'alternative', flirting with dissident communists to this end, but finally decided to cease its activities at its last congress in 1989. (**Susan Collard**)

Psychoanalysis   Psychoanalysis has been more influential in France since the Second World War than in any other European country – the result of the dominance (not to say the stranglehold) of one key figure, Jacques LACAN. Lacan's development and deployment of Freudian theory lay especial stress on the importance of language. If 'the unconscious is structured like a language,' to cite one of his most celebrated and approachable dicta, then this implies that like language (at any rate the Saussurean version of it to which Lacan adhered), it is dependent for its very existence on the silences and ambiguities by which it is systemically riven. This is at the antipodes of what Lacan derided as the American model of psychotherapy, with its stress on the conscious and on wholeness, rather than on the fractured and warring drives of/in the unconscious.

Lacan's implicit anti-Americanism, his brazen INTERTEXTUAL promiscuity purloining phrases and concepts from figures as disparate as Pascal, Dali, LÉVI-STRAUSS and Heidegger, and the theatrical flamboyance with which his regular public seminars were conducted, made of him a guru-like figure in the PARIS of the 1960s and 1970s in particular. The sexism, which characterized his professional practice and his personal life alike, the sectarianism spiked with maliciousness that led to numerous dissolutions of and expulsions from the groups he formed (most notably the *École Freudienne de Paris*) and the infamously costly and sometimes insultingly brief sessions he accorded his analysands make it very difficult to think of him as a guru nowadays. Yet his influence remains profound and abiding, not least in the field of film theory where his stress on the field of vision – so crucial in the 'mirror-phase' of a child's development – has made him a key player. FEMINISM, POST-MODERNISM, GENDER and queer theory successively have worked against Lacanian psychoanalysis and the phallocratic reductionism of which it is widely accused. Yet they have done so using Lacan's own concepts and tools, as the work of IRIGARAY and DERRIDA among a host of others suggests. Psychoanalysis may no longer be *de rigueur* among the Parisian intelligentsia as it was a quarter century ago, but it remains a massively important part of the contemporary French cultural landscape. (**Keith Reader**)

Further reading

Bowie (1991). An excellent critical introduction. Turkle (1979). Places Lacan in his specifically French context.

Psych et po   Founded 1968. A component of the women's liberation movement (MLF), which combined MARXIST and LACANIAN theories, from which it took its full title *Psychanalyse et politique* (Psychoanalysis and Politics). Active in book and periodical publishing, the group was ferociously partisan in its battles with other currents of the movement, to the point of registering exclusive copyright of the title MLF in 1979.

Publishing   Even as France currently experiences the latest, electronic revolution in publishing along with the rest of the world, the old-guard publishing houses, GALLIMARD, SEUIL, Flammarion, stand strong. Gallimard, founded in 1911 as the publishing organ of the young literary journal *LA NOUVELLE REVUE FRANÇAISE*, is the best known both in France and abroad. Gaston Gallimard made his mark by publishing unknown writers for their intellectual value as well as their sales potential. The one notorious mistake made by the editorial board was to initially reject Marcel PROUST's *A la recherche du temps perdu* (*Remembrance of Things Past*, 1913–27) (Andre GIDE was the particular naysayer). When Gallimard bought the rights back from the Grasset house, he inaugurated the first commercial competition between publishers in France.

During The Second World War, publishers in occupied PARIS found themselves in a quandary: to continue to function was tantamount to collaboration. Gallimard came upon the strategy of placing Pierre DRIEU DE LA ROCHELLE, one of his authors whose views were in line with those of the Nazis, in the position of director of *La nouvelle revue française*. The censorship board thus allowed Gallimard to maintain control of the book publishing side of his house, and to somewhat avoid sullying his own name. Less cannily, some of the other venerable Parisian publishers collaborated overtly with the Nazis. Bernard Grasset, for example, urged his colleagues in print to accept German censorship, and was charged as a COLLABORATOR during the purges (*ÉPURATION*) that followed the LIBERATION.

During the OCCUPATION, a trio of RESISTANCE fighters and sympathizers created the clandestine Éditions de MINUIT (Midnight Press). With these impeccable credentials, Minuit positioned itself initially against the compromised Grasset and Gallimard, but would eventually forge links with the Gallimard house. In 1954–55, the editorial strategy at Minuit changed: increasingly the house became a forum for AVANT-GARDE writers like Georges BATAILLE, Pierre Klossowski, and Maurice BLANCHOT, and for a so-called new school of experimental fiction christened the 'New Novel' (*NOUVEAU ROMAN*). Minuit novels have rarely sold well, but the house has succeeded enormously in the face of financial difficulty.

Prior to the most recent global innovation in publishing, the advent of the electronic book, multimedia groups came to dominate French publishing in the 1980s: Lagardère-Hachette and Vivendi (*Presses de la Cité*). Though many bemoan the demise of publishing houses marked by personality *à la Gallimard*, it is testimony to French intellectual life that all these houses large and small can co-exist. (**Susan Weiner**)

Further reading

Assouline (1988). Intellectual biography of the publisher Gallimard and his house.

Putsch (April 1961)   In April 1961, a group of French generals opposed to Algerian independence attempted to seize power in the capital, Algiers. This putsch took place at a pivotal moment as France, the colonial occupier, was in the process of negotiating self-determination with the Algerian provisional government. The uprising was crushed.

France had been in an undeclared war with increasing numbers of Algerian nationalists since 1954 when a *Front de Libération Nationale* (FLN, National Liberation Front) was formed to oppose France's continued colonial presence in ALGERIA. After the upheavals of the Second World War, colonial powers, like France and BRITAIN, were forced into emancipating overseas territories over which they had ruled for hundreds of years, exploiting their natural resources and indigenous peoples. In the case of Algeria, this was a particularly painful process as a large and articulate French settler population, known as the *pieds noirs*, waged a sustained campaign to save an *Algérie française* (French Algeria). With pressure growing to secure a resolution to the Algerian crisis, General DE GAULLE returned to power in 1958 as President of the FIFTH REPUBLIC. His election seemed to promise a reprieve to those opposed to Algerian independence and the accelerated process of French DECOLONIZATION between 1945 and 1962. Yet in a broadcast of 16 September 1959, de Gaulle declared that a 'great nation' like France was obliged to offer self-determination to the Algerian people. When General MASSU, an outspoken critic of Algerian self-determination, was recalled to PARIS in January 1960, *pieds noirs* extremists and rebel army officers launched a general strike in Algiers. This was followed in April 1961 by the putsch, led by General SALAN, and a union with the hard-line settlers who formed the *Organisation de l'armée secrète* (OAS, Secret Army Organization). Algeria gained independence in 1962 with the ÉVIAN AGREEMENTS. (**Claire Gorrara**)

Further reading

Gildea (1996). Overview of developments in French national identity since 1945.

Que sais-je? A popular paperback series launched in 1948. It presents a collection of short works, each of which aims to give an accessible and informative account of a particular topic.

Québec Majority French-speaking province in CANADA.

Queneau, Raymond 1903–76. Writer. Inspired by SURREALISM, and founder of the OULIPO movement, he wrote novels which combined popular language with complex literary techniques. His *Exercises du style* (*Stylistic Exercises*, 1947) rewrite a simple incident in 99 different styles, and his best-known novel, *Zazie dans le métro* (*Zazie on the Tube*, 1959), was adapted as a film by Louis MALLE (1960).

Race and ethnicity Terms used in describing group affiliations and differences. Ethnicity sometimes serves as an umbrella term, covering ideas of 'racial' differences, generally based on visible or supposed biological features, as well as culturally-based notions of group identities. Widely used during the COLONIAL period, notions of separate biological races are now scientifically discredited, though they continue to influence popular attitudes and Extreme-Right parties such as FRONT NATIONAL. Ethnicity and a number of related terms are also generally avoided by French officialdom, in whose eyes they are associated primarily with group IDENTITIES that are considered to lack the legitimacy accorded to national communities.

Growing pressure to recognize the role of perceived ethnic differences in structuring social relationships is closely connected with the politicization of IMMIGRATION during the past twenty years. Working on an implicit assumption that ASSIMILATION into the national community is the natural destiny of immigrants and their descendants, politicians and civil servants have traditionally refused to grant any official recognition to group identities based on separate places of origin or associated cultural differences such as religion or language. Recognizing such differences would, it is feared, encourage *communautarisme* (ethnic separatism), thereby weakening national unity. In official statistics and documents such as those compiled by the census authorities, the only criterion generally taken into account is nationality. But the attitudes and behaviour of many ordinary inhabitants are built on assumptions of racial or ethnic differences which significantly affect the everyday lives of many people, particularly those of minority ethnic origin, who frequently suffer from discriminatory treatment by members of the majority ethnic population. In attempting to combat racial discrimination, policy-makers have been taking tentative but still hesitant steps towards the recognition of ethnic differences in official analyses and regulations. (**Alec Hargreaves**)

Further reading

Pluriel recherches, (1993), (1994), (1997). This annual publication, subtitled 'Vocabulaire historique et critique des relations inter-ethniques', contains dictionary-type entries providing a critical account of key terms. Numbers 1 (1993), 2 (1994), and 5 (1997) are particularly helpful.

Radicalism *(Parti radical)* Radicalism was a political ideology and organization, which deeply marked the modern French style of DEMOCRACY. The *Parti républicain radical et radical-socialiste* (1901) is the oldest French party; its foundation gave a loose organization to groups of deputies who stood for a left-wing version of republicanism, seeking parliamentary primacy over government, disestablishment of the CATHOLIC church, and an end to denominational schooling. The first two aims were achieved by 1905, when Émile Combes's government passed the Act of Separation. As well as expressing the Church–State cleavage, radicalism had a social basis, speaking increasingly for the provincial middle classes and parts of the peasantry (*PAYSANS*); it showed particular strengths in those areas of France (South-West, South-East, Centre) which had been dechristianized after 1789.

Radicalism remained the major party until 1940, increasingly ready to form governments with the Right and operate conservative ECONOMIC and social policies. It still proclaimed its leftist credentials by militant secularism and praise of *les petits* against *les gros*. It provided premiers such as CLÉMENCEAU, CHAUTEMPS, HERRIOT and DALADIER. Discredited by the collapse of the THIRD REPUBLIC, which it had come to symbolize, radicalism recovered after 1945 through leaders like MENDÈS-FRANCE, only to succumb to the influence of the COLONIALIST lobby which overthrew the regime in 1958. Since then the party has become a mere spectre, splitting into two, with a Right-wing *valoisien* tendency (named after the site of the party offices) and a leftish *Parti Radical-Socialiste*, dominated by the Baylet family who run the long-established daily *La Dépêche de Toulouse*. Both factions elect a few deputies as allies of the mainstream Right or Left. That a Radical party still exists demonstrates how organizations can survive long after the disappearance of the social and political circumstances which produced them. (**David Hanley**)

Further reading

Berstein (1982). An exhaustive study of radical ideology and politics. Zeldin (1973). A concise overview.

Radio, independent The original independent radio stations of the 1920s and 1930s did not survive the Second World War. Following deregulation of French radio by the SOCIALISTS (1981–84), the new independent sector has become dominated by commercial networks, to the detriment of independent local or community radio, which is surviving only thanks to protection from the BROADCASTING regulator, the CSA (*Conseil supérieur de l'audiovisuel*, Higher Broadcasting Council). The break-up of the STATE monopoly allowed an explosion of new private local radios, many of which have since been taken over by major networks, themselves now concentrated into three groups, the newer *NRJ* group and the two long-standing *périphériques* (over-the-border radios), *Europe 1* and the Luxembourg-based *RTL*. The latters' expertise and financial weight allowed them to survive the initial competition for audience from the new music radios, and now each (like *NRJ*) owns further networks of FM stations. Cross-media ownership of the *périphériques* means the major international media companies Matra-Hachette and CLT-UFA effectively control much of French commercial radio. Deregulation also saw the fall of the dominant model of the generalist station in favour of the formatted, thematic station, the most common format being 'music-and-news', aimed at a segment of the national audience divided up by age. *Skyrock*, *Fun* and *NRJ* target the under-25s; *Chérie FM*, *Europe 2*, *RTL 2* share the 25–45 audience; *Nostalgie* aims at the over-45s. Despite this concentration of ownership and loss of many stations since 1981, some 1200 different broadcasters still share the air-waves, ensuring the French radio landscape offers considerable variety. This is less the case in the regions, where the networks dominate, than in PARIS. Recent regulatory issues have included the sexual content of phone-in shows and the amount of American popular music being played by youth radio to the detriment of FRENCH LANGUAGE song. (**Geoff Hare**)

Further reading

Dauncey and Hare (1999a).

Radio, state   Radio is listened to regularly by over 80 per cent of the French NATION. STATE (or public service) radio is once again competing against an independent sector. After the pre-war mix of public and private radio stations, a state BROADCASTING monopoly was born, when the political regime emerging from OCCUPATION and LIBERATION was determined to protect such a vital means of communication from private capital and foreign influence. In the 1950s the state radio audience dwindled through competition with the freer and livelier tone of the commercial *périphériques* (*RTL*, *Europe 1* and *Monte-Carlo*), broadcasting in French from across the borders. The creation in 1963 of the generalist station *France-Inter* and two high culture, low audience channels, *France Culture* and *France Musique*, re-established the ORTF state radio as a major broadcaster, but without silencing its critics. Social demand grew for more independence and a more varied diet of programme. The election of MITTERRAND in 1981 at last saw the authorization of 'private local radios' and soon of national commercial music networks. State radio reacted to the new competition as the radio audience was being fragmented over a huge number of new stations. *Radio-France* (as state radio is now known) rapidly created a network of local radios (*radios décentralisées*), now numbering 39 and covering half the territory of France, and a very successful 24-hour rolling news station *France Info* (1987). *Radio-France* is developing web broadcasting, DAB radio, and satellite digital broadcasting, and its modernization is lately symbolized by adding an 's' to make *France Musiques* (with a wider remit). Its other national stations are *FIP* (music and traffic information for motorists) and *Radio Bleue* for older listeners. *RFI* is state radio's world service. **(Geoff Hare)**

Further reading

Hare (1998). Recent technological developments in French radio.

Radiodiffusion-télévision française (RTF)   1945–64. French state BROADCASTING company which exercised a monopoly in French-based RADIO and TELEVISION broadcasting.

Raï   Musical style developed in ALGERIA, combining traditional Arab forms with rock instruments and rhythms. Popular from the 1980s in the *BEUR* community.

Railways   French railways are dominated by the state-owned *Société nationale des chemins de fer* (SNCF, National Railway Company) and the *Régie autonome des transports parisiens* (RATP, Paris Transport Corporation). Railways expanded until the 1930s and have since contracted, but rail travel and freight have always been integral to national TRANSPORT, as the success of the TGV high-speed train since the 1980s illustrates. The *service public* mission of SNCF and RATP has allowed railways to serve republican objectives of subsidized travel and regional development, but this is threatened by EU competition policy. In 1934 the *Compagnie de Paris-Orléans* and the *Compagnie du Midi* merged, the STATE having since 1921 encouraged the numerous private rail companies to rationalize. The railways were originally run as state–private sector collaboration, in which private companies built and ran national or local lines as state concessions, but by 1937, depressed economic activity had closed so many lines and so weakened private companies that government created the nationalized SNCF. Although railways contributed to INDUSTRIALIZATION in post-war decades, their pre-eminence was challenged by road transport, causing closure of thousands of kilometres of local lines. Rising petrol prices and the SOCIALIST administration's commitment to railways in 1981 stemmed contraction, as did the TGV (1981), but passengers deserted non-TGV national lines during the 1980s and 1990s and new *transports express régionaux* (TER) struggled to maintain local travel. TGVs excel at city-to-city passenger travel (competing with airlines), but competition from road carriers means the SNCF carries only some 25 per cent of freight. The SNCF and RATP are heavily subsidized by the state and have suffered from over-staffing and inefficient management. The SNCF restructured in 1997 with the *Réseau ferroviaire français* (RFF) responsible for the track network. As transport becomes increasingly European, SNCF-RFF and RATP need to continue their MODERNIZATION. **(Hugh Dauncey)**

Further reading

Goussot (1999). Brief overview of all forms of transport, placing railways in their economic, geographical and political context.

Rainbow Warrior   A Greenpeace ship sent to disrupt French nuclear tests in the Pacific, it was blown up while in harbour in New Zealand in 1985, killing a worker. A scandal ensued when it emerged that the French secret services were involved in the attack.

Ramadier, Paul   1888–1961. Socialist politician. He was a minister in many governments from the 1930s to the 1950s, and was Prime Minister in 1947.

Ravel, Maurice   1875–1937. Composer. Noted for his compositions for piano and his orchestrations. His best known piece is *Bolero*, originally composed for a ballet in 1928.

Realism   A style of representation, which attempts to persuade the reader or spectator that they recognize it as a true and honest picture of life. Realism is often a label applied by critics to narratives that focus on WORKING-CLASS life and social issues. In this sense, it includes the 'social realism' of ETCHERELLI's description of the life of Algerian immigrants in a car factory, in the novel *Élise ou la vraie vie* (*Elise or Real Life*, 1967). It may also include the 'neo-realism' of Jean RENOIR's films, like *Les Portes de la nuit* (*The Gates of Night*, 1946), whose sets faithfully reproduce the district of Barbès-Rochechouart. It was also extended in the concept of SOCIALIST REALISM to include the depiction of social life with a strongly signalled political message.

Regionalism   How to balance the unique identity of each of the diverse regions that make up the NATION with a singular national IDENTITY? This tension has been more pressing for France in modern times than it has been for many of its neighbours, and originates in the Revolution of 1789. Republicanism sought to override local particularities and languages and create a national whole, but PARIS came to occupy centre position. It was not until the turn of the twentieth century, in reaction to this excessive centralization and URBANIZATION as well as to the Franco-Prussian War, that literary and political defenders of regional particularities began to be heard. These voices came largely from the Right. Most notorious among them was Maurice BARRES, who made his native Lorraine the symbolic projection of an ideal France. For the Right, loyalty to one's region was the authentic allegiance from which national identity derived: a point of view that intentionally excluded all who were not born in France (and their children, and their children's children), and led naturally to xenophobia and racism. This vision culminated in VICHY government state policy.

Such unsavoury ideological associations began to fade in the flourishing economic climate of the 1950s, when the FOURTH REPUBLIC instituted a programme of 'functional regionalization', focusing on each region's specific potential for INDUSTRIAL and AGRICULTURAL growth. Only in 1986 did the 22 regions of metropolitan France and the four overseas (Guadeloupe, Guyana, Martinique, Réunion) acquire administrative jurisdiction over their own territory.

Regions in France today have a strong sense of identity that is political, economic, and cultural. *Radio Pays* has been broadcasting in Occitan, Basque, Corsican, Catalan, Breton, Alsacian, and Flemish since 1981. In CORSICA and the Basque country, an unfortunate result of regionalism has been violent separatist movements. BRITTANY, on the other hand, provides one of the strongest positive formations of regional identity, from the revival of the Breton language and folk music (street signs in Quimper are bilingual; there is talk of a Breton-language television show), to its exceptional development of the agricultural and telecommunications industries, not to mention the myriad and internationally reputed summer festivals that have made Brittany such a popular TOURIST destination. Each region bears a unique place on the national scene; how they will function as a composite in the new EUROPE remains to be seen. (**Susan Weiner**)

Further reading

Nora (1996–97). Three chapters in particular give an overview of the connection between geography, national identity, and historical memory in the question of the spatial composition of France and its representation: 'The Region' (Jacques Revel), 'The Local' (Thierry Gasnier); and 'Paris-Province' (Alain Corbin). Lebovics (1992). Has a particular focus on ethnographic aspects.

Regional languages   There are eight principal regional languages in France: Alsatian, Basque, Breton, Catalan, Corsican, Flemish, Francique and Occitan. Francique, spoken in parts of Lorraine, is frequently omitted from lists or is bracketed together with Alsatian. However, it is a distinct language and probably more widely spoken in France than Flemish or Basque. Occitan is the name given to a series of related dialects spoken in the Southern third of France, from Gascon on the Atlantic coast to Provençal in Provence. Occitan with over 2 million speakers and Alsatian with over 1 million are the most widely spoken, while Flemish and Basque have the smallest number of speakers in France, although both are spoken in neighbouring countries, BELGIUM and Spain respectively. However, it is notoriously difficult to obtain accurate figures regarding the use of minority languages.

From the French Revolution up to the 1950s, successive French governments did their utmost to discourage the use of regional languages which were considered to be detrimental to national unity and a relic of pre-revolutionary ignorance. After the introduction of compulsory education in the 1880s, the school system became the principal method for promoting the FRENCH LANGUAGE at the expense of the regional languages. In many cases speaking in a regional language (or in *PATOIS*) at school was punished. This attitude did not change until the *loi* DEIXONNE was passed in 1951 which permitted the teaching of Basque, Breton, Catalan and Occitan. This was extended to all regional languages in 1982. Linguistic discrimination has often proved a rallying point for regionalist movements: precisely what central government policy-makers were seeking to avoid. Today, language issues are still important to many regionalist political groups, for example in CORSICA and BRITTANY. Nevertheless, social and economic developments and the influence of the MASS MEDIA are conspiring against the long-term survival of France's regional languages. All are under threat, with the position of Flemish, Basque and Francique perhaps the most precarious. (**James Minney**)

Further reading

Lodge (1993). Traces the development of French, with several sections dealing with regional languages. Walter (1988). General introduction to language issues in contemporary France.

Reinhardt, Django   1910–53. Musician. A JAZZ guitarist with a Gypsy background, he was a star of the Hot Club de France (1934–39), despite lacking two fingers of his left hand, and performed often with violinist Stéphane GRAPPELLI.

Relève, la   1942. Campaign by the LAVAL government to recruit workers voluntarily for German industry. For every three workers recruited, one French prisoner-of-war would be released; 90 000 PoWs were freed as a result. A limited success, it was replaced by labour conscription (STO).

Renaud   Born 1952. Singer and songwriter. His songs, reflecting the life of young people in deprived WORKING-CLASS suburbs, were popular in the 1980s. He uses irreverent humour and a good deal of urban slang.

Renaud, Madeleine   1900–94. Actor. After a career in the COMÉDIE FRANÇAISE, she founded the Renaud-Barrault theatre company in 1946 with her husband Jean-Louis BARRAULT, and starred in many AVANT-GARDE productions, including BECKETT's *Oh les beaux jours* (*Happy Days*, 1963).

Renault   Motor manufacturing company, founded by Louis Renault (1877–1944) and his brothers in 1899 at Billancourt in the Paris suburbs. Since it had produced military equipment for the German army, it was NATIONALIZED in 1945 and is still the largest French car maker. See also AUTOMOBILE INDUSTRY.

Renoir, Jean   1894–1975. Film director. A leading film-maker of the 1930s, he dealt with WORKING-CLASS subjects in a REALIST style, which included sharp social comment and linked him to the POPULAR FRONT. His opposition to war is exemplified in his most influential film, *La Grande Illusion* (*The Great Illusion*, 1937). He worked mainly in Hollywood after the war.

Resistance   Between 1940 and 1944, the Resistance developed from small beginnings into a major force which played an important role in the LIBERATION of France. After the traumatic defeat of June 1940, the French were primarily concerned with picking up the threads of daily life; refugees struggled home, and prisoners of war made efforts to be freed or to escape. Resistance was on the whole the fact of individuals, writing tracts or refusing to be co-operative. Only in the North, where the memory of the long years of German occupation from 1914–18 was still very fresh, did an organized, anti-German resistance devoted to sabotage, and to escape networks for Allied soldiers, get under way quickly.

Gradually Resistance movements, often grouping people of the same political sympathies, and Resistance information and escape networks working with London, grew in importance. After GERMANY invaded the Soviet Union in the summer of 1941, the French COMMUNIST PARTY threw itself, with its extensive network and organizational skills, into Resistance activities, including direct action against the German Army. In 1942, the widespread arrests of JEWS in both southern and northern zones accelerated the disaffection with the VICHY government. So did the creation of the STO, *Service du Travail Obligatoire*, seeking effectively to deport large numbers of young people to work in Germany, which had the effect of swelling the numbers joining the *maquis*. From June to September 1944, these forces were engaged across the country, though at times to ill-effect because of the paucity of their arms and experience. Battles between the Resistance and the MILICE, Vichy's para-military French force devoted to fighting the Resistance, left the bitter legacy characteristic of a civil war.

The Resistance also developed importance political and cultural activities. Newspapers such as COMBAT or *Défense de la France* were printing up to 450 000 and 100 000 copies respectively by the end of the OCCUPATION. Clandestine presses also produced poems and short stories, by ÉLUARD, ARAGON, VERCORS, and TRIOLET among many others. (**Margaret Atack**)

Further reading

Prost (1997). A very good range of articles on Resistance history and methodology. Kedward (1978). A classic study of the development of resistance movements in the southern zone.

Resnais, Alain Born 1922. Film director. Associated with the NOUVELLE VAGUE, he made many films with AVANT-GARDE writers, including *Hiroshima mon amour* (*Hiroshima my love*, 1959, with Marguerite DURAS). His documentary on concentration camps, *Nuit et brouillard* (*Night and Fog*, 1955) is still often shown.

Restaurants du cœur Launched in 1985 by the comedian COLUCHE, these soup-kitchens for the destitute became one of France's best-supported charities.

Revel, Jean-François Born 1924. Writer and journalist. He wrote for *L'EXPRESS*, which he directed for a time (1979–81) and for *Le POINT* (since 1980). A liberal democrat, he is well known for his polemical editorials. He also writes literary and philosophical essays.

Revolution A radical transformation of society. The French Revolution of 1789 inaugurated the revolutionary tradition in France, and it has since been part of the IDEOLOGY of successive Republics. The political revolutions of the nineteenth century (1830, 1848, 1871) were generally accompanied by fighting in major cities, especially PARIS, and for many French people, this appeared as the main element in revolution, confirmed by the Bolshevik Revolution in Russia (1917). INDUSTRIALIZATION came belatedly to France, during the nineteenth century, and is sometimes thought of as a revolution. From the early twentieth century, some SOCIALISTS, such as Charles Péguy (1873–1914) argued that political revolution needed to focus on moral (or spiritual) change, and later Christian socialists, like MOUNIER, believed that gradual, long-term changes were a more fundamental kind of revolution than political upheavals.

During the 1930s, many right-wing groups called for the revolutionary overthrow of the social order, and in 1940, Marshal PÉTAIN adopted the label of *RÉVOLUTION NATIONALE* (National Revolution) to describe his programme of authoritarian reform. At the same time, the RESISTANCE movements planned radical changes at the LIBERATION, which they saw as revolutionary. The moderate movement, COMBAT, for example, adopted the slogan *De la Résistance à la Révolution* (From resistance to revolution), which appeared on the masthead of its newspaper at the Liberation.

The events of MAY '68 appeared to many participants as a revolution, not least because of the barricades and street fighting. Much controversy raged over whether the situation was ripe for political revolution in the MARXIST sense, but later commentators point to the transformation in attitudes which it provoked as being a social (or cultural) revolution.

Historians like François Furet have reassessed the French Revolution (1789), pointing to the long-term nature of many of the changes it introduced. But for many people in France today, it is the rapid scientific and technological changes that seem to be best fitting the idea of revolution as a radical transformation of society. (**Michael Kelly**)

Further reading

Kelly (1996). Pilbeam (1999).

Révolution nationale   Launched after the defeat of France in 1940 by Marshal PÉTAIN, it was the declared strategy of his regime, based in VICHY, and replaced the slogan of the 1789 Revolution (*Liberté, Égalité, Fraternité*) with the alternative *Travail, Famille, Patrie* (Work, Family, Fatherland). Intended as a movement of national renewal and a radical break with the democratic Republican past, it was gradually abandoned as the war progressed.

Reynaud, Paul   1878–1966. Right-wing politician. A minister in several governments from the 1930s to the 1950s, and Prime Minister briefly at the Fall of France (1940).

Ricoeur, Paul   Born 1913. Philosopher. Concerned initially with developing an ethical philosophy in the tradition of Husserl, his later *Temps et récit* (*Time and Narrative*, 1983–85) has been widely influential. He was the progressively-minded rector at Nanterre when the events of MAY '68 broke out.

Rif War   In 1925–26 France was engaged, alongside Spain, in a war to suppress the Berber tribes of Morocco. The origins of this conflict date back to 1912 when France established a Protectorate, and the Spanish a Sub-Protectorate, in this part of North Africa. Spanish incompetence sparked off a Berber rebellion led by the journalist, Abd el-Krim. In 1921, Spanish armies suffered a catastrophic setback at Anual, a defeat credited with the collapse of the Spanish monarchy and the advent of Primo de Rivera's dictatorship (1925). Historians cannot agree whether the Berber revolt was a tribalist revolt or a war of national independence. Whatever the case, Paris fretted that the trouble might spread to French Morocco and Algeria. Yet reinforcing French troops along the boundaries of the Spanish Sub-Protectorate only precipitated a Berber attack (April 1925). The Resident-General of Morocco, the experienced colonial administrator Marshal Lyautey, promised some measure of self-rule, but this proposal was rejected by the insurgents who sought an independent republic, and went down badly in Paris which wanted complete control. Lyautey was replaced by Marshal PÉTAIN, hero of the First World War and later head of the VICHY government. He agreed on a combined Franco-Spanish military operation and deployed the tactics of the trenches, although historians stress it was the improvised campaign of Spanish officers such as Franco that proved more effective. In May 1926 Abd el-Krim, confronted by superior force, conceded defeat. While the war prefigured those uprisings that affected the French EMPIRE after 1945, it also influenced Pétain who was enamoured of Primo's dictatorship and was angered by the support COMMUNISTS, such as Jacques DORIOT, gave the Berbers. Pétain's loathing for Doriot, who in 1940 became a leading collaborator and sympathizer of the Marshal, stemmed from this dispute. (**Nicholas Atkin**)

Further reading

Woolman (1968). Still the standard work on the subject, despite its age.

Robbe-Grillet, Alain   Born 1922. Writer. Leading figure and theorist of the NOUVEAU ROMAN. He challenged traditional narrative techniques in novels such as *La Jalousie* (*Jealousy*, 1957) and films like *L'Année dernière à Marienbad* (*Last Year at Marienbad*, 1961, directed by Alain RESNAIS).

Rocard, Michel   Born 1930. Socialist politician. Moving from the Far Left PSU to the SOCIALIST Party, he led an important faction and served in several governments, including a period as Prime Minister, (1988–91).

Rochefort, Christiane   Born 1917. Writer. She explores the attempts of WOMEN to overcome the pressures and constraints upon them, in novels like *Les Petits enfants du siècle* (*Little Children of the Age*, 1961).

Rohmer, Eric   Born 1920. Film director. Initially a NOUVELLE VAGUE director, his films like *Ma nuit chez Maud* (*My Night with Maud*, 1969) explore characters, rather than plot or action, focusing on the intimate workings of personal relationships, with self-questioning, self-deception and moral dilemmas.

Rolland, Romain   1866–1944. Writer. His reputation as a novelist, biographer and playwright was confirmed by the award of a Nobel Prize in 1915. In the inter-war period, he was a committed PACIFIST, and admirer of Gandhi. He contributed to launching the ANTI-FASCIST movement in France and more widely in Europe.

Romains, Jules   1885–1972. Writer. He wrote many novels, poems, film-scripts and plays. He is remembered for a long series of novels, *Les Hommes de bonne volonté* (*Men of Good Will*, 1932–47) and for *Knock* (1923), a much-performed comic play, satirizing doctors.

Roudy, Yvette   Born 1929. Socialist politician. A supporter of François MITTERRAND, who appointed her as the first Minister for Women's Rights (1981–86).

Roy, Claude   1915–97. Writer. His poems, novels and literary criticism reflect his political interests, which shifted across the political spectrum during his lifetime. He is best-known for his often acerbic memoirs, including *Moi je* (*Me, I*, 1969).

RPF (*Rassemblement du peuple français*)   (Rally of the French People). Launched in April 1947 by Charles DE GAULLE, not as a party but as a political movement, because of his animosity towards political parties in general, which he considered to represent sectional rather than national interests. De Gaulle had resigned as Prime Minster of the PROVISIONAL GOVERNMENT in January 1946 in protest at the type of regime that was being proposed by the Constituent Assembly, and he sought through the RPF to rally support across a wide spectrum of voters on both Right and Left. However, since it was strongly ANTI-COMMUNIST in orientation, its appeal drew essentially from within the ranks of the MRP and RADICAL PARTY on the right of the political divide. RPF candidates initially met with considerable electoral success: in the municipal elections of 1947, they won 40 per cent of the vote, and 31 per cent in the *cantonales* the following year, taking the cities of PARIS, MARSEILLE, Lille, Strasbourg and Bordeaux. In the legislative elections of June 1951 this dropped to 22.3 per cent which gave them 119 *députés*, but they were immediately confronted with the paradox of being part of a system (that of the FOURTH REPUBLIC) which they officially opposed. As the RPF began to increasingly behave like any other political party, de Gaulle withdrew his support and in 1955 the movement ceased its activities. The parliamentary group took the name of *Union des républicains d'action sociale*, and Jacques CHABAN-DELMAS became its president.

In 1999, the letters RPF were consciously used as part of the acronym of a new '*souverainiste*' movement (*Rassemblement Pour la France et l'Indépendance de l'Europe*, RPF-IE) created by the GAULLIST Charles PASQUA and the dissident liberal Philippe de Villiers after their successful joint list in the European elections. However, leadership rivalry caused de Villiers to leave. (**Susan Collard**)

Further reading

Morelle (1998); and Mazzuccheti and Fredj, (1995). Both provide a clear synopsis. Charlot (1971); and Hartley (1972). Both give an analysis of Gaullism in its heyday.

RPF–IE *Rassemblement Pour la France et l'Indépendance de l'Europe*   (Rally for France and Independence from Europe). Consciously borrowing the GAULLIST acronym, this '*souverainiste*' movement (opposed to further European integration) was launched by Charles PASQUA and the dissident liberal Philippe de Villiers after their successful joint list in the European elections.

Further reading

See its website on:
www.rpf-ie.org

RPR (*Rassemblement pour la République*)   The name RPR (Republican Rally) was given to the GAULLIST party by Jacques CHIRAC in 1976. It had previously been called UDR (*Union pour la Défense de la République*, Union for the Defence of the Republic). Following his resignation as Prime Minister to Valéry GISCARD D'ESTAING, he sought to position himself for the next presidential election by reasserting his authority over the Gaullist party. He reorganized the party structure, strengthening the leadership structures and launched a successful campaign to increase membership. But electoral success was harder to achieve, and in the legislative elections of 1978 the party lost seats to the new presidential federation of non-Gaullist parties, the UDF (*Union pour la Démocratie Française*, Union for French Democracy) which was beginning to challenge the Gaullist hegemony on the Right. This trend continued at the presidential election of 1981 and at the subsequent legislative elections when the RPR suffered a dramatic loss of seats, from 153 to 83. Despite a reversal of fortunes in the 1986 elections, which brought Chirac into office as the first Prime Minister of a COHABITATION government, it did not secure him victory in the presidential election of 1988, and it was not until the departure of François MITTERRAND in 1995 that the leader of the RPR finally achieved this ambition. The party leadership was then taken over by Alain JUPPÉ, who was replaced by Philippe SEGUIN in 1997, who in turn was replaced in 1999 by the first female leader, Michèle Alliot-Marie.

In recent years the RPR has been dogged by political scandals and internal rivalries, leading to the breaking away of various splinter groups (such as the RPF-IE). The party's methods of financing its activities have been at the heart of the problems, and the personal implication of Chirac in these dealings, mostly while he was also Mayor of PARIS (1977–95), may have very serious consequences for the party. (**Susan Collard**)

Further reading

The party has an informative website:
www.rpr.org

Rugby   Rugby football arrived in France from across the Channel towards the end of the nineteenth century. Contrary to the 'public school' image that rugby union often has in England or Scotland, in France *Rugby à quinze* was and still is a largely WORKING-CLASS sport with its stronghold in the south. Despite being a member of the Five Nations tournament from its creation in 1910, France was rarely victorious in the early years: of the 78 matches played between 1906 and 1929, they won only 13. Rugby league (*Rugby à treize*) has been played in France since 1934, but it by no means boasts the enthusiasm and financial situation that surround the game in northern England.

The fortunes of the national rugby union team increased after the Second World War, leading to a glory era in the 1970s. France won the Grand Slam (*Grand Chelem*) in 1968, 1977 and 1981, the latter under the captainship of Jean-Pierre Rives, with Wales their principal rivals of the time. More recently, *les Bleus* were Grand Slam champions in 1997 and 1998. They were also finalists of the first rugby World Cup (1987) and of the 1999 tournament, losing to New Zealand and Australia respectively. The 1999 defeat came as an anticlimax after France's 43–31 semi-final victory against New Zealand, this being the highest number of points the All Blacks had ever conceded. Since 1920 Rugby in France has been governed by the FFR (*Fédération Française de Rugby*). The *Fédération*'s current aim is to popularize the sport further and make it more accessible to all. The latter policy may be in the wake of the success of the nation's culturally diverse football team, or of the key role of players of non-metropolitan origin, such as Émile Ntamack and Abdelatif Benazzi.

At club level the principal competitions are the *Championnat de France*, a league championship, with a knockout competition for the final stages, and the *Coupe de France* (cup competition). France's main teams include Toulouse (eight championship titles from 1960–99), Béziers (eleven titles) and Agen (six titles). Toulouse were also European club champions in 1996, as were Brive the following year. On the whole, professionalism has hit rugby less in France than, say, England, a fact reflected even in the seat prices at the *Stade de France* (as low as 50 francs for a Six Nations international match). The *troisième mi-temps* ('third half', or post-match socializing) is still an essential part of a rugby tradition noted for its flair but also for its indiscipline. (**Laurence Grove**)

Further reading

Sommerville (1997). Few books in English are dedicated entirely to French rugby, but many, including this one, will have at least one chapter on the French tradition.
The FFR's official website, offering full up-to-date information including pages in English is: www.ffr.fr

Sagan, Françoise   Born 1935. Her first novel, *Bonjour Tristesse* (*Hello Sadness*, 1954) is still her most popular, but she has written many novels, plays and autobiographical memoirs.

Saint-Exupéry, Antoine de   1900–44. Writer and aviator. In novels like *Vol de nuit* (*Night Flight*, 1931) he depicted the life and challenges of aviation pioneers. His Christian HUMANIST perspective emerges clearly in his popular children's book *Le petit prince* (*The Little Prince*, 1943). He was killed on a wartime flying mission.

Saint-Germain-des-Prés   Area of LEFT BANK PARIS within the 6th *arrondissement* (district), with a high concentration of cultural institutions, PUBLISHERS, CAFÉS, and restaurants. It was traditionally a centre of INTELLECTUAL and cultural life, made famous by the fashion for EXISTENTIALISM in 1945.

Saint-Jean-Perse   1887–1975. Poet. A career diplomat, his poems often deal with exile and migration. His best-known volume, *Anabase* (*Anabasis*, 1924), was translated into English by T.S. Eliot, and he received the Nobel Prize in 1960.

Saint-Laurent, Yves   Born 1936. Fashion designer. After working with Dior, he opened his own FASHION house in 1962, and made an impact with designs inspired by contemporary ART. His mass-produced ready-to-wear clothes for men and women remain popular.

Saint-Phalle, Niki de   Born 1930. Artist. Her paintings and sculptures often have gaudy colours and provocative themes, and have particularly explored the representation of WOMEN.

Salacrou, Armand   1899–1989. Playwright. Inspired by EXISTENTIALIST themes, his plays satirize BOURGEOIS life and manners.

Salan, General Raoul   1899–1984. Soldier. A highly decorated General, he was appointed Commander-in-Chief in Algeria (1956–58) and led the insurrection against the FOURTH REPUBLIC. Involved in the 1961 'PUTSCH' and the terrorist Secret Army Organization (OAS), he was tried and imprisoned (1962–68).

Salut les copains   1960s' radio programme on *Europe 1*, and music magazine (from 1962) which promoted pop music (*musique yé-yé*).

Sans-papiers   Foreigners living in France without legal authorization. The term gained widespread currency during the mid-1990s. Before then, a more common expression was *immigrés clandestins* (illegal immigrants) or simply *clandestins*. Their status is a consequence of the complex interaction between the economic, political and legal framework within which IMMIGRATION is regulated and the personal aspirations and itineraries of individual migrants.

In times of rapid economic growth and labour shortages, immigration controls have often been relaxed. This was the case, for example, during the 1960s, when large numbers of immigrant workers were permitted to enter France and take up jobs without the normal documents. Once they had found jobs these undocumented migrants were allowed to 'regularize' their situation by applying for residence and work permits. With the onset of a more difficult economic climate in the mid-1970s, those previously referred to as *irréguliers* now became known by the more sinister label of *clandestins*. Despite the legal ban on non-European labour migration introduced in 1974, undocumented migrants from relatively poor Third World countries continued to enter France in search of better economic opportunities. Many were granted an amnesty when the Left came to power in 1981, but later Centre-Right governments cracked down on them with increasing firmness. The toughest regulations of this kind, the 1993 PASQUA laws, provoked widespread criticism on the grounds of inhumane treatment. It was during this period that the label *sans-papiers* began to replace *clandestins* as a more sympathetic descriptor. On returning to office in 1997, the Left partially reversed the Pasqua laws, and granted an amnesty to most of the *sans-papiers* who had asked to be regularized, while retaining strong measures designed to prevent further inflows of unauthorized migrants. (**Alec Hargreaves**)

Further reading

Fassin, Morice and Quiminal, (1997). A wide-ranging collection of articles mainly sympathetic to the *sans-papiers*.

Sarraute, Nathalie   1900–99. Writer. An early exponent of the NOUVEAU ROMAN, in novels like *Le Planétarium* (1959) she explores human subjective experience, focusing on the often instinctive and unarticulated movements which affect it. She wrote several plays, and an AUTOBIOGRAPHICAL narrative, *L'enfance* (*Childhood*, 1983).

Sartre, Jean-Paul   1905–80. Writer. The leader of the EXISTENTIALIST movement from 1945, he wrote prolifically, producing novels and plays that are still often read or performed, as well as philosophical treatises and literary criticism. He founded and directed the influential monthly review, *LES TEMPS MODERNES* (*Modern Times*, founded 1945). He remains the exemplar of the COMMITTED INTELLECTUAL, intervening with authority on most political, social and cultural issues of his time, and often setting the agenda for public debate.

Satellite and cable broadcasting   French high technology policy has been closely linked to BROADCASTING developments and consequently to issues of national cultural sovereignty. Satellite and cable broadcasting took off in the late 1990s after much private sector investment, a decade after ambitious state-led cable and satellite plans had stumbled. Deregulation of broadcasting allowed the private companies *Vivendi* and *Suez-Lyonnaise* to invest initially in a lower-tech cable infrastructure and in new thematic channels. Since 1997, France has two major digital satellite systems (*Canal Satellite*, using the subscription expertise of *Canal Plus*, and *TPS*) offering around 100 channels and interactive services. Cable television is also converting to digital, offering a mix of services from different satellites, plus INTERNET access. Over 2 million homes subscribed to a satellite television service in 1999, and 2.75 million to cable TV. The new delivery platforms of satellite and cable have in practice changed broadcasting economics and consumption: subscription television and pay-per-view are turning broadcasting into a commodity, and competing strongly with universal access public service television. Whereas TELEVISION has been the MASS medium *par excellence*, technological change is leading to a demassification (or individualization) of its usage as viewers construct their own schedules. The major 'free' terrestrial channels are losing their audience little by little in this new competitive environment. The huge increase in channels, the convergence of broadcasting with telecommunications and the Internet, and the GLOBALIZATION of the industry are posing new regulatory problems. As Internet broadcasting becomes a reality, the STATE will find it increasingly difficult to regulate what people watch. The MODERNIZATION of French broadcasting and high technology is thus in conflict with traditional protection of the FRENCH language, cultural sovereignty, and an indigenous French AUDIOVISUAL INDUSTRY. **(Geoff Hare)**

Further reading

Hare (1999).

Savary, Jérôme   Born 1942. Theatre director. Founder in 1965 of the *Grand Magic Circus* theatre company, which specialized in experimental and often provocative productions.

Scènes nationales   See MAISONS DE LA CULTURE.

Schuman, Robert   1886–1963. Centrist politician. A CHRISTIAN DEMOCRAT, he was minister in many post-war governments, including Prime Minister (1947–48). An unusually long-serving Foreign Minister (1948–53) he played a key role in EUROPEAN integration.

Schumann, Maurice   1911–98. Centrist politician. A CHRISTIAN DEMOCRAT, he held ministerial posts in the 1950s. A successful writer, he was also elected to the ACADÉMIE FRANÇAISE.

Science fiction   Science fiction is the term given to a group of NOVELS, short stories and films which assume a technological or scientific advance, or make use of an imagined and often catastrophic change in our human environment. Although such concerns were expressed in earlier literary texts, it was not until the late nineteenth century that science fiction emerged in a form that we would recognize today. One of the most influential writers at this time and subsequently was Jules Verne (1828–1905) with classics such as *Voyage au centre de la terre* (*Journey to the Centre of the Earth,* 1864).

   During the twentieth century, science fiction in France and elsewhere has reflected scientific progress and its possible consequences. Common themes include interplanetary travel, robots, androids and the fear of machines replacing humans. Those texts that focus on technological advances often highlight their capacity to destroy the world, such as NUCLEAR weaponry, and carry with them an apocalyptic message about humankind's self-destructive tendencies. In terms of a French tradition of science fiction, it was only in the 1950s that specialized collections were established which, in their early days, functioned mainly as vehicles for British and American translations. As with DETECTIVE FICTION, the development of French science fiction as a genre was hampered by the view that it was no more than pulp fiction with little literary merit. However, by the late 1960s, a group of writers had begun to use the conventions of science fiction to investigate present-day social and ecological issues with a clearly political purpose in mind. Unlike Britain and America, a long-favoured medium for French science fiction has been the adult *BANDE DESSINÉE,* with writers like Moebius (Jean GIRAUD) who tend to exploit the fantasy aspects of science fiction writing, playing with parallel universes and time/space distortions. The prevalence of science fiction in such a variety of forms testifies to its importance for contemporary French popular culture. (**Claire Gorrara**)

Sculpture   Sculpture, like ARCHITECTURE, is a peculiarly public art, destined as much for outdoor as indoor exhibition. In France, whose roll-call of distinguished practitioners extends from David d'Angers and Landowski via Rodin and Maillol to

PICASSO and GIACOMETTI, its historic high-water mark was reached with the *statuomanie* of the THIRD REPUBLIC between 1870 and 1914. Though the short-lived Revolution of 1848 had commissioned representations of the Republic (works by Daumier and Soitoux), the consolidation of the regime after 1870, the extension of democracy to the *communes* in 1884, and the 1889 centenary created a mass market which a plethora of talented artists was ready to satisfy. Bartholdi and Dalou, Landowski and Falguière, Injalbert and Gautherin among others created statues of Liberty and busts of MARIANNE for town halls and honoured major figures of art, science and philosophy such as Arago, Comte, Diderot, Lavoisier, Claude Bernard, Cuvier, Pasteur and Raspail. Sculpturally, the values of progress and democracy, industry and enlightenment were republican.

After 1919, and during the OCCUPATION (1940–44) when many statues were demolished, official sculpture suffered an eclipse which lasted until the 1980s, when an ambitious presidential cultural policy and STATE patronage (*mécénat*) combined with the renewal of city-centre sites (*aménagement, espaces verts*) to create the conditions for revival. If the abstract or ludic has displaced the allegorical (Niki de SAINT-PHALLE, Yves Klein, Buren's columns at the Palais-Royal), contemporary naturalism is the keynote of public *hommages* to SARTRE and Léon BLUM, MAURIAC, POMPIDOU and MENDÈS-FRANCE. Sculpture has acknowledged wartime RESISTANCE and FREE FRENCH heroes such as Jean MOULIN, General Leclerc, Bertie Albrecht and offered reparation for a problematic past: Tim's Dreyfus combines the cartoonist's vision and the subject's vulnerability, while in Spitzer's 1994 memorial to the Jewish victims of the round-up of the *VEL D'HIV* (1942) a suitcase and a child's doll capture the banality of evil and the holocaust of small hopes and dreams. (**Bill Kidd**)

Further reading

Curtis (1999); Hargrove (1989).

Sécurité sociale   The system of social insurance (the equivalent to the British welfare state) to ensure a more equal society, where extreme poverty would be eliminated. Set up in 1945, it is divided into three branches, to cover sickness, and child benefits and pensions (but not unemployment, which has a different regime run by the UNEDIC). There are separate schemes for salaried WORKERS, farmers and agricultural workers (*PAYSANS*) and the self employed. Some 98 per cent of the population is covered by a complex system of separately run but interdependent *caisses* (funds) whose management has seats for elected representatives of employers and employees. The majority of the funding comes from employer and employee contributions at a fixed rate per salary. Governments interfere with the funding and regulation of the system at their peril, as Prime Minister Alain JUPPÉ discovered in November 1995. His government's attempted reform brought the country to a standstill for three weeks in a public sector strike with the rallying cry *Touche pas à mon Sécu!* (Hands off my welfare!).

While the benefits to those in work are generous, there is a gap between those covered and able to top up insurance with private schemes, and those who are no longer eligible for benefits (see EXCLUSION). The *Sécurité sociale* finances have been under increasing strain from an ageing population, soaring unemployment and increasing medical costs, (see HEALTH), as it cannot borrow to source the debt and it has been under increasing attack as it has failed to eliminate the poverty gap, and social exclusion. Michel ROCARD introduced reforms which are still in place. They include the RMI of 1988 (*revenu minimum d'insertion*, minimum social income), to grant an allowance to those marginalized by long-term unemployment; and the CSG (*contribution sociale généralisée*, a supplementary income tax) of 1991, to raise revenue for the funds. (**Márie Cross**)

Further reading

Reland (1997). An analysis of the December 1995 crisis. Hirsch (1994). A good work for explaining the weaknesses of the system.

Seguin, Philippe   Born 1943. Centre-Right politician. On the Left of the GAULLIST movement, he was Minister for Social Affairs, 1986–88.

Semiology and semiotics   Semiology is the science of signs, their structure, inter-action and interpretation. There are two traditions of sign study. One was instituted by the Swiss linguist Ferdinand de Saussure in his seminal *Cours de linguistique générale* (Course in General Linguistics, 1916). Saussure recognized that language was one of several sign systems and he divided the sign into its twin aspects of *signifiant* (signifier: acoustic or visual aspect) and *signifié* (signified: concept or idea). This greatly enhanced the scope of semiotic analysis. The other tradition, Semiotics, was inspired by the American philosopher Charles Sanders Peirce (1839–1914), who elaborated a triadic concept linking sign, object and interpretant. Peirce also facili-tated analysis of the visual sign by dividing it into three fundamental classes: icon, index and symbol. The essential difference between Peirce and Saussure was that Peirce included the object as a vital component of the signifying system, whereas Saussure excluded it.

On the whole, it is the Saussurian semiological tradition that has predominated in France. It has been used in literary and cultural studies, for example, by Roland BARTHES in his *Mythologies* (1957) and *L'Empire des signes* (1970); in social and polit-ical studies, for example, by Jean BAUDRILLARD in his *Pour une critique de l'économie politique du signe* (*For a Critique of the Political Economy of the Sign*, 1972); and in PSYCHOANALYSIS, for example by Jacques LACAN in his *Écrits* (1966, 1971), and by Julia KRISTEVA in her *Pouvoirs de l'horreur* (*Powers of Horror*, 1980).

Other fruitful branches of sign study include the semiology of communication (the intentional, denotative aspect of signs) and the semiology of meaning (sign interrelationships). The latter in particular has enriched our understanding of CINEMA (Christian METZ) and advertising (Jean-Marie Floch). Modern semiotics, notably after Umberto Eco, embraces both, with a noticeable current interest in the problem of the way the 'objective' meaning of the sign is problematized by the SUBJECTIVITY of the receiver. It is here that Peircian analysis of the 'interpretant' becomes increasingly relevant. As late CAPITALIST, post-industrial society engages increasingly in the exchange, not of objects but of signs, semiotic analysis of the image is an increasingly pressing concern. (**David Scott**)

Further reading

Costantini (1995); Deledalle (1979).

Senghor, Léopold Sédar   Born 1906. Writer and politician. With CÉSAIRE, he led the *NÉGRITUDE* movement in the 1930s, writing poems and essays which explored the condition of black people and the bankruptcy of the COLONIAL powers from a broad HUMANIST perspective. After its independence, he became President of his native Senegal (1960–80).

Serge, Victor   1890–1947. Writer. A participant in the Russian Revolution, he was opposed to Stalin and lived in exile for a period in France. His essays and novels reflect his political COMMITMENTS and the difficulties faced by INTELLECTUALS in revolutionary situations.

Série noire   A collection of mainly THRILLERS and DETECTIVE novels, edited by Marcel Duhamel for Gallimard. It has published over 2000 volumes, including many translated American novels.

Serres, Michel   Born 1930. Philosopher. His work has mainly analysed the history of science, and the relations between scientific and artistic investigation, particularly in their aesthetic and ethical implications.

Servan-Schreiber, Jean-Jacques   Born 1924. Liberal politician. Co-founder in 1953 of the weekly *L'EXPRESS*, he was strong supporter of MODERNIZATION, best known for his book *Le Défi américain* (The American Challenge, 1967), which warned against European complacency.

Sétif   1945. Algerian town where a pro-nationalist demonstration, followed by riots, was brutally repressed by the French security forces on VE (Victory in Europe) Day, May 1945.

Seuil, Éditions du   Publishing house, founded 1935. Initially specializing in progressive Catholic studies on political and cultural issues, it developed during the 1960s to become one of the biggest French publishers of books in the arts and humanities and social sciences.

Sexuality   The term *sexualité* began to be used widely in France in the decades that followed the LIBERATION, that is during the post-war period of rapid MODERNIZATION. The CATHOLIC Church had always represented sexual desire as an obstacle to salvation, an unavoidable aspect of procreation within marriage, but sinful if detached from its God-given purpose. As the influence of the Church declined, as the legalization of CONTRACEPTIVE devices (1967) and ABORTION (1975) dissociated sex from procreation, and the CONSUMER society increasingly legitimized the pursuit of personal pleasure, so it became more possible to speak not just of sex but of different sexualities.

Simone de BEAUVOIR's *Le Deuxième Sexe* (*The Second Sex*, 1949) scandalized many readers, and delighted others, by its frank discussion of female sexuality that included a detailed account of the female orgasm and a sympathetic treatment of lesbianism. The post-1968 FEMINIST movement also made sexuality a central campaigning theme, attacking the assumption that male sexuality was naturally, hence uncontrollably, aggressive, refusing the objectified representations of the female body that both encouraged sexual violence and denied women's own sexual agency. Some feminists of the *PSYCH ET PO* tendency argued that female sexuality had been so repressed by patriarchal culture that the most urgent task was to explore women's BODIES, women's desires, outside the constructions and fantasies imposed upon them. Writing female sexuality from a woman's perspective was part of this project: sexuality was linked to *textuality*.

The feminist agenda was shaped in part by lesbian women who formed groups such as the *Gouines rouges* (Red Dykes). Homosexual men also organized to defend and celebrate what soon came to be re-named gay (*gai*) sexuality: the first French Gay Pride march took place in 1977, and the age of consent was equalized for hetero sexual and homosexual relations in 1982. In the late twentieth century sexualities have been a recurring and important theme of French theory, literature and cinema, from Michel FOUCAULT's three-volume *Histoire de la sexualité* (*History of Sexuality*, 1976–84), to Marguerite DURAS's best-selling *L'Amant* (*The Lover*, 1984), and 1990s' films such as Cyril Collard's *Les Nuits fauves* (*Savage Nights*, 1992), Josyane Balasko's comedy film *Gazon Maudit* (*French Twist*, 1995), Catherine Breillat's *Romance* (1999). (**Diana Holmes**)

Further reading

Duchen (1986). Heathcote *et al.* (1998).

SFIO (*Section française de l'internationale ouvrière*) See SOCIALIST PARTY.

Short story The successful short story (*conte* or *nouvelle*) explores not only the aesthetic and narrative virtues of brevity, but the symbolic values that can be convincingly associated with brevity. In so far as the characters featured by short story writers have tended to live overlooked, isolated lives, lived at the edge (geographically, socially, economically, psychologically, etc.), the theme of marginality would appear to have forged a firm symbolic link with short fiction. Given the problems of marginalization and EXCLUSION affecting the post-industrial era (not least in French society), short fiction is unlikely in the near future to lose its compelling attraction as a literary form.

Having passed through its 'golden age' in the nineteenth century, French short fiction fell out of favour with writers, readers, and publishers over the course of the twentieth century. Writers renowned above all for their short fiction are few in number. Pre-war exceptions include Marcel Arland, Marcel AYMÉ and COLETTE (whose skills as a short story writer went unacknowledged for many decades), and, in the post-war period, Daniel Boulanger, Georges-Olivier Châteaureynaud, and Annie Saumont. The genre has often appeared to survive mainly on the strength of one-off collections of stories by major novelists, as in SARTRE's *Le mur* (The Wall, 1939), Camus's *L'Exil et le royaume* (*Exile and the Kingdom*, 1957), and Alain Robbe-Grillet's *Instantanés* (*Snapshots*, 1962).

A key characteristic of the contemporary period has been the shift away from the generic self-confidence of the 'short story' (*nouvelle*) to a practice of writing that is less intent on being narrative, and therefore more open to interaction with neighbouring short forms (e.g. the prose poem). Genre-mixing has even led the short story to overcome its resentment against its 'big brother', the novel, as in Georges Perec's brilliant *La vie mode d'emploi* (*Life: A User's Manual*, 1978), at once a novel and a volume of *nouvelles*. Young women writers, including Marie Desplechin, Pierrette Fleutiaux, Catherine Lépront, and Linda Lê, have figured prominently in the revitalization of French short fiction since 1970. (**Johnnie Gratton**)

Further reading

Flower (1998). Covers a range of authors from Sartre to the present. Gratton and Le Juez (1994). An anthology of stories from 1830 to the present, with an introduction and notes in English.

Signoret, Simone   1921–85. Actor. She took the leading female role in many French films, and also used her star status, with her husband Yves MONTAND, to support many political campaigns on the Left.

Simon, Claude   Born 1913. Writer. Associated with the *NOUVEAU ROMAN*, in novels like *La Route des Flandres* (*The Flanders Road*, 1960), he presents a fragmented and ambiguous narrative, which explores historical catastrophe and human responses to it. He was awarded the Nobel Prize in 1985.

Situationism   An AVANT-GARDE artistic movement which was closely associated with the new ways of thinking and radical politics of the 1960s in France. The Situationist International was founded in 1957 by artists from several European countries, some of whom belonged to the French *lettrist* avant-garde movement. Over the next 15 years, the Situationalist International promoted a critique of what it saw as the ALIENATION, CONSUMERISM and boredom of post-war society. Drawing on DADAISM and SURREALISM, the situationists sought to tear art away from its conventional forms, and reconstitute it at the level of EVERYDAY LIFE. In this way, they aimed to initiate a range of activities that would give rise to a series of creative and imaginative 'situations'. For example, inspired in part by De Quincey's intoxicated journeys around London, they advocated the practice of the *dérive*, a spontaneous rambling through the streets of PARIS, the aim of which was to reinvent a new city with each *dérive*. Allied to this creation of situations was a project of utopian urbanism, which drew upon certain modernist tendencies in ARCHITECTURE. In a world apparently increasingly dominated by objects and spectacles, which required only passive consumption, the situationists sought to introduce elements of autonomy, authenticity, imagination, *détournment*, spontaneity and creativity into the practice of everyday life. For these reasons, their ideas fed into the outpouring of social and political unrest and utopian theorizing which constituted the events of MAY '68 in France.

Paradoxically perhaps, given its mistrust of authority, the Situationist International itself was characterized by a fairly strict control of membership and a history of ruthless expulsions. Guy DEBORD emerged as the leading light and effective head of the movement, publishing *La Société du spectacle* in 1967. In the aftermath of 1968, with DE GAULLE's party back in power, it seemed to Debord that the historical moment of the Situationist International had passed, and he and his colleagues dissolved the movement in 1972. (**John Marks**)

Further reading

Blazwick (1989). A catalogue to accompany the exhibition 'On the passage of a few people through a brief period of time', shown in Paris and London. Knabb (1981). A comprehensive collection of writings by members of the Situationist International.

Socialist Party, *Parti socialiste* (PS)   Born in 1905, the PS was known as the SFIO (*Section française de l'Internationale Ouvrière*) until 1969. A merger between various small groups, it was always subject to tension between MARXIST revolutionaries, led by Jules Guesde, and reformists seeking to use republican democracy to push society gradually towards socialism; Jean Jaurès personified this approach. Always smaller than most of its social-democratic counterparts in EUROPE, SFIO was a party of protest and principled opposition until the threat of FASCISM in the 1930s led it to head a short-lived governing coalition with COMMUNISTS and RADICALS. After 1945, with the PCF sidelined by the COLD WAR, SFIO was a key member of coalitions alongside Radicals, CHRISTIAN DEMOCRATS and moderates as it strove to preserve the FOURTH REPUBLIC.

When the Fourth Republic collapsed, SFIO shared much of its unpopularity before reinventing itself thanks to an imaginative programme, the charismatic leadership of François MITTERRAND and a dynamic electoral pact with its long-standing PCF competitor. Mitterrand's 1981 victory heralded 14 years of his presidency, during which time the PS was confirmed as a major governing party, having learned that traditional socialist recipes based on tax-and-spend policies and interventionist economic management are unsustainable in today's global economy. Nowadays the PS heads a 'plural Left' coalition including PCF (no longer a threat since the demise of Soviet communism), Radicals and Greens, which won office in 1997. Its militant Marxist-tinged rhetoric has given way to a more moderate, managerial discourse as, like its sister parties, the PS seeks an expression of socialism appropriate to today. (**David Hanley**)

Further reading

Bell and Criddle (1987). Ladrech and Marlière (1999). Both books give solid and up-to-date accounts.

Socialist realism   As its name suggests, the aim of socialist realism in art is to present a realistic portrayal of society with clear indications of how it might be improved through the introduction of revolutionary socialist values. Such art has a clear didactic dimension. As a doctrine, socialist realism was first introduced into France from the Soviet Union in the early 1930s in the wake of the Revolutionary Writers'

Congress in Moscow in 1934. This was attended, among others, by NIZAN and ARAGON, who became socialist realism's principal proponents for the next decade. Translations of articles by Russian theorists were carried in the COMMUNIST-inspired periodical *Commune*. Aragon published a series of lectures under the title *Pour un Réalisme Socialiste* (*For a Socialist Realism*, 1935).

A second phase of socialist realism developed from the late 1940s when the ideologically driven directives on ART, literature and music by Andrei Zhdanov, Stalin's Minister of Culture, were translated into French. These were followed by similar works by Laurent Casanova and Jean Kanapa, the intellectual commissars of the French Communist party and by articles and debates published in *La NOUVELLE CRITIQUE* and *Les LETTRES FRANÇAISES*. There was now a greater emphasis on political orthodoxy than in the 1930s and the focus was sharper with communism being offered as the panacea for all social ills. In literature, the result was a series of novels and stories by writers such as André Stil and Pierre Courtade in which the weaknesses and evils of CAPITALIST, BOURGEOIS society were ruthlessly – but often simplistically – exposed. In painting there was an excessive adulation of André Fougeron's paintings of WORKING-CLASS life. Socialist realism never provoked more than a minority interest, however, and several who publicly gave their support to it as part of communist doctrine were in private far more cynical and critical. By the early 1960s it had disappeared. (**John Flower**)

Sociology   First coined by Auguste Comte (1798–1857) in 1830, the French term *sociologie* is defined as 'the scientific study of social phenomena, including social forms (structures and functions) and their evolution', which belies the rich and complex history of a field that is essentially a French creation. 'Daughter of the Revolution of 1789', sociology's ancestors include the revolutionary social thought of the Enlightenment philosophers Montesquieu, Condorcet, and Rousseau, as well as the counter-revolutionary lineage represented by de Bonald and de Maistre. This double heritage informed the work of Comte as well as Saint-Simon in the early part of the nineteenth century until its formalization as a modern discipline in the last decades by Émile DURKHEIM. The common thread linking the founding fathers is the notion of *crisis*, and the concomitant need for a scientific basis for the moral equivalent to religion in the reconstruction of a fractured social body.

This is the motivation for Durkheim's early classic treatises on the social division of labor (1893) and suicide (1897) as well as his subsequent turn towards the ethnographic study of archaic religion in *The Elementary Forms of Religious Life* (1912), to elucidate the basis for social solidarity in the modern world. By integrating an 'ethnographic detour' to address contemporary social issues, Marcel MAUSS extended sociology to a new generation of cultural iconoclasts in the inter-war period. Rather than accentuate the paralysing effects of social determinism, the French school assumes that social forms are *enabling*, and provide the basis for experience and knowledge otherwise inaccessible to the individual.

After the Second World War, sociology expanded rapidly as an academic discipline, driven by the demand for social understanding to inform social policies of the STATE and CONSUMER strategies of business. It was strongly influenced by American theories, focused on social behaviour, and by MARXIST theories, focused on social CLASSES. These approaches were challenged by the social repercussions of the nation's rapid MODERNIZATION. Its identity crisis was underscored when the events of MAY '68 erupted among sociology students at Nanterre, inspired by Henri LEFEBVRE. More recently, Pierre BOURDIEU situates his wide-ranging studies within the Durkheimian comparative tradition by claiming that even when reference to another culture is not explicit, *sociologie* maintains critical relevance by imposing upon one's own society the objectification usually reserved for others. (**Michèle Richman**)

Further reading

Lemert (1981). Bourdieu (1993).

Sollers, Philippe   Born 1936. Writer. Influential critic, and editor of *TEL QUEL* monthly review, which published radical literary CRITICAL THEORY. He has also written several novels.

Sorbonne   The University of Paris, it grew from a college founded in the LATIN QUARTER during the thirteenth century by Robert de Sorbon, whose name it eventually adopted. It was, with Nanterre, at the epicentre of the events of MAY '68. As part of the ensuing reforms, it was divided into several institutions, which are among the many universities in and around Paris.

Soupault, Philippe   1897–1990. Writer. A DADAIST and SURREALIST during the inter-war period, he wrote poems, essays and novels. From the 1930s, he combined this with working as a radio broadcaster and producer.

Soustelle, Jacques   1912–90. GAULLIST politician. He opposed the agreements to end the ALGERIAN WAR, and after a period of exile returned to France as a symbol of the Extreme Right. He was elected to the *ACADÉMIE FRANÇAISE*.

Space programme   The French space programme reflects successive French governments' 'national' approaches to science and TECHNOLOGY policy, industry, and guaranteeing France's place in the world. Originally closely linked to development of NUCLEAR DETERRENCE, the space programme and industry have developed more civilian applications, and French space is closely linked with the EUROPEAN space effort. Although captured German V2 rocket technology helped French interest in ballistic missiles in the 1940s, it was in the late 1950s that serious work on creating missile vectors for the French nuclear deterrent began. The military procurement agency and its specialized laboratories and industrial facilities worked with the *Commissariat à l'énergie atomique* (Atomic Energy Commission, CEA) to design rockets which gave the land- and sea-based ballistic missiles of the independent *FORCE DE FRAPPE* created by DE GAULLE in the 1960s. The French national space agency CNES (*Centre national d'études spatiales*, National Centre for Space Studies) was founded in 1961. Space programmes have civil and international aspects as well as contributing to defence. France has always led in developing space science and commercial applications of space technologies (telecommunications, remote sensing) and has always stimulated interest in the European space programme run since 1975 by the European Space Agency (ESA). The ESA is an inter-governmental body in which France is the leading partner by virtue of her substantial domestic space industry and of French governments' strong support for space technologies. The successful ESA rocket *Ariane* (launched from French Guiana) is European, but was planned and heavily supported by France. As cross-national mergers of previously 'national champion' aerospace companies have proliferated across Europe, traditional French claims that 'French space policy is European space policy' become harder to deny, but France remains the European country whose nuclear deterrent maintains her need for continuing independent expertise in space technologies. (**Hugh Dauncey**)

Further reading

RIIA (1988). An overview of European space policy, placing the French space programme in context.

Spanish Civil War   1936–39. This conflict greatly exacerbated the growing tension between Left and Right in France in the 1930s, and acted as a prelude to the divisions in the country which the defeat of 1940 would bring. The Spanish Civil war broke out in July 1936 as a result of a coup by General Franco against the Republican Government of Spain. The resulting war tore the country apart, and engaged the international attention of foreign governments and of European and American INTELLECTUALS. The two ideological blocs of the 1930s, FASCISM and COMMUNISM, supported opposing sides, the Italians and Germans sending arms to the Franco insurgents, and the Russians giving aid to the Republican Government. Many French left-wing idealists enlisted in the pro-Republican military units, the International Brigades.

At the outbreak of the Civil War, the French Government, a POPULAR FRONT coalition of the Left, had wanted to send help to the Spanish Republicans. However, British diplomatic pressure and French public opinion prevented this, and instead the government adopted a non-intervention policy, which came to mean turning a blind eye to the clandestine despatch of aid across the border. French intellectuals became deeply committed to what they believed to be a just war. On the Left, intellectuals like André MALRAUX supported the efforts of the Republicans, chronicling in his book, *L'Espoir* (*Days of Hope*, 1937) the optimism, and disappointments of war. On the Right, intellectuals like Robert BRASILLACH extolled the Spanish fascist leader, José Antonio Primo de Rivera, as an example of what France needed.

For many French intellectuals, the Spanish Civil War was the beginning of choices which were to come to a climax in the defeat of France in 1940. Malraux, for example, would become a Resister and subsequently a minister of CULTURE in post-war France. Brasillach would write for a COLLABORATIONIST newspaper in the war, and face a firing squad in 1945 in the *ÉPURATION* (purge) of the LIBERATION. (**Hilary Footitt**)

Further reading

Malraux (1937). A classic evocation of the emotions of the period. Bernanos (1938). The political impact of the War on a conservative French Catholic.

Spelling, orthography   French spelling still reflects the pronunciation of the medieval language, for which it was designed. In the eleventh century, the word for 'water' actually *was* a sequence of three vowels (*e-a-u*), there *was* an audible *e-n-t* at the end of *chantent* ('they sing'), and so on. Today's mismatch is caused by the failure of orthography to keep up with rapid pronunciation changes, particularly in the fourteenth and fifteenth centuries, when many consonants disappeared and many vowel sequences were simplified. Complications were even introduced deliberately, either to make hastily written manuscripts more legible (the *h* of *huit*, 'eight') or to emphasize links with Latin (the *g* of *doigt*, 'finger').

Other languages, not least English, also have conservative orthographies. But in French, grammatical information conveyed by spelling (e.g. the *-s* on plural nouns) may not be there in the pronunciation, or may be indicated in a different way. For example, in speech, it is the *le/les* contrast that tells us whether a noun is plural or not. So written grammar can be very unlike spoken grammar, which causes difficulties for children learning to write, and even for adults. The verb endings *-é*, *-és*, *-ée*, *-ées*, *-er*, *-ai*, *-ais*, *-ait*, *-aient*, for instance, are pronounced in the same way by many speakers, who are therefore unsure which spellings to use.

The fascination of such complications, and innumerable minor irrationalities (*imbécile*, but *imbécillité*, etc.), helps to explain the popularity of the annual televised spelling contest *Les Dicos d'or* (*Golden Dictionaries*) and the fact that Scrabble is a major national pastime. And it may well be public affection for traditional orthography (as well as the conservatism of the ACADÉMIE) that has halted even the most timid attempts at reform – most recently in 1989–90. (**Rodney Ball**)

Further reading

Ball (2000). Differences between written and spoken forms. Pivot (1989). Concise history of French spelling and spelling reform.

Sport   Sociologically important, but often intellectually derided, sport is played by one in ten French people (half of them under 18 years), whereas three out of ten have never practised any sport. Many modern sports were imported from Britain in the late nineteenth century by the middle and upper classes. Their popularity spread throughout the nation with INDUSTRIALIZATION and URBANIZATION. As in other developed countries, they were commercialized as spectator sports, with input from the PRESS (particularly the sports daily *L'Equipe*). Certain sporting competitions (especially FOOTBALL) have recently become key commodities in the competition for viewers between TELEVISION companies. Televised sport, especially when the national team is involved, commands the largest television audiences: half the nation watched the 1998 World Cup Final. The consequent interest of sponsors and advertisers and the steeply rising cost of transmission rights for a narrow range of sports have brought business attitudes and practices into sports that had long been run by volunteers, and governed under the 1901 law on non-profit-making associations. This in turn has created growing inequalities between rich and poor sports, and made certain sports more independent of the state and local authority subsidy (and therefore less subject to public control). Sports Ministers have endeavoured to tread the thin line between allowing French sports to 'modernize' and become competitive internationally (by allowing professional clubs to become businesses) and maintaining STATE regulation to preserve a sporting and public service ethos. The fight against drugs in sport (highlighted in the 1998 TOUR DE FRANCE) has become a key element of government policy – in contrast to the emphasis of GAULLIST and later government policy of imitating Eastern bloc countries' use of sport as an instrument of national *grandeur*, notably in competitions like the OLYMPIC GAMES. **(Geoff Hare)**

Further reading

Holt (1981). Still the best history of French sport in English.

Stadia French sports stadia have traditionally been multi-use, and owned by municipalities rather than by sporting clubs. In these ways, they reflect differences between French organization of SPORT, and British and US traditions of stadia devoted to a single sport. The 1998 soccer World Cup gave a boost to modernizing many French stadia. France has traditionally used both sport and ARCHITECTURE to create *grandeur*: the prestigious hosting of the 1924 OLYMPICS, the 1938 World Cup, the 1984 European Soccer Championships and the 1998 soccer World Cup developed stadia in Paris and regionally. Modern stadia appeared as early as 1924, when Colombes (Paris suburbs) hosted the Olympics, but building a national stadium was an ongoing problem. In the 1930s and 1940s various high-capacity stadia were unsuccessfully proposed around PARIS, although the *FRONT POPULAIRE*'s promotion of sport proliferated municipal stadia in the late 1930s.

In the 1950s a stadium honouring RESISTANCE hero Jean MOULIN was considered, but only after an appeal from DE GAULLE, did POMPIDOU decide (1962) on a stadium publicly funded and managed by the *Ville de Paris* and *Caisse des dépôts*. However, this was shelved until the mid-1980s and Paris's application for the 1992 Olympics. Failure to attract the Olympics led to successful bidding for the 1998 soccer World Cup, to the creation of the *Stade de France*, and the improvement of stadia in provincial cities. The *Stade de France* encapsulates many of the debates over French stadia: funded in partnership by government and the private sector, and run as a profit-making business, it reflects new principles of managing sport. After long debate over its name, its final appellation reflects a more politically neutral approach to sport than that of municipalities in previous decades, anxious to celebrate heroes of sport or politics. A multi-use venue, it continues the role of stadia as fora for sports, popular music CONCERTS and political meetings. **(Hugh Dauncey)**

Further reading

Vigneau (1998). Overview of sporting infrastructures, including stadia.

Standardization (of the French language)

The importance of grammarians in francophone culture dates from the seventeenth and eighteenth centuries, when the fluctuations and uncertainties of earlier usage were regularized in accordance with classical principles of logic, clarity and consistency. All kinds of questions were gradually resolved – from the gender of *période* to the compulsory use of *pas* in negatives. The outcome was the grammar of today's standard language, then used only by the upper classes, mainly in the Paris region. The rest of the population continued to speak a multitude of dialects and REGIONAL languages. Standardized French came to be regarded, rightly or wrongly, as clearer and more logical than other languages. Pioneering grammarians like Malherbe or Vaugelas, so influential in seventeenth-century Court circles, are still household names.

With the norm largely in place, it was felt essential to preserve it in its 'perfect' state, and, after the 1789 Revolution, to induce all citizens to use it. Hence the modern grammatical tradition. In its most conservative or *normative* form this is enshrined in school grammar books, with their emphasis on the intricacies of SPELLING, and in countless guides to correct usage for adults (e.g. Jacques Capelovici's *Le Français correct*). Some grammarians (called *dirigistes*) take a more accommodating approach towards variation than their normative colleagues, seeking to guide (*diriger*) rather than impose hard-and-fast rulings, and preferring to discuss non-standard forms rather than dismiss them out of hand. Well-known modern *dirigistes* are Maurice Grevisse (*Le Bon Usage*) and Joseph Hanse (*Dictionnaire des difficultés de la langue française*). But, whether normative or *dirigiste*, all these grammarians are committed to furthering the standard. They command widespread respect (even fear) from the general public, who often worry about having an inadequate grasp of grammatical rules. See LINGUISTICS for the very different 'descriptivist' approach. (**Rodney Ball**)

Further reading

Lodge (1993). The norm, from early days to the present.

State   The political structure which controls and regulates the life of society. There are many theories of what a state is and how it functions. The LIBERAL view is that the state is an administrative convenience to facilitate the orderly pursuit of freely chosen activities by citizens in 'civil society'. At the other end of the spectrum, the MARXIST view is that the state is an instrument for the most powerful CLASS to secure its domination over the whole of civil society.

The French state has five main aspects. It provides a structure for power to be negotiated between different social groups, regulating the political operation of democracy. It provides institutions of law and order, including a legal framework for regulating behaviour and relationships, and repressive forces needed to enforce compliance (such as the police, courts and prisons). It provides essential services for the education, health and welfare of the people, including schools, hospitals and social security. It intervenes to regulate and support the economy, through fiscal controls, direct investment and planning. And it deploys military and diplomatic resources to support and defend itself, and the interests of the country. In each of these aspects, the state has the ability to compel people to comply, but an increasing amount of its effort is devoted to persuading people to do so.

The state has traditionally played a key role in the development of French society, and all French people expect to have a direct relationship to it in most of its aspects, ranging from the *carte d'identité* (identity card) to military service, which was compulsory for all young French men until 1997. As a result the relationship between the state and the NATION is particularly close, and major national crises tend to result in changes to the constitutional form of the state, for example in 1940, 1944 and 1958. The transfer of significant state functions to the institutions of the European Union may lead to further changes in the nature of the French state. **(Michael Kelly)**

Further reading

Rosanvallon (1992); Cerny and Schain (1985).

Stavisky affair   The aftermath of the January 1934 death of the financier and theatre owner Alexandre Stavisky (also known as Serge Alexandre) led to the downfall of two French governments and precipitated the 6 FEBRUARY 1934 riots in PARIS. Stavisky was born in the Ukraine in 1886 and moved to Paris as a child. After serving time in prison for minor crimes, he emerged in the late 1920s as the founder and director of the municipal pawnshop in city of Bayonne on the Atlantic coast in Southwestern France. A December 1933 audit implicated Stavisky and a number of RADICAL PARTY politicians in a scheme to use the pawn shop as a clearinghouse for worthless bonds. Stavisky fled Paris and died on 8 January 1934 of a gunshot wound in a chalet outside Chamonix. Some called his death a suicide; others claimed that he had been 'suicided' by those in the government who had abetted his shady financial ventures. Right-wing groups saw his death as an attempt to cover up a major government scandal. The fact that Stavisky had transformed himself from a petty crook into a theatre owner, high-stakes gambler and would-be financier further heightened suspicions concerning the circumstances of his death. The fact that his parents had converted from JUDAISM to CATHOLICISM like-wise fuelled suspicions among those for whom Stavisky embodied the decadence of a French NATION increasingly corrupted by Jews, foreigners and Freemasons. After demonstrations on the evening of 6 February 1934 resulted in several deaths, groups on the political Left and Right mobilized. COMMUNIST, SOCIALIST and RADICAL Party members soon began working with the independent Left to form what would become known a year later as the POPULAR FRONT. Throughout the 1930s, the popularity of Stavisky's wax figure at the *Musée Grévin* was a testament to his impact on collective memory of the period. Renewed interest followed the release of Alain Resnais's 1974 feature film, *Stavisky*, with Jean-Paul BELMONDO in the main role. **(Steven Ungar)**

Further reading

Weber (1995). Cogent narrative account of the decade organized around topics rather than by chronology.

STO, *Service du Travail Obligatoire*   STO (*Service du Travail Obligatoire*, compulsory labour) operated from February 1943, and was a prime example of the French State's COLLABORATION with the German occupiers in the Second World War. Under the programme of STO, Frenchmen between the ages of 18 and 50, and French women between 21 and 35 were liable to be called up and sent to work either in GERMANY or in German factories in France. Previous voluntary measures, such as the RELÈVE, to deliver the number of workers the Nazi regime required had been unsuccessful, which was why the compulsory call-up of STO was instituted by the VICHY Prime Minister, Pierre LAVAL.

In fact, STO proved to be an enormous asset to the RESISTANCE because it provoked huge disaffection with the Vichy regime among substantial parts of the French population, with every family affected by its implications. The clandestine press called on the population to boycott the call-up, and there was widespread non-compliance, supported at every level of French society. Massive numbers of people evaded STO (*les réfractaires* or draft dodgers), and the underground Resistance movement helped to create support networks for those who went into hiding rather than go to Germany. In some areas, these groups were to be the nucleus of armed Resistance groups, called *maquis*, after the scrubland scenery of the mountains in which many of them were located.

In total about three-quarters of a million French workers were sent to Germany, around half the number originally demanded by the Germans. When the STO workers returned from Germany at the end of the war, there was some national uncertainty about how they should be viewed: were STO workers themselves guilty of collaboration because they had chosen not to disobey a law passed by a collaborationist government? **(Hilary Footitt)**

Further reading

Kedward (1993). The first chapters provide an excellent picture of the response to STO on the ground.

Structuralism   The name given to the intellectual movement that succeeded EXISTENTIALISM and dominated French thought from the late 1950s until the mid-1970s. The initial ambition of structuralism was to establish a new scientific model applicable to all fields of human activity, such that the human and social 'sciences' might fully accede to the status implied by their name. The ANTHROPOLOGIST Claude LÉVI-STRAUSS set an influential example by applying models drawn from structural LINGUISTICS to the study of kinship and MYTH. Linguistics rapidly gained prestige, enforcing the view that the key object of study should no longer be isolated terms, but the relations between these terms and the systems expressed by these relations. By the 1960s, methodologies inspired by linguistics were being applied in a wide range of areas, including literary criticism (as notably exemplified by Roland BARTHES, Gérard GENETTE and Tzvetan Todorov), Freudian PSYCHOANALYSIS (as reworked by Jacques LACAN), and MARXIST critique (as overhauled by Louis ALTHUSSER).

The achievement of 'scientificity' (*scientificité*) required that the structural analyst dislodge the human SUBJECT from the privileged position it had enjoyed in SARTRE's existentialism and MERLEAU-PONTY's phenomenology. Inasmuch as the structures constituting any given field are held to be 'deep' structures, they are not available to the consciousness of an experiencing subject. As the structuralist pantheon expanded to make room for the competing radicalisms of Althusser, Barthes, DERRIDA, Lacan and FOUCAULT, so it became more and more clearly dominated by anti-humanism, centred on the ambition to disempower the 'subject'.

By the mid-1970s, in the wake of the upheaval of MAY '68, the structuralist mixture of scientificity and anti-humanism was beginning to look unattractive and austere. Structuralism was duly succeeded by POST-STRUCTURALISM, DECONSTRUCTIONISM, and the *TEL QUEL* movement, but, beyond these, new ways and reasons were being proposed throughout the arts and social sciences for the reintroduction of the factors forsaken by structuralism: those of human agency and subjective experience. (**Johnnie Gratton**)

Further reading

Culler (1975). A classic account of structuralism's impact on literary theory and critical practice. Dosse (1997). A two-volume study, thoroughly researched and offering invaluable insights.

Students France's higher education system has always been sharply polarized between the élite GRANDES ÉCOLES and the generally over-stretched UNIVERSITIES, who tend to recruit students from the local geographical catchment area. The latter operate a broad-based admission policy, with selection taking place (some would say wastefully) by repeated failure and dropping-out after entry. Yet until 1968, students in France were regarded as a largely passive not to say inert mass. France's most prestigious institution of higher education, the ÉCOLE NORMALE SUPÉRIEURE, had had a long left-wing tradition, and there had been a degree of student opposition to the ALGERIAN WAR throughout the country. But any suggestion that a student-led movement could bring the government, indeed the STATE, to its knees would have been relegated to the realms of science fiction. Yet, that is precisely what happened in MAY '68. Large-scale university expansion accompanied by insufficient funding, of institutions and individuals alike, caused widespread student dissatisfaction, and the intellectual hegemony of MARXISM along with the growing number of courses in the social sciences provided the academic seedbed for revolt. While *les événements* (the events) would not have been so important as they were without the massive participation of the industrial WORKING CLASS, they were in the first instance a university phenomenon, issuing in substantial restructuring and DEMOCRATIZATION of the system.

Since then, successive French governments have lived in scarcely disguised fear of student unrest. This was most clearly seen in late 1986, when proposals to restrict access to higher education and charge market-based fees brought vast numbers of student demonstrators on to the streets. They may have chanted *68, c'est vieux – 86, c'est mieux!* (68 is old, 86 is better), but their debt to their more revolutionary predecessors was obvious. After the death of a student, the proposals were withdrawn, and any government seeking to introduce such measures now would have to brace itself for similar manifestations of discontent. (**Keith Reader**)

Further reading

Reader with Wadia (1993). A comprehensive overview.

Subject and subjectivity Terms used in modern Continental philosophy to argue for a certain essence of human being. The 'subject' (*le sujet*) designates that which is considered to found itself as both consciousness and self-consciousness, and to realize itself in the exercise of its capacity for acquiring knowledge through experience, thought and meaningful action. The subject so conceived is often characterized by historians of philosophy as going back to Descartes and passing most notably through the work of Kant, Hegel and Husserl.

How, then, did the 'subject' come to emerge as such a key issue in the broader panoply of post-modern critical thought? The answer lies in the huge impact that two decades of French intellectual history, the 1960s and 1970s, had on a whole generation of academics, writers and activists. This was a period during which, under the sway of STRUCTURALISM, the 'subject' became a common item of critical parlance, and, more precisely, a familiar term for what was now felt in Parisian circles to be one of the most retrograde products of HUMANIST philosophy. For structuralism and its heirs (notably POST-STRUCTURALISM and DECONSTRUCTIONISM), the subject is less a foundation than a pernicious yet shaky construct, simultaneously dependent on and undermined by forces or structures outside it, ranging from the LINGUISTIC (as determined by Saussureanism) to the socio-economic (as determined by MARXISM) and the unconscious (as determined by Freudian PSYCHOANALYSIS).

Although the (post-)structuralist critique of the subject has continued to vitalize important areas of intellectual debate, more and more voices have been raised since the late 1970s expressing the need for a 'post-deconstructive' subject. FEMINISM, multiculturalism, and the 'new ethics' in late twentieth-century philosophy are just some of the areas of contemporary thought in which a relatively re-empowered subject, capable of resisting, intervening, and choosing, has begun to receive intellectual and theoretical validation. Significantly, such calls for change have themselves increasingly been characterized by the adoption of first-person forms of critical discourse. (**Johnnie Gratton**)

Further reading

Critchley (1999). A volume of essays charting the passage from a deconstructive to a 'post-deconstructive' approach to the question of the subject. Gifford and Gratton (2000). A collection of essays written in the context of contemporary debates about the status of the subject.

Suez Crisis   The Suez Crisis of 1956 saw the governments of the UK (led by the conservative Sir Anthony Eden) and France (led by the SOCIALIST Guy MOLLET) engaged at the beginning of November in a joint military adventure with Israel to reclaim the Suez Canal. The Suez Canal Company, in which BRITAIN and France had controlling interests, had just been nationalized by the government of Egypt under President Nasser. This outbreak of what Stanley Hoffman described as 'disimperial dyspepsia' brought universal condemnation across the world led by AMERICA and the USSR and the UN. The French and British governments were obliged to bow to international pressure and withdraw their forces a day after the invasion began. Suez marks the end of an era in European history.

For the French government of Mollet, the consequences of this action impacted principally on the conduct and process of the war for independence in ALGERIA, but also on relations with Britain which was blamed for bowing to American pressure. Elected in January 1956, Mollet's socialist-dominated coalition was seen as offering the last chance for a peaceful political solution to the ALGERIAN WAR, which had begun in 1954. Mollet's electoral platform of political reform rather than military oppression for Algeria was seriously undermined by participation in the Suez Crisis, and any faith that the FLN might have had in promises of genuine democratic reform in Algeria vanished. Indeed, the FLN from that time onwards adopted the tactics of violence that culminated in the Battle of Algiers in 1957. The action in Suez also helped the FLN in heightening the international dimension of the Algerian war, setting it in the wider context of pan-Arabism promoted by Nasser himself, and thereby increasing the flow of arms to their military units.

The effect on the French army, defeated in Vietnam in 1954 and humiliated at Suez, was considerable. It exacerbated their distrust of the 'weak' governments of the FOURTH REPUBLIC, made them more resistant to political control, and led to the strategic involvement of senior officers in the collapse of the Republic in 1958. (**Bill Brooks**)

Further reading

Williams (1968).

Surrealism   An AVANT-GARDE collective that emerged in post-First World War PARIS as an offshoot of DADAIST non-conformity among writers and artists surrounding André BRETON, Louis ARAGON, and Philippe SOUPAULT. The group's 1924 *Manifesto of Surrealism* invoked Freud's writings on the interpretation of dreams as a model for mobilizing the unconscious against a tradition of reason it deemed oppressive to the full range of human experience. Experiments in alternative poetics explored methods of producing images for non-literary and non-artistic ends in order to address foundational, that is, metaphysical questions of IDENTITY and creation. By the late 1920s, the early emphasis on poetics yielded to concerns with politics and IDEOLOGY. Throughout the 1930s, the group struggled to resolve ongoing tensions between artistic freedom and ideological COMMITMENT. When Paris fell to the Germans in June 1940, Breton was in the French army. A year later, he arrived in New York City after stops in MARSEILLE, Martinique and Guadeloupe.

Breton returned to Paris in May 1946 after an absence of almost five years. He led new surrealist groups increasingly at odds with the partisan and cultural orthodoxies of COLD WAR Europe. Where surrealism's early call to an existence elsewhere and its assertion of convulsive beauty had been essential to the European avant-garde between the wars, post-war attempts to revive the group failed to overshadow its growing inability to meet/fulfil the revolutionary ambitions to which Breton continued to lay claim. At the same time, ongoing exhibitions and scholarship attest to surrealism's impact on innovative practices in popular and fine arts from poetry, ART and film to advertising, ARCHITECTURE and performance. (**Steven Ungar**)

Further reading

Beaujour (1988). A concise and informed account of the group's first decade. Foster (1993). Incisive analyses of automatism and objective chance with reference to Freudian concepts of the uncanny and the death drive.

Switzerland   Switzerland is a confederation of 23 cantons which came together over the last 700 years around an original nucleus of Uri, Schwyz and Unterwalden in 1291. The Swiss Confederation achieved independence and neutrality at the Treaty of Westphalia in 1648, though Napoleon conquered the country in 1798, founding the Heletevian Republic. Though a small country (41 000 sq. km) with a population of barely 7 million, Switzerland has exploited its central position in EUROPE, its neutrality and its cultural diversity to establish itself as one of the richest DEMOCRACIES in the world. With its spectacular Alpine scenery and many beautiful lakes, Switzerland is especially celebrated as a resort for both winter sports and summer touring, though it is also a highly industrialized country.

Bordering Italy, France, Germany, Liechtenstein and Austria, Switzerland recognizes four national languages – German (spoken by 65 per cent of the population), French (18 per cent), Italian (12 per cent) and Romansch (1 per cent). It uses a fifth language, Latin, for federal identification: its stamps are marked 'Helvetia' and the initials' CH' (Confederatio Helvetii) appear on Swiss automobile international identification plates. The Jura in the west and the Lake Geneva region in the southwest constitute the main French-speaking areas, with Geneva and Lausanne being the chief Francophone cities. It is however, the German-speaking regions of the North and East that contain the largest and most industrialized cities – Basel, Zürich and the capital, Bern. The Protestant city of Geneva provided a haven for the French religious reformer, John Calvin (1509–64) for the latter part of his life, and counts among its famous sons the philosopher Jean-Jacques Rousseau (1712–78), the artist, theoretician and inventor of the strip cartoon, Rodolphe Töpffer (1799–1846), the linguist, Ferdinand de Saussure (1857–1913), while the sculptor Alberto GIACOMETTI (1901–66) studied there before moving to PARIS.

Although Switzerland has through the centuries attempted positively to embrace its diverse linguistic and cultural traditions, some strain still persists in the relationship between French- and German-speaking regions. (**David Scott**)

Further reading

Pro Helvetia (1991).

Tapie, Bernard Born 1945. A wealthy and successful business man and owner of the MARSEILLES football club, he served as a SOCIALIST minister before becoming embroiled in sporting and business scandals, which led to his conviction and imprisonment.

Tardieu, André 1876–1945. Centrist politician. Minister in several inter-war governments, he was briefly Prime Minister three times.

Tardieu, Jean 1903–94. Writer. He published many poems during the inter-war period, and wrote some moving clandestine poems during the OCCUPATION. Working as a broadcaster after the LIBERATION, he wrote experimental plays, including radio plays, and translated poetry, notably Hölderlin.

Tati, Jacques   1908–82. Film director and actor. In comedy films like his Oscar-winning *Mon oncle* (*My Uncle*, 1958), he played the main character, the ungainly and naïve Hulot. His knockabout comedy and witty observation of manners satirized France's experience of MODERNIZATION.

Tavernier, Bertrand   Born 1941. Film director. His films combine social comment and nostalgia for time gone by, like *La vie et rien d'autre* (*Life and Nothing Else*, 1989).

Taylorism   A system of industrial organization which began in AMERICA at the turn of the century but which has had considerable impact on French social, economic and cultural life. Under the system developed by American engineer, Frederick Winslow Taylor (1856–1915), jobs were broken down into a series of simplified tasks for which norms of speed and movement were set by engineers, on the basis of time and motion studies. The WORKER's conformity to the system was ensured by a combination of supervision, bonuses and penalities, and the ultimate sanction for the worker who did not meet production targets was dismissal. One of the central features of the system was its tendency to shift control of the task away from workers towards managers and engineers. Another innovation was the emphasis on analysing the movements of the working body.

The French engineer, Henry Le Chatelier (1850–1936), began promoting Taylorism in France shortly before the First World War, with limited success. Between the wars, a number of French engineers and industrialists sought to adapt Taylor's methods and develop their own vision of what they termed the 'rationalization' or 'scientific organization' of work, often drawing on methods devised by French psychologists and physiologists. A movement led by Paulette Bernège also sought to apply Taylorist techniques to housework. More industrialists were now experimenting with 'scientific organization', but many remained reticent until the national drive for increased productivity and economic growth after the Second World War accelerated the process of Taylorization.

Taylorism often encountered opposition from workers, who sought ways of reasserting control over their own work on an everyday basis, as well as resorting to strike action in certain cases. Many French writers and intellectuals (for example, Émile Pouget (1860–1931), Georges DUHAMEL, and Emmanuel MOUNIER) have also been critical of Taylorism, arguing that it exploited workers and treated human beings like machines. At the same time, the scientific study of the moving body at work inspired modern artists, like Fernand LÉGER, who were fascinated by machines, movement and the body. (**Jackie Clarke**)

Further reading

Merkle (1980). Considers Taylorism and the French scientific organization movement in an international perspective. Pouget (1914). A classic critique written in response to early experiments with Taylorism in French industry.

Tchatche   See ARGOT.

Technology   France is a high-tech economy whose technological expertise grew rapidly post-1945. The STATE has always played a leading role in the development of French technology. Late and incomplete INDUSTRIALIZATION in the nineteenth century meant that French technology was found lacking in the First World War. Between the wars, industry and technologies remained generally backwards compared with GERMANY and BRITAIN, although French science was often strong. Uneven technological development in the 1930s was exemplified by the MAGINOT LINE'S modern construction technologies, although DE GAULLE simultaneously called unsuccessfully for a mechanized army. Post-1945, governments acknowledged France's technological gap, and exploiting French traditions of *grands corps* of engineers and scientists, used technocracy and planning to stimulate technology. The *Commissariat à l'énergie atomique* (Atomic Energy Commission, 1945) leading the nuclear energy and ATOMIC WEAPONS programmes exemplified this *DIRIGISME* and *volontarisme*. As the ECONOMY and industry modernized during the FOURTH REPUBLIC, France acquired key industrial technologies, and during the 1960s, GAULLIST emphasis on French *grandeur* further encouraged high technology, fearing a technology gap with AMERICA. Industrial concentration and 'national champion' state firms (such as, RENAULT, Elf, Aérospatiale) in key sectors led technology during the 1960s and 1970s, but France lacked technologies such as computing. Generally, two approaches were common: the *grand programme* addressed sectoral development, often directed by a state agency; the *grand projet* targeted specific technological applications. Thus space technologies evolved through a SPACE PROGRAMME led by the national space agency, in which civilian, military, public and private interests combined, whereas the TGV high-speed train exemplified a project where a nationalized company (the SNCF) developed a specific technology. As EUROPEAN collaboration between high-tech firms increased in the 1990s and as French *dirigisme* declined under EU pressure, French approaches to technology became less distinctive, but still marked by state-driven origins. (**Hugh Dauncey**)

Further reading

Kellermann (1988). A comparative overview of technology policy.

Teilhard de Chardin, Pierre   1881–1955. Philosopher and scientist. A Jesuit priest, he specialized in the study of fossils, and attempted to reconcile the science of evolution with Christian theology. Most of his writings, including the well-known *Le Phénomène humain* (*Phenomenon of Man*, 1955) were published after his death, when they made an international impact.

Television   Television was established in France as early as 1935, although regular broadcasts did not commence until after the Second World War. Despite the continuation of earlier MEDIA (PRESS and RADIO), by the late 1950s television had become the major source of entertainment and information for the public. The French BROADCASTING system consisted of only one channel until 1964 when a second national channel was launched. A third (*France Régions 3*), developed to focus on

France's regions, was established in 1972. From the outset both radio and television broadcasting were state monopolies administered first by the RDF (*Radiodiffusion Française*, established in 1945 and later known as RTF, RADIODIFFUSION-TÉLÉVISION FRANÇAISE), and then from 1964 by the ORTF (*Office de Radiodiffusion-Télévision Française*). French television was then a state-owned public service and this situation remained largely unchanged until the early 1980s when the state monopoly of broadcasting finally came to an end.

In 1986 the main channel, *TF1*, was privatized making it the first public television channel in EUROPE to pass into the private sector. Today French terrestrial television consists of four public channels (*France 2* and *3*, the Franco-German *Arte* and the educational channel *La Cinquième*) and three private channels (*TF1*, *M6* and the subscription channel *Canal Plus*). Cable and SATELLITE broadcasting are also playing an increasingly important role in the televisual landscape.

The early state monopoly of television meant that it became a vital tool in the construction of a national IDENTITY and more specifically in the battle for political power. General DE GAULLE was one of the first French politicians to exploit television as a means of transmitting and supporting his political message. Although the contemporary televisual landscape is radically different from its predecessors of the 1950s, 1960s and 1970s, offering much more diversity and choice, it continues to play a major role in the construction and dissemination of national identities and agendas through scheduling and different types of programming. (**Lucy Mazdon**)

Further reading

Kuhn (1995). Provides a useful overview of the main developments in the media industries, including television. Lecomte and Scriven (1999). A collection of articles analysing and comparing various aspects of recent French and British television.

Television drama   Since the expansion of the number of channels in the mid-1980s, the most rapidly expanding programme genre on French television has been 'fiction', which the French divide into the categories of films (made initially for the cinema), *téléfilms* (made specifically for television), *séries*, and *feuilletons* (serials and soaps). The increase in series and serials (cheaper to make than longer fiction) was spectacular. Demand also increased: French viewers now spend over a third of their viewing time watching fiction. The 1950s saw TV versions of classical drama, and the beginnings of socially conscious drama, as produced by Marcel Bluwal, and of detective fiction, such as *Les Cinq Dernières Minutes* (*The Last Five Minutes*), a genre famously carried on later with *Les Enquêtes du commissaire Maigret* (*The Investigations of Inspector Maigret*, based on the Simenon character, and played by Jean Richard). In the 1960s and 1970s staple items were recorded or live performances from the theatre, filmed adaptations of historical novels by Dumas, Troyat and Druon (*Les Rois maudits*, *The Cursed Kings*), and historical dramas (*Thierry la Fronde*), and cult imports such as *Columbo* and *The Avengers* (*Chapeau melon et bottes de cuir*). In the 1980s and 1990s, American imports increased (*Dallas*, *Dynasty*, *the Cosby Show*), and new home-produced drama series for the adolescent audience appeared, such as *Premiers baisers* (*First Kisses*) and *Hélène et les garçons* (*Helen and the Boys*) on *TF1*, with re-runs of *Belle et Sébastien* on *M6*. Most channels have serious cinema slots, for example, *Le cinéma de minuit* (*Midnight Cinema*) on *France 3*. The cultural channel *Arte* gives a special place to classic films, while first showings on TV of recent cinema films are on the subscription channel *Canal Plus*. In 1999 apart from world sporting events and the odd news bulletin, the most popular programmes were police or detective fiction (*Julie Lescaut* and *Navarro*) and American blockbuster films such as *Pretty Woman*. The seasoned British or American viewer, when confronted with French television drama schedules, notices a dearth of long-running French-made television soaps and situation comedy. (**Geoff Hare**)

Tel Quel 1960–83. An AVANT-GARDE literary review, it advocated formalist and STRUCTURALIST methods of analysis, and became associated with radical left-wing politics and intellectual MAOISM. During the 1970s it turned to personal experience and PSYCHOANALYSIS as the subject of experimental writing.

Temps, le 1861–1942. The leading liberal newspaper of the THIRD REPUBLIC. Its national position and format were taken over by LE MONDE after the Second World War.

Temps modernes, les A monthly intellectual review, founded in 1945 by SARTRE, BEAUVOIR and MERLEAU-PONTY, it was the main platform for EXISTENTIALISM, and advocated left-wing political COMMITMENT by writers and artists. It has continued to be influential in many intellectual movements and public debates.

Tennis Tennis is France's second participatory SPORT after FOOTBALL, and the sport most practised by WOMEN. Introduced to France by the British in the nineteenth century, tennis developed gradually until the mid-1970s, when interest grew spectacularly for some ten years, partially DEMOCRATIZING a mostly upper-class sport. Tennis was initially practised by leisured classes in private sporting clubs founded by British expatriates on the Riviera, or in areas where business brought foreign contacts (PARIS, Bordeaux, LYON, Normandy). Events bringing tennis to wider public notice included Suzanne Lenglen's successes during the 1920s and the exploits of the *Quatre Mousquetaires* (Borotra, Brugnon, Cochet, Lacoste) victorious in the Davis Cup 1927–29. From 1920 the *Fédération française de tennis* (FFT) oversaw a sport of gentlemen-amateurs and rare professionals. The 1927 Davis Cup victory over the USA stimulated building of the Roland-Garros stadium in Paris. Tennis was mainly urban and coastal, reflecting imported origins and upper-class holidays, and spread slowly down the urban hierarchy and into the countryside. FRONT POPULAIRE policies to encourage LEISURE and sports benefited tennis, as did the *Patronages* (youth clubs) among Catholic youngsters.

Sport was facilitated post-war by government, but after steady (albeit socially uniform) inter-war growth, numbers of tennis clubs declined until the mid-1960s, as tennis remained essentially private, costly and upper-class, despite France's social and demographic transformation. After MAY '68 new social aspirations coincided with the 'Open' era in tennis and changes at the FFT. As professional tennis became more visible, FFT and local authorities widened access: between 1970 and 1980 the number of clubs tripled to 15 000 and *licenciés* (registered players) quintupled to 800 000. Influenced by demography, MASS MEDIA coverage of tennis – *TF1* introduced full TV coverage of the Roland-Garros (the French Open) in 1978 – and star professionals such as Yannick Noah, players peaked at 1.4 million in the mid-1980s, subsequently falling slightly. (**Hugh Dauncey**)

Further reading

Waser (1995). A study of the social aspects of tennis.

Territoires d'outre-mer   See TOM.

Theatre   The middle decades of the century saw a renaissance of theatre in France. Before the First World War the director Jacques COPEAU decried the shameless commercialism and mediocre artistic standards of the time. His reforming campaign bore fruit in the late 1920s: Louis Jouvet's production of Jean GIRAUDOUX'S *Siegfried* (1928) was a new dawn. Thereafter, directors pursuing similar anti-realist ideals, such as DULLIN, Pitoëff, Baty and then BARRAULT and VILAR, created an era of great theatre, in which poetry, fantasy and cosmic leaps in time and space were the vehicles for the exploration of profound moral and philosophic themes, sometimes given impetus by the theories of Antonin ARTAUD on the 'Theatre of Cruelty'. The best plays of Giraudoux, CLAUDEL, COCTEAU, ANOUILH, GENET, MONTHERLANT, SALACROU, CAMUS and SARTRE are still performed. Contemporary social and political subjects were far from excluded (and prominent in the three last named); but only with the 'discovery' of Brecht in the 1950s did a more stridently political theatre using systematic agitprop techniques develop. Roger PLANCHON directed his own plays and those of Adamov and Gatti from a MARXIST perspective, notably in the working class LYON suburb of Villeurbanne. Much similar work was produced outside PARIS in 'decentralized' theatres and in front of new left-wing audiences in the challenging climate leading up to MAY '68.

Simultaneously, 'ABSURD' or 'NEW' THEATRE, very different ideologically, appeared in small Paris LATIN QUARTER theatres, where Roger BLIN and Jean-Marie Serreau notably championed the plays of IONESCO, BECKETT and the early Adamov. The universe of the 'new' theatre is artistically challenging and morally disturbing; it avoids (and subverts or parodies) scenic REALISM and the classic, Aristotelian norms of logical dialogue and plot construction, inventing alternative (and appropriately 'absurd') theatrical means to mirror the metaphysical anguish of man in the twentieth century. (**Ted Freeman**)

Further reading

Bradby (1991). A comprehensive study, which has no equal in France.

Theatre Festivals   Since 1947 AVIGNON in Provence has been the site of the most prestigious theatre festival in France if not in the world. It owes its origins and immediate success to an *animateur* of genius, Jean VILAR (1912–71). From 1951 to

1963 he was also the director of the Paris-based THÉÂTRE NATIONAL POPULAIRE (TNP), and took its productions for three weeks each summer to the courtyard of the historic Papal Palace in Avignon. Against this outdoor backdrop, on a stage with no wings or décors, Vilar made an imaginative use of costume, lighting projectors, drapes and banners. Thus were the classics of French and world repertory, as well as new plays, performed by stars such as Gérard PHILIPPE and Maria Casarès before 3000 enthusiastic spectators. Vilar wanted theatre to be a great collective experience rather than an exclusive cultural thrill for a Parisian ÉLITE. Avignon coincided with a general DECENTRALIZING movement of high culture. As National Dramatic Centres were established in a growing number of places (e.g. Saint-Étienne, Toulouse, Rennes), so summer festivals proliferated: a World Student Festival at Nancy (created by Jack LANG long before he became MITTERRAND'S Minister of CULTURE), Francophone Theatre in the Limousin, Sacred Theatre in Annecy, among others. Those that have survived exist precariously, enjoying only a fraction of Avignon's 60 per cent subsidised budget. They are often expected to be a tourist attraction, thus not too AVANT-GARDE or politically contentious. And local authority financing has been problematic in areas where the NATIONAL FRONT has influence. None has ever had the scale, generous resources and mass carnival atmosphere of Avignon, where hundreds of performances now take place in every conceivable venue scattered throughout the city. (**Ted Freeman**)

Further reading

The official web site of the Avignon Festival: www.festival-avignon.com/fr
A website giving details of a range of festivals:
fr.dir.yahoo.com/Arts du spectacle/Theatre/Festivals

Théâtre National Populaire (TNP) For twelve years from 1951 under the charismatic Jean VILAR, the *Théâtre National Populaire* was one of the most adventurous theatre companies in France. It was first founded in 1920 by Firmin Gémier, one of many progressive INTELLECTUALS and theatre practitioners seeking quality French theatre that was socially welcoming, and cheap enough for ordinary citizens. Hopelessly under-funded, and situated in the unsuitable Trocadéro, Gémier's TNP attracted few new theatre-goers, being little more than a passing home for other companies' productions; things got no better under his successors. But the cultural climate improved after the Second World War: few disputed that theatre needed subsidizing if it was to find new audiences. Driven by a liberal HUMANIST dream of theatre as a great unifying force, Vilar responded to this challenge energetically, liaising with TRADE UNIONS to recruit WORKING-CLASS audiences in the 'red' PARIS suburbs. He took to them high quality productions of French and foreign classics, Corneille, Molière, Shakespeare, Brecht, Kleist, performed by stars like Gérard PHILIPPE. And in his base, the 2900 seat Chaillot Theatre with which he was saddled (the same Trocadéro site on the right bank), and at his prestigious AVIGNON summer theatre FESTIVAL, going to the theatre was no longer intimidating. For example, plays began punctually, and no harpy-like usherettes would scrounge tips. Vilar retired from the TNP in 1963 to concentrate on Avignon; it limped along under Georges Wilson but was a victim of the events of May 1968. It transferred to the *Théâtre de la Cité* in the LYON suburb of Villeurbanne, where the committed Marxist Roger PLANCHON had directed many hard-hitting political plays (his own and plays by Brecht, ADAMOV, Gatti, Vinaver and others). Here the TNP had a new lease of life under rising star directors, Patrice Chéreau and Georges Lavaudant. Its former home in Paris became the *Théâtre national de Chaillot.* (**Ted Freeman**)

Further reading

Vilar (1975): Godard (1998).

Theatres (major venues) The cultural prestige of the NATION being a high priority for politicians, the theatre from DE GAULLE and MALRAUX onwards has had considerable STATE organizational support and funding to match. Five companies have the status of *Théâtre Dramatique National.* The largest subsidy (over 100 million francs per year) goes to the COMÉDIE FRANÇAISE, dating back to the seventeenth century. Also housed in a great historic theatre is the *Théâtre national de l'Odéon-Europe,* charged with performing new work as well as French and international classics. The *Théâtre national de Chaillot* is the third large PARIS company, located in the theatre first made famous as the THÉÂTRE NATIONAL POPULAIRE (TNP) in 1951 by the great Jean VILAR. The *Théâtre national de la Colline* is an oasis in what was called a cultural desert, the Eastern Paris suburbs. The only provincial National Theatre among the five is the *Théâtre national de Strasbourg.* All except the *Colline* have a vast main theatre as well as a studio theatre.

Boosted by the national policy of DECENTRALIZATION, some 30 *Centres dramatiques nationaux* also provide high quality theatre in the provinces and Paris suburbs. Some enjoy historic prestige, such as Saint-Étienne, Toulouse, Rennes, and Roger PLANCHON'S *Théâtre de la Cité* in Villeurbanne, LYON, which inherited the TNP designation in 1972 after it fizzled out in Paris. Scores of private theatres survive in Paris, mainly ornate nineteenth-century proscenium arch establishments (*à l'italienne*) such as the Antoine, Bouffes-Parisiens, Marigny, and Mathurins, specializing in artistically unadventurous vehicles for star performers. Most large provincial cities have an equivalent theatre, hosting the same plays on tour. (**Ted Freeman**)

Further reading

Quid. This annual 2,000 page encyclopaedia is stuffed with facts, statistics, and historical summaries. The comprehensive section 'Le Théâtre en France' is an excellent example of the format.

Third Republic The Third Republic (1870–1940) established parliamentary government, built an EMPIRE and maintained world power status. Originating in an insurrection against the Second Empire (1852–70), it was consolidated after 1875 by constitutional laws reflecting a class compromise. A republic suited monarchists from business, financial and commercial ÉLITES as well as the rising professional middle classes and, thanks to the political marketing skills of Gambetta, also suited the most numerous class, the peasantry. The republic was a LIBERAL CAPITALIST economy with minimal STATE intervention, except for economic protectionism and EDUCATION, where republicans combated THE CATHOLIC Church influence in schools, and provided the upwards social mobility central to their doctrine. Its political system was coalition government, with weak premiers and a dominant parliament, composed of flexible miniparties; as most politicians were lawyers or professionals, and the electorate was entirely male, such practices proved ideal for brokering conflicting interests within society. Even the volatile Church–State question was defused by the Separation of 1905. Abroad, the republic allowed private interests to build up an Empire cheaply. It tied France into alliance with BRITAIN and Russia, as part of its strategy to contain GERMANY and recover the provinces of ALSACE-LORRAINE amputated in 1871.

The republic survived the Great War victorious, but with huge loss of life and economic damage. The inter-war years, with economic depression and the rise of FASCISM, tested a system which seemed ideal for a slowly evolving, inward-looking society; but the republic survived until defeat by the Nazi armies panicked the parliamentarians into voting special powers to Marshal PÉTAIN in July 1940, abolishing DEMOCRACY. Thus began the trend of blaming the republican system for all French shortcomings, a simplistic view of a regime which is still the longest-lasting since 1789, precisely because it suited the society it served. (**David Hanley**)

Further reading

Mayeur and Rebérioux (1984). Bernard and Dubief (1985).

Thorez, Maurice   1900–64. Communist politician. From a mining background, he was General Secretary of the PCF (1930–64), leading it to be a powerful national force. Close to Stalin, he spent the war in Moscow, and on his return enjoyed a personality cult of his own in France. He served as a minister (1944–47).

Thriller   Suspense, criminality, doom, and transgression, these are the characteristics of a genre whose ill-defined borders are encapsulated in the range of terms applied to it: *roman noir, polar* (derivative of *policier*), *néo-polar, roman à suspense,* and thriller. The genre has never lost its links with the French traditions of the *roman policier* (DETECTIVE novel) marked by obsessive psychology, atmospheric settings, be they urban or rural, and fine writing.

The thriller is inextricably linked to the *Série noire* collection launched for Gallimard by Marcel Duhamel in 1945, publishing primarily translations of American and English writers such as Hadley Chase, Hammett and Chandler. It is also inextricably linked to the cinema: the gangsters and psychological suspense of the American B-movie, dubbed *film noir* by French critics in the 1940s, was a powerful influence on French *film noir* and on the French thriller; in turn, many thrillers were successfully adapted for the cinema.

By the 1970s, the *polar* was well established as a racy investigation of the modern world and its urban woes. ALIENATION, social deprivation, and violence were its stock-in-trade, along with a sophisticated exploitation of the FRENCH LANGUAGE, as the inventiveness of contemporary slang was mixed with word-play, puns, and literary references – a new language to render the hard-boiled American themes in a French context, and also a springboard to a place in the canon of 'high culture'. After 1968, the genre was exploited politically; Jean-Patrick Manchette, a left-wing writer who coined the term *néo-polar*, and A.D.G., who was on the political Right, were the leading authors of this renewal, which pointed to the STATE and its institutions, the judiciary, and the police as dark forces and agents of repression and criminality. In recent times, Didier Daeninckx and Sebastien Japrisot have found rich material in French history, and particularly in crimes and repressed memories associated with the German OCCUPATION and the ALGERIAN WAR. (**Margaret Atack**)

Further reading

Roman noir: Pas d'orchidées pour les T.M., special number of *Les Temps modernes*, (1997) which gives an excellent thematic and historical overview of the genre, arguing strongly for its political and social importance. Reuter (1997). Includes detailed chapters on *le roman noir* and *le roman à suspense*, and gives excellent attention to questions of narrative and generic structure

TNP   See THÉÂTRE NATIONAL POPULAIRE.

TOM   Although constitutionally part of the French Republic, the TOM (*territoires d'outre-mer*, overseas territories) have greater autonomy than the DOM (overseas departments). Like the DOM, this new status granted to former colonies was first recognized under the terms of the 1946 constitution. The TOM benefit from economic and social support from France, while enjoying greater control over their own affairs. With individual statutes tailored to their local situations, they are 'associate' members of the European Union and their citizens have French nationality. Their inhabitants are represented by a locally elected *Assemblée territoriale* and a *Conseil de gouvernement* and do not necessarily elect their metropolitan representatives directly. Areas of responsibility are divided between the French Republic and local authorities. Two TOM are in the South Pacific (French Polynesia and Wallis-and-Futuna), and there are also the TAAF (*Terres Australes et Antarctiques Françaises*) made up of the French possessions in Antarctica and four islands in the southern Indian Ocean. Towards the end of the twentieth century, metropolitan France could not ignore the existence of the TOM. The independence movement in New Caledonia (officially a TOM until 1999) was particularly active in the late 1980s, when a series of violent incidents led to a period of direct rule from Paris. As a result of the Matignon Accord, regional and territorial assemblies were suspended and a High Commissioner controlled this TOM for a year. New Caledonia (no longer a TOM) now has a unique status, which will allow a progressive transfer of power to local institutions. In 2014, voters who have been on the archipelago for at least twenty years will be consulted on full independence. The constitutional flexibility of the TOM permits a range of possibilities, from direct rule to a greater degree of self-government (for example, in Wallis-and-Futuna, where some control is still exercised by local chieftains and royalty). In relation to their colonial history, the TOM remain at an intermediate stage, with options for either independence or *départementalisation*. Of a similarly semi-detached status are the *collectivités territoriales* (CT). These are made up of Saint-Pierre-et-Miquelon (two islands close to Newfoundland, which were a DOM until 1985) and Mayotte (an island in the Indian Ocean). (**Charles Forsdick**)

Further reading

Aldrich and Connell (1992). The only major English-language study of the DOM-TOM, giving an excellent overview with individual chapters devoted to politics, economics and future status. Belorgey and Bertrand, (1994). Provides a useful account of the emergence of the TOM, and devotes a chapter to each territory (as well as to the CT). www.outre-mer.gouv.fr/domtom/ – website of the *Secrétariat d'État à l'Outre-mer*, with comprehensive and regularly updated pages on each TOM and CT.

Toubon, Jacques   Born 1941. GAULLIST politician. Minister of CULTURE (1993–95), known for the 1994 FRENCH language legislation (*loi Toubon*), which sought to limit the use of English in France, and earned him the nickname 'Mr Allgood' from French satirists.

Tour de France   The Tour annually attracts millions of spectators and television viewers. It is an iconic sporting phenomenon and important commercial and MASS MEDIA event. Changes to the Tour have reflected the development of French CYCLING, SPORT and society. Founded in 1903 by the newspaper *L'Auto*, the Tour was suspended from 1915 to 1918, and many pre-war champions died in action. Inter-war, the competition developed *villes-étapes*, the *grande boucle* ending in PARIS, time trials, and sprint and climbing competitions. Short-lived innovations included national and regional teams, but from 1930 the accompanying 'caravan' of promotional vehicles demonstrated the growing commercial importance of the competition. Suspended 1940–46, after the war the Tour developed under the sponsorship of *L'Équipe* and *Parisien Libéré*, managed by often tyrannical sporting directors (Goddet, Lévitan and Leblanc). In 1969 the formula of teams sponsored by cycling-related companies or any firm using the Tour as advertising was finalized. During the 1970s the Tour initiated occasional stages outside France, and in 1975 introduced the finale on the Champs Élysées. The Tour was 'spectacularized' as mass media coverage, particularly RADIO and TELEVISION, developed internationally. Interest was stimulated domestically and abroad by dramatic exploits, epic rivalries, and French champions such as Anquetil (five-times winner) and Hinault (five-times winner). Poulidor was loved for repeatedly finishing second or third, but never winning. The Tour reflects the social history of French cycling through riders' origins: initially professional riders were recruited from the Parisian proletariat; inter-war riders came from urban working classes nationally; post-war recruitment came from rural and urban working classes. The Tour has been analysed as *carnaval* in which noble proletarian competitors confront a 'system' imposed by the organizers, in symbolic consecration of existing social CLASS relations. Originally a celebration of INDUSTRIALIZATION, the Tour has become a spectacle of commercialized sport undermined by drug scandals and cheating champions. (**Hugh Dauncey**)

Further reading

Vigarello (1992). Barthes (1957) The Tour in France's collective imagination.

Touraine, Alain   Born 1925. Sociologist. Specialising initially in the SOCIOLOGY of work and of post-industrial society, he has analysed the production of social meaning and argued that the individual human SUBJECT is an important agent for social change.

Tourism and travel   Since travel in Europe before the eighteenth century was dangerous, uncomfortable and slow, it was not undertaken by most people except when absolutely necessary. With the improvement of road and the development of steam-powered transport – first rail and then sea – after the Industrial Revolution, travel to distant places in EUROPE and the Mediterranean became a more agreeable and practical prospect. Improved communications coincided with, and accelerated, the development of European COLONIAL interests, particularly in North Africa and the Middle East, with the result that travel both for political reasons or for pleasure vastly increased. The British and French were pioneers in this domain and produced an extensive literature, part politically, part aesthetically motivated, with the result that, in France for example, there were few important writers from Chateaubriand to Flaubert who did not produce an account of their ORIENTAL voyage.

With Thomas Cook's mid-nineteenth century initiation of organized group travel to Egypt and various parts of Europe, tourism began to develop the mass potential that it manifests today. In France, tourism coincided with the rediscovery of the monuments and antiquities within the home frontiers, as well as the increasing popularity of foreign travel. The development of first popular CYCLING and then (at the beginning of the twentieth century) motoring, brought with it the publication of numerous tourist maps and guides (the most famous of which were by Michelin), while the initiation of paid holidays by the FRONT POPULAIRE in 1936 opened tourism to mass society.

After the Second World War, travel and tourism were an important part of the _TRENTE GLORIEUSES_ years of prosperity, accelerated by European integration, cheap air travel and increased LEISURE time. During the summer, France is one of the most popular destinations for inbound mass tourism, from the rest of Europe as well as from America and Japan, and the tourism industry is now a major factor in the economy, particularly in some rural areas.

Despite the banality that Disneyland, theme parks and the package HOLIDAY have brought to late twentieth-century tourism, travel writing is still a widely popular genre, taken seriously by many writers, including anthropologists (Claude LÉVI-STRAUSS), sociologists (Jean BAUDRILLARD, Pierre Sansot) and semioticians (Roland BARTHES). A recent development has been the discovery of the exotic of the everyday (Marc Augé, François MASPÉRO, Jean Rolin). **(David Scott)**

Further reading

Augé (1992), and (1997); Bouvier (1992). Urbain (1991), and (1994).

Tournier, Michel   Born 1924. Writer. His many novels explore personal and social IDENTITIES, often starting with themes from MYTH or literature, as in his _Vendredi, ou les Limbes du Pacifique_ (_Friday, or the Pacific Limbo,_ 1967), which reuses the story of Robinson Crusoe, and which he also rewrote as a children's book.

Tours, Congress of   On 25–30 December 1920, the French SOCIALIST party (SFIO) assembled at Tours for its eighteenth congress, an acrimonious affair that led to schism and the launching of the French COMMUNIST PARTY (PCF) which embraced the 21 conditions of the Moscow-dominated Third International (Comintern). This split highlighted the quarrel that had long dogged European socialist movements: whether to pursue the democratic path to power or opt instead for revolution. The Bolshevik Revolution in 1917 emboldened the Left in the SFIO. Yet reformists held firm and, at the party's seventeenth congress at Strasbourg in February 1920, few supported the Comintern. Historians illustrate how circumstances changed in the ensuing months and usually stress the following: the economic downturn; dissatisfaction with new voting procedures which, in the 1919 elections, discriminated against the Left; unease at the Right's control of government; the collapse of the May 1920 strikes which undermined revolutionary syndicalism and led to a drop in union membership; the growing influence of the *patronat* (employers); and the attitude of many new SFIO members who, after the excitement of the trenches, were not averse to violence. Favourable reporting on the situation in the USSR by SFIO visitors further ensured that three-quarters of the votes cast at Tours favoured schism. In 1921 the trade union organization (CGT) also split, with the creation of a communist-led CGTU. Not until the late 1920s did the SFIO regain the upper hand, yet a bitter mistrust endured between Communists and Socialists. An embittered debate also goes on among historians. Whereas some argue that schism was only possible because of a 'conjunctural accident', that is the unique circumstances of 1920, others believe it reflected the revolutionary tradition present within France since 1789. (**Nicholas Atkin**)

Further reading

Magraw (1992). Volume 2 provides the wider context and the detail.

Trade unions   Organizations of working people, formed to improve their rights and working conditions. Most French trade unions are grouped into congresses or confederations, which reflect particular IDEOLOGICAL tendencies. The largest groups are the COMMUNIST-led CGT, the SOCIALIST-led *FORCE OUVRIÈRE*, and the independent socialist CFDT.

Around 2 million people in France, about 8 per cent of the working population, are members of a trade union (*syndicat*). This is one of the lowest rates of unionization in Europe. The small numbers, together with the fragmented organization and inter-union competition, have made French trades unions relatively weak. However, they have played an important role in social and political change at key moments in French history.

In 1920, the initial division of the French Left between communists and socialists was reflected in corresponding splits in the labour movement, which have continued to influence relations to the present day. The shift towards co-operation between trade unions was an important factor in cementing the electoral alliance of the POPULAR FRONT. Trade unions played a significant role under the German OCCUPATION, particularly in orchestrating actions by transport workers, miners and manufacturing workers to impair the German war effort, through sabotage, intelligence-gathering and other methods. At the LIBERATION, trade unions were prominent in campaigns to rebuild the economy, and soon afterwards took a leading role in the strikes and demonstrations that heralded the beginning of the Cold War.

Taken by surprise by the events of MAY '68, the unions were slow to support the call for a general strike, suspecting the motives of BOURGEOIS students. But their role in the Matignon negotiations ensured that workers achieved significant improvements in wages and conditions before agreeing to return to work.

In recent years, the strength of the trade unions has declined, but they none the less retain the ability to mobilize workers in collective action. They have continued to be the main channel through which employers and governments have secured the assent of the workforce in matters of social and economic policy. (**Michael Kelly**)

Further reading

Milner (1999a) and (1999b).

Transport   Transport in France has been determined by a historical legacy of road and rail networks, changing technologies, INDUSTRIALIZATION and MODERNIZATION of the ECONOMY, decline of EMPIRE and increased French trade with European partners. In the 1990s, French attachment to public service in transport was reassessed in the light of EU moves towards LIBERALIZATION. In the 1920s, French road and rail systems were well developed but exhibited traditional centralized patterns dominated by Paris and radial provincial links. During the *ENTRE-DEUX-GUERRES*, governments failed to modernize the RAILWAYS (although the SNCF was formed in 1937) and to realize the growing importance of road transport (the first motorway was started only in 1939) or of air transport (despite the creation of Air France in 1933). OCCUPATION prevented improvements to road and rail, but post-war reconstruction and growth, modernization through electrification, track replacement and high-speed locomotives transformed the rail network. The plan autoroutier of 1961 targeted 3000 km of new motorways by 1976, and rail freight and passenger transport competed increasingly with road transport as car ownership expanded and private motorway companies developed the motorway network to 8500 km by the 1980s. The TGV high-speed train entering service in the 1980s represented French innovation in TECHNOLOGY led by the public service SNCF and traditional post-war concerns for regional development. High development costs of the TGV and its tendency to concentrate benefits in narrow transport corridors seem outweighed by its encouragement of rail traffic. TGV links with neighbouring rail networks (including the UK) demonstrate France's centrality to European transport, as EU integration encourages cross-border transport axes. However, EU competition and liberalization policies challenge France's public service tradition and egalitarian pricing policies for rail and air transport: the SNCF has been restructured but has not been privatized (1997) and debate continues over the PRIVATIZATION of Air France. (**Hugh Dauncey**)

Further reading

Sykes (1987). Covers the main forms of transport and general issues.

Trenet, Charles   1913–2001. Singer and songwriter. During his long career, he enjoyed huge popularity for his smooth and lyrical performances, combining traditional French and modern international styles and rhythms. *La Mer* (Somewhere beyond the sea, 1945) was his greatest success and he influenced many later singers.

Trente glorieuses, les   Derived from the title of Jean Fourastié's 1979 study, the expression *les trente glorieuses* (thirty glorious ones) refers to the period of dramatic transformations spanning 1946 to 1975. It also contains a reference to the overthrow of the restoration monarchy in July 1830 during three 'glorious days' of revolution (*trois glorieuses*). Over this 30-year period, benefiting from an exceptionally high economic growth rate and full employment, the end of DECOLONIZATION, the political stability of the FIFTH REPUBLIC, IMMIGRANT labour and new markets opened by the population explosion, France acquired the characteristics of a CONSUMER society already initiated in the pre-war period in other industrialized nations.

Focusing primarily on *la révolution invisible*, the invisible revolution in rural areas, Fourastié's study cleverly presents a comparison between a typical village of a relatively underdeveloped nation with that of a modern advanced one. In fact, the two were the same village in the Lot region, which had undergone a metamorphosis over a 30-year period. Improved sanitation, health care and diet, the mechanization of labour, introduction of the telephone, television and automobile, all contributed to moving a lifestyle close to the eighteenth century into one recognizably of the twentieth. By 1965, Henri Mendras also questioned if this revolution did not usher in the numerical as well as cultural 'disappearance of the peasantry'.

Despite the overall improvements to the average individual's economic prosperity and physical well-being, the statistical charts do not easily account for the perverse effects of rapid socio-economic change manifested in the psychological *morosité* (moroseness) and social unrest leading to the events of MAY '68. *Les trente glorieuses* also marks the generational divide between those born before and after 1945. Reeling from the petrol crises that started in 1973, plagued by stagflation and unemployment, France none the less remained the world's fourth economic power even as the *glorious thirty* became a distant memory for the 'sacrificed' generations that followed them. (**Michèle Richman**)

Further reading

Fourastié (1979); Mendras (1970).

Triolet, Elsa   1896–1970. Novelist. Russian-born, partner of Louis ARAGON, with whom she organized the RESISTANCE paper *Les LETTRES FRANÇAISES*. She is best known for her clandestine novels and short stories, and her satires of modern CONSUMERISM.

Tripartism   The term given to a government coalition of the MRP (*Mouvement républicain populaire*), SFIO (*Section française de l'Internationale ouvrière*) and PCF (*Parti communiste français*), which ruled between 20 January 1946, after the resignation of DE GAULLE as head of government, and 5 May 1947. The three parties which each enjoyed almost equal electoral support and parliamentary strength had in common the experience of the RESISTANCE movement against GERMANY and VICHY (1940–44). Of the three, the MRP was a new centrist Catholic party. The SFIO and the PCF had previously formed an electoral coalition in 1935 on an ANTI-FASCIST ticket. The zeal for reconstruction and MODERNIZATION saw the tripartite government push through many crucial economic reforms begun during the previous PROVISIONAL GOVERNMENT such as NATIONALIZATION of key industries and the Banque de France and the establishment of the *SECURITÉ SOCIALE* (French equivalent to the British National Health Service). The tripartite government lasted as long as the three parties were willing to compromise over their fundamental ideological differences to ensure support in parliament. However, common experience of Resistance was not enough to negate the fundamental ideological differences especially between the MRP and the PCF with the SFIO often acting as broker. The MRP was European in outlook, favoured moderate social and economic reform and STATE support for Catholic schools. The SFIO contained a reformist wing close to the MRP and an anti-clerical MARXIST wing close to the PCF. The tripartite government fell victim to the COLD WAR which eventually drove the PCF from government leaving the SFIO to find new allies, an increasingly difficult task as the MRP struggled to retain the Centre-Right ground. (**Máire Cross**)

Further reading

Gildea (1996). Contains an excellent account of Tripartism in the context of Fourth Republic parliamentary procedures and institutional practices. Larkin (1997). Also gives a very clear account of a complex political situation in post-war France.

Trotskyism   A MARXIST doctrine of communism based on the theories and political methods of Leon Trotsky (1879–1940) who was one of the revolutionary Bolshevik leaders in November 1917. He successfully directed the Red Army and was one of the first to devise a theory to explain how the first successful communist revolution had occurred in an underdeveloped country rather than an advanced capitalist one as Marx had predicted. He clashed with Stalin, urging the absolute necessity for a permanent revolution and overthrow of all institutions in all countries for communism to succeed. This resulted in his expulsion from the USSR in 1929 and eventual assassination in Mexico in 1940. Trotskyism is internationalist and claims to be more DEMOCRATIC, more radical in defence of human rights, less bureaucratic and less centralist. Often prone to bitter internal feuds, however, Trotskyism has always been weak in France as an effective political force especially as it refused to enter any broad Left parliamentary alliance during the 1970s when the PS-PCF alliance came close to winning an electoral majority. It did enjoy a revival during and after MAY '68 when the cultural hegemony of Marxism that the PCF hitherto enjoyed was seriously challenged. Since the decline of the PCF as a radical force there has been a slight increase in the Trotskyist appeal as an alternative protest vote. Thanks to the European electoral system of proportional representation and the single list which favours small parties, when two of the many small Trotskyist groups united (Alain Krivine's *Ligue communiste révolutionnaire* and Arlette LAGUILLER's *Lutte ouvrière*), they gained five seats in the 1999 European elections. Trotskyists insist on workers' political autonomy and the relevance of the CLASS struggle and are active in many grass-roots campaigns to defend illegal IMMIGRANTS (les *SANS-PAPIERS*), unemployed, immigrants, and WOMEN. (**Máire Cross**)

Further reading

> Frank (1979); Laguiller (1996). An autobiographical account of the Trotskyist leader who regularly stands as a presidential candidate, a working-class bank employee with some acknowledgement of gender politics.

Truffaut, François   1932–84. Film director. Initially a film critic, he led the NOUVELLE VAGUE movement, with films like *Les Quatre cents coups* (*Four Hundred Blows*, 1959) and *Jules et Jim* (1962). His films explore themes of love and death, and often reflect on the film-making process, as in *La nuit américaine* (*Day for Night*, 1973).

Tzara, Tristan   1896–1963. Writer. Romanian-born founder of the DADA movement in 1916, he wrote his *Manifeste Dada 1918* in French. Living in Paris, he joined the SURREALISTS before moving towards COMMUNISM after the Second World War.

Uderzo, Albert   Born 1927. Cartoonist. Creator of the *Adventures of Astérix the Gaul*, with GOSCINNY. He continued to produce Astérix albums after the latter's death (1977).

UDF (*Union pour la Démocratie Française*)   The UDF (Union for French Democracy) is a failed attempt to organize the parties of the non-Gaullist Right. Desperate to combat RPR hegemony, President GISCARD D'ESTAING cajoled a number of parties into an alliance for the 1978 elections. He hoped the resulting 'federation' would become a united party. UDF combined Giscard's own liberal *Parti républicain*, the CHRISTIAN DEMOCRATS of the CDS, the *valoisien* RADICALS and sundry groups; there are even a very few direct members. Despite elaborate structures, UDF never developed as a united organization, because of ideological and historical differences between partners, but above all because of fear of losing existing positions in a merger. UDF remains a loose grouping of small parties dominated by provincial notables, embedded in local government. It can produce an electoral programme and negotiate deals with RPR on candidacies and, when victorious, on seats in government; but it always comes second to the more united and better-off GAULLISTS. In the last two presidential contests it could not field a candidate from its own ranks. The bipolarized two-ballot electoral system, with the second round usually a straight contest between Right and Left, has forced UDF to ally with the Right, despite periodic talk of an 'opening' towards the Left. The most UDF has ever dared is to have its own lists for the European elections of 1989 and 1999; significantly, these are held on proportional representation. The future of this failed party remains doubtful. The liberals (now called *Démocratie libérale*) withdrew in 1999. Despite the current crisis of the French

Right, especially within the RPR, UDF's failure to find a credible presidential candidate, *pace* the ambitions of leader François Bayrou, plus its chronic divisions, seem to condemn it to its eternal second place. (**David Hanley**)

Further reading

Hanley (1999).

Union française   An administrative structure which officially replaced the Empire in 1946, combining France and its overseas dependencies.

Universalism   A model which has informed France's conception of its culture and its place in the world since the eighteenth century, and which arguably has its roots in Cartesian rationality. Universalism underpins the idea of the republican model of the nation and culture, which develops out of the ideals of the French Enlightenment and the Revolution. According to these ideals, the power of reason and science, nurtured in France, would provide an environment in which humanity, conceived of as an abstract citizenship, would flourish. The dissemination of these values would be France's historical mission. The THIRD REPUBLIC (1870–1940) in particular sought to create a unified NATION in which equality would be guaranteed by the driving forces of rationality and progress. It was in the Third Republic that universalism became indissolubly linked with EDUCATION. The role of the pedagogic STATE is to create a neutral and egalitarian public space. In this way, the republican tradition has become associated with the 'universal' values of abstract equality, citizenship and secularism (*LAÏCITÉ*). Some commentators compare the universalist French model of nationaility to a more ethnic and particularist German model. Alain FINKIELKRAUT, a contemporary advocate of French universalism, claims that 'France is made up of a set of values offered to human intelligence.'

As several critics have argued, the concept of universalism depends upon a strict opposition between the universal and the particular, whereby the latter is devalued. This means that, in the post-war period, as the '*grand narratives*' of Enlightenment and progress have been challenged by the effects of IMMIGRATION, mass culture, GLOBALIZATION, post-industrialization and CONSUMERISM, universalism has come under attack. Some would argue that the universalist tradition no longer offers simply a neutral egalitarian space for the citizen, but favours a nationalistic and ÉLITIST model. At the very least, the republican model of INTEGRATION is seen by many to be inadequate to the task of engaging with the reality of a new, multicultural France. (**John Marks**)

Further reading

Finkielkraut (1995). A passionate defence of French universalism in the face of post-modern 'dumbing-down'. Silverman (1999). A comprehensive analysis of some of the important debates concerning modernity and postmodernity in contemporary French thought.

Universities   There are 3600 higher education establishments in France, of which 90 are universities. At the beginning of the twentieth century, the term *l'Université* was used to refer to the entire French state education system, which at that time included the SORBONNE and 16 other universities, mostly established in the nineteenth century. However, with the growth of the GRANDES ÉCOLES and other third-level institutions, the modern university has become the lower level of a two-tier system, and frequently a staging post for students preparing entry to a *grande école*.

Until the 1960s, university education was reserved for a small ÉLITE, generally from wealthier social backgrounds. In 1960 there were around 300 000 students in higher education, mostly in universities in PARIS and the larger cities. This increased fourfold over 20 years to 1.2 million in 1980, and almost doubled again to 2.2 million in 1995, from which it has since slightly declined. The major wave of expansion in the 1960s included the building of many new universities, often on out-of-town campuses. The lack of social facilities and overcrowding of classrooms on large campuses such as Nanterre or Vincennes, in the Paris suburbs, was a major contributory factor in the uprising of MAY '68. Subsequent waves of expansion have developed further new universities as well as a growing range of specialist and vocational institutions of higher education.

Entry to university is based on gaining the BACCALAUREAT, which is now achieved by nearly 80 per cent of candidates. Enrolment fees are minimal, and most French students study at a university close to home, often combining study with part-time, or sometimes full-time work. There is a high level of failure in studies, with a quarter of students abandoning at first year level, and less than two-thirds getting beyond second year. The high levels of graduate unemployment are also a matter of concern. French universities have a long record of educating overseas students, and are active participants in exchange schemes, particularly with their EU partner countries.

Universities undertake research across all academic disciplines, and in science and technology especially, they have developed partnerships with local authorities and with business, as well as with national research funding agencies such as the CNRS (*Centre national de la recherche scientifique*). (**Michael Kelly**)

Further reading

Duclaud-Williams (1993). Renaut (1995).

Urban planning   Town planning is the means by which CITIES are organized in the most appropriate way for their population, and development across the country is carried out to serve the best interests of the NATION. Urban planning in France began in the first years of the twentieth century, with Tony Garnier's *La Cité industrielle* and the formation of the *Musée* social group. These early planners were concerned with housing and hygiene, the separation of residential and industrial zones and means of dealing with traffic flow. Planning of Paris and other major cities in the inter-war years was not a complete sucess, mainly because of a lack of adequate legislation. Housing, often of a poor quality, spread in an uncontrolled manner on the outskirts of cities. There were, however, attempts to meet the need for decent cheap housing through the HBM (*Habitation bon marché*, cheap housing) movement, the forerunner of the HLMs (*Habitation à loyer modéré*, low rent dwelling) of the post-war era, and in the Parisian suburb of Suresnes, the mayor, Henri Sellier, established a garden city.

In the period following the Occupation, France modernized rapidly and its cities grew rapidly as a consequence. In order to house this new urban population, the French adopted the policy of huge residential units (*grands ensembles*), loosely derived from LE CORBUSIER's concept of the *ville radieuse* (radiant city), often characterless, remote from town and city centres and with few amenities. The declining state of these *grands ensembles*, often inhabited by IMMIGRANT communities, has led to considerable social unrest in the 1990s in the *BANLIEUES* (suburbs). In the PARIS region, the situation was mitigated in the 1970s by the creation of a number of new towns (*villes nouvelles*) linked by the high-speed RER metro system. (**Nicholas Hewitt**)

Further reading

Bosma and Hellinga (1997). Contains an excellent short analysis of French planning.

Uriage, École des cadres   1940–42. School set up under the VICHY regime to train young people in leadership. Loyal to PÉTAIN but hostile to COLLABORATION, many of its staff and graduates were influential after the LIBERATION.

Vailland, Roger   1907–65. Writer. An early SURREALIST who moved to COMMUNISM, his novels, like *325 000 francs* (1955) deal with the tension between individual happiness and social circumstances, often, as in *Drôle de jeu* (*Strange Game*, 1945) exploring the ambiguities and multiple levels of human motivation.

Vaillant-Couturier, Paul   1892–1937. Writer. A COMMUNIST INTELLECTUAL, twice editor of *L'HUMANITÉ*, he led several left-wing movements, including CLARTÉ and the AEAR. He was an early French advocate of the POPULAR FRONT strategy of a broad Centre and Left alliance.

Valéry, Paul   1871–1945. Writer. His poems, like *Le cimetière marin* (1920) and others collected in *Charmes* (1922), develop symbolist themes and explore the nature of the self and consciousness. His essays and notebooks contain dense and cerebral meditations on philosophical, religious and artistic themes. He received many honours, including a state funeral.

Varda, Agnès   Born 1928. Film director. The leading woman director of the NOUVELLE VAGUE, her films, like *L'Une chante, l'autre pas* (*One Sings, the Other Doesn't*, 1977), use techniques of distanciation, emphasizing visual composition and disrupting the perceptions of time and space.

Vartan, Sylvie Born 1944. Singer. A star of 1960s' pop music, her hairstyles and dress were widely imitated. She was for a time married to Johnny HALLYDAY.

Vasarély, Victor 1908–97. Artist. Associated with the Op Art movement of the 1960s, his paintings used optical illusions, striking colour contrasts and intricate geometrical patterns.

Veil, Simone Born 1927. Gaullist politician. A survivor of the concentration camps, she served as Health Minister and introduced the *loi Veil* which legalized ABORTION in 1975. She was Speaker of the European Parliament (1979–82).

Vél d'Hiv July 1942. 13 000 French Jews were arrested by the French police in a series of raids and imprisoned in the *Vélodrome d'Hiver* sports stadium in Paris. Almost all were deported and died in Nazi concentration camps. President CHIRAC finally acknowledged the responsibility of the French state in the *rafle* (round-up) in 1995.

Vercors 1902–91. Writer. Jean Bruller, a graphic artist, jointly founded the clandestine *Éditions de* MINUIT (Midnight Press), which began by publishing his own short novel, *Le Silence de la mer* (*The Silence of the Sea*, 1942) under the pen-name Vercors. After the war, he kept the name and contributed to many left-wing publications and campaigns.

Verlan See ARGOT

Versailles Treaty Treaty settling arrangements with GERMANY after the First World War, signed in June 1919. See PARIS PEACE SETTLEMENT.

Vian, Boris 1920–59. Writer and jazz musician. A prominent member of the EXISTENTIALIST circle in SAINT-GERMAIN-DES-PRÉS, he was an ardent player and supporter of American JAZZ. His novels, like *L'Écume des jours* (*Froth on the Daydream*, 1947), combine SCIENCE FICTION and SURREALIST fantasy and gained a cult following in the 1960s, as did his anti-war song *Le Déserteur* (The Deserter, 1954), his plays, and his American-style crime fiction.

Vichy regime The Vichy regime was the French government established after Nazi German forces overran and occupied France in June 1940. Committed to COLLABORATION with the Germans, the Vichy regime was headed by the First World War hero Marshal Philippe PÉTAIN until it was swept away by the LIBERATION of August 1944.

With the invasion of France in June 1940, the THIRD REPUBLIC government abandoned PARIS and settled in Vichy, a resort town known for spas and mineral water. There Pétain and his supporters replaced the Republic with the more authoritarian *État Français* (French State), launched under the programme of a *RÉVOLUTION nationale* (National Revolution), intended to collaborate with Germany and eliminate COMMUNISTS, Freemasons, and JEWS from French public life. Vichy controlled the unoccupied southern two-fifths of France, the navy, and the North African EMPIRE.

Resistance at first was rare but it grew following the German invasion of the Soviet Union in June 1941, and after the Allied landings in French North Africa in November 1942, when the Germans occupied all metropolitan France. Vichy scuttled the French fleet at Toulon in response. The loss of the previously unoccupied zone, the navy, and the empire deprived the regime of any independent leverage against the Germans. As the war turned against the Germans, they intensified demands on French industry, agriculture, and labour. Vichy officials collaborated and also deported Jews and other enemies of Germany to extermination camps. By 1944, the Vichy government had become a satellite FASCIST state.

Ironically, Vichy's mere existence and the enthusiasm for French collaboration may have helped stop the German advance towards Spain, Gibraltar, and North Africa which might have disrupted the British Empire. Instead, the Germans chose to occupy a rump Vichy when they later needed their military resources for use in Russia. (**Bertram M. Gordon**)

Further reading

Paxton (1982). Gordon (1998). For the general context, see the Preface.

Viêtminh   Founded 1941. The Vietnamese Independence Front, led by Hô Chi Minh, and combining communist and nationalist forces. It was responsible for the guerrilla army which defeated French forces at DIEN BIEN PHU.

Vilar, Jean   1912–71. Theatre director. A successful actor on stage and screen, he was particularly influential as the director of the THÉÂTRE NATIONAL POPULAIRE and founder, in 1947, of the annual AVIGNON FESTIVAL.

Villiers, Philippe de   Born 1949. Right-wing politician. *Député* for the Vendée region, founder of the nationalist *Mouvement pour la France* (1994), and co-founder with Charles PASQUA of the RPI-IE, he is a leading spokesman for opposition to further European integration.

Vlaminck, Maurice de   1876–1958. Painter. Member of the Fauves group, he was noted for his bold use of colour.

Waechter, Antoine Born 1949. Politician. A leading figure in the ECOLOGY movement, he stood unsuccessfully for President in 1988.

Wall Street Crash On 29 October 1929, shares plummeted on Wall Street, the New York Stock Exchange, immediately plunging much of the industrialized world into depression. This downturn took time to reach France (1931), possibly because PARIS possessed huge gold reserves following the stabilization of the FRANC (1926), and possibly because French firms were smaller, with fewer international links, than those in Europe and America. While most countries had escaped the crisis by 1935, in France the Depression endured until 1938, as governments were frightened to devalue the currency and were wary of massive public reconstruction. Historians stress that the impact of the Depression was gradual rather than sudden. Unemployment, although high at 1 million in 1935, never reached the levels seen elsewhere, and those in work benefited from the collapse in prices. Large businesses also rode out the crisis. Worst hit were IMMIGRANTS and women, who were turned out of jobs, and small shopkeepers, artisans and PAYSANS (peasants). It is sometimes suggested that the crisis helped modernize the ECONOMY, encouraging the growth of innovative TECHNOLOGY and the establishment of larger businesses, yet there is little evidence of this. The RADICAL-dominated government of 1932 responded by orthodox economics which caused friction with its SOCIALIST allies and the breakdown of reform. Power thus slipped to the extra-parliamentary leagues, most famously the CROIX-DE-FEU, which on 6 FEBRUARY 1934 exploited the scandal surrounding a minor crook Serge STAVISKY to demonstrate against the THIRD REPUBLIC on the streets of Paris. The rise of the Extreme Right, at home and abroad, frightened the French Left which, under the impetus of the COMMUNIST Party, formed the POPULAR FRONT alliance that won the 1936 elections. (**Nicholas Atkin**)

Further reading

Jackson (1985). Provides a well-rounded guide to the many aspects of the Depression.

Weil, Simone 1909–43. Philosopher. Active in the SOCIALIST movement, she converted to Christianity and attempted to combine a radical engagement in social issues with Christian mysticism. She died of self-imposed starvation in solidarity with the suffering of occupied France.

Western A cinematic genre much beloved of the CAHIERS DU CINÉMA critics, for whom it represented, along with the *film noir*, the quintessence of AMERICAN moviemaking. Directors such as Howard Hawks and John Ford were prominent figures in the *Cahiers* pantheon of *auteurs* – the former a prototypical *auteur* working across a variety of genres of which his Westerns (notably *Red River* and *Rio Bravo*) were but one example, the latter the supreme Western specialist, whose *Stagecoach* and *The Searchers* were considered among the finest examples of the genre.

Yet the direct influence of the Western on French film-making was, and remains, small. It was to take Sergio Leone, Clint Eastwood and the Italian 'spaghetti westerns' of the 1960s to give European cinema its first major instances of the genre. Unsuitable landscape (parts of the South notwithstanding) and consequent high production costs were an obvious reason for this; the *film noir* was far more easily transplanted to PARIS. GODARD directed a 'Marxist western', *Vent d'est* (*East Wind*, 1969), co-scripted by Daniel COHN-BENDIT, but it received very limited distribution. Manuel Poirier's *Western* (1997), despite its title, owes very little to the genre, being a road-movie set in the (Western) province of Brittany. With the seeming demise of the Western as an American genre, it is difficult to see this situation changing. (**Keith Reader**)

Wine   Although seriously challenged in recent years by the wines of the New World and, increasingly, by those of South America, French wine manages still to be pre-eminent in the eyes of most serious and professional connoisseurs. Frequently described and marketed by regional type – Burgundy, Bordeaux, Champagne, and so on – French wine defies such simple classification. In France as elsewhere, the wine of any vintage is the result of a mysterious alchemy in which weather, soil and grape variety all play their part together with the skills of the maker (*viticulteur*). A late frost, too much rain at the critical moment just before the grapes are picked (*vendange*), or an attack of blight, can result in disaster. The origins of winemaking can be traced back to the Romans and today, with the exception of the most northerly departments, wine is produced almost everywhere. Traditional methods of production have long prevailed but the last decade has seen the introduction of modern techniques and equipment, often initiated by Australian winemakers. To a degree, improved methods have led to a rise in the quality of cheaper wines, but little interferes with the distinctive aromas and tastes of French wines at their best: the spicy, cedar and liquorice qualities of *Médoc*; the round and altogether softer tones of *Pomerol* and *St. Émilion*; the flintiness of *Pouilly-Fuissé*; the cherry flavours of *Beaujolais* at its chilled best; the tang of hung game in a great *Vosne-Romanée* or the honeyed richness of *Sauternes*, for example. Quality controls, which include the amount of wine produced from given areas of vines, and blending (*assemblage*) are imposed by law for all wines except the cheapest *vin de table* and allow them to be categorized as A.O.C. (*Appellation d'origine contrôlée*) or V.D.Q.S. (*Vin de qualité supérieure*). (**John Flower**)

Winter sports   Winter sports in France are popular, attract foreign holidaymakers, and are an important sector of the TOURISM industry. Socially, skiing has traditionally separated BOURGEOIS and proletarian France, but prosperity has helped reduce this distinction. Development of resorts has reflected trends in French society and the place of SPORT and LEISURE. Some 25 per cent of French households take winter HOLIDAYS, and 10 per cent of the population practise winter sports. Between 1960 and 1980, French skiing holidaymakers multiplied sixfold, but in the mid-1980s' economic downturn, numbers of registered skiers fell. In the early 1990s ski holidays declined and resorts and ski accessory companies failed as unreliable snow undermined winter sports. The 1992 Albertville Winter OLYMPICS helped the industry, although structural and climatic problems remained.

Winter sports are provided by networks of Alpine (and other) resorts whose development has followed evolving thinking by government and private industry about sport and leisure. Skiing was bourgeois leisure during the early twentieth century, but during the period 1920–60 resorts developed, catering for diversified demand. After the 1924 Chamonix Olympics, during the 1930s, the POPULAR FRONT's encouragement of sports, improving TRANSPORT and URBAN PLANNING, and ski stations such as Val-d'Isère widened the appeal of winter sports, but cost deterred mass interest.

Superlioran (Massif central), Gourette (Pyrénées) and Courchevel (Savoie) were resorts where public–private planned infrastructures aimed to increase popular participation but saw influxes of wealthier tourists. In the 1960s and 1970s, high-altitude integrated resorts (Avoriaz, Flaine) developed as the government stimulated the ski industry to attract foreign currency and widen social demand for winter sports by the *Plan neige*. High-altitude resorts concentrated on 'Alpine' skiing popularized by heroes such as Killy (three gold medals at the 1968 Chamonix Olympics); other stations diversified into other activities. Winter sports have seemed unable to consistently attract sufficient numbers of holidaymakers and are now increasingly obliged to respect costly environmental requirements. (**Hugh Dauncey**)

Further reading

Dailly *et al.* (1992). The 1992 Winter Olympics and French winter sports.

Women   Though necessarily intertwined with that of men, women's history in the twentieth century has also followed a separate narrative, that of the struggle for emancipation. In 1918, French women had no part in the nation's political life, having neither the vote nor the right to stand in elections. They were excluded from many educational establishments and qualifications, and could only sit a low status, girls-only BACCALAURÉAT. If married, they could not open a bank account, obtain a passport or take employment without their husband's permission, and parental rights over children belonged only to the father. Women's inferior status was enshrined in the law and the Constitution as well as in social practice. By the end of the twentieth century, *les Françaises* had not only won the vote and equal right to stand as political candidates (1944), but the *parité* law (1999) had been passed to enforce equality of parliamentary representation between the sexes, a goal that mere equality of opportunity had failed to achieve (in 1999 only 59 of the 577 MPs were women). A series of legal reforms had extended civil rights to women (1938, 1965, 1970); educational provision no longer made any distinction between the sexes; the legalization of CONTRACEPTION and ABORTION (1967, 1974) had acknowledged women's sexual and reproductive rights. Equal pay was, at least theoretically, established (in the Constitutions of both FOURTH and FIFTH REPUBLICS) and the Ministry for Women's Rights (1983–86) extended employment legislation to outlaw discrimination in recruitment and promotion. The principle of sexual equality has been established, even though in practice unequal pay, women's disproportionate responsibility for domestic labour and high rates of male violence against women mean that women continue to suffer certain disadvantages as a sex. Different histories produce different cultures: women artists have expressed their vision of the world in books, paintings, music, films throughout the century, with the numbers of women writers and film-makers increasing dramatically over the last three decades. (**Diana Holmes**)

Further reading

Duchen (1994). Fallaize (1993). Laubier (1990). McMillan (1981).

Workers and working class   Workers are a social group composed of people who earn their living by working for an employer, in return for a wage or salary. In present-day France, this now includes nine-tenths of the working population, including many professional and managerial staff (CADRES). Most wage or salary earners would accept that they are workers (*travailleurs*), but the majority would not identify themselves as members of the working CLASS (*classe ouvrière*, or *prolétariat*).

Until the twentieth century, most manual workers in France were hired farm workers, but as the industrial revolution developed momentum the numbers of rural workers declined, while the urban working class grew, particularly in the mining and manufacturing industries. By the end of the Second World War, manual workers had grown to nearly a third of the working population, rising to a peak of 38 per cent by 1975, before declining to the current 23 per cent. As traditional industries such as mining began to decline, the automation of industrial production also reduced the need for manual workers, replacing them with service personnel and managers. The booming service sector also expanded the number of white-collar jobs, to the point where 55 per cent of the workforce are now in clerical, technical and managerial positions.

Social and political theorists have a surprisingly wide range of views about whether the changing composition of the workforce means that the working class is vanishing or expanding to become all-inclusive. The answers have political implications. Traditionally, the SOCIALIST and COMMUNIST PARTIES and the TRADE UNIONS appealed to the class solidarity of manual and non-manual workers in pressing for improvements in working conditions and increased democratic involvement in issues related to work. They are now having to find more differentiated political strategies to match the increasingly varied life experience and aspirations of working people. (**Michael Kelly**)

Further reading

Todd (1991); Mendras and Cole (1991).

Working time   The question of working time has often been an important social and political issue in France and is closely linked to questions about LEISURE and CONSUMPTION. At the turn of the century it was not unusual for WORKERS to work ten hours a day or more. It was only in 1919, following an unprecedented campaign by labour activists and social reformers both before and after the First World War, that legislation was passed which established the eight-hour day as standard in France. Another major advance came in 1936 when the left-wing alliance known as the POPULAR FRONT introduced a 40-hour week and statutory paid holidays. While this was seen on the Left as a moment of great liberation, employers and right-wing governments immediately tried to reverse or undermine these measures. More recently, the French Left has returned to the idea of reducing the working week, as the government of Lionel JOSPIN (elected in 1997) has sought to introduce a 35 hour week in response to France's unemployment problem.

Working time takes on particular significance in the context of TAYLORISM and FORDISM. In twentieth-century France, the worker may have spent fewer hours at work than his/her nineteenth-century counterpart, but the worker's time became increasingly controlled by engineers, managers and performance targets. Reduced working hours meant more opportunity for leisure and consumption, thereby creating a larger market for leisure industries such as the CINEMA, TRAVEL and MUSIC businesses. For example, the introduction of paid holidays allowed many working class people to go on HOLIDAY for the first time. (**Jackie Clark**)

Further reading:

Cross (1989).

Writer   See AUTHOR.

Yourcenar, Marguerite   1903–87. Writer. The first woman elected to the *ACADÉMIE FRANÇAISE*, though she spent much of her career outside France. Her historical novels, like *Mémoires d'Hadrien* (*Memoirs of Hadrian*, 1951), are respected rather than popular.

Youth   *La jeunesse* (youth) in contemporary France is a word whose definitions have often been politically motivated. In the early decades of the twentieth century, 'youth' meant young male students. Students ceased to dominate politicized perceptions of the category of youth in the 1930s and 1940s, when Left and Right eagerly reached out to the less economically privileged. Léo LAGRANGE, in the post of Under-Secretary of Sport and Leisure created by the POPULAR FRONT, had stadiums, youth hostels, and sports centres built, the goal being to expose urban WORKING-CLASS youth to high culture, sports, and the great outdoors. Under the COLLABORATIONIST government at VICHY, youth became a major preoccupation of the STATE. State-sponsored youth centres and centres for professional development reinforced the policy decisions of the Youth Commissioner as well as the Vichy cult of the land.

With this most recent unsavoury connection to FASCISM, policies directed towards youth were absent from FOURTH and FIFTH REPUBLIC platforms. Young people instead became increasingly invisible in the expanding MASS media, first as particularly traumatized victims of wartime and COLD WAR paranoia, then as a carefree and apolitical CONSUMER group in their own right, though at the same time the majority of young men were obliged to perform military service in the ALGERIAN WAR. It was consumer society's unmet promises of prosperity and gainful employment, along with the poor condition of France's educational institutions, that led students and workers alike to the uprisings of MAY '68. Every ten years or so, French INTELLECTUALS debate the results and benefits of the 'events of May', but the politicized image of youth has shifted once again. In the 1980s and 1990s, unemployment and the rise in violent crime among the young residents of low-income suburbs (*la BANLIEUE, la cité*), must be understood in light of RACIAL tension in France today, since this social group is largely composed of second and third generations from France's former colonies. Their sense of disenfranchisement has yielded a new political term: *insertion*, a place in the social fabric: a daunting goal which local and national governments have yet to meet. (**Susan Weiner**)

Further reading

Weiner (2001). Focuses on the question of gender in the emergence of the teenager as a category of identity in the mass media. Reader, with Wadia (1993). The important texts of the 'revolution', accompanied by the authors' analyses.

Youth culture   The leisure activities, language, values, and forms of sociability specific to teenagers and young adults, usually thought to result from the common experiences of adolescence (school, rejecting parental authority, sexual awakening, and so on) and to end with adulthood, work and independence. In its contemporary sense, it is a post-1945 Western phenomenon, related to the onset of the CONSUMER society (which gave French youth a higher disposable income), the raising of the school-leaving age from 14 to 16, and a massive increase in the number of UNIVERSITY entrants, which culminated in the uprising of May '68. Americanization has also played a major part, from Hollywood movies in the 1940s to McDonald's (*Macdo* in youth slang), computer games, baseball caps, and rap today.

Sociologists sometimes question the notion of a 'CLASS' culture specific to youth. Certainly, surveys provide evidence of common activities and tastes. Cinema-going is the most popular outing (87 per cent of 15–19-year-olds went at least once in 1997 compared to 49 per cent of French generally); also fairgrounds (69 per cent), clubbing (56 per cent) and – a notable newcomer – karaoke nights (40 per cent). Popular music, however, is the main vehicle of identification, with 90 per cent of 15–19s expressing a preference for some form of pop in 1997. None the less, the romantic belief, common in the 1960s, that music generates a homogeneous and distinctive identity needs challenging. First, statistics indicate that young people's musical tastes are significantly differentiated by social background, GENDER and educational attainment. Second, since the 1960s, successive generations have carried their adolescent pop tastes into adulthood and middle age, thereby making pop much less age-specific than it was. One important consequence of this is that youth culture has in the past 40 years proved to be a locomotive of cultural change generally in France. (**David Looseley**)

Further reading

Donnat (1998b). The Cultural Practices of the French: Survey (1997): statistical source with plenty of data regarding youth culture.

Z

Zazous, les   Familiar label applied to groups of young people in PARIS during the OCCUPATION and LIBERATION, who celebrated their independence in an unconstrained and occasionally scandalous life-style. In many cases, their BOURGEOIS families had withdrawn to the country or fled abroad.

Zidane, Zinedine   Born 1972. Currently France's most famous and popular FOOTBALL (soccer) player, known affectionately as 'Zizou', and regarded as a role model for French Algerian young people. He played for Cannes and Bordeaux, before moving to Juventus (Turin) in 1996. He scored twice to secure French victory in the 1998 World Cup Final, and captained the French team that won the 2000 European Championships.

Bibliography

Abadie, M. (1988) *Minitel story : les dessous d'un succès*, Lausanne: P.-M. Favre.

Adamthwaite, A. (1995) *Grandeur and Misery: France's Bid for Power in Europe, 1914–1940*, London: Arnold.

Adereth, Max (1984) *The French Communist Party: A Critical History (1920–1984)*, Manchester: Manchester University Press.

Ades, Dawn (1984) *The 20th-Century Poster. Design of the Avant-garde*, New York: Abbeville Press.

Ager, Dennis (1996) *'Francophonie' in the 1990s: Problems and Opportunities*, Clevedon: Multilingual Matters.

Ageron, Charles-Robert (1991) *La décolonisation française*, Paris: Armand Colin.

Agulhon, Maurice (1979) *Marianne au combat: l'imagerie et la symbolique républicaines de 1789 à 1880*, Paris: Flammarion.

Agulhon, Maurice (1989) *Marianne au pouvoir: l'imagerie et la symbolique républicaines de 1880 à 1914*, Paris: Flammarion.

Agulhon, Maurice and Bonte, Pierre (1992) *Marianne: les visages de la République*, Paris: Gallimard.

Albera, François (1995) *Albatros: Des Russes à Paris 1919–1929*, Paris: Gnématheque française.

Albert, Pierre (1990) *La Presse française*, Paris: La Documentation française.

Albistur, Maïté and Armogathe, Daniel (1978) *Histoire du féminisme français*, Paris: Editions des femmes.

Aldrich, Robert (1993) *France and the South Pacific since 1940*, London: Macmillan.

Aldrich, Robert (1996) *Greater France: A History of French Overseas Expansion*, London: Macmillan.

Aldrich, Robert and Connell, John (1992) *France's Overseas Frontier: Départements et Territoires d'Outre-Mer*, Cambridge: Cambridge University Press.

Alexander, Martin (ed.) (1999) *French History since Napoleon*, London: Arnold.

Althusser, Louis (1971) 'Ideology and Ideological State Apparatuses,' in *Lenin and Philosophy and Other Essays*, London: New Left Books.

Amouroux, Henri (1976) *La Grande Histoire des Français sous l'occupation*, vol. 1 'Le Peuple du désastre 1939–1940', Paris: Le Grand livre du mois.

Andrew, Dudley (1978) *André Bazin*, New York: Oxford University Press.

Andrieu, Claire, Le Van, L. and Prost, A. (eds) (1987) *Les nationalisations de la Libération: de l'utopie au compromis*, Paris: Presses de la fondation nationale des sciences politiques.

Apollonio, Umbro (ed.) (1973) *Futurist Manifestos*, New York: Viking Press.

Ardagh, John (2000) *France in the New Century*, Harmondsworth: Penguin.

Ariès, P. and Duby, G. (eds) (1999) *Histoire de la vie privée Vol. 5. De la première guerre mondiale à nos jours*, Paris: Seuil.

Arthus, P. *et al.* (1998) *Euro: les enjeux pour la France*, Paris: Economica.

Assouline, Pierre (1988) *Gaston Gallimard: A Half-Century of French Publishing*, San Diego: Harcourt, Brace, Jovanovich.

Atack, Margaret (1999) *May 68 in French Fiction and Film: Rethinking Society, Rethinking Representation*, Oxford: Oxford University Press.

Atlas de la langue française (1995) Paris: Bordas.

Augé, Marc (1992) *Non-lieux. Introduction à une anthropologie de la surmodernité*, Paris: Seuil. Translated as *Non-Places: Introduction to an Anthropology of Supermodernity*, London: Verso 1995.

Augé, Marc (1997) *L'Impossible Voyage: le tourisme et ses images*, Paris: Payot/Rivages.

Austin, Guy (1996) *Contemporary French Cinema*, Manchester: Manchester University Press.

Azéma, Jean-Pierre (1979) *De Munich à la libération (1938–1944)*, Paris: Editions du Seuil.

Badinter, Elizabeth (1986) *L'Un est l'Autre, des relations entre hommes et femmes*, Paris: Odile Jacob.

Badinter, Elizabeth (1992) *XY: De l'identité masculine*, Paris: Odile Jacob.

Bakhtin, M. (1968) *Rabelais and his World*, Cambridge, MA: Harvard University Press.

Ball, Rodney (2000) *Colloquial French Grammar*, Oxford: Blackwell.

Barbrook, Richard (1995) *Media Freedom*, London: Pluto Press.

Barcellini, Serge and Wieviorka, Annette (1995) *Passant, souviens-toi! Les Lieux du souvenir de la Deuxième guerre mondiale*, Paris: Plon.

Bargiel, Réjane (1991) *Quand l'affiche faisait de la réclame! L'affiche française de 1920 à 1940*, Paris: Réunion des musées nationaux.

Barker, A.J. (1977) *Dunkirk : The Great Escape*, London: Dent.

Barré, R. and Papon, P. (1993) *Economie et politique de la science et de la technologie*, Paris: Hachette.

Barry, Peter (1995) *Beginning Theory: An Introduction to Literary and Cultural Theory*, Manchester: Manchester University Press.

Barsam, Richard M. (1992) *Non Fiction Film*, revised edition, Bloomington: Indiana University Press.

Barthes, Roland (1957) 'Le Tour de France comme épopée', in *Mythologies*, Paris: Seuil.

Barthes, Roland (1966) *Critique et vérité*, Paris: Seuil.

Barthes, Roland (1967) *Système de la mode*, Paris: Seuil.

Barthes, Roland (1973a) *Le Plaisir du texte*, Paris: Seuil.

Barthes, Roland (1973b) *Mythologies*, London.

Barthes, Roland (1980) *La chambre claire: Note sur la photographie*, Paris: Cahiers du Cinéma/Gallimard/Seuil, available in English as *Camera Lucida: Reflections on Photography*, trans. R. Howard (1982) London: Jonathan Cape.

Bauberot, Jean (1995) 'Le débat sur la laïcité', *Regards sur l'actualité*, nos 209–210, March-April , pp. 51–62.

Baudrillard, Jean (1970) *La Société de consommation*, Paris: Denoël.

Baudrillard, Jean (1988) *America*, London: Verso.

Bayart, Jean-François (1984) *La Politique africaine de François Mitterrand*, Paris: Karthala.

Beaujour, M. (1988) 'From text to performance: André Breton publishes the *Manifeste du surréalisme* and launches, with his friends, *La Révolution Surréaliste*', in D. Hollier, (ed.), *A New History of French Literature*, Cambridge, MA: Harvard University Press.

Beauvoir, S. de (1949) *Le Deuxième Sexe*, Paris: Gallimard (translated as *The Second Sex*, London: Penguin 1953).

Behr, Edward (1993) *Thank Heaven for Little Girls: The True Story of Maurice Chevalier's Life and Times*, London: Hutchinson.

Bell, D.S. and Criddle, Byron (1987) *The French Socialist Party: The Emergence of a Party of Government*, Oxford: Clarendon Press.

Bell, D.S. and Criddle, Byron (1994) *The French Communist Party in the Fifth Republic*, Oxford: Clarendon Press.

Bell, David, Johnson, Douglas and Morris, Peter (eds) (1990) *A Biographical Dictionary of French Political Leaders since 1870*, Hemel Hempstead: Harvester Wheatsheaf.

Bell, P.M.H. (1996) *France and Britain, 1900–1940: Entente and Estrangement*, London: Longman.

Bell, P.M.H. (1997) *France and Britain, 1940–1994: The Long Separation*, London: Longman.

Belorgey, Gérard and Bertrand, Geneviève (1994) *Les DOM-TOM*, Paris: La Découverte.

Ben Jelloun, Tahar (1999) *French Hospitality*, New York: Columbia University Press.

Benbassa, Esther (1999) *The Jews of France: A History from Antiquity to the Present*, Princeton, NJ: Princeton University Press.

Bernanos, Georges (1938) *Les Grands Cimetières sous la Lune*, Paris: Plon.

Bernard, P. and Dubief, H. (1985) *Decline of the Third Republic, 1914–38*, Cambridge: Cambridge University Press.

Berstein, Serge. (1982) *Histoire du Parti Radical*, 2 vols, Paris: Presses de la fondation nationale des sciences politiques.

Berstein, Serge and Milza, Pierre (1991) *Histoire de la France au XXe siècle, 1945–1958*, Paris: Editions Complexe.

Bertrand, Claude-Jean (ed.) (1995) *Médias*, Paris: Ellipses.

Beti, M. (1972) *Main basse sur le Cameroun*, Paris: Maspéro.

Betts, Raymond F. (1991) *France and Decolonization: 1900–1960*, Basingstoke: Macmillan.

Bigsby, C.W.E. (1971) *Dada and Surrealism*, London: Methuen.

Birkett, Jennifer and Kearns, James (1997) *A Guide to French Literature: From Early Modern to Postmodern*, London: Macmillan.

Birnbaum, Pierre. (1982) *The Heights of Power: An Essay on the Power Elite in France*, Chicago: University of Chicago Press.

Birnbaum, Pierre (1992) *Anti-Semitism in France: A Political History from Léon Blum to the Present*, Oxford: Blackwell.

Blampain, Daniel *et al.* (1997) *Le Français en Belgique*, Louvain-la-Neuve: Duculot.

Blatt, Joel (ed.) (1998) *The French Defeat of 1940: Reassessments*, Providence: Berghahn.

Blazwick, Iwona, (ed.) (1989) in consultation with Mark Francis, Peter Wollen and Malcolm Imrie, *An Endless Adventure, an Endless Passion, an Endless Banquet: A Situationist Scrapbook*, London: ICA/Verso.

Bloom, Harold (1994) *The Western Canon*, Basingstoke: Macmillan.

Bodier, M. and Crenner, E. (1996) 'Partir en vacances', *Données sociales 1996*, Paris: INSEE.

Boltanski, Luc (1987) *The Making of a Class: Cadres in French Society*, Cambridge: Cambridge University Press.

Borne, Dominique and Dubief, Henri (1989) *La crise des années 30*, Paris: Seuil.

Bosma, Koos and Hellinga, Helma (eds) (1997) *Mastering the City, II: North European City Planning 1900–2000*, The Hague: EFL Publications.

Bourdieu, Pierre (1989) *La Noblesse d'état: Grandes écoles et esprit de corps*, Paris: Minuit.

Bourdieu, Pierre (1993) *Sociology in Question*, London: Sage.

Bouvier, Nicolas (1992) *L'Usage du monde*, Paris: Payot.

Bové, José (1999) *Le monde n'est pas une marchandise*, Paris: La Découvertte.

Bowie, Malcolm (1991) *Lacan*, London: Collins.

Boyce, Robert (ed.) (1998) *French Foreign and Defence Policy, 1918–1940*, London: LSE/Routledge.

Boyer, Alain (1998) *L'Islam en France*, Paris: Presses universitaires de France.

Bradby, David (1991) *Modern French Drama, 1940–1990*, Cambridge: Cambridge University Press.

Brasillach, Robert (1941) *Notre Avant-Guerre*, Paris: Plon.

Britton, Celia (1992) *The Nouveau Roman: Fiction, Theory and Politics*, London: Macmillan.

Bürger, Peter (1984) *Theory of the Avant-garde*, Manchester: Manchester University Press (first published in Germany in 1974).

Burrin, Philippe (1996) *France under the Germans: Collaboration and Compromise*, New York: New Press.

Caffier, Michel (1994) *L'Académie Goncourt*, Paris: Presses universitaires de France.

Caute, David (1964) *Communism and the French Intellectuals 1914–1960*, London: Macmillan.

Cerny, Philip G. and Schain, Martin A. (eds) (1985) *Socialism, the State and Public Policy in France*, London: Frances Pinter.

Certeau, Michel de (1984) *The Practice of Everyday Life*, Berkeley, CA: University of California Press.

Césaire, Aimé (1995) *Notebook of a Return to My Native Land*, trans. Mireille Rosello and Annie Pritchard, Newcastle: Bloodaxe.

Césaire, Aimé (2000) *Discourse on Colonialism*, trans. Joan Pinkham, New York: New York University Press.

Cesari, Jocelyne (1998) *Musulmans et républicains: les jeunes, l'islam et la France,* Brussels: Editions Complexe.

Chadwick, Kay (ed.) (2000) *Catholicism, Politics and Society in Twentieth-Century France,* Liverpool: Liverpool University Press.

Charlot, Jean (1971) *The Gaullist Phenomenon: The Gaullist Movement in the Fifth Republic,* London: Allen and Unwin.

Charlton, Donald (ed.) (1979) *France: A Companion to French Studies,* 2nd edn, London: Methuen.

Charon, Jean-Marie (ed.) (1991) *L'Etat des médias,* Paris: La Découverte.

Charon, Jean-Marie (1996) *La presse quotidienne,* Paris: La Découverte.

Chaudenson, Robert (1995) *Les Créoles,* Paris: Presses universitaires de France.

Chebel d'Appolonia, Ariane (1991) *Histoire politique des intellectuels en France, 1944–1954,* 2 vols, Paris: Editions Complexe.

Cholvy, Gerard (1991) *La religion en France de la fin du XVIIIe à nos jours,* Paris: Hachette.

Cixous, Hélène (1974) *The Laugh of the Medusa,* in Warhol, Robyn R. and Herndl, Diane Price, *Feminisms An Anthology of Literary Theory and Criticism,* New Brunswick, Rutgers: Rutgers University Press 1991, pp. 334–49.

Clark, Graham (1997) *Oxford History of Art: The Photograph,* Oxford: Oxford University Press.

Clarke, Jackie (2001) 'Engineering a new order in the 1930s: the case of Jean Coutrot', *French Historical Studies,* February.

Clayton, A. (1994) *The Wars of French Decolonization,* London: Longman.

Cleary, M.C. (1989) *Peasants, Politicians, and Producers: The Organisation of Agriculture in France since 1918,* Cambridge: Cambridge University Press.

Clifford, James (1988) *The Predicament of Culture. Twentieth-Century Ethnography, Literature, and Art,* Cambridge, MA: Harvard University Press.

Cohn-Bendit, Daniel and Cohn-Bendit, Gabriel (1968) *Le Gauchisme: remède à la maladie sénile du communisme,* Paris: Seuil.

Cointet, Michèle (1988) *Histoire culturelle de la France 1918–1958: Regards sur l'histoire,* Paris: SEDES.

Collard, Susan (1996) 'Politics, culture, and urban transformation in Jacques Chirac's Paris, 1977–1995', in *French Cultural Studies,* vii.

Collard, Susan (1998) 'Architectural gestures and political patronage: the case of the Grands Travaux', *The European Journal of Cultural Policy,* 5.1 Autumn.

Compagnon, Antoine (1994) *The Five Paradoxes of Modernity,* New York: Columbia University Press (*Les Cinq paradoxes de la modernité,* Paris: Seuil, 1990).

Conan, Eric and Rousso, Henry (1994) *Ce Passé qui ne passe pas,* Paris: Fayard.

Cook, Malcolm (ed.) (1993) *French Culture since 1945,* London: Longman.

Cook, Malcolm and Davie, Grace (eds) (1999) *Modern France: Society in Transition,* London and New York: Routledge.

Cornick, M. (1994) 'The myth of perfidious Albion', in Dutton, D. (ed.), *Statecraft and Diplomacy in the Twentieth Century: Essays Presented to P.M.H. Bell,* Liverpool: Liverpool University Press.

Costantini, Michel (1995) 'Six ou sept choses que l'on croit savoir sur les signes et l'image', *Eidos. Bulletin international de sémiotique de l'image*, vol. 11.

Cousquer, Jean-Yves and Picard, Jeanine (1996) *Brittany*, French Regional Studies, London: Bristol classical.

Crawford, Stephen (1989) *Technical Workers in an Advanced Society: The Work, Careers and Politics of French Engineers*, Cambridge: Cambridge University Press.

Crémieux-Brilhac, Jean-Louis (1990) *Les Français de l'an 40*, vol 1: *La Guerre Oui ou Non?*, Paris: Gallimard.

Critchley, Simon (1999) *Ethics–Politics–Subjectivity: Essays on Derrida, Levinas and Contemporary French Thought*, London: Verso.

Cross, Gary (1989) *A Quest for Time: The Reduction of Work in Britain and France, 1840–1940*, Berkeley, CA: University of California Press..

Cross, Máire (2000) 'Women in politics', in Gregory, Abigail and Tidd, Ursula (eds) *Women in France*, Oxford: Berg.

Crouzet, F. (1993) *The Economic Development of France since 1870*, Aldershot: Edward Elgar.

Crozier, Michel (1987) *État modeste, état moderne*, Paris: Fayard.

Culler, Jonathan (1975) *Structuralist Poetics: Structuralism, Linguistics and the Study of Literature*, London: Routledge and Kegan Paul.

Curtis, Penelope (1999) *Sculpture 1900–1945: After Rodin*, Oxford: Oxford University Press.

Dachy, Marc (1990) *The Dada Movement, 1915–1923*, New York: Rizzoli.

Dailly, D. *et al* (1992) *Albertville 92: l'empreinte olympique*, Grenoble: Presses universitaires de Grenoble.

Dalloz, Jacques (1990) *The War in Indo-China: 1945–54*, New York: Barnes and Noble.

D'Angelo, M. (1997) *Socio-économie de la musique en France*, Paris: La Documentation française.

Darier, Eric (1987) 'The gay movement in French society since 1945', *Modern and Contemporary France*, 29.

Dauncey, Hugh and Hare, Geoffrey (1999a) 'French youth talk radio: the free market and free speech', *Media, Culture and Society*, vol. 21, no. 1, pp. 93–108.

Dauncey, Hugh, and Hare, Geoff (eds) (1999b) *France and the 1998 World Cup*, London: Frank Cass.

Davies, Peter (1999) *The National Front in France: Ideology, Discourse and Power*, London: Routledge.

Debord, Guy (1992) *La Société du spectacle*, Paris: Gallimard. First published in 1967.

Debray, Régis (1981) *Teachers, Writers, Celebrities: The Intellectuals of Modern France*, New York: Verso.

De Certeau, Michel (1984) *The Practice of Everyday Life*, Berkeley, CA: University of California Press.

DeClair, Edward G. (1999) *Politics on the Fringe: The People, Policies and Organization of the French National Front*, Durham, NC: Duke University Press.

De Gaulle, Charles (1980) *Memoires de Guerre*, Paris: Plon.

Deledalle, Gérard (1979) *Théorie et pratique du signe. Introduction à la sémiotique de Charles S Peirce*, Paris: Payot.

Delphy, C. (1993) 'Rethinking sex and gender', *Women's Studies International* Forum, vol. 16, no. 1, pp. 1–9.

Descombes, Vincent (1990) *Modern French Philosophy*, Cambridge: Cambridge University Press.

Dewitte, Philippe (ed.) (1999) *Immigration et intégration: l'état des savoirs*, Paris: La Découverte.

Dine, Philip (1998) 'Sport and the state in contemporary France', *Modern and Contemporary France*, vol. 6, no.3, pp. 301–11.

Directory of European Film and Audiovisual Festivals/Annuaire européen des festivals de cinéma et audiovisuel, Bonnières sur Seine, Carrefour des Festivals published annually.

Donnat, Olivier (1998a) 'Temps libre et pratiques culturelles', in *L'État de la France 98–99*, Paris: La Découverte.

Donnat, Olivier (1998b) *Les Pratiques culturelles des Français: enquête 1997*, Paris: La Documentation française.

Dosse, François (1997) *History of Structuralism*, Minneapolis: University of Minnesota Press. (*Histoire du structuralisme*, Paris: La Decourverte, 1991–92)

Duchen, Claire (1986) *Feminism in France: From May'68 to Mitterrand*, London: Routledge.

Duchen, Claire (1994) *Women's Rights and Women's Lives in France 1944–1968*, London and New York: Routledge.

Duchen, Claire (ed. and trans.) (1987) *French Connections: Voices from the Women's Movement in France*, London: Hutchinson.

Duclaud-Williams, Roger (1993) 'Education', in *France Today*, edited by J.E. Flower, London: Hodder and Stoughton.

Ducrot, Oswald, *et al.* (1995) *Nouveau Dictionnaire encyclopédique des sciences du langage*, Paris: Seuil.

Duhamel, Georges (1931) *America the Menace: Scenes from the Life of the Future*, Boston: Houghton Mifflin.

Durand, J.P. and Taylor, A. (1990) 'Information technology and the legacy of Taylorism in France', *Work, Employment and Society*, vol. 4, no. 3, pp. 407–27.

Eagleton, Terry (1983) *Literary Theory: An Introduction*, Oxford: Blackwell.

Eck, J.-F. (1988) *Histoire de l'économie française depuis 1945*, Paris: Armand Colin.

Eck, J.-F. (1996) *La France dans la nouvelle économie mondiale*, Paris: Presses universitaires de France.

Edwards, John (ed.) (1998) *Language in Canada*, Cambridge: Cambridge University Press.

Elias, Norbert (2000) *The Civilizing Process: Sociogenetic and Psychogenetic Investigations*, Oxford: Blackwell.

Esslin, Martin (1991) *The Theatre of the Absurd*, revised and enlarged edition, Harmondsworth: Penguin.

Evans, Richard (1987) *Comrades and Sisters: Feminism, Socialism and Pacifism in Europe 1870–1914*, Brighton: Wheatsheaf.

Evrard, Franck (1996) *Lire le roman policier*, Paris: Dunod.

Fallaize, Elizabeth (1993) *French Women's Writing Recent Fiction*, London: Macmillan.

Fanon, Frantz (1967) *Black Skins, White Masks*, New York: Grove Press (*Peau noire, masques blancs*, Paris: Seuil 1952).

Fassin, Didier, Morice, Alain and Quiminal, Catherine (1997) *Les lois de l'inhospitalité: les politiques de l'immigration à l'épreuve des sans-papiers*, Paris: La Découverte.

Faujas, Alain (1994) *Trigano: l'aventure du Club Med; avec une postface de Gilbert Trigano*, Paris: Flammarion.

Featherstone, Mike *et al.* (eds) (1991) *The Body: Social Process and Cultural Theory*, London: Sage.

Ferro, Marc (1997) *Colonization: A Global History*, London: Routledge.

Feyel, Gilles (1999) *La Presse en France des origines à 1944*, Paris: Ellipses.

Finkielkraut, Alain (1995) *The Defeat of the Mind*, New York: Columbia University Press.

Flandrin, Jean-Louis and Montanari, Massimo (eds) (1999) *Food: A Culinary History from Antiquity to the Present*, New York: Columbia University Press.

Flood, Christopher and Bell, Laurence (eds) (1997) *Political Ideologies in Contemporary France*, London: Pinter.

Flood, Christopher and Hewlett, Nick (eds) (2000) *Currents in Contemporary French Intellectual Life*, London and New York: Macmillan and St. Martin's Press.

Flower, J.E. (ed.) (1998) *Short French Fiction: Essays on the Short Story in the Twentieth Century*, Exeter: Exeter University Press.

Flower, J.E. (1993a) 'Religion', in J.E. Flower (ed.) *France Today*, London: Hodder and Stoughton.

Flower, J.E. (ed.) (1993b) *France Today*, 7th edn, London: Hodder & Stoughton.

Fohlen, C. (1966) *La France de l'entre-deux-guerres (1917–1939)*, Paris: Casterman.

Footitt, Hilary and Simmonds, John (1988) *France 1943–45*, Leicester: Holmes and Meier.

Forbes, Jill, Hewlett, Nick and Nectoux, François (eds) (2001) *Contemporary France. Essays and Texts on Politics, Economics and Society*, 2nd edn, London: Longman.

Forbes, Jill and Kelly, Michael (eds) (1995) *French Cultural Studies: An Introduction*, Oxford: Oxford University Press.

Foster, H. (1993) *Compulsive Beauty*, Cambridge, MA: MIT Press.

Fourastié, Jean (1979) *Les Trente Glorieuses ou la révolution invisible*, Paris: Fayard.

Francastel, Pierre (1977) *Peinture et société*, 3 vols, Paris: Denoël-Gonthier.

Francastel, Pierre (1984) *Histoire de la peinture française*, 2 vols, Paris: Denoël.

France, Peter (ed.) (1995) *The New Oxford Companion to Literature in French*, Oxford: Clarendon Press.

Frank, Pierre (1979) *The Fourth International: the Long March of the Trotskyists*, (translated from French), London: Ink Links.

Freeman, Ted (1997) *France and the Cold War*, special number, *French Cultural Studies*, vol. 8, part 1, February, 1–140.

Frizot, Michel (ed.) (1998) *A New History of Photography*, Cologne: Konemann.

Fysh, P., 'Gaullism and Liberalism', in Flood, C. and Bell, L. (eds) (1997) *Political Ideologies in Contemporary France*, London: Pinter.

Gaffney, John (1988) *France and Modernisation*, Aldershot: Avebury.

Gane, Mike (2000) *Jean Baudrillard: In Radical Uncertainty*, London: Pluto.

Gaspard, Françoise (1992), 'Assimilation, insertion, intégration: les mots pour "devenir français"', in *Hommes et Migrations*, no. 1154, May, pp. 14–23.

Gibson, R. (1995) *Best of Enemies: Anglo-French Relations since the Norman Conquest*, London: Sinclair-Stevenson.

Gifford, Paul, and Gratton, Johnnie (eds) (2000) *Subject Matters: Subject and Self in French Literature from Descartes to the Present*, Amsterdam and Atlanta: Rodopi.

Gildea, Robert (1996) *France since 1945*, Oxford: Oxford University Press.

Girardet, Raoul (1972) *L'Idée coloniale en France de 1871 à 1962*, Paris: La Table ronde.

Giudici, N. (1998) *Le Problème corse*, Toulouse: Éditions Milan.

Giusti, Ada (1997) *La langue française*, Paris: Flammarion.

Godard, Colette (1998) *Chaillot un théâtre national et populaire*, Paris: Norma.

Goetschel, P. and Loyer, E. (1995) *Histoire culturelle et intellectuelle de la France au XXe siècle*, Paris: Armand Colin.

Gordon, Bertram M. (1980) *Collaboration in France during the Second World War*, Ithaca, New York: Cornell University Press.

Gordon, Bertram M. (ed.) (1998) *Historical Dictionary of World War II France: The Occupation, Vichy and the Resistance, 1938–1946*, Westport, CT: Greenwood Press.

Gordon, Bertram M. (1999) 'The decline of a cultural icon: France in American perspective', *French Historical Studies*, vol. 22, no. 4 (Fall), pp. 625–51.

Gordon, F. and Cross, M. (1996) *A Passion for Liberty: Early French Feminisms 1830–1940*, London: Edward Elgar.

Goussot, M. (1999) *Les transports en France*, Paris: Armand Colin.

Graham, Peter (1968) *The New Wave*, London: Secker and Warburg.

Gramsci, Antonio (1971) 'Americanism and Fordism' in Hoare, Q. and Nowell Smith, G. (eds), *Selections from the Prison Notebooks of Antonio Gramsci*, London: Lawrence & Wishart.

Gratton, Johnnie and Le Juez, Brigitte (eds) (1994) *Modern French Short Fiction*, Manchester: Manchester University Press.

Green, Christopher (1987) *Cubism and its Enemies*, New Haven, CT: Yale University Press.

Green, D. (1981) *Managing Industrial Change? French Policies to Promote Industrial Adjustment*, London: HMSO.

Hallmark, R. (1998) 'Educational elitism: the grandes écoles', in Hughes, A. and Reader, K. (eds), *Encyclopedia of Contemporary French Culture*, London: Routledge, pp. 180–1.

Hammond, Brian and O'Connor, Patrick (1988) *Josephine Baker*, London: Cape.

Hamon, Hervé and Rotman, Patrick (1987 and 1988) *Génération*, 2 vols, Paris: Seuil.

Hanley, D.L. and Kerr, A.P. (eds.) (1989) *May 68: Coming of Age*, London: Macmillan.

Hanley, D.L., Kerr, A.P. and Waites, N.H. (1979) *Contemporary France*, London: Routledge and Kegan Paul.

Hanley, David (1994) *Christian Democracy in Europe: A Comparative Perspective*, London: Pinter.

Hanley, David (1999) 'Compromise, party management and fair shares: the case of the French UDF', *Party Politics*, vol. 5, no. 2, pp. 167–85.

Hantrais, Linda (1982) *Contemporary French Society*, London: Macmillan.

Hantrais, Linda (1999) 'Paid and unpaid work', in Cook, M. and Davie, G. (eds) *Modern France: Society in Transition*, London: Routledge.

Hare, Geoffrey (1998) 'Digitisation and the hybridisation of French radio', *Web Journal of French Media Studies*, November. Website: wjfms.ncl.ac.uk

Hare, Geoffrey (1999) 'Towards demassification of French broadcasting in the 21st century?', *Modern and Contemporary France*, vol. 7, no. 3, pp. 307–17.

Hargreaves, Alec G. (1995) *Immigration, 'Race' and Ethnicity in Contemporary France*, London: Routledge.

Hargreaves, Alec G. (1996) 'A deviant construction: the French media and the "banlieues"', *New Community*, vol. 22, no. 4 (October), pp. 607–18.

Hargreaves, Alec G. (1997) *Immigration and Identity in Beur Fiction: Voices From the North African Immigrant Community in France*, 2nd edn, Oxford: Berg.

Hargreaves, Alec G. and McKinney, Mark, (1997) *Post-Colonial Cultures in France*, London: Routledge.

Hargrove, June (1989) *The Statues of Paris: An Open-air Pantheon*, New York: Vendome Press.

Harland, Richard (1987) *Superstructuralism: The Philosophy of Structuralism and Post-structuralism*, London: Methuen.

Harman, N. (1980) *Dunkirk: The Necessary Myth*, London: Hodder and Stoughton.

Harris, Sue (2000) 'Festivals and *fêtes populaires*', in Kidd, William, and Reynolds, Siân (eds) *Contemporary French Cultural Studies*, London: Arnold, pp. 220–8.

Harrison, Alexander (1989) *Challenging De Gaulle: The OAS and the Counterrevolution in Algeria*, New York: Praeger.

Hartley, Anthony (1972) *Gaullism: The Rise and Fall of a Political Movement*, London: Routledge and Kegan Paul.

Haut Conseil de la Francophonie, *Etat de la Francophonie*, Paris: La Documentation française.

Hayward, Susan (1993) *French National Cinema*, London: Routledge.

Hazareesingh, Sudhir (1991) *Intellectuals and the French Communist Party 1945–1989*, Oxford: Clarendon Press.

Hazareesingh, Sudhir (1994) *Political Traditions in Modern France*, Oxford: Oxford University Press, 1994.

Heathcote, O., Hughes, A. and Williams, J.S. (eds) (1998) *Gay Signatures: Gay and Lesbian Theory, Fiction and Film in France, 1945–1995*, Oxford and New York: Berg.

Henissart, Paul (1973) *Wolves in the City: The Death of French Algeria*. London: Paladin.

Hewitt, Nicholas (1996) *Literature and the Right in Postwar France: the Story of the 'Hussards'*, Oxford and Washington, DC: Berg.

Hewitt, Nicholas (ed.) (2000) *La France et les pays de l'Est*, special number, *French Cultural Studies*, vol. 11, part 3, October, pp. 291–430.

Hewlett, Nick (1998) *Modern French Politics. Analysing Conflict and Consensus since 1945*, Cambridge: Polity Press.

Hinchcliffe, Arnold (1969) *The Absurd*, London: Methuen.

Hirsch, Martin (1994) *Les enjeux de la protection sociale*, Paris: Montchrestien.

Hirschfeld, Gerhard and Marsh, Patrick (eds) (1989) *The Collaboration in France*, London: Berg.

Hirst, Paul Q. and Thompson, Graham (1996) *Globalisation in Question*, Cambridge: Polity Press.

Hobsbawm, Eric (1992) *Nations and Nationalism since 1780*, Cambridge: Cambridge University Press.

Hollier, Denis (ed.) (1989) *A New History of French Literature*, Cambridge, MA and London: Harvard University Press.

Holmes, Diana (1996) *French Women's Writing 1848–1994*, London: Athlone.

Holt, Richard (1981) *Sport and Society in Modern France*, London: Macmillan.

Horne, Alistair (1985) *A Savage War of Peace: Algeria 1954–1962*, Harmondsworth: Penguin.

Howorth, Jolyon and Chilton, Paul (eds) (1984) *Defence and Dissent in Contemporary France*, London: Croom Helm.

Hughes, Alex and Reader, Keith (eds) (1998) *Encyclopedia of Contemporary French Culture*, London and New York: Routledge.

Hulten, Pontus (1987) *Futurism and Futurisms*, London: Thames and Hudson.

Immergut, Ellen (1992) *Health Politics: Interests and Institutions in Western Europe*, Cambridge: Cambridge University Press.

Irigaray, Luce (1977) *Ce sexe qui n'en est pas un*, Paris: Minuit.

Jack, Belinda (1996) *Negritude and Literary Criticism*, Westport, CT: Greenwood Press.

Jackson, Julian (1988) *The Popular Front in France: Defending Democracy 1934–38*, Cambridge: Cambridge University Press.

Jackson, Julian (1985) *The Politics of Depression in France, 1932–36*, Cambridge: Cambridge University Press.

Jackson, Stevi (1996) *Christine Delphy*, London: Sage.

Jeancolas, Jean-Pierre (1993) 'L'Arrangement Blum-Byrnes à l'épreuve des faits', in *1895*, no. 13, December, pp. 3–49.

Jeannin, Pierre (ed.) (1964) *Le livre d'or de l'Ecole Normale Supérieure*, Paris: Office français de diffusion artistique et littéraire.

Jenkins, Brian (1990) *France: Class and Nation since 1789*, London: Routledge.

Jennings, Jeremy (1990) *Syndicalism in France: A Study of Ideas*, Basingstoke: Macmillan.

Johnson, Douglas and Johnson, Madeleine (1987) *The Age of Illusion: Art and Politics in France, 1918–1940*, London: Thames & Hudson.

Jones, Colin (1994) *The Cambridge Illustrated History of France*, Cambridge: Cambridge University Press.

Jones, Rosalind Ann (1986) 'Writing the body: towards an understanding of *l'écriture féminine*', in Showalter, Elaine (ed.), *The New Feminist Criticism: Essays on Women, Literature and Theory*, London: Virago.

Judt, Tony (1986) *Marxism and the French Left*, Oxford: Clarendon Press.

Judt, Tony (1992) *Past Imperfect. French Intellectuals 1944–1956*. Berkeley & Los Angeles: California University Press.

Julliard, Jacques and Winock, Michel (eds) (1996) *Dictionnaire des intellectuels français*, Paris: Seuil.

Kandinsky, Wassily (1989) *Du spirituel dans l'art, et dans la peinture en particulier*, Paris: Denoël. First published 1910.

Kandinsky, Wassily (1970) *Point, ligne plan. Pour une grammaire des formes*, Paris: Denoël-Gonthier, First published 1926.

Kaplan, Alice and Ross, Kristin (eds) (1987) *Everyday Life*, special number of *Yale French Studies*, no. 87, Yale University Press.

Kedward, H.R. (1978) *Resistance in Vichy France*, Oxford: Oxford University Press.

Kedward, H.R. (1993) *In Search of the Maquis*, Oxford: Clarendon Press.

Kedward, H.R. and Wood, Nancy (1995) *The Liberation of France: Image and Event*, Oxford: Berg.

Keefe, Terry and Smyth, Edmund (eds) (1995) *Autobiography and the Existentialist Self: Studies in Modern French Writing*, Liverpool: Liverpool University Press.

Kellermann, E.W. (1988) *Science and Technology in France and Belgium*, Harlow: Longman.

Kelly, Michael (1979) *Pioneer of the Catholic Revival: The Ideas and Influence of Emmanuel Mounier*, London: Sheed and Ward.

Kelly, Michael (1982) *Modern French Marxism*, Oxford: Blackwell.

Kelly, Michael (1996) 'Revolution, renaissance, redressement: representations of historical change in post-war France', in Bartram, Graham, Slawinski, Maurice and Steel, David (eds), *Reconstructing the Past: Representations of the Fascist Era in Postwar European Culture*, Keele: Keele University Press.

Kemp, Anthony (1981) *The Maginot Line: Myth and Reality*, London: Warne.

Klejman, Laurence and Rochefort, Florence (1989) *L'Egalité en marche: le féminisme sous la Troisième République*, Paris: Presses de la fondation nationale des sciences politiques.

Knabb, Ken, (ed.) (1981) *Situationist International Anthology*, Berkeley, CA: Bureau of Public Secrets.

Kuhn, Raymond (1995) *The Media in France*, London: Routledge.

L'État de la France (1998) Paris.

Ladrech, R., and Marlière, P. (1999) *Social-Democratic Parties in the European Union*, London: Macmillan.

Laguiller, Arlette (1996) *C'est toute ma vie. Une femme dans le camp des travailleurs*, Paris: Plon.

Lallaoui, Mehdi (1993) *Du bidonville aux HLM*, Paris: Syros.

Lane, C. (1995) *Industry and Society in Europe: Stability and Change in Britain, Germany and France*, Aldershot: Brookfield.

Larkin, Maurice (1997) *France since the Popular Front*, 2nd edition, Oxford: Oxford University Press.

Laubier, Claire (1990) *The Condition of Women in France: 1945 to the Present*, London and New York: Routledge.

Lavenir, Catherine Bertho (1999) *La Roue et le Stylo: Comment nous sommes devenus touristes*, Paris: Odile Jacob.

Laver, James (1982) *Costume and Fashion: A Concise History*, London: Thames and Hudson.

Lebovics, Herman (1992) *True France: The Wars Over Cultural Identity 1900–1945*, Ithaca, New York: Cornell University Press.

Lecomte, Monia and Scriven, Michael (1999) *Television Broadcasting in Contemporary France and Britain*, Oxford: Berghahn.

Leeman-Bouix, Danielle (1994) *Les Fautes de français existent-elles?* Paris: Seuil.

Lefebvre, Henri (1991) *Critique of Everyday Life*, London: Verso (first published in 1947).

Lefebvre, Marcel and Laisney, François (eds) (1998) *Archbishop Lefebvre and the Vatican, 1987–1988*, 2nd edn, Kansas City: Angelus Press.

Lefort, Claude (1988) *Democracy and Political Theory*, Cambridge: Polity.

Le Lannou, Maurice (1978) *La Bretagne et les Bretons*, Paris: Presse universitaires de France.

Lemert, Charles C. (ed.) (1981) *French Sociology: Rupture and Renewal since 1968*, New York: Columbia University Press.

Le Petit Larousse illustré (2000) Paris: Larousse.

Leppert, Richard (1996) *Art and the Committed Eye: The Cultural Functions of Imagery*, Boulder, CO: Westview Press.

Le Québécois de poche (1998) Chennevières-sur-Marne: Assimil.

Letamendia, P. (1995) *Le Mouvement Républicain Populaire*, Paris: Beauchesne.

L'Etat de la France 98–99 (1998) Paris: La Découverte.

Lévi-Strauss, Claude (1955) *Tristes Tropiques*, Paris: Plon; (English translation, Harmondsworth: Penguin, 1978).

Lévi-Strauss, Claude (1969) *Elementary Structure of Kinship*, Boston: Beacon Press.

Lévi-Strauss, Claude (1977) *Structural Anthropology*, Harmondsworth: Penguin.

Levy, J.D. (1999) *Tocqueville's Revenge: State, Society, and Economy in Contemporary France*, Cambridge, MA and London: Harvard University Press.

Lodge, R.A. (1993) *French: From Dialect to Standard*, London: Routledge.

Looseley, David (1995) *The Politics of Fun: Cultural Policy and Debate in Contemporary France*, Oxford and New York: Berg.

Lottman, Herbert R. (1982) *The Left Bank: Writers, Artists and Politics from the Popular Front to the Cold War*, London: Heinemann.

Loubet del Bayle, Jean-Louis (1969) *Les Non-conformistes des années trente*, Paris: Seuil.

Luc, J.-N. and Barbé, A. (1982) *Des normaliens: histoire de l'École normale supérieure de Saint-Cloud*, Paris: Presses de la fondation nationale des sciences politiques.

Lyotard, Jean-François (1993) *The Postmodern Explained to Children: Correspondence, 1982–1985*, London: Turnaround.

Magraw, Roger (1992) *A History of the French Working Class*, Oxford: Blackwell.

Malraux, Andre (1937) *L'Espoir*, Paris: Gallimard.

Marie, Michel (1997) *La nouvelle vague*, Paris: Nathan.

Marks, Elaine and Courtivron, Isabelle de (eds.) (1981) *New French Feminisms*, Brighton: Harvester Wheatsheaf.

Marlière, Philippe (1997) 'Social suffering "in their own words": Pierre Bourdieu's sociology of poverty', in Perry, Sheila and Cross, Máire (eds) *Voices of France: Social, Political and Cultural Identity*, London: Pinter, pp. 46–58.

Marrus, Michael and Paxton, Robert (1981) *Vichy France and the Jews*, New York: Basic Books.

Martel, F. (1996) *Le Rose et le noir*, Paris: Seuil.

Martin, B. (1999) *France and the Après-Guerre, 1918–1924: Illusions and Disillusionment,* Baton Rouge: Louisiana State University Press.

Mathieu, Jean-Luc (1993) *Histoire des DOM-TOM,* Paris: Presses universitaires de France.

Matthews, Eric (1996) *Twentieth-Century French Philosophy,* Oxford: Oxford University Press.

Mayeur, J.-M. and Rebérioux, M. (1984) *The Third Republic from its Origins to the Great War, 1871–1914,* Cambridge: Cambridge University Press.

Mazower, Michael (1998) *The Dark Continent,* London: Allen Lane.

Mazzuccheti, D. and Fredj, C. (1995) *Le Gaullisme de 1940 à nos jours,* Paris: Hatier.

McCarthy, Patrick (ed.) (1993) *France-Germany, 1983–1993,* London: Macmillan, and New York: St Martin's Press.

McLintock, J.D. (1983) *Renault: The Cars and the Charisma,* Cambridge: Stephens.

McMillan, James F. (1992) *Twentieth-century France: Politics and Society 1898–1991,* London: Arnold.

McMillan, James F. (1981) *Housewife or Harlot: The Place of Women in French Society 1870–1940,* Brighton: Harvester.

Mende, Tibor (1973) *From Aid to Re-colonization: Lessons of a Failure,* New York: Pantheon Books.

Mendras, Henri (1970) *The Vanishing Peasant: Innovation and Change in French Agriculture,* Cambridge, MA: MIT Press.

Mendras, Henri and Cole, Alistair (1991) *Social Change in Modern France. Towards a Cultural Anthropology of the Fifth Republic,* Cambridge: Cambridge University Press and Paris: Editions de la Maison des Sciences de l'Homme.

Merkle, Judith A. (1980) *Management and Ideology: The Legacy of the International Scientific Management Movement,* Berkeley, CA: University of California Press.

Merle, Pierre (1996) *L'Argot,* Paris: Hachette.

Merle, Pierre (1999) *Le Dico du français branché,* Paris: Seuil.

Michel, Henri (1980) *Histoire de la France libre,* Paris: Presses universitaires de France.

Milner, Susan (1999) 'Trade unions', in Cook, Malcolm and Davie, Grace (eds) *Modern France: Society in Transition,* London and New York: Routledge, pp. 132–50.

Milner, Susan (1999) 'What about the workers? The trade unions' "short century"', in Alexander, Martin (ed.) *French History since Napoleon,* London and New York.

Mitterand, Henri (1986) *Zola et le naturalisme,* Paris: Presses universitaires de France.

Moi, Toril, (ed.) (1987) *French Feminist Thought: A Reader,* Oxford: Blackwell.

Monaco, James (1976) *The New Wave,* Oxford: Oxford University Press.

Montreynaud, Florence (1992) *Le 20ème siècle des femmes,* Paris: Nathan.

Moores, Pamela (1997) '*La presse SDF*: voice of the homeless?' in Perry, Sheila and Cross, Máire (eds.), *Voices of France: Social, Political and Cultural Identity,* London: Pinter, pp. 157–71.

Moreau Defarges, P. (1999) *La Mondialisation,* Paris: Presses universitaires de France.

Morelle, Chantal (1998) *De Gaulle, le Gaullisme et les Gaullistes,* Paris: Armand Colin.

Morris, Alan (1989) *Collaboration and Resistance Reviewed: Writers and the mode rétro in Post-Gaullist France,* London: Berg.

Morris, Frances (ed.) (1993) *Paris Post War: Art and Existentialism 1945–55,* London: Tate Gallery.

Morris, Peter (1994) *French Politics Today,* Manchester: Manchester University Press.

Mossuz-Lavau, Janine (1998) *Femmes/Hommes pour la parité,* Paris: Presses de Sciences Po.

Mouron, Henri (1985) *Cassandre,* London: Thames and Hudson.

Murard, Numa (1993) *La protection sociale,* Paris: La Découverte.

Nemeth, Charles (1994) *The Case of Archbishop Marcel Lefebvre: Trial by Canon Law,* Kansas City: Angelus Press.

Nora, Pierre (ed.) (1997) *Les Lieux de mémoire,* Paris: Gallimard.

Nora, Pierre (ed.) (1996–97) *Realms of Memory,* New York.

Norindr, Panivong (1996) *Phantasmatic Indo-China: French Colonial Ideology in Architecture, Film and Literature,* Durham, NC and London: Duke University Press.

Norris, Christopher (1982) *Deconstruction: Theory and Practice,* London: Routledge.

Novick, Peter (1968) *The Resistance Versus Vichy: The Purge of Collaborators in Liberated France,* New York: Chatto and Windus.

OECD (1998) *France's Experience with the Minitel: Lessons for Electronic Commerce over the Internet,* Paris, Working Papers 1022–2227 v.6, no. 88.

Ory, Pascal (1994) *La Belle illusion,* Paris: Plon.

Ory, Pascal and Sirinelli, Jean-François (1986) *Les intellectuels en France, de l'affaire Dreyfus à nos jours,* Paris: Armand Colin.

Ozouf, M (1995) 'La singularité française' in *Les Mots des femmes, essai sur la singularité française,* Paris: Fayard.

Pallud, Jean-Paul (1988) 'The Maginot Line', *After the Battle,* No. 60.

Pastoureau, Michel (1998) *Les Emblèmes de la France,* Paris: Bonneton.

Pavy, Didier (1999) *Les Belges,* Paris: Grasset.

Paxton, Robert O. (1982) *Vichy France: Old Guard and New Order, 1940–1944,* New York: Columbia University Press.

Payne, Michael (1996) *A Dictionary of Cultural and Critical Theory,* Oxford: Blackwell.

Picq, Françoise (1993) *Libération des femmes, les années-mouvement,* Paris: Seuil.

Pilbeam, Pamela (1999) 'Revolution, restoration(s) and beyond: changes, continuities and the enduring legacies of 1789', in Alexander, Martin (ed.) *French History since Napoleon,* London and New York: Arnold.

Pivot, Bernard (1989) *Le Livre de l'orthographe,* Paris: Hatier.

Pluriel recherches: Vocabulaire historique et critique des relations inter-ethniques nos 1 (1993), 2 (1994) and 5 (1997).

Poidevin, Raymond and Bariéty, Jacques (1977) *Les Relations franco-allemandes 1815–1975,* Paris: Armand Colin.

Ponting, C. (1990) *1940: Myth and Reality,* London: Hamilton.

Portes, Jacques (1986) 'Les origines de la légende noire des accords Blum-Byrnes' in *Revue d'histoire moderne et contemporaine,* April-June pp. 314–329.

Posner, T.R. (1991) *Current French Security Policy: The Gaullist Legacy,* New York: Greenwood Press.

Poster, Mark (1975) *Existential Marxism in Postwar France: From Sartre to Althusser,* Princeton, NJ: Princeton University Press.

Pouget, Emile (1914) *L'Organisation du surménage (le système Taylor),* Paris: Rivière.

Powrie, Phil (1997) *French Cinema in the 1980s: Nostalgia and the Crisis of Masculinity*, Oxford: Clarendon Press.

Prédal, René, (ed.) (1987) 'Le documentaire français', *CinémAction* 41, January.

Prendiville, B. (1997) 'Ecologism' in Flood, C. and Bell, L. (eds) *Political Ideologies in Contemporary France*, London and Washington: Pinter, pp. 140–61.

Price, Roger (1993) *A Concise History of France*, Cambridge: Cambridge University Press.

Pro Helvetia, (1991) *Arts et culture visuels en Suisse*, XIII vols, Disentis: Editions Desertina.

Prost, Antoine (ed.) (1997) *La Résistance: une histoire sociale*, Paris: Editions de l'Atelier/Editions ouvrières.

Proud, J. (1995) 'Ecology parties in France' in Addinall, N.A. (ed.) *French Political Parties*, Cardiff: University of Wales Press, pp. 131–52.

Quel président pour les femmes? Réponses de F. Mitterrand à Choisir, (1981) Paris: Gallimard.

Quid, Paris: Robert Laffont, published annually.

Rauch, André (1996) *Vacances en France de 1830 à nos jours*, Paris: Hachette.

Reader, Keith A. (1987) *Intellectuals and the Left in France since 1968*, London: Macmillan and New York: St Martin's Press.

Reader, Keith, with Wadia, Khursheed (1993) *The May 68 Events in France: Reproductions and Interpretations*, London: Macmillan.

Reland, J. (1997) 'The social security headache: the necessary but elusive reform', in Cross, Máire and Perry, Sheila (eds) *Population and Social Policy in France*, London: Pinter, pp. 170–86.

Renaut, A. (1995) *Les révolutions de l'université. Essai sur la modernisation de la culture*, Paris: Calmann-Lévy.

Reuter, Yves (1997) *Le Roman policier*, Paris: Nathan.

Reynolds, Siân (1996) *France Between the Wars: Gender and Politics*, New York: Routledge.

Reynolds, Siân (1998) 'Women and political representation during the Mitterrand presidency or the Family Romance of the Fifth Republic', in McLean, Mairi (ed.) *The Mitterrand Years: Legacy and Evaluation*, London: Macmillan.

Rigby, Brian (1991) *Popular Culture in Modern France*, London: Routledge.

RIIA (1988) *Europe's Future in Space: A Joint Policy Report*, London: Routledge and Kegan Paul.

Rioux, Jean-Pierre (1980) *La France de la Quatrième République*, vol. 1, Paris: Seuil.

Rioux, Jean-Pierre (1987) *The Fourth Republic 1944–1958*, Cambridge: Cambridge University Press.

Rioux, Jean-Pierre (ed.) (1990) *La Guerre d'Algérie et les Français*, Paris: Fayard.

Rioux, L. (1994) *50 ans de chanson française*, Paris: L'Archipel.

Robbe-Grillet, Alain (1988) *For a New Novel: Essays on Fiction*, trans. Richard Howard, Evanston, Ill.: Northwestern University Press.

Robinson, Christopher. (1995) *Scandal in the Ink*, London: Cassell.

Rochefort, Christiane (1961) *Les Petits Enfants du siècle*, Paris: Livre de Poche.

Rochefort, Christiane (1963) *Les Stances à Sophie*, Paris: Livre de Poche.

Rochefort, Christiane (1966) *Une Rose pour Morrison*, Paris: Livre de Poche.

Rochefort, R. (1995) *La Société des consommateurs*, Paris: Odile Jacob.

Roman noir: Pas d'orchidées pour les T.M. (1997) special number of *Les Temps modernes*, août-septembre-octobre 1997, no. 595.

Rosanvallon, Pierre (1992) *L'Etat en France de 1789 à nos jours*, Paris: Seuil.

Roskill, Mark (1985) *The Interpretation of Cubism*, Philadelphia: Art Alliance Press.

Ross, G., Hoffmann, S. and Malzachert, S. (eds) (1987) *The Mitterrand Experiment: Continuity and Change in Socialist France*, Oxford; Polity.

Rousso, Henry (1987) *Le Syndrome de Vichy*, Paris: Seuil.

Roy, Jules (1965) *The Battle of Dienbienphu*, New York: Harper & Row.

Sadoul, Georges (1973) *Histoire générale du cinéma*, 3rd edn, vol. 2, Paris.

Sadoul, Georges and Breton, Emile (1990) *Dictionnaire des cinéastes*, Paris: Microcosme/Seuil.

Said, Edward (1993) *Culture and Imperialism*, New York: Knopf, Vintage Books.

Sansot, Pierre (1991) 'La Légende dorée du Tour de France', in *Les Gens de peu*, Paris: Presses universitaires de France.

Sartre, Jean-Paul (1988) '*What is Literature?' and Other Essays*, Cambridge, MA: Harvard University Press.

Schalk, David (1979) *The Spectrum of Political Engagement*, Princeton, NJ: Princeton University Press.

Scott, David (1995) *European Stamp Design: A Semiotic Approach*, London: Academy Editions.

Segalen, Martine (1996) *Sociologie de la famille*, Paris: Nathan.

Sellars, Susan (1991) *Language and Sexual Difference. Feminist Writing in France*, New York: Macmillan.

Sellers, Susan (ed.) (1994) *The Hélène Cixous Reader*, preface by Hélène Cixous and foreword by Jacques Derrida, London: Routledge.

Serreau, Geneviève (1966) *Histoire du 'nouveau théâtre'*, Paris: Gallimard.

Service des Droits des Femmes (1995) *Les Femmes: Contours et caractères*, Paris: INSEE.

Sheringham, Michael (1993) *French Autobiography: Devices and Desires*, Oxford: Clarendon Press.

Shields, James (2000) 'The Poujadist movement: a faux "Fascism"', *Modern and Contemporary France*, vol. 8, no. 1 pp. 19–34.

Shohat, Ella and Stam, Robert (1994) *Unthinking Eurocentrism. Multiculturalism and the Media*, London: Routledge.

Silverman, Dan (1972) *Reluctant Union: Alsace-Loraine and Imperial Germany, 1871–1918*, Pennsylvania: Pennsylvania State University Press.

Silverman, Hugh J. (ed.) (1989) *Derrida and Deconstruction*, London: Routledge.

Silverman, Max (1999) *Facing Postmodernity*, London and New York: Routledge.

Sommerville, Donald (1997) *The Encyclopedia of Rugby Union*, London: Aurum.

Soucy, Robert (1985) *French Fascism: The First Wave, 1924–1933*, New Haven, CT: Yale University Press.

Soucy, Robert (1995) *French Fascism: The Second Wave, 1933–1939*, New Haven, CT: Yale University Press.

Souton, Georges-Henri (1994) "France," in *The Origins of the Cold War in Europe: International Perspectives*, edited by David Reynolds, New Haven: Yale University Press.

Spang, Rebecca L. (2000) *The Invention of the Restaurant: Paris and Modern Gastronomic Culture*, Cambridge, MA: Harvard University Press.

Stevens, Anne (1996) *The Government and Politics of France*, 2nd edn, London: Macmillan.

Stora, Benjamin (1993) *Histoire de la guerre d'Algérie (1954–1962)*, Paris: La Découverte.

Stora, Benjamin (1994) *Histoire de l'Algérie depuis l'indépendance*, Paris: La Découverte.

Story, Jonathan (ed.) (1993) *The New Europe*, Oxford: Blackwell.

Strenski, Ivan (1987) *Four Theories of Myth in Twentieth Century History: Cassirer, Eliade, Lévi-Strauss and Malinowski*, London: Macmillan.

Sturrock, John (1987) *Structuralism*, London: Grafton.

Sturrock, John (1998) *The Word from Paris: Essays on Modern French Thinkers and Writers*, London: Verso.

Suleiman E. (1978) *Elites in French Society*, Princeton, NJ: Princeton University Press.

Sykes, B. (1987) *Transport in France*, London: Harrap.

Thody, Philip (1995) *Le Franglais*, London: Athlone.

Thompson, I. B. (1970) *Modern France: A Social and Economic Geography*, London: Butterworths.

Thomson, Ian (1971) *Corsica*, Newton Abbott: David and Charles.

Tocqueville, A. de (1887) *Democracy in America*, London and New York: Longman Green.

Todd, Emmanuel (1991) *The Making of Modern France: Politics Ideology and Culture*, transl. A. and B. Forster, Oxford: Blackwell.

Todd, Loreto (1990) *Pidgins and Creoles*, London: Routledge.

Todorov, Tzvetan (1994) *On Human Diversity: Nationalism, Racism, and Exoticism in French Thought*, Cambridge, MA: Harvard University Press.

Tombs, Robert (1999) *The Paris Commune 1871*, London and New York: Longman.

Touraine, Alain (1994) *Qu'est-ce que la démocratie?*, Paris: Fayard.

Turkle, Sherry (1979) *Psychoanalytic Politics: Freud's French Revolution*, London: Burnett and Deutsch.

Turnbull, P. (1978) *Dunkirk: Anatomy of Disaster*, London: Batsford.

Unwin, Tim (ed.) (1997) *The Cambridge Companion to the French Novel*, Cambridge: Cambridge University Press.

Urbain, Jean-Didier (1991) *L'Idiot du voyage. Histoires de touristes*, Paris: Plon.

Urbain, Jean-Didier (1994) *Sur la plage. Mœurs et coutumes balnéaires*, Paris: Payot.

Verschave François-Xavier (1998) *La Françafrique, le plus long scandale de la 5ème République*, Paris: Stock.

Vigarello, G. (1992) 'Le Tour de France', in P. Nora (ed.), *Les lieux de mémoire* vol. III, Paris, pp. 886–925.

Vigneau, F. (1998) *Les espaces du sport*, Paris: Presses universitaires de France.

Vilar, Jean (1975) *Le Théâtre, service public*, Paris: Gallimard.

Vinen, Richard (1996) *France 1934–1970*, Basingstoke: Macmillan..

Waites, N. (1984) 'Defence policy: the historical context', in Howorth, J. and Chilton, P. (eds) *Defence and Dissent in Contemporary France*, London: Croom Helm.

Wall, Irwin M. (1991) *The United States and the Making of Postwar France*, Cambridge: Cambridge University Press.

Walter, Henriette (1988) *Le Français dans tous les sens*, Paris: Robert Laffont.

Warner, Marina (1981) *Joan of Arc. The Image of Female Heroism*, London: Penguin.

Waser, A.-M. (1995) *Sociologie du tennis: genèse d'une crise 1960–1990*, Paris: L'Harmattan.

Watkins, K (1992) *Fixing the Rules*, London: Catholic Institute for International Relations.

Weber, Eugen (1962) *Action Française: Royalism and Reaction in Twentieth-Century France*, Stanford, CA: Stanford University Press.

Weber, Eugen (1995) *The Hollow Years: France in the 1930s*, New York: Norton, and London: Sinclair-Stevenson.

Webster, Roger (1990) *Studying Literary Theory*, London: Arnold.

Weiner, Susan (2001) *Enfants Terribles: Femininity, Youth, and the Mass Media in France, 1945–1968*, Baltimore: Johns Hopkins University Press. .

Welton, Donn (1999) *The Body*, Oxford and Cambridge, MA: Blackwell.

Willaime, Jean-Paul (1998) 'Le protestantisme, un christianisme de la modernité', in *L'Etat de la France 98–99*, Paris: La Découverte.

Williams, A. (1968) *Britain and France in the Middle East*, London: Macmillan.

Williams, Alan (1992) *Republic of Images*, Cambridge, MA and London: Harvard University Press.

Williams, Glyn (1999) *French Discourse Analysis: The Method of Post-structuralism*, London: Routledge.

Williams, Philip (1958) *Politics in Post-war France*, 2nd edn, London: Longman.

Williams, Philip (1964) *Crisis and Compromise : Politics in the Fourth Republic*, London: Longman.

Wilson, Emma (1999) *French Cinema since 1950*, London: Personal Histories.

Winchester, Hilary P.M. (1993) *Contemporary France*, London: Longman.

Winock, Michel (1998) *Nationalism, Anti-Semitism, and Fascism in France*, Palo Alto: Stanford University Press.

Wood, Paul (ed.) (1999) *The Challenge of the Avant-Garde*, London: Open University Press.

Woolman, David S. (1968) *Rebels in the Rif*, Stanford, CA: Stanford University Press.

Young, Robert (1996) *France and the Origins of the Second World War*, London: Macmillan.

Zahariadis, N. (1995) *Markets, States and Public Policy: Privatization in Britain and France*, Ann Arbor, MI: University of Michigan Press.

Zelden, Theodore (1973) *France, 1848–1945*, Oxford: Oxford University Press.

Zeldin, Theodore (1983), *The French*, London: Collins.

Zuccotti, Susan (1999) *The Holocaust, the French, and the Jews*, Lincoln, NE: University of Nebraska Press.